Becoming an

Effective Christian Counselor

A Practical Guide for Helping People

Walter and Trudy Fremont

Bob Jones University Press
Greenville, S.C. 29614

Library of Congress Cataloging-in-Publication Data

Fremont, Walter, 1924–
    Becoming an effectvie Christian counselor / Walter and Trudy
Fremont.
        p.   cm.
    Includes bibliographical references and index.
    ISBN 0-89084-890-4
        1. Counseling—Religious aspects—Christianity.   I. Fremont,
Trudy, 1926– .   II. Title.
BR115.C69F74   1996
253.5—dc20   96-30409
                                                                    CIP

NOTE:
The fact that materials produced by other publishers are referred to in this volume
does not constitute an endorsement by Bob Jones University Press of the content
or theological position of materials produced by such publishers. The position of
Bob Jones University Press, and the University itself, is well known. Any references and ancillary materials are listed as an aid to the reader and in an attempt to
maintain the accepted academic standards of the publishing industry.

Becoming an Effective Christian Counselor

Edited by Becky J. Smith
Cover and illustrations by Chris Hartzler

© 1996 Bob Jones University Press
Greenville, South Carolina 29614

Printed in the United States of America
All rights reserved

ISBN 0-89084-890-4

15   14   13   12   11   10   9   8   7   6   5   4   3   2   1

To Elaine Marie Fremont, our loving, effervescent daughter, whose expert editing skills made this book a reality. Just before this book went to the publishers, Elaine went on to rejoice with the saints in glory as they offer praises to Jesus Christ for His creation and redemption (Rev. 4:10-11; 5:9-12).

Table of Contents

Tables

Foreword

It gives me great pleasure to write a few words in the endorsement of this superb and significant book. Both the subject and the authors are dear to my heart. Counseling is an essential part of the Christian life. In Proverbs 11:13 we are told that where no counsel is, people fall, but in the multitude of counselors there is safety. Here we see the words *counsel* and *counselors* used together in one sentence. The Hebrew word from which these words are translated is used over seventy times in the Old Testament. It is a verb which means "to give counsel, to deliberate, to give purpose, or to determine." From a Christian perspective, with this definition we can then say that counseling is to deliberate over a problem and determine its cause, then give a plan for the solution of that problem and an escape from its consequences.

In Isaiah 9:6 the Lord Jesus is called "Counselor." In Psalm 33:11 we read, "The counsel of the Lord standeth for ever, " and all through Scripture we see that God uses men to give the counsel of His Word to other men. True biblical counseling comes from a concerned Christian who over the years has earned a position of spiritual leadership—a person who possesses wisdom gleaned from a sincere study of God's Word, a person who has applied these truths in his own life, a person of spiritual wisdom and spiritual discernment who has learned to search the Scripture to find common experiences which allow him to identify problems, institute plans, and then implement the procedures that will free men from sin and its consequesnces. I know of no couple in the service of the Lord that is better qualified to bear the title of "Christian counselors" than Walt and Trudy Fremont. Over the years they have extracted many Bible Action Truths and given us simple, straightforward, practical applications of those principles to be used for resolving both the common and the complicated problems of life.

A myriad of spiritually restored lives around the world offer "proof" of the Fremonts' effective ministry. *Becoming an Effective Christian Counselor* contains the truths they have gleaned from a lifetime of study and application of God's Word. I can heartily recommend it to all who know and love the Lord and His Word, and to those who have a sincere desire to practice the gift of exhortation as it is described in the Scripture. It is my prayer that in the future there will be many blessings and rewards in the lives of others as a result of the Fremonts' wonderful labor of love.

Bob M. Wood
Executive Vice President
Bob Jones University

Preface

The twentieth century will be known in church history as the age when psychological thinking displaced biblical thinking, self-centeredness displaced Christ-centeredness, concern for personal needs displaced concern for the needs of others, feelings displaced mental attitudes, self-esteem displaced humility and favor with God, and health-and-wealth Christianity displaced sacrifice-and-service Christianity. This has resulted in Christians who have a multitude of seemingly unsolvable problems.

We wrote this book to provide biblical answers for the common personal problems in today's confused and valueless culture. The Bible has eternal values, sure direction, and answers (at least in principle) to every nonmedical problem that people experience. Our book identifies the thirty-five most common problems, categorized under seven biblical root causes: bitterness, fornication, materialism, rejection, lying, imagination, and doubt. The chapters on addiction, cruel men, suffering and grief, and depression are separate because of their length, but each falls under one of the root causes. Family problems are listed in three separate chapters because each may be a result of several root causes. There are enough suggested solutions to each problem that, by using the appropriate solution, the counselor can help the counselee find God's solution to the problem, no matter what the situation. The case studies are essentially true regarding the symptoms, diagnoses, solutions, and outcomes. However, to protect the counselees' privacy, the names, genders, places, and details have been fictionalized.

Information and principles are drawn from the Word of God, secular studies, and the authors' experience in forty-two years of counseling. The Bible principles, if the correct interpretation has been made, are dependable and trustworthy, since they are based on the inspired, inerrant Word of God. Other studies are only as good as the scope and breadth of the study and their interpretation by the authors. The experience of the authors is colored by a literal interpretation of the Bible as the Word of God and their educational backgrounds and experiences.

Dr. Fremont's background is in the field of psychology and counseling, and he taught those subjects at Bob Jones University for forty-one years. Mrs. Fremont's background is in the field of health care and family relations, and she has taught in the Division of Nursing at BJU for thirty-six years. Walter Fremont, B.S., M. S., D. Ed., and his wife, Trudy, R.N., B.S., M.S., C.F.L.E., were turned from a "secular psychological viewpoint" acquired from graduate study in psychology and counseling courses at the University of Wisconsin, Pennsylvania State University, and the University of North Carolina, to a Bible-oriented viewpoint by thorough study of the Bible, conversations with leading Christians in the psychology and counseling fields, and attending the seminars and reading the books of these men.

Clyde Narramore, an active soulwinner who taught at a Christian college in the early 1940s, was about the only one in the 1950s who was trying to relate psychology to the Bible. Henry Brandt in the 1960s, especially in his book *Struggle for Peace,* gave emphasis to the biblical viewpoint. In the early 1970s Bill Gothard, Larry Coy, and the Bob Jones University education and psychology teachers emphasized Bible principles as the solution to mental problems and confusion. The turning point toward biblical counseling came with Jay Adams's book *Competent To Counsel,* published in 1972, and its companion volume *The Christian Counselor's Manual,* published in 1973. In these two books, he laid the groundwork for thousands of pastors and counselors around the country with his biblical nouthetic counseling approach, which was devoid of the taint of secular psychology. His books have been used as textbooks in many Christian colleges and universities. Charles Solomon, with some of his ideas on rejection and the biblical solution of identification with Christ, made a further contribution. In the 1980s books by Hunt and McMahon, *The Seduction of Christianity* and *Beyond Seduction,* and the Bobgans' books, *Psychoheresy* and *Prophets of Psychoheresy II,* helped direct Christians away from secular and "Christian" psychology and toward the biblical viewpoint of counseling others.

We designed this book to be a resource for Christian laymen who want to solve their own problems and who wish to counsel others. It is a useful textbook for church counselor-training classes, for pastors, deacons, Sunday school teachers, Christian school teachers, and camp counselors. It is designed for Christian colleges to use as a textbook in their ministerial training and beginning counseling courses. Anyone wishing to help other believers along the path to a more intimate relationship with Jesus Christ and a life of peace, happiness, and joy can use this book as a tool. Helping people God's way has great rewards with eternal results.

Our appreciation and thanks go to Dr. Robert Bell, Dean Jim Berg, Dr. Greg Mazak, Dr. Jean Saito, and Dr. Bob Wood for their valuable comments and suggestions as they reviewed all or parts of the manuscript.

Chapter 1

Christian Counseling—
Biblical or Secular?

All mature Christians do some counseling. If they are involved in the evangelization or edification program of their local churches, they will come in contact with people who have problems. Spiritual Christians can have a tremendous influence on younger, immature Christians if they are willing to make the sacrifice of time necessary for helping others in a counseling ministry. The Bible says, "Brethren, if a man be overtaken in a fault, ye which are spiritual, restore such an one in the spirit of meekness; considering thyself, lest thou also be tempted. Bear ye one another's burdens, and so fulfill the law of Christ" (Gal. 6:1-2). Pastors also do a great amount of counseling as a regular part of their pastoral ministry. However, most Christians need assurances that they can become effective Christian counselors using only Bible principles and concepts without training in the field of psychology.

To be an effective Christian counselor, one must be aware of the following: (1) the goal of counseling; (2) the basic causes of problems; (3) general biblical concepts about the nature and behavior of people; (4) medical problems that affect behavior; (5) the present forces in society that people allow to shape and mold their behavior; (6) the common categories of problems that affect people's lives, such as doubt, discontentment, rejection, depression, anger and bitterness, fear and panic, addiction, sex problems, marriage and family problems, and discipline of children; and (7) the principles in the Word of God so that he may continually apply God's wisdom to solutions of problems and maladjustment.

The Word of God Is Sufficient

It is concerning the last point that most Christian counselors fail because they are not willing to trust the Word of God as sufficient to solve the problems of life. Second Peter 1:3-4 says that God "hath given unto us all things that pertain unto life and godliness." The Scriptures are sufficient to so change and enhance the mind (thought), emotions (feelings), and behavior (actions) that a Christian may properly adjust to live a life of holiness.

God gave Joshua a three-point formula for prosperity and good success: (1) do not let the book of the law depart out of your mouth, (2) "meditate therein day and night," (3) "observe to do according to all that is written therein" (Josh. 1:8). Psalm 19:7-10 indicates that the Word of God is "perfect, converting the soul"; is "sure, making wise the simple"; is "right, rejoicing the heart"; is "pure, enlightening the eyes." It is to be desired more than fine gold, and it is "sweeter also than honey and the honeycomb." Psalm 119:9 and 11 say that if we will take heed to the Word of God, it will cleanse our soul; and if we will hide the Word of God in our hearts, it will keep us from sin. Verses 98 and 99 say that the commandments will make us wiser than our enemies and give us more understanding than our teachers. Second Timothy 3:16 gives the four main uses of Scripture in counseling: "All scripture is given by inspiration of God, and is profitable for doctrine, for reproof, for correction, for instruction in righteousness."

The goal of the counselor should be to help the man of God to be conformed to the image of Christ, as stated in Romans 8:29: "For whom he did foreknow, he also did predestinate to be conformed to the image of his Son." He is also helping the counselee to be prepared for the work of the ministry, to be a stable, mature Christian (Eph. 4:11-13) and to be "perfect [adequate], and throughly furnished unto all good works" (II Tim. 3:16-17). Therefore, to solve nonorganic, nonmedical problems, the effective Christian counselor needs only the Word of God. God's Word, in principle, applies to every problem that man experiences, for God is the Creator of man and knows all of the problems that mankind will ever encounter.

Three Types of Christian Counselors

Many Christian psychologists and counselors have a thorough knowledge of the theories of psychology, which are products of the creature and not of the Creator. They claim that all truth is God's truth. But they hardly ever consider the converse: all error is the Devil's error. If psychological theories do not agree with the Word of God, they are the Devil's error and not God's truth. These counselors use psychological theories rather than the Word of God to attempt to solve the problems of mankind. While they are born-again Christians who want to do the will of God, man's wisdom and knowledge is the foundation for their "professional" ministry.

A second group of Christian psychologists and counselors, who are well schooled in psychology, do use certain Bible principles, which they try to integrate with psychological theories and ideas. They are called integrationists.

A third group of Christian counselors, who may have considerable knowledge of psychology, nevertheless realize that psychologists may be only good observers of behavior. The psychologist may (or may not) have garnered some accurate general principles about the behavior of man from laboratories, surveys, and research studies; but he is not qualified to draw accurate conclusions about the solutions to man's problems, nor can he categorize and label problems accurately if he does not do so according to biblical categories. Man's mental and behavioral problems are spiritual and must be solved spiritually. The Bible states, "But the natural man receiveth not the things of the Spirit of God: for they are foolishness unto him: neither can he know them, because they are spiritually discerned" (I Cor. 2:14). To solve counselees' problems, the effective Christian counselor decides to use only Bible principles in solving the nonorganic or nonmedical problems of those whom he counsels. He bases his counseling on the spirit-flesh model (see Table I) instead of the medical or moral model.

In trying to determine the basic cause of problems, Sigmund Freud came to some conclusions, which have been called the

Medical Model: mental and moral problems are labeled as illnesses or sick behaviors. According to Freud, "mental illness" is caused by early environmental experiences in family and society; therefore, a person is not responsible for his behavior. Freud further concludes that only a qualified psychiatrist or therapist can give proper treatment, which consists largely of ventilation of feelings.

O. H. Mowrer, in his book *The Crisis in Psychiatry and Religion,* rejected Freud's Medical Model and proposed the Moral Model: problems are caused by guilt, which results from an individual's violating his conscience or his own moral standards (not necessarily God's standards). The individual, then, is responsible for his behavior and can cure himself by changing his behavior and confessing his sin (at least to someone).

Spirit-Flesh Model

Christian counselors reject both the Medical Model and the Moral Model, proposing instead the Spirit-Flesh Model (Gal. 5:17-26) (see Table I): problems are caused by guilt resulting from sinful attitudes and behavior in direct violation of God's standards as revealed in the Bible.

All people, including Christians, have the flesh within that motivates them to sin. The Christian also has the Holy Spirit within to give him victory over the flesh. Thus, in the Christian's life, the flesh is continually warring against the Spirit. Paul in Galatians 5:16-17 gives this admonition: "This I say then, Walk in the Spirit, and ye shall not fulfil the lust of the flesh. For the flesh lusteth against the Spirit, and the Spirit against the flesh: and these are contrary the one to the other: so that ye cannot do the things that ye would." The Christian counselor asserts that the individual is responsible for his problems when he gives in to the flesh and sins by violating God's laws and will. God works in repentant men who confess sin and trust Jesus Christ for complete forgiveness. A person then must crucify self daily, as indicated in Luke 9:23: "And he said to them all, If any man will come after me, let him deny himself, and take up his cross daily, and follow me." Again Galatians 5:24 says, "And they that are Christ's have crucified the flesh with the affections and lusts."

TABLE I
SPIRIT-FLESH MODEL: THE BATTLE WITHIN

Serve Sin—Flesh	Serve Righteousness—Spirit
False gospel—works	True gospel—faith, blood of Christ
Feeling oriented	Mind oriented
Rebellion	Obedience
Hate, bitterness, revenge	Love, forgiveness
Lust—fornication	Purity—one flesh in marriage
Dissatisfaction—love of money	Contentment—peace
Pride	Humility
Unreality—TV, fiction	Reality—servanthood, loving people
Sensual music—rhythm	Uplifting music—melody, balance
Temporal high—drugs, alcohol	Joy in the Lord—praise

```
0   1   2   3   4   5   6   7   8   9   10
|---|---|---|---|---|---|---|---|---|---|
```

Sin ⟵⟶ Holiness

Worldliness (I John 2:5-17)

Which direction?

Dedication (Romans 12:1-2)

Self reigns

Rev. 3:15-16
Gal. 5:24
Rom. 6:11-13; 7:15-25
James 1:8

Self crucified (Luke 9:23; Gal. 2:20; 5:22-23)

Two forces beat within my breast.
The one is foul, the other blest.
The one I love, the one I hate.
The one I feed will dominate.

Jesus Christ conquered the Devil, death, and the flesh at the cross. Because of that victory, the flesh does not have a stranglehold on Christians. They depend on the power of Christ, walk in the Spirit, and do not make provision for the flesh to fulfill lusts (Rom. 13:14; 6:11-13; Gal. 5:24).

The Spirit-Flesh Model does not apply to some organic problems that are the result of the consequences of sin (Exod. 20:5), or of a sovereign God's working out His perfect will in a life (Job 23:10), or of demon possession, which Christ treated in a different way (Mark 9:29). Pastors and Christians who know the Word of God are best qualified to counsel people who are having problems. If the problem is caused by physical difficulties, the counselee should be referred to a physician while he continues to meet with a biblical counselor. A thorough understanding of the spirit and the flesh is necessary for proper biblical counseling to take place (see Table II).

The Flesh

The Christian's battle with the flesh has been chronicled in the Bible since the beginning of time. Adam and Eve disobeyed the Lord even though they were in a perfect environment. Lot got drunk and committed incest. Abraham lied about his wife. Jacob deceived his father. Moses committed murder and later disobeyed God. David, a man after God's own heart, nevertheless committed adultery and murder. And Solomon, the wisest man, became involved with ungodly women and false idols. The various kings of Israel and Judah went into idolatry. Elijah, after a great spiritual victory, went into deep depression. Even the disciples who walked with Jesus and converts of Paul had their problems with the flesh. Five of the disciples left their commitment and went back to fishing after the crucifixion. Peter denied the Lord, and Thomas doubted. John Mark was rebellious, and Demas went back into the world. All of these were leaders and men of God.

Satan reaches Christians by appealing to the flesh. The flesh includes the mind and the physical body of man, which are habituated to sin. Self, man's tendency to operate from his own resources and in his own strength instead of trusting God's power, is a characteristic of the flesh. It is weak and tends toward corruptness.

TABLE II
THE SPIRIT-FLESH AND THE WORLD

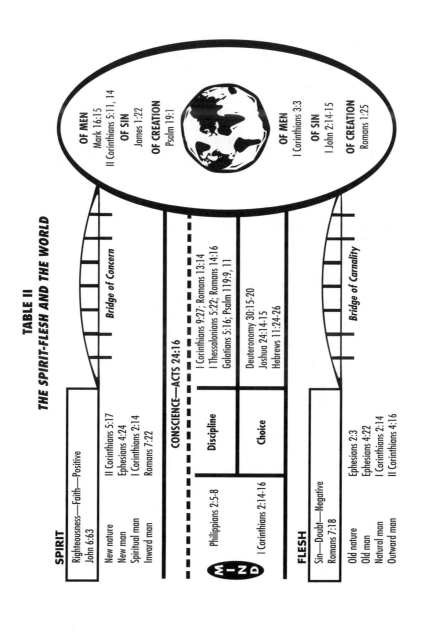

SPIRIT

Righteousness—Faith—Positive
John 6:63

New nature
New man
Spiritual man
Inward man

II Corinthians 5:17
Ephesians 4:24
I Corinthians 2:14
Romans 7:22

Bridge of Concern

CONSCIENCE—ACTS 24:16

Discipline

I Corinthians 9:27; Romans 13:14
I Thessalonians 5:22; Romans 14:16
Galatians 5:16; Psalm 119:9, 11

Choice

Deuteronomy 30:15-20
Joshua 24:14-15
Hebrews 11:24-26

Philippians 2:5-8

I Corinthians 2:14-16

MIND

FLESH

Sin—Doubt—Negative
Romans 7:18

Old nature
Old man
Natural man
Outward man

Ephesians 2:3
Ephesians 4:22
I Corinthians 2:14
II Corinthians 4:16

Bridge of Carnality

OF MEN
Mark 16:15
II Corinthians 5:11, 14
OF SIN
James 1:22
OF CREATION
Psalm 19:1

OF MEN
I Corinthians 3:3
OF SIN
I John 2:14-15
OF CREATION
Romans 1:25

The Devil uses the world of sin as an appeal to stir up and entice the flesh. Paul wrote in Romans 7:18, "For I know that in me (that is, in my flesh,) dwelleth no good thing." John 6:63 says, "The flesh profiteth nothing." Matthew 26:41 indicates that "the spirit indeed is willing, but the flesh is weak." Galatians 5:17 and 21 point out that "the flesh lusteth against the Spirit, and the Spirit against the flesh." The flesh is, in reality, a built-in crime system in each person. As someone quipped, "We have met the enemy; he is us."

Psychologists use the term *latent* to refer to the tendencies of some people who have unexpressed, corrupt desires hidden deep in their subconscious waiting to explode. For example, they speak of latent homosexuality, latent incest, or latent homicidal tendencies. The existence of Freud's concept of the subconscious mind is under criticism by both secular psychologists and Christian counselors. These corrupt tendencies which exist in everyone, even Christians, can be better explained by the biblical term *flesh.* Any human is capable of doing anything imaginable in the right circumstances, given the right provocation and failure to trust Christ. For example, suppose a man walking through a park on his way home hears a cry. He sees a man in the act of raping a teenage girl, whose face is a bloody mess. He grabs a big stick and then realizes that the teenage girl is his daughter. It would be safe to say that the father would probably continually beat the rapist until he died. While the law would call it justifiable homicide, the father would have to deal with the guilt of having killed a human being.

Psychologists study addiction and call it a disease. The Bible calls addiction the bondage of sin (II Peter 2:19). Everybody, even a Christian, is susceptible to coming under bondage to something—be it food, sex, alcohol, tobacco, gossip—because all have the flesh within, motivating them to become enslaved to sin. But Christ has freed all from such bondage. Christians need not give in to such sins. They are no longer sin's slaves. The Bible warns Christians to guard themselves against the flesh and to make no provision for it (Rom. 13:14).

The Bible refers to the flesh as lust in Ephesians 2:3: "Among whom also we all had our conversation in times past in the lusts of our flesh, fulfilling the desires of the flesh and of the mind." The Bible refers to the flesh as "the old man" in Ephesians 4:22: "That ye put off concerning the former conversation [habitual way of life] the old man, which is corrupt according to the deceitful lusts." The flesh does not improve with age or experience. If it is not constantly kept under control by the Holy Spirit's ruling the thoughts and actions, there can be an eruption of corruption at the most unexpected times (Gal. 5:16). God does not reform the flesh; He condemns it. But He gives the Holy Spirit so that the Christian can have victory over the flesh (Rom. 8:12-13; Gal. 5:24; Col. 3:5, 12).

The World

The Bible talks about the world as being the world of men (John 3:16), the world of sin (I John 2:14-15), and the world of creation (Rom. 1:20). The Devil uses the world to appeal to the person over the bridge of carnality. The fleshly person looks upon the world of men with envying, strife, and divisions, which result from his carnality (I Cor. 3:3). He looks upon the world of sin with the lust of the eyes, the lust of the flesh, and the pride of life (I John 2:16). He looks upon the created world, worshiping the creature more than the creator (Rom. 1:25). All humans are born with a sinful nature, which, until given a new nature, goes on wrongly (sinfully) habituating the body. The flesh keeps operating within until the person dies, even though he becomes a Christian.

The Spirit

The flesh is contrasted with the Holy Spirit, who comes into every born-again Christian the minute he is saved. The Spirit indwelling the life results in the new nature or new creature, as written in II Corinthians 5:17: "Therefore if any man be in Christ, he is a new creature: old things are passed away; behold, all things are become new." This new nature produces the new man, also referred to as the spiritual man and the inward man (Eph. 4:24; I Cor. 2:15; Rom. 7:22).

The Spirit reaches out over the bridge of concern to the world of men by reaching men with the gospel: "And he said unto them, Go ye into all the world, and preach the gospel to every creature" (Mark 16:15). The new nature interacts with the world of sin by activism. "But be ye doers of the word, and not hearers only" (James 1:22). The new nature responds to the world of God's creation, which reveals God, by thoroughly enjoying God's great creation. "The heavens declare the glory of God; and the firmament sheweth his handywork" (Ps. 19:1). God gives tremendous blessings to Christians through His creation.

Conscience

God has given all human beings a conscience to determine right from wrong. However, the reaction and the response of the conscience depend on early moral training and the extent to which one has habitually and consistently given a right response to the promptings of the conscience. When the conscience is violated by sinning, it can be seared and defiled and rendered ineffective (I Tim. 4:2; Titus 1:15). Early training can be evil training so that the conscience is not activated when evil is done. For example, certain Islamic sects teach that heavenly rewards await one who has killed an unbeliever. Therefore, in good conscience, sect members can kill and feel no remorse.

The conscience of a believer, trained in the moral principles of the Word of God, acts as a buffer to keep the world from having an undue influence and the flesh from erupting into corruption. The Christian, like Paul, should "have always a conscience void of offence toward God, and toward man" (Acts 24:16). The conscience is, however, only a warning light. The Christian must trust the sure Word of God and not depend on his conscience to distinguish right from wrong and to determine whether the flesh, the world, or the Devil is motivating behavior. The world culture says, "Let your conscience be your guide." For the Christian this saying should be changed to "Let the Word of God be your guide." The Scriptures must become the rule by which conscience evaluates thoughts, attitudes, and behavior.

The Choice

The flesh is in opposition to the Spirit, and the Christian is continually making choices between them. The Bible cites Moses as making the right choices: Moses chose "rather to suffer affliction with the people of God, than to enjoy the pleasures of sin for a season" (Heb. 11:25). Joshua made the right choices and then appealed to God's people to do the same: "And if it seem evil unto you to serve the Lord, choose you this day whom ye will serve; whether the gods which your fathers served that were on the other side of the flood, or the gods of the Amorites, in whose land ye dwell: but as for me and my house, we will serve the Lord" (Josh. 24:15).

To serve God according to God's Spirit requires daily discipline of body and mind, as Paul urged in his epistles: "But I keep under my body, and bring it into subjection" (I Cor. 9:27; cf. Rom. 13:14); "let not then your good be evil spoken of" (Rom. 14:16); "abstain from all appearance of evil" (I Thess. 5:22). God gave victory over the flesh at the cross where the flesh was crucified. The Christian is no longer in bondage to the flesh, but he still must make daily choices and observe discipline in his life to have victory. God's three-point formula for victory is found in Romans 6:11-13. The Christian is to (1) reckon himself dead to sin because the sin nature was crucified at the cross. Christ had complete victory over sin at the cross; therefore, the Christian has the power to (2) overthrow the reign of sin in his mortal body and to (3) make the choice not to yield his members as instruments of unrighteousness.

Biblical counselors realize not only that the Scriptures are sufficient for changing and enhancing the mind, feelings, and behavior toward godly adjustment but also that they help the counselee to make the right choices and decisions—those that are in line with God's will. Early conditioning, early environmental influences, and early emotional reactions to experiences may have a strong influence in shaping and directing his present actions and reactions. However, humans are not animals at the mercy of these forces. They are beings with minds and wills that can overcome the past. Christian counselors help counselees understand how they have allowed past situations to shape their present mental attitudes, feelings, and behavior. Although early influences, conditioning, and environment do bias present behavior, they are not excuses for sinful behavior or continuing in that behavior.

After confronting the counselee about his sinful attitudes and behavior, the counselor helps him to make scriptural choices and to find God's will. The one great choice is whether the person is going to serve God or the Devil (Matt. 6:24, 33; Josh. 24:14-15; Heb. 11:24-26). As Moses did, the counselee must choose whether to be led of the Holy Spirit and go God's way or to respond to the flesh and go the way of the world. God promises that if the Christian goes God's way, he will be blessed (Josh. 1:8). Deciding to go after idols and false gods brings difficulty, judgment, and even destruction. That same promise holds true today. The counselee must *make up his mind* to follow biblical principles if he hopes to have success in pleasing God by clearing up his problems. Spiritual living is a matter of making right choices for God in line with biblical principles. Fleshly living is choosing against God and His Word and serving idols of the world.

Seven Decisions

There are seven important decisions that are helpful in setting a person's attitude toward continually making the right daily choices.

1. **Salvation**—This is the most important decision and the beginning of a new life in Christ. Turning from sin to Jesus Christ; believing that He is God, that His blood was shed on Calvary's cross as a payment for sin, and that He was buried and bodily rose from the dead; accepting Him into one's life; and trusting Him as a personal Savior is the only way to eternal life (John 1:12; 3:36; I John 5:11-13).

2. **Scripture study**—Paul instructed Timothy to *"study* [be diligent] to show thyself approved unto God, a workman that needeth not to be ashamed, rightly dividing the word of truth" (II Tim. 2:15; cf. Ps. 119:9, 11, 15, 17). Deciding to have devotions, systematically studying and memorizing Scripture, and putting into practice Bible principles are important means for Christian growth.

3. **Separation**—The Bible emphasizes this idea: "For the grace of God that bringeth salvation hath appeared to all men, teaching us that, denying ungodliness and worldly lusts, we should live soberly, righteously, and godly, in this present world" (Titus 2:11-12); and "Be ye not unequally yoked together with unbelievers: for what fellowship hath righteousness with unrighteousness? . . . Wherefore come out from among them, and be ye separate, saith the Lord, and

touch not the unclean thing: and I will receive you "(II Cor.
6:14-17). Recognizing God's holiness and His desire for the
holy life in every believer, the born-again Christian decides
to practice personal and ecclesiastical separation.

4. **Surrender**—Paul appeals to Christians in Romans 12:1-2:
"I beseech you therefore, brethren, by the mercies of God,
that ye present your bodies a living sacrifice, holy, acceptable
unto God, which is your reasonable service. And be not
conformed to this world: but be ye transformed by the renewing of your mind, that ye may prove what is that good, and
acceptable, and perfect will of God." God wants total commitment and dedication. Every believer should surrender his
life for service and crucify self daily (Luke 9:23).

5. **Soulwinning**—The Bible says, "Awake to righteousness,
and sin not; for some have not the knowledge of God: I speak
this to your shame" (I Cor. 15:34), and "Go ye therefore, and
teach all nations, baptizing them in the name of the Father,
and of the Son, and of the Holy Ghost: teaching them to
observe all things whatsoever I have commanded you: and,
lo, I am with you alway, even unto the end of the world.
Amen" (Matt. 28:19-20). Deciding to obey the Great Commission, the Christian invites others to gospel services, carries and passes out tracts, witnesses at every opportunity, and
actively engages in some sort of gospel ministry.

6. **Sacrifice of praise**—The writer of Hebrews states, "By him
therefore, let us offer the sacrifice of praise to God continually, that is, the fruit of our lips giving thanks to his name"
(Heb. 13:15). Other Scriptures emphasize the importance of
praise: "Oh that men would praise the Lord for his goodness,
and for his wonderful works to the children of men!" (Ps.
107:8); "Speaking to yourselves in psalms and hymns and
spiritual songs, singing and making melody in your heart to
the Lord; giving thanks always for all things unto God and
the Father in the name of our Lord Jesus Christ" (Eph.
5:19-20). Deciding to praise the Lord in song, voice, and
spirit brings about a positive faith attitude that underlies a
well-adjusted, stable Christian.

7. **Service of love**—Jesus said, "A new commandment I give
unto you, That ye love one another; as I have loved you, that

ye also love one another. By this shall all men know that ye are my disciples, if ye have love one to another" (John 13:34-35; cf. Matt. 22:37-40). Deciding to live an unselfish, self-sacrificing life, understanding and meeting the needs of others, is the only way to show forth the great love God put into the heart of the Christian at salvation (Rom. 5:5).

If the counselee has made these basic decisions, it is much easier for him daily to make other right decisions for God and be biblically adjusted. It also helps if the person early in his Christian life makes certain specific decisions, such as "I will not be immoral in my actions; I will not smoke; I will not drink any alcoholic beverage; I will read my Bible and pray every day; I will tithe; I will witness at every appropriate opportunity." This type of decision can insulate the Christian against peer pressure, temptations of the flesh, or just negligence in focusing on the Lord. Care must be taken not to bind oneself in a legalistic system of rules to gain favor with God or as a substitute for God's grace.

Making the right choices by having a Spirit-filled, disciplined mind is the only way that a Christian can experience victory over the flesh. Galatians 5:16 says, "Walk in the Spirit, and ye shall not fulfill the lust of the flesh." This is the desire of every Christian. When he gives in to the flesh, he is sure to have mental and behavioral problems. He then brings upon his life the correcting hand of God. But praise the Lord, He has given the Christian confession (as explained in I John 1:9) as the remedy for sinful choices which result in sinful behavior.

The story is told about a rooster that left the barnyard through a hole in the fence and wandered into the zoo next door. He came upon an ostrich egg and was amazed. He slowly and laboriously rolled it back to the barnyard through the hole in the fence. Standing by the egg he called the fifteen hens together and said to them, "Girls, I am not complaining, but I just wanted you to see what the competition next door is doing."

Some evangelical leaders have rolled a humanistic, psychological ostrich egg from the worldly zoo into the Christian barnyard, encouraging Christians to follow the example of the world. Biblical Christians more and more are realizing that trying to follow psychology and psychiatry principles, giving them the name "Christian," is an impossibility. Using psychological principles in their counseling is not producing the results that they wanted or desired. One cannot use nonbiblical principles and methods to bring about spiritual results. The Holy Spirit is the One who brings about change, and He will not bless nonbiblical ways, since He always works in accordance with the Word of God. Psychological techniques and methods can and do produce change, but it is worldly change and not the kind of change that God wants in a life (Rom. 8:8), for it is self-centered and not God-centered.

Chapter 2

The Goal of Counseling—
Christlikeness

Christlikeness is the goal of counseling (Rom. 8:29). Man was created perfect and was conformed to God's will in the Garden of Eden. Adam was in a perfect relationship with God, his environment was perfect, and his relationship with his wife was perfect. There was no problem with his feelings about himself. When Adam and Eve failed the test that God allowed and chose to rebel against God, they became hostile to God, others, self, and the environment. Ever since that original sin, mankind has had problems that, if not derived from medical causes (which include chemical causes) or organic causes, such as brain tumors, are a result of wrong relationships to God and one's neighbor. People experience maladjustment in this way because they deliberately sin against a holy God and reap the resulting guilt or fear.

A spiritual Christian is rightly related to God through Christ and is well adjusted to others and to life because he follows God's principles under the leadership of the Holy Spirit and acts and reacts exactly as God intended. The natural man is not rightly related to God and has problems because of his sin. However, the believer who serves the flesh while serving the Spirit of God may have more problems than the natural man. This dichotomy causes a double-mindedness. James 1:8 emphasized this idea long before psychology was ever developed: "A double-minded man is unstable in all his ways." A natural man who has been brought up in a moral environment with moral teaching, which may include God's standards, can violate these standards and become doubleminded and, therefore, maladjusted and besieged with many problems. Sin, which is a violation of God's law, causes guilt and fear of judgment and results in maladjustment. Most people in mental hospitals are not sick; they are sinful. They have become so maladjusted that authority figures decide that they cannot function in normal society and must get treatment.

The Christian counselor's ministry is to help people to achieve Christlikeness by conforming to God and His will and by making biblical adjustments to others, to self, to circumstances, and to the various stages of life.

Conformity to God and His Will

Salvation is the initial step in conformity to God. The world believes that salvation is obtained by works—joining a church, getting baptized, giving to charity, reforming outward behavior, or by a variety of other deeds or ceremonies. The Bible says, however, "All our righteousnesses are as filthy rags" (Isa. 64:6). Ephesians 2:8-9 also says, "For by grace are ye saved through faith; and that not of yourselves: it is the gift of God: Not of works, lest any man should boast."

To be saved, or born again, one must believe certain things about Jesus Christ. First, he must realize that Jesus Christ is God and the only begotten Son of God. Second, he must realize that God loved him enough to send His Son down to earth to suffer, bleed, and die for his sins, as told in John's gospel: "For God sent not his son into the world to condemn the world; but that the world through him might be saved" (John 3:17). Christ's purpose for coming to earth was not to live a perfect, sinless life, condemning others by His example; rather, He came to shed His blood on Calvary's cross as payment for man's sins. Third, Christ was buried and rose again the third day for man's justification. Everyone must believe these things in order to be saved.

Moreover, to obtain salvation, one must understand that believing includes receiving Christ as personal Savior. He must accept Christ into his life as indicated in John 1:12: "But as many as received him, to them gave he power to become the sons of God, even to them that believe on his name." There must be a time when he repents of his sin and asks Christ to come into his heart—a time when he receives Christ as his personal Savior. As the Bible explains, "To whom God would make known what is the riches of the glory of this mystery among the Gentiles; which is Christ in you, the hope of glory" (Col. 1:27). Salvation is repenting (or turning from one's sins to Christ) and accepting Him by faith. The moment a person does so he is saved; Christ immediately gives him eternal life. He becomes part of Christ, and the believer is said to be in Christ, a new creation. The Bible affirms this truth: "Therefore if any man be in Christ, he is a new creature: old things are passed away; behold, all things are become new" (II Cor. 5:17), and he becomes a partaker of Christ's divine nature.

At the same time a person accepts Christ, the Holy Spirit comes into a person's heart to comfort and empower him to do righteous deeds through Christ. Neither the decision to accept Christ nor the indwelling of the Holy Spirit completely eliminates all temptation to sin, but it will completely eliminate condemnation for sin. As the Scripture assures in Romans 8:1, "There is therefore now no condemnation to them which are in Christ Jesus." A Christian can be assured that his sins—past, present, and future—have been paid for and that he is washed white as snow by the blood of Christ.

When a Christian sins following salvation, he hurts his fellowship with Christ and needs to confess his wrongdoing (I John 1:9). He need not, however, struggle through life, working to maintain righteousness before God by virtue of his own resources. Through forgiveness, he lives by faith, trusts Christ as Savior, and looks to God's Word for guidance and direction in his daily walk with Christ. The believer's desire is to glorify Jesus Christ as the Lord of his life (I Cor. 10:31). His goal is to be conformed to the image of Christ (Rom. 8:29). He progressively realizes the goal as he does four things: (1) obeys the principles of the Word (John 14:21); (2) has fellowship with Christ (I John 1:7); (3) studies the character of Christ in the Word and experiences the Holy Spirit's transformation (II Cor. 3:18); and (4) equips himself to do the work of the ministry (II Tim. 3:16-17).

Dedication is critical in knowing and doing the will of God. Many make this dedication decision at the time of their salvation. If a counselor has a right view of a Christian's future, which is service for God, he will counsel each Christian to make a decision to surrender to God. However, both the counselor and the counselee must be aware that the decision to surrender always results in sacrifice. Presenting one's body to Jesus Christ for full-time service is a continuous process (Rom. 12:1-2). It is dying to self (Gal. 2:20), taking up the cross daily, and following Christ (Luke 9:23).

Some Christians dedicate their lives to the Lord within a year or two of their salvation decision. Some persons in a good Christian environment will dedicate themselves to God several times, each time giving another area of their lives to His control, but not surrendering their lives for service. Many Christians in the church are simply self-centered, carnal Christians and do not seem to be interested in serving Christ. Lack of dedication causes many problems in a Christian's life.

A dedicated Christian is in a position to be filled daily with the Spirit and can begin manifesting the fruit of the Spirit defined in the Bible as "love, joy, peace, longsuffering, gentleness, goodness, faith, meekness, temperance: against such there is no law" (Gal. 5:22-23). Often, Christians who do not manifest the fruit of the Spirit have sin in their lives and are not dedicated to the Lord. When a person dedicates his life to the Lord, he usually becomes serious about Bible study and prayer. His lifestyle changes as he becomes fully aware of God's presence in his life (Titus 2:11-15). He also becomes interested in proclaiming the gospel (I Cor. 15).

A man that has a right relationship to God is also content with the way God has made him, the life that has been given him, and the environment into which he has been put. The Bible says, "But godliness with contentment is great gain" (I Tim. 6:6; cf. Phil. 4:11). He continually works to overcome adverse circumstances and to improve his situation while recognizing the sovereignty of God and His will (Rom. 8:28; I Thess. 5:18). It is God's will that a man live God's way and not his own way.

After salvation and dedication, it is imperative that the Christian develop four important attitudes.

1. **An attitude of positive faith, which carries one through life's uncertainties.** Faith is positive, for true faith is in a great and mighty God who will bring all things to pass: "but with God all things are possible" (Matt. 19:26). Faith must develop from the point of childlike faith at salvation to

mature biblical faith that will stand the test of life's trials, tragedies, and tribulations (Heb. 11).

2. **An attitude of love that reaches others.** Man must be filled with the Holy Spirit so that he can manifest the love of God in his everyday life. Genuine love reaches a lost world with the gospel (John 4:34-35). Evangelism is one evidence of real love helping to relieve man's deepest fears—how to cope with death and judgment (Heb. 9:27-28).

3. **An attitude of hope that results in goalsetting.** The mind operates best when it is focused on goals. The writer of Proverbs says, "Hope deferred maketh the heart sick: but when the desire cometh, it is a tree of life. . . . The desire accomplished is sweet to the soul" (13:12, 19). God's goals give hope, which motivates the soul. The goals must glorify God in everything that is done (I Cor. 10:31).

4. **An attitude of obedience that fully recognizes God's holiness.** Man must order his life in line with Bible principles if he is to walk God's way and to do God's will. The Bible admonishes the believer: "Trust in the Lôrd with all thine heart; and lean not unto thine own understanding. In all thy ways acknowledge him, and he shall direct thy paths" (Prov. 3:5-6; cf. John 14:21).

Adjustment to Others

Man must not only have a right relationship to God but also become properly related to others. He first must learn how to give and receive love since he is born very self-centered. If he is bonded to a caring mother and father, he learns to receive and accept love from them, and he begins to develop his own expressions of love. The caring on the part of the parents includes discipline, which is part of training a child. When discipline is lacking because the parents are busy, unconcerned, or absent, the child's potential to receive and give love may be damaged. The child may feel rejected and insecure. He may find it difficult to develop a loving relationship with people. Such a child would often rather work with things than with people. Salvation can change these rejection feelings as the person begins to realize that he is fully accepted in the beloved by God. This is affirmed in Ephesians 1:6-7: "To the praise of the glory of his grace, wherein he hath made us accepted in the beloved. In whom we have redemption through his blood, the forgiveness of sins, according to the riches of his grace."

The Christian realizes that he is a child of God (I John 3:1) and that God is his Father (Rom. 8:15-16). He realizes after his salvation that his sins are washed in the blood of Christ and he is no longer under the condemnation of God (Rom. 8:1).

Everyone loves himself and has a strong self-focus as several Scripture passages point out: "No man ever yet hateth his own flesh" (Eph. 5:29); "And the second is like unto it, Thou shalt love thy neighbour as thyself" (Matt. 22:39). Every Christian must learn that at some time in his Christian growth he must overcome this self-focus by dedicating his life (Rom. 12:1), which is in reality becoming dead to self (Gal. 2:20), and daily denying self (Luke 9:23). Only then can he unleash to others the love that God has "shed abroad in our hearts" at salvation (Rom. 5:5).

To have a right relationship to others, the child of God must learn to engage in positive social interaction, which includes godly communication techniques. The Bible teaches, "Let no corrupt communication proceed out of your mouth, but that which is good to the use of edifying, that it may minister grace unto the hearers" (Eph. 4:29). This social interaction is best learned at home, in the preschool years, in the loving, caring interaction of the parents with the child. Dating techniques and basic principles of love and marriage are important if one is to live eventually in a close family relationship. Relating to others also involves a proper relation to one's church, work, school, community, and government. The Bible has definite principles concerning each area of relationships, whatever the circumstances or situation.

Adjustment to Self

After rightly relating to God and to others, the Christian must have a scriptural attitude toward himself to have an appropriate identity or self-awareness. Christians find their identity in Christ (Gal. 2:20) as they identify with the death, burial, and resurrection of Christ by submitting daily to His control (Luke 9:23). The Bible gives John the Baptist's testimony, which should be followed by all Christians: "He must increase, but I must decrease" (John 3:30).

This right attitude toward self includes an accurate self-appraisal of one's body, intelligence, talents, gifts, strengths, and weaknesses in humility before God, realizing that it is God that is working in and through the believer after salvation (Phil. 2:13). He does not think of himself more highly than he ought to think (Rom. 12:3) and does not compare himself to others (II Cor. 10:12).

Self always tries to promote itself and its rights at others' expense. The Spirit-filled person denies self to follow Christ. Nowhere in the Bible is it even suggested for the Christian to love self. Self-love has become the plague of modern man. However, man should not degrade or deprecate the great creation that God has performed in each human. Instead, this creation of God, including the gifts and talents, should be used to His glory (I Cor. 10:31), and praise should be given to God for the results. "Oh that men would praise the Lord for his goodness, and for his wonderful works to the children of men!" (Ps. 107:8).

Having a right attitude toward self means becoming an independent person under the Lordship of Christ and His Word. He is then able to make godly decisions in line with Bible principles instead of bowing to peer pressure and the world system. The independent person controls the environment instead of being controlled by it.

A scriptural attitude toward self also involves learning to control one's feelings by having proper attitudes. The Christian should learn to use his feelings in a God-directed way. An appropriate attitude toward self also means keeping a healthy body and learning to accept the bodily changes that take place in the various stages of life. Through proper rest, nutrition, and exercise, the Christian keeps his body functioning as efficiently as possible.

Adjustment to Circumstances

The Christlike Christian knows how to face reality with all of its frustrations, tragedies, difficulties, and heartaches. The Bible gives comforting assurances and instruction: "When my father and my mother forsake me, then the Lord will take me up" (Ps. 27:10); "In every thing give thanks: for this is the will of God in Christ Jesus concerning you" (I Thess. 5:18); "Giving thanks always for all things unto God and the Father in the name of our Lord Jesus

Christ" (Eph. 5:20); "And we know that all things work together for good to them that love God, to them who are the called according to his purpose" (Rom. 8:28). There are many calamities over which a person has no control, such as war, earthquakes, tornadoes, hurricanes, and death. There are also life-threatening circumstances, such as disease, accidents, and terminal illness. There are also humiliating or embarrassing situations that occur in everyone's life. In addition, the Bible reminds us that godly Christians will be persecuted (II Tim. 3:12).

People have a misconception that life should be fair because God is fair and good. Life is not fair, but God is always fair and good. If people confuse God with the reality of life and expect financial success or good health, their faith in God is going to be shattered when they have a financial reversal or a terminal disease. Heaven, of course, is perfect, and it helps man to focus on eternal things rather than on the temporary frustrations and troubles of life.

Adjustments to Various Stages of Life

Through the various stages of life, problems spring from the crucial changes that are taking place in the body and the person's ongoing life situation. These include adolescence, launching into a career, marriage, having and rearing children, midlife crisis, retirement, declining health, and death.

Most adjustments have to be made by the adolescent as he goes from childhood to adulthood. Some of these adjustments are as follows: (1) accepting his physical development and sex role, (2) controlling his emotions, (3) becoming socially accepted, (4) finding his identity as a uniquely created person, (5) becoming independent and making choices while still respecting authority and seeking wise counsel, (6) gaining financial responsibility, (7) establishing his character, (8) learning to set goals, (9) developing positive faith attitudes and eliminating negative doubt attitudes, (10) assuming the unselfish attitude of a servant, and (11) developing his own moral and spiritual values.

Parents have the main responsibility for counseling their teenage son or daughter; however, Christian school teachers, youth workers, pastors, and other Christian leaders who work with youth can be of vital assistance in helping the adolescent to make these adjustments.

Choosing a vocation or career, getting the necessary training and experience, getting started with the right company or organization, and making advancements require many adjustments in a short time.

Marriage involves many adjustments, from dating and choosing the right mate to the adjustments necessary in the engagement period and through the wedding. There are many adjustments in early marriage, which include finances, communication, sexual relations, proper relationships with the in-laws, new routines and different responsibilities, and a changed social life. These adjustments must be made if the marriage is going to be happy and stable.

When children come along, there is financing, training, schooling them through college, and the many other adjustments that rearing children forces upon the parents.

The midlife period requires dramatic adjustments. The change in hormones for both men and women causes for many a midlife crisis and severe temptations to sin. It has been suggested that sex hormones increase just before they begin a gradual decline in midlife. As the children leave home, some parents experience the empty-nest syndrome and must develop a new relationship with each other.

Retirement has its own sets of problems for the wife. Many wives are faced with having a husband underfoot trying to control the home that he has ignored for forty or more years. Various adjustments have to be made regarding hobbies and part-time work for the man and possibly a change in lifestyle because of reduced finances. Usually there must be adjustments to declining health at this time as well as the care and the death of parents, the death of a spouse, or even the tragedies and deaths of the children and their families.

Since these situations do not occur all at once but are spread out over a period of fifty or sixty years, most people are capable of making the necessary adjustments. However, some people do need help, especially if a number of crucial situations and changes occur at one time. When it rains, it often pours. Christians must be ready to help and bear one another's burdens (Gal. 6:1-2). The Christian who knows the Lord can make these situations a good point of contact for the gospel, being ever ready in love to lend a helping hand and to present the claims of Christ to people who are ready to listen.

The Christian counselor's ministry is to help people to achieve Christlikeness by conforming to God and His will and by adjusting to others, to themselves, to their circumstances, and to the various stages of life. Christian counselors usually accomplish their ministry in four stages: identification, confrontation, teaching, and decisive action.

1. **Identification**—Like good detectives, counselors listen and ask questions, searching for clues so that the basic problem can be revealed. They are especially aware of any sin that might be causing the problem. They are also alert to any physical problems that might be causing or contributing to the problem so that they can determine whether it is necessary to refer the person to a physician. The Holy Spirit, through the Word of God, guides the counselor as he analyzes the problem and discerns the solution.

2. **Confrontation**—After the basic problems have been identified, counselors must confront the individual with the sinful, inadequate, or mistaken behavior, motive, attitude, or belief that has caused the problem. The counselor must explain the cause of the problem, which may be the result of sinful thinking, decisions, behaviors, or wrong childhood and teenage attitudes, behaviors, or responses that have carried over into the present and contributed to the problem.

3. **Teaching**—This is best done by applying God's principles to the problem and showing what behavior or action or attitude must be eliminated or changed because it is not in accord with God's Word.

4. **Decisive action**—This stage involves a commitment on the part of the counselee to take definite action to change his behavior and eliminate the problem. Counselor follow-up is necessary for answering questions and challenging and encouraging the counselee to follow through with the necessary changes to achieve proper adjustment.

Many people act and react on the feeling level, and adverse situations, problems, and circumstances throw them into a confusing turmoil. Many think through life's problems but make decisions based on wrong or inadequate principles and, therefore, do not make the best adjustments in life. Real adjustment for an individual is brought about as he makes right decisions and follows the will of God by obeying the principles in the Word of God. Jesus clearly explained how to identify His disciple: "He that hath my commandments, and keepeth them, he it is that loveth me; and he that loveth me shall be loved of my Father, and I will love him, and will manifest myself to him" (John 14:21). Having a right relationship with God and obedience to God's Word are the keys to Christlikeness.

Chapter 3

The Brain and the Functioning of the Mind

The brain is probably the most intricate mechanism that God ever created. The wonder and complexity of the human brain defies all imagination. Although the average brain weighs three pounds, it does most of its work through the neurons, which are too small to be measured. The latest estimate of the number of neurons in the brain is from 50 to 100 billion. These neurons carry millions of signals, and the electrochemical reaction that occurs in the gap between neurons—called a synapse—happens millions of times in a day's thought process. "There may be from 10 trillion to 100 trillion synapses in the brain, and each one operates as a tiny calculator that tallies signals, arriving as electrical impulses."[1] Communication between the neurons is electrochemical. The chemical signal or the neurotransmitter is converted back into an electrical impulse as it reaches the other neurons. As Richard Restak states in his book *The Brain,* "The total number of connections within the vast network of the brain's neuronal system is truly astronomical."[2]

The main control panel of the brain is the hypothalamus, which is a link between the body and the brain. It is situated just at the base of the brain and at the top of the spine and controls the basic drives of the body, such as sex and hunger. The hypothalamus also controls the pituitary gland, which governs the production and circulation of hormones for the body. The hypothalamus is also the switchboard mechanism for all the nerves of the body, transmitting impressions from the five senses and from the various organs of the body concerning body movement and sensory information. No one is fully aware of the complexity and minuteness of this feeding of information to the brain. It is thought that even the individual components of the hormone system are measured and secreted according to the needs of the body and the immune system.

The brain is the only organ in the body that cannot be transplanted (if medical science could solve all the complex problems of a brain transplant) without completely changing the person, for the mind which contains the conscience, the spirit, and the very identity of a person resides in and operates through the brain. The brain controls every action of the body, and there is a continuous interaction between the brain and the body.

Brain Research

To understand the functioning of the mind, one must understand the brain; therefore, scientists, who know very little about the brain, are developing tools to increase their understanding. In the past they had the use only of electroencephalograms, or EEGs. Using a scanner that records gamma rays from decaying radioactive isotopes, scientists have developed Positron Emission Tomography (PET), and Single-Photon Emission Computed Tomography (SPECT), which allow them to map the brain by measuring changes in the brain's glucose consumption. PET and SPECT scans prove useful in the diagnosis of Alzheimer's disease and a few other mental conditions. "CT scans are certainly the best known of the new wave of diagnostic devices. . . . A series of X-ray beams on a rotating axis . . . take computer-generated pictures of different segments . . . of the brain or body."[3] Another promising technique for the study of the brain is Brain Electrical Activity Mapping (BEAM), a way of enhancing the amount of information available on a standard EEG. This device enables one to watch information go through the brain from recognition to cognition. A closely related technique is Significant Probability Mapping (SPM), which provides a highly sensitive way to diagnose schizophrenia and a few other severe mental disorders. Another diagnostic tool is the Nuclear Magnetic Resonance (NMR), now called Magnetic Resonance Imaging (MRI), which measures the responses of hydrogen protons within brain tissue to applied radio frequency pulses. Extensive research is being done at the Brain Research Institute at UCLA, where 140 UCLA faculty members in 135 research laboratories are involved in brain research.[4]

The late neurosurgeon Wilder Penfield did extensive research with electrical probes in human beings at the Montreal Neurologic Institute in Canada. Although brain researchers equate the mind with the brain, Penfield and others in their later years tended to the dualistic position that the mind is independent of the brain, though it works through the brain and is dependent on the brain's activity.[5]

These scientists have found that the brain contains a vast memory bank. They have discovered through electrical brain probes that if a certain part of the brain is touched, any memory can be brought to the conscious mind. This memory includes the feelings and sensations that happened at the event, whether it was a fourth birthday or a twelfth Christmas. Scientists have been unable to determine how much, if any, storage loss occurs in the memory bank. They also know that when a thought is occurring, several parts of the brain are activated simultaneously so that there is a tremendous exchange of information involving most of the brain in the various thought patterns.

When most people use the term *mind,* they are thinking of a mind independent of a brain. However, in this life the mind is indeed dependent on the brain since mind activity is recognized as emanating through the function of the brain.

Dr. Norman Cousins, working closely with the Brain Research Institute at UCLA, said in his book *Head First,* "Brain researchers now believe that what happens in the body can affect the brain and what happens in the brain can affect the body. Hope, purpose, and determination are not merely mental states. They have electro-chemical connections that play a large part in the workings of the immune system and indeed in the entire economy of the total human organism."[6] He goes on to say that "the human brain serves as a control center for millions of messengers carrying instructions to the body's organs without intruding on the conscious intelligence. Recent research tends to emphasize communication rather than connection to describe the process by which the brain interacts with the body. . . . Directions being given by the brain travel along heavily trafficked electrochemical pathways. These directions are augmented by delivery of specific activating substances to the glands . . . called neuropeptides, [and] serve as information carriers to coordinate the function of the brain's plans and immune systems."[7] Counselors dealing with people who have life-threatening and psychosomatic diseases must be fully aware of the effect of mental attitudes on the body and its organs as well as the reaction of these organs and bodily processes to mental attitudes.

How the Mind Works

One way to describe the mind and the brain is to compare them to the advanced computer, which can work on many problems at the same time. Although this complex mechanism cannot parallel the marvelous functioning of the mind and the brain, the comparison will be made for the purposes of simplicity. (See Table III.)

How the mind works as it uses the brain is largely a matter of speculation and theory. Some surmise that the brain uses memory bits that are drawn from the memory bank to form thought patterns, and that these thought patterns tend to be opposites, either positive or negative, pain or pleasure, or true or false. Jeremy Bentham, an English philosopher, wrote in 1789, "Nature has placed mankind under the governments of two sovereign masters, pain and pleasure. It is for them alone to point out what we ought to do as well as to determine what we shall do." Restak comments on that statement: "But I wonder if that is entirely so. I prefer to think of it in terms of a predisposition on our part always toward thinking in opposites, good and bad, painful and pleasureful, and so on. Since this is the way our mind works, these are the kinds of observations that come naturally to brain researchers. The animal (or research subject) must be either seeking pleasure or avoiding pain."[8]

The will in the conscious mind is the operator of this giant computer (processing mind) and determines what bits of information will be drawn from the memory bank to form these thought patterns. A person can decide which thought patterns he wants to have and which he wants to eliminate. He can refuse to think about the thought patterns that have been formed, or he can alter the thought patterns any way he decides. He can also combine some thought patterns with others to form complex thinking, including creative thinking.

TABLE III
THE MIND AS A COMPUTER

Dreams

Although there is no scriptural basis for this theory, the authors' belief is that dreams, which reveal man's inner depravity, serve to cleanse the computer mind of unwanted thought patterns. The average person dreams five dreams a night, and these dreams are usually couched in symbols. There are no universal dream symbols, so God evidently wants to camouflage these thought patterns that are being purged from the mind. A person tends not to remember his dreams unless he wakes up during a dream and recalls the details within the first ten minutes of awakening. One should not try to remember his dreams, for that process feeds the dream material back into the brain.

When a person wants to get rid of a sinful thought pattern, he must confess that thought pattern to Jesus Christ, who forgives and cleanses the thought pattern with His blood. God may then use dreams to remove it from the mind. A person can, of course, reconstruct the thought patterns any time he chooses. There are also wish-fulfillment thoughts that are not in line with God's goals and that will not do a person any good in his life or in his future service for God. God takes those thought patterns out of the mind in dreams. God also uses dreams as a legitimate means of releasing sexual tension. Most men and about 20 percent of women have at times regularly experienced this type of dream. One should not try to remember or interpret his dreams but rather thank God for eliminating the corrupt or bizarre thoughts, the fear, the wish fulfillment, the tension, and the useless material from the mind.

The Conscious and the Processing Mind

The authors believe that the mind is composed of two parts: the conscious mind and the processing mind, which operates through the automatic functioning of the brain and the nervous system. (See Table III.) The conscious mind is the decider, the programmer, or the will. The conscious mind is used to make observations, gather information, evaluate incoming data from the senses, form value judgments, pose problems, and categorize information. Through major and minor decisions, the conscious mind programs into the processing mind the life directions and the goals to be achieved. Since man is a goal-oriented being, his mind functions best as it aims toward a goal and solves the necessary problems to reach the goal (Prov. 13:12, 19); the mind should be focused on the eternal goal (Phil. 3:13).

In numerous places, the Scriptures give clear instruction about focusing the conscious mind on one's life direction and goals. Christians are commanded in the Bible to choose (Heb. 11:25; Josh. 24:14), to purpose in their hearts (II Cor. 9:7), to be renewed in the spirit of the mind (Eph. 4:23), to be transformed by the renewing of their minds (Rom. 12:2), and to set their affections (attitudes of feeling) on things above and not on things on this earth (Col. 3:2). This latter verse also indicates that a Christian can completely control his feelings through the proper use of the conscious mind. The conscious mind poses problems and identifies problems but it does not solve them.

The processing mind acts as a giant computer storing information, stimuli, impressions, and ideas, all of which are cataloged and stored in the memory bank for future retrieval. Like a computer, it also solves problems, using the stored information that has been fed into it by the conscious mind. Although God has programmed into the human computer certain instincts that help man to survive, man himself continually programs additional data into the processing mind. What is put into this computer determines what eventually becomes one's life action. One can get out only what is put in.

Life Control

God has given each person a powerful mind, which in this life operates through the brain and nervous system, to be used in controlling his life. Unlike animals, humans are neither controlled by the environment nor governed only by immediate stimuli. A person controls his own actions and activities and, subsequently, his life by what he thinks. He is what he thinks, for thoughts eventually are acted out in life. Man is commanded to "keep thy heart with all diligence; for out of it are the issues of life" (Prov. 4:23), and he is reminded that "of the abundance of the heart his mouth speaketh" (Luke 6:45). "A good man out of the good treasure of the heart bringeth forth good things: and an evil man out of the evil treasure bringeth forth evil things" (Matt. 12:35). The heart in these three verses refers to both the conscious mind and the processing mind. What man thinks in his conscious mind is stored in his processing mind and automatically directs his life actions. Regardless of the environmental pressures, one can determine how he is going to respond in any situation. Because God will hold humans accountable for their lives, He created people so that they are responsible for making decisions and carrying them out. The means of controlling one's life, therefore, is the conscious mind.

Two Types of Thoughts

Most thoughts are of two types: "positive faith thoughts" that are God-directed and based on the principles of the Word of God and that result in wholesome actions; or "negative doubt thoughts" that reject God, His Word, His will, and ultimately have unwholesome and sinful results. (See Table IV.) The Bible alludes to these thought patterns as either "godly thought patterns"—"Finally, brethren, whatsoever things are true, whatsoever things are honest, whatsoever things are just, whatsoever things are pure, whatsoever things are lovely, whatsoever things are of good report; if there be any virtue, and if there be any praise, think on these things" (Phil. 4:8)—or "devilish thought patterns"—"Casting down imaginations, and every high thing that exalteth itself against the knowledge of God, and bringing into captivity every thought to the obedience of Christ" (II Cor. 10:5).

Positive Faith Thoughts

Some Christian counselors, including the authors, equate positive thought patterns with positive faith thoughts. They make this parallel on the basis that faith thought in God is always positive. One cannot think of faith in God without being positive. A description of faith in the Bible indicates this connection: "Now faith is the substance of things hoped for, the evidence of things not seen" (Heb. 11:1). The Christian has every reason to have a positive attitude, because he has a firm, solid faith based on Jesus Christ and His Word. He is positive about death and eternity because of a strong faith in Jesus Christ, who is going to take him to heaven. As stated in the Gospel of John, "He that believeth on the Son hath everlasting life: and he that believeth not the Son shall not see life; but the wrath of God abideth on him" (John 3:36). He is positive about life because of the promise in the Bible that all things work

TABLE IV
THE THINKING MAN

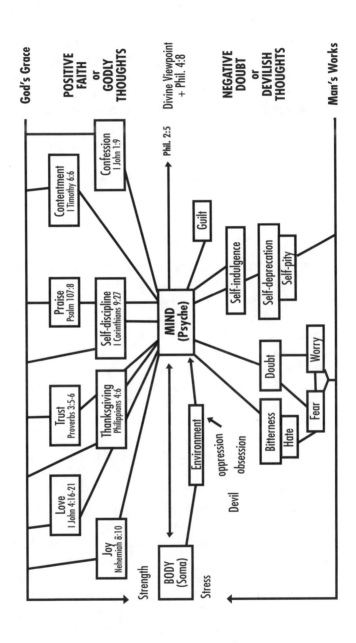

God's Grace

POSITIVE
FAITH
or
GODLY
THOUGHTS

Divine Viewpoint
+ Phil. 4:8

NEGATIVE
DOUBT
or
DEVILISH
THOUGHTS

Man's Works

Phil. 2:5

Contentment
I Timothy 6:6

Confession
I John 1:9

Guilt

Self-indulgence

Self-deprecation

Self-pity

Praise
Psalm 107:8

Self-discipline
I Corinthians 9:27

MIND
(Psyche)

Doubt

Worry

Trust
Proverbs 3:5-6

Thanksgiving
Philippians 4:6

Bitterness

Hate

Fear

Love
I John 4:16-21

Environment

oppression
obsession

Devil

Joy
Nehemiah 6:10

BODY
(Soma)

Strength

Stress

together for the good of them that are called of God according to His purpose (Rom. 8:28). A Christian can be positive about self because he knows from Paul's letter to the Ephesians that he is God's "workmanship, created in Christ Jesus unto good works" (Eph. 2:10; Ps. 139). A Christian can be positive toward people because of God's love shed abroad in his heart and his faith in God's plan, which can change the sinner's behavior (II Cor. 5:17). He can be positive about provisions because he knows that God has created and prepared great and good things for the Christian (I Cor. 2:9; Ps. 84:11).

A positive faith attitude is based on the finished work and resurrection power of Jesus Christ (I Cor. 15:17; Phil. 3:10) and His grace (Eph. 2:8-9).

Negative Doubt Thoughts

The negative doubt or devilish thoughts of rebellion, discontentment, bitterness, pride, doubt, hate, lust, and fear are to be cast out and every thought subjected to the obedience of Christ (II Cor. 10:5). With Christ in his heart, a Christian should not be under the influence of the Devil's negative thoughts regarding man's most dominating fears: fear of death and judgment (Heb. 9:27; John 3:16; Rom. 5:8), fear of defeat and lack of power (Phil. 4:13; Eph. 3:20), fear of poverty (Matt. 6:31-32; Phil. 4:19; Prov. 3:9-10), and fear of rejection and loneliness (I John 3:1-3; John 10:27-29; Eph. 1:6-7). Although unsaved men may have partially minimized these fears in their lives, only the Christian can fully and finally defeat them. Jesus Christ took away the spirit of fear and replaced it with power, love, and a sound mind (II Tim. 1:7; I John 4:18). The Christian should avoid negative "if only," "why?" "why me?" "why now?" and "what if?" attitudes, such as "We would have won the game if only I had made the extra point," and purposely think positive "next-time" and "thank-God-for-His-will-being-done" thoughts. Some negative, bitter people have a tendency to dwell on negative thoughts—"black rocks" of hatred, bitterness, and revenge. They are like a man going down the road with a sack on his back, looking for these "black rocks." Every black rock he finds he puts into his sack. (See Table V.) The sack becomes heavy, so he sits down to rest and takes a "negative memory rag" from his pocket and begins polishing the "black rocks." As he continues his trek

TABLE V
THE NEGATIVE, BITTER PERSON

Flesh
(Self)

SEEDS
of
GOD'S
LOVE

down the road, his load gets heavier and heavier. He must now decide: if he is to have rest and peace, he must let the Lord take the load of black rocks, and he must not pick up and polish any more. Instead of picking up black rocks, the Christian needs to be planting seeds of God's love. If negative, devilish thoughts are programmed into the processing mind, negative, sinful actions will result, for the processing mind or computer must work with the input it has received (Ps. 101:3).

Importance of a Proper Mind Set

Negative doubt thoughts put tremendous stress on the body and create many problems, both physical and mental. The authors believe that negative doubt thought patterns and attitudes that lead to sinful behavior could cause a chemical imbalance in the brain affecting the neurotransmitters. This condition may set up a predisposition, which could be inherited, toward certain types of severe mental problems. Habitual positive faith thoughts, or godly thoughts, tend to free the body and the mind to work at optimum level, resulting in peace and strength (Rom. 8:6; Neh. 8:10). (See Table IV.) The Christian's conscious mind should be set on the positive faith attitudes of "love, joy, peace, longsuffering, gentleness, goodness, faith, meekness, and temperance" found in Galatians 5:22-23, as well as the thoughts found in Philippians 4:8. If one programs positive faith thoughts from God's Word into the processing mind, the results will be works that honor the Lord and reflect His glory. Positive faith thoughts or attitudes and negative doubt thoughts or attitudes stem from basic beliefs. When there is a dependence on the grace of God, positive faith thoughts are the natural result and become a source of strength. When there is a dependence on the works of man, negative doubt thoughts arise and become a source of stress.

Positive Anticipation

The processing mind, or computer, makes no differentiation between thoughts about real situations and thoughts about anticipated experiences. For example, athletes "psych themselves up" by eagerly anticipating a winning situation and by carefully practicing in their minds how they are going to act in the game to bring about a winning situation. As a result, the underdog often upsets the favored team because the processing mind works toward the goal of winning. On the other hand, by anticipating negative situations and failure, many people are programming failure into the processing mind so that when a similar situation actually occurs, the processing mind works toward the goal of failure.

The principle can be used effectively for success if a person will anticipate possible successful situations and biblically determine the steps necessary to accomplish the successful goals. For example, if a Christian decides that he wants to overcome bad reactions to a close neighbor, he must first confess the reactions as sin and determine from God's Word to do what God wants him to do in the matter. Then he must mentally anticipate the next contacts with the neighbor and think through an immediate Christlike response to the neighbor's snide remarks and belligerent behavior.

Making up one's mind in anticipated situations has the same effect as playing out an actual situation. For this reason the Bible directs Christians to meditate on the Word of God. Such meditation helps a Christian to determine how God wants him to act and react in various situations. It helps him to think through how certain "Bible Action Truths" apply in each life situation.

The principle can be used in overcoming temptation by thinking about a Christlike biblical response that should be given in a tempting situation. For example, a traveling Christian businessman unlocks his hotel door and finds a beautiful woman in a negligee lying on the bed. If, prior to that situation, he has meditated on Joseph's reaction to a similar situation, he will likely flee to the hotel desk. Slogans, mottos, and verses such as "Do right now" or "Smile, for there's a great day coming" or "Think positive faith thoughts" or "The battle is the Lord's" or "I can do all things through Christ which strengtheneth me" can be recorded through repetition into the processing mind and will automatically operate at the appropriate time.

People who dwell on the negative through dissatisfaction, griping, and failure-orientation are going to experience defeat and difficulty because they actually program into their processing mind these thoughts, which eventually come out in actions. Successful people think about their successes; people who fail dwell on their failures.

Habits

Once a behavior is programmed into the brain and practiced over and over again, habit patterns are established that are hard to break. New thought patterns must be put into the processing mind by the will. Only as the Christian, claiming the power of the resurrected Christ, decides to "put off" the old and "put on" the new can longstanding sinful habit patterns be broken (Eph. 4:22-24; Rom. 6:11-13). Much of the counseling of the typical Christian counselor involves trying to change habituated sinful thought patterns that result in habituated sinful behavior and become enslaving habits. Habits that have been continually associated with pleasure are especially difficult to break.

The world and a segment of evangelical Christianity have taken some of these scriptural ideas and twisted them to extremes until they have become "New Age," "occult," and even "Other God" ideas. [See Martin and Deidre Bobgan's book *Psychoheresy*[9] and Dave Hunt's book *The Seduction of Christianity*[10] for a full discussion of these extremes.]

Spirit, Soul, and Body

The Bible indicates that man is composed of three parts: spirit, soul, and body (see Table VI), as indicated in I Thessalonians 5:23: "And the very God of peace sanctify you wholly; and I pray God your whole spirit and soul and body be preserved blameless unto the coming of our Lord Jesus Christ." This threefold division is further presented in Hebrews 4:12: "For the word of God is quick, and powerful, and sharper than any twoedged sword, piercing even to the dividing asunder of soul and spirit, and of the joints and marrow, and is a discerner of the thoughts and intents of the heart." The spirit is the part of man given by God at conception and is not to be equated with the Holy Spirit of God, who is received by Christians at the time of conversion.

The Spirit

The spirit of man is the vehicle for communion with God, as Jesus explained: "But the hour cometh, and now is, when the true worshippers shall worship the Father in spirit and in truth: for the

TABLE VI
THE TRIUNE MAN

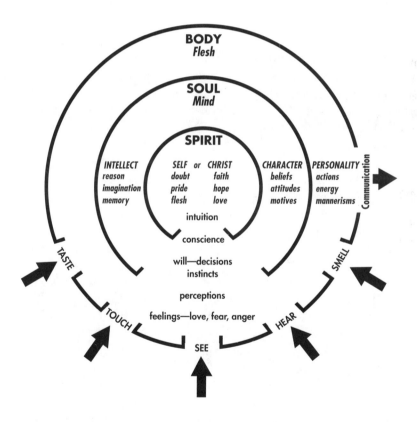

Father seeketh such to worship him" (John 4:23). The spirit of man also includes the conscience and the perceptive or intuitive powers. According to Romans 2:15, conscience is the capacity that enables man to make self-evaluations. The conscience, which the authors believe is the door between the soul and the spirit, judges every action and initiates responses that warn a person of his guilt or innocence in violating a prelearned value system. The Bible refers to a good conscience (I Pet. 3:16, 21; Heb. 13:18; Acts 23:1; I Tim. 1:5, 19) and a pure conscience (I Tim. 3:9; II Tim. 1:3). If a person fails to heed his conscience, it becomes weak (I Cor. 8:7, 10, 12) and then defiled (Titus 1:5) and evil (Heb. 10:22), and eventually it may become seared (I Tim. 4:2). The spirit of man also provides perceptions or intuitions. Christ perceived in His spirit while the scribes were reasoning in their minds (Mark 2:8). The Holy Spirit, which is received at the time of salvation, works in the spirit of man. The Devil also works through the spirit and the mind of man, and one needs to test every perception or intuition to make sure that it is in line with the Word of God. The Bible cautions Christians to try the spirits to see whether they be of God (I John 4:1). The spirit of man is naturally ruled by self, which is manifested in attitudes of doubt, pride, and fleshly lusts. This rule of self continues after a person becomes a born-again Christian until he decides to yield his life to God. Then the Holy Spirit can rule and manifest Himself in attitudes of faith, hope, and love.

The Soul

The soul of man has three functions. Proverbs 19:2 and Psalm 139:14 refer to the *mind* or the intellectual aspect of the soul which includes reason, imagination, and memory. Job 6:7 and Job 7:15 refer to the *will* or the ability of the soul to choose or make decisions. The third function of the soul is character, which includes a person's beliefs, attitudes, and motives. The door between the soul and the body are the perceptions that are determined from the sensory input to the body. Song of Solomon 1:7, II Samuel 5:8, and Colossians 3:2 refer to emotional attitudes that are manifested in the body as certain feelings.

The soul also contains instincts that are programmed into the brain of every human being before birth by God Himself. These instincts could also be called drives or essential needs: food, water, air, rest, and certain behavioral instincts such as sucking. The sex instinct is programmed into the brain before birth, and if not awakened prematurely, it manifests itself automatically after puberty. Certain emotional attitudes are also preprogrammed into the mind, such as the attitudes of fear, anger, love, and curiosity or the desire to learn new things. The early training of the first four to five years helps the child to use properly these natural, God-given instincts. A lack of proper training tends to confuse the child and may result in mental problems later on in life.

The Body

The body receives sensory input through the five senses, and the mind makes certain perceptions. The body includes the feelings which are the result of the attitudes in the mind. The personality of the body is manifested by one's actions, energy, and mannerisms and is exhibited to the world through the door of communication.

The Heart

The word *heart* is mentioned more than eight hundred times in the Old Testament and New Testament, appearing as the Hebrew word *lev* or *levab* and the Greek word *kardia.* It refers to the immaterial part of man or the wellspring of life (Prov. 14:30). The word *heart* has various meanings in Scripture. Sometimes it refers to the mind (II Cor. 4:6), to understanding (Prov. 4:23), to the will (Dan. 1:8), to emotions (Isa. 65:14), to conscience (Heb. 10:22), and sometimes to the material body (Prov. 14:30). Generally speaking it refers to the soul of man, which is the moral center of the person and morally guides the entire person. The heart is not based on intellect but is based on a person's belief in God. However, the word *heart* includes the more specific term *the mind,* mentioned less than one hundred times, which generally refers to one's moral initiative, moral judgment, and moral reasoning, which embodies one's relationship with God.[11] Ruth Beechick, in *A Biblical Psychology of Learning,* makes a point that the heart and the mind may be different. She points out that there is only one place in Scripture where heart is referred to as an area of mental activity involving the brain, and that is in Daniel 2:28 and 30 "where Daniel talked to the king about visions of his head and in the same conversation called them thoughts of his heart."[12] She cites the Lacey Experiment, which indicated a difference between the mind and the heart.[13]

The central theme of the counselor in his dealings with the counselee should be *Keep your heart right with God and your mind disciplined to the Word of God,* with the admonition *Make up your mind.*

Attitudes, Beliefs, and Motives

Life's decisions are made by the will and depend on one's attitudes, beliefs, and motives, which compose his character. Decisions that one makes result in behavior. Behavior then usually precedes feelings, whether painful (e.g. guilt) or pleasurable (e.g. euphoria or satisfaction). Counselors must realize that sinful behavior in the client stems from wrong decisions made by the will. These wrong decisions are a result of wrong Devil attitudes that may be based on wrong beliefs or wrong motives. The counselee will readily reveal his feelings, behavior, and some of his decisions that he thinks caused the problem. However, the counselor searches below the surface for the wrong attitudes, motives, beliefs, and decisions which contributed to the wrong behavior. The Christian counselor is not interested in merely changing a person's sinful behavior resulting from wrong decisions. A person's behavior is just the tip of the iceberg. (See Table VII.) Underneath the surface are attitudes, based on beliefs and motives, which affect decisions on how the person is going to behave and conduct his life. When a person makes up his mind to change these three things, the decisions that follow will be right, and the behavior that follows the decisions will be right. Good feelings will then follow right behavior. Attitudes to a great extent determine behavior. (See Table VIII.)

Human beings are not locked into a specific kind of behavior. They can make up their minds to change at any time. The mind has great power to control the body and behavior through a person's attitudes, beliefs, and motives, which determine the decisions that he makes. If he lets them, environment, fleshly desires, and stress can drastically affect a person's behavior. But the Spirit-filled mind has the power to overcome any environment, no matter how bad; any desire, no matter how strong; or any stress, no matter how acute. Human beings with a Spirit-filled mind able to make godly decisions

TABLE VII
THE ICEBERG OF THE MIND

TABLE VIII
ATTITUDES DETERMINE BEHAVIOR

Right actions follow right attitudes.
Good feelings follow right actions.

ATTITUDES	ACTIONS	FEELINGS
Love (right)	Obedience Morality Generosity Sacrifice	Righteous Pure Unselfish Noble
Faith (strength)	Appreciation Belief Trust	Content Secure Assured
Hope (gain)	Setting goals Reaching goals	Purposeful Successful
Anger (wrong)	Corruptness Vengefulness Hatefulness	Guilty Mean Bitter
Fear (weak)	Unthankfulness Indecisiveness Worry Doubt Greed	Discontented Confused Anxious Defeated Selfish
Depression (loss)	Procrastination Despair	Aimless Helpless

can act and react exactly as God tells them to in His Word. Christians have the Word of God to guide them and the power of the Holy Spirit to help them make right decisions that will result in right behavior.

.

Chapter 4

Predisposing Factors, Root Causes of Mental Problems, and Basic Solutions

Effective Christian counselors are always looking below the surface for root problems or basic causes for each surface problem that is presented in their counseling office. They are also alert to factors that may affect each problem. The counselor can be compared to a tree surgeon treating a barren fruit tree. Though the tree has dying branches and is losing leaves prematurely, the surgeon does not necessarily treat the leaf or the limb first. He considers, rather, all the factors affecting the tree: moisture or rain, insects, heat or cold, or some superficial damage to the tree. Then he looks at the roots. Are the roots getting enough fertilizer? Is some insect or animal damaging the roots? So the Christian counselor looks at the factors affecting the client's problem in addition to searching for root causes.

Predisposing Factors

Because of certain factors, some people are predisposed to specific types of problems. (See Table IX.) The Christian counselor should be aware of these factors, for they will have a bearing on the most serious problems with which he will deal. The problems themselves cannot be blamed on these factors, for each person is a rational human being with a choice; but these factors may affect the choices and decisions a person makes.

The first factor is heredity or genetics. A child born with certain physical deformities, appearance, or diseases may react to an environment in a way that is different from the way a person who is born without the inherited problems reacts. Children also inherit characteristics, such as intelligence and certain personality traits, as well as a predisposition to certain disorders of the brain, such as schizophrenia. Studies of identical twins who are reared away from their parents and in separate environments have indicated that some mental problems are due mainly to heredity and not just to the environment.

A second factor affecting present problems is the environment in which the person was reared. The Bible indicates in Proverbs 22:6, 29:15, and 23:13-14 that parental training, love, and firm discipline are vital factors in that child's adjustment. The danger of parental abuse, either physical, verbal, or sexual, is indicated in Ephesians 6:4, especially the possibility of the father's being the main perpetrator of this abuse. Traumatic childhood experiences, such as a serious accident, rape, or the suicide of a sibling or a parent, which are not properly handled at the time of the experience, can affect a person's later adjustment.

Any serious disruption of the cohesive family unit, such as parental substance abuse, divorce, or death, can affect a child's immediate and later adjustment, depending on his reactions to it. For example, at the death of one or both parents, some become angry at God and some feel guilty, especially if they have ever wished their parents dead. Other children feel insecure because death was a problem that even Dad could not solve. While the family is most influential on the child's later adjustment, the church, school, and community must also be considered.

The effects of environment upon a life are illustrated by Lot's downfall. Three times in II Peter 2:7-8 he is called righteous, but he chose an environment which predisposed him to choose sin. Instead of choosing the land to the north or south that Abraham suggested, he chose for himself the well-watered plains of the east near the Jordan River, outside Canaan, and moved his family into the city of Sodom (Gen. 13:6-13; 14:12). Influenced by his worldly, sinful environment, he chose to offer his virgin daughters to the wicked men who were storming his house. He also lost his honor,

TABLE IX
THE PERSONAL PROBLEMS OF MAN

FACTORS, ROOT CAUSES, AND SOLUTIONS

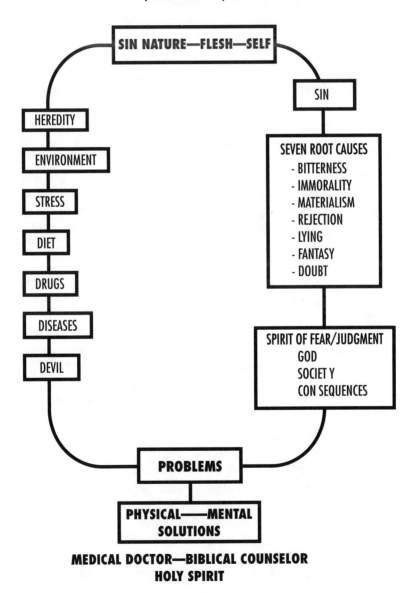

family, and wealth, ended up drunk, and committed incest with his two daughters (Gen. 19:1-38).

An individual is responsible for his reaction to situations and cannot excuse himself by blaming childhood environment; however, environment is a factor that must be considered in explaining the problem. Environment may even determine the solution that is suggested to solve the problem.

The third factor that affects the person's problem is the present stress that he is under. The authors believe that stress is a result of sinful negative doubt thoughts about life's circumstances (Isa. 25:3). In 1967 Holmes and Rahe developed a scale for ranking the impact of stress in a counselee's recent lifestyle. They assigned certain value points to each stress-causing situation. For example, the seven situations with 50-point value or above are as follows: death of spouse, 100; divorce, 73; marital separation, 65; jail term, 63; death of a close family member, 63; personal injury or illness, 53; marriage, 50. Farther down the list are such situations as beginning or ending school, 26; change in schools, 20; change in residence, 20; change in recreation, 20. Many stresses occurring in a year's time totaling over 150 points can be a predisposing cause of health problems and other problems.

A person can bring stress into his own life by procrastination or by overscheduling. Parents, older siblings, peers, and coworkers cause stress, especially when their goals and values do not match the counselee's. There is also self-inflicted stress when a person continually verbalizes a negative attitude toward his own actions and behavior. For example, the person might say, "I'm stupid" or "That was a dumb thing to do" or "I can never do anything right." One author called this type of negative doubt thinking "stinking thinking."

Other factors which can influence adjustment and have a significant effect on mental problems are diet, drugs, a variety of diseases, and the Devil. All of the above factors can have a bearing on the problems that are presented to the counselor. (See Table IX.) The effect of diet, drugs, and disease on mental problems is discussed in Chapter 5.

The Devil is a very important factor affecting mental problems. During Christ's time, the Devil was active and affecting the behavior of people. Many of Christ's and the disciples' miracles dealt with the Devil and demonic activities. The Devil is still active today and Christians are warned in Scripture to "be sober, be vigilant" (I Pet. 5:8-9), to stand against the wiles of the Devil by putting on the whole armor of God (Eph. 6:11), and to resist the Devil in order to force him to flee (James 4:7). The authors believe that many of the mental problems labeled *psychosis* are actually demon possession and are very difficult to treat. Even the disciples had difficulty dealing with this kind of problem (Matt. 17:14-21). When Jesus was told about it, He replied that "this kind goeth not out but by prayer and fasting" (Matt. 17:21). The authors do not recommend that the average counselor get involved in dealing with this kind of problem because of the danger of the inexperienced Christian's becoming susceptible to demonic pressure, which would include demon obsession and demon oppression. Some of the more difficult and seemingly unsolvable cases should be referred to godly pastors or mature believers who are knowledgeable in this area and know how to handle this type of problem the scriptural way.

Main Cause of Mental Problems—Sin

Sin, or going against God's commandments, in the Word of God, is the primary cause of stress, which may eventually cause mental problems and disrupt normal adjustment. (See Table IX.) If a Christian wishes to be free from mental problems, he must walk in the light of God's Word with sins confessed and live a life to the glory of God (I John 1:5-10). He must also dwell in love because the Bible says, "Beloved, let us love one another: for love is of God; and every one that loveth is born of God, and knoweth God. He that loveth not knoweth not God; for God is love" (I John 4:7-8).

Reacting incorrectly to life's pressures causes negative devilish attitudes and produces wrong behavior called sin. God's Word explains: "But every man is tempted, when he is drawn away of his own lust, and enticed. Then when lust hath conceived, it bringeth forth sin: and sin, when it is finished, bringeth forth death" (James 1:14-15). This sin reacts against the conscience, which produces a spirit of fear. This fear should not be a part of a Christian's life, as Paul told Timothy, "For God hath not given us the spirit of fear; but of power, and of love, and of a sound mind" (II Tim. 1:7). This fear is of God's judgment, of being found out by society and loved ones, or of the natural consequences of sin. The spirit of fear can be manifested in the body by certain physical problems (Ps. 51). The fear can also be intensified by conditioning in a certain place or with a certain thing or in a certain circumstance. It then becomes a phobia or anxiety and can result in panic attacks. Depending on the root cause of the sin, the spirit of fear can cause various types of mental problems. Good adjustment (the abundant life) and the spirit of fear are mutually exclusive (Phil. 4:6). Behind the spirit of fear are seven root causes found in Scripture. (See Table IX.)

The Scriptures teach that all born-again Christians have **peace with God:** "Therefore being justified by faith, we have peace with God through our Lord Jesus Christ" (Rom. 5:1). But to be well-adjusted, they also need the **peace of God:** "Be careful for nothing; but in every thing by prayer and supplication with thanksgiving let your requests be made known unto God. . . . And the peace of God, which passeth all understanding, shall keep your hearts and minds through Christ Jesus" (Phil. 4:6-7). That peace can be secured by being identified with Christ and filled with the Holy Spirit.

Seven Root Causes of Problems

When a counselor deals with people's problems, he will find that they can usually be traced to one or more root causes. Three root causes are found in Hebrews 12:15-16: bitterness, fornication, and materialism. A fourth root cause is found in Psalm 27:10: rejection feelings. A fifth cause is found in Romans 1:21-22: imagination and fantasy. A sixth root cause is found in James 1:5-7: doubt. A seventh cause is found in I Timothy 4:2: lying.

Bitterness

The first root cause is given in Hebrews 12:15: "Looking diligently lest any man fail of the grace of God; lest any root of bitterness springing up trouble you, and thereby many be defiled." The root of bitterness springs up first against parents and usually begins in the teen years. It soon spreads to others. A whole family, neighborhood, or church can be defiled by one person's bitterness, which in reality is rebellion and bitterness against God. The forgiveness principle of Ephesians 4:30-32, Matthew 5:23-24, and

Matthew 18:15-17 is a help in dealing with this problem. This basic cause is discussed further in Chapter 10.

Fornication

A second root cause is mentioned in Hebrews 12:16: "Lest there be any fornicator, or profane person, as Esau, who for one morsel of meat sold his birthright." It is also found in I Corinthians 6:18 and Romans 7:24-27. This word *fornication* is a comprehensive word covering all kinds of sex sins. It includes necking and petting, masturbation, pornography, incest, homosexuality, premarital sex, adultery, and various sexual perversions.

Pastors and counselors know that people who attempt suicide or have severe guilt feelings or certain psychosomatic diseases usually are involved in or have been involved in some sex sin. First Corinthians 6:18 gives the reason for the severe consequences of these sins.

The purity principle as found in I Thessalonians 4:1-7 is a help in dealing with the sin of fornication. This basic cause is discussed further in Chapters 11 and 12.

Materialism

Hebrews 12:16 also reveals a third root cause of problems: a worldly viewpoint, that money and things will unlock the door to sensual pleasure and satisfaction. This results in profane, feeling-oriented, pleasure-mad, and Epicurean behavior demanding instant gratification. People who are hooked on rock music, drugs, sports, and possessions have this materialistic viewpoint. They are in the "fast lane"; and money, things, and sensual pleasure are more important than God's standards, self-respect, or their testimony for Christ. Rebellion and discontentment are symptoms of this viewpoint. An understanding of the Kingdom of God principle as found in Matthew 6:19-34 and of the contentment principle found in I Timothy 6:6-10 is helpful for dealing with materialism and the resulting sensuality. This basic cause is discussed further in Chapter 13.

Rejection

A fourth root cause of problems is rejection, expressed in the Psalms: "When my father and my mother forsake me, then the Lord will take me up" (27:10). It is referred to indirectly by Jesus Christ in Matthew 19:14. Negative rejection feelings are usually based on self-centeredness and selfishness. Most people feel rejected at one time or another in their lives, beginning in childhood and peaking in the teen years. Careless negative comments and even vicious cutting remarks made by parents, siblings, peers, or teachers about a child's appearance, abilities, skills, social status, and personality can cause some children to feel rejected. Situations such as divorce, a new school, loss of a friend, death of a loved one, or loss of a job can bring about rejection feelings. The typical reaction is to withdraw and become selfish and self-centered. The cure is the God-acceptance principle found in Ephesians 1:6-7, I John 3:1, and Romans 8:1 and the Identification with Christ principle found in Galatians 2:20 and Ephesians 2:4-7. This basic cause is discussed further in Chapter 14.

Fantasizing

A fifth root cause is Devil-directed imagination, resulting in sinful, humanistic fantasizing. There are several references to this in the New Testament: "Casting down imaginations, and every high thing that exalteth itself against the knowledge of God, and bringing into captivity every thought to the obedience of Christ" (II Cor. 10:5; cf. Rom. 1:21-22). The attitude behind this thinking is man's reasoning about life's situations, giving little or no weight to God's control, His intervention, or His claims on the affairs of man. When situations develop or crucial events take place, the average man does not look to the principles of the Word of God for guidance about how he is to act and react. Instead he constructs a pattern of thinking that is largely fantasy and involves his wishes, his sinful desires, unreal goals, and a make-believe world. This pattern of thinking is usually negative, for it goes against positive faith principles. When this fantasizing is acted out in real life, it results in tremendous difficulties. Television tends to accentuate the problem, for the average person finds it hard to distinguish fantasy from God's reality after filling his brain with humanistic fantasy twenty-five to thirty hours a week. Many times this thinking is a cover-up for guilt feelings. A cure for this root problem is found in II Corinthians 10:5 and also in Philippians 4:8. In Chapter 16 this problem will be discussed in detail.

Doubt

The sixth basic cause is doubt. The Bible instructs: "If any of you lack wisdom, let him ask of God, that giveth to all men liberally, and upbraideth not; and it shall be given him. But let him ask in faith, nothing wavering. For he that wavereth is like a wave of the sea driven with the wind and tossed. For let not that man think that he shall receive any thing of the Lord" (James 1:5-7; cf. I Cor. 10:3-10; Acts 12:5). The Word of God is the only sure foundation for faith. A person who rejects the inerrancy of Scripture is open to doubting. He thinks about the promises of God as mere probabilities rather than God's promises. Then the person begins to doubt God's power and His past performance. Soon this doubt spreads to other areas, such as any authority figure, starting with parents. These people either become cynics or tend to become insecure, worried, fearful, and depressed. They can even become suicidal. This basic cause will be discussed in Chapter 17.

Lying

A seventh root cause underlying mental problems is lying. The Scriptures give numerous warnings about this: "Now the Spirit speaketh expressly, that in the latter times some shall depart from the faith, giving heed to seducing spirits, and doctrines of devils; Speaking lies in hypocrisy; having their conscience seared with a hot iron" (I Tim. 4:1-2; cf. Acts 5:1-4). First Timothy 4:2 seems to indicate that lying bypasses the conscience which has become seared. Continual lying is the sure road to hypocrisy and even to departing from the faith. These types of people are the typical con men with no conscience about what they say or do. The treatment for lying is found in Ephesians 4:25. This problem will be discussed in Chapter 15.

Physical causes

There may be physical causes for some problems (see Chapter 5). A brain tumor or a blow to the head could affect behavior. However, more subtle physical problems, such as allergies, neurotransmitter and hormone disturbances, drugs, anemia, vitamin deficiencies, fatigue, and upset blood sugar levels can seriously affect a person's actions and reactions. When a counselor suspects a physical problem because the person does not respond to counseling, he should suggest that the person see a medical doctor for a checkup.

Basic Solutions

There are certain basic solutions that can be recommended and used over and over again, depending on the specific problem. These solutions can be classified as physical or spiritual.

Physical

Adequate Rest: Most people with physical and mental problems are not getting enough sleep. In fact, when a person is hospitalized for mental breakdown, the standard treatment is to give medication which allows for dreaming sleep and which keeps the patient sleeping for twenty-four hours straight. The dreams seem to clear the mind enough so that the person can then be properly counseled.

With some married couples, the husband needs only five to six hours of sleep a night, while the wife's sleep needs are eight to nine hours. The tendency for the wife is to keep going, trying to satisfy the husband's and children's demands. The husband may have a second job, and the demands from church, job, and home prevent him from getting more than four or five hours of sleep a night. Over a period of time, this sleep debt can wreak havoc in a person's life. If the wife has three or four preschool children, the husband might be able to hire a high-school girl to come in and take care of the children or do some housework while the wife takes a nap every day. Taking the phone off the hook and trimming the family's schedule helps by giving time for naps.

Proper Nutrition: Another important treatment is a proper diet. Some mental problems are caused by lack of specific vitamins, especially the B complex, and certain minerals. Skipping meals, eating an imbalanced diet, and excessive eating also cause problems. Getting adequate and regular nutrients can be helpful in alleviating some problems. Cutting down on excess sugar and caffeine may be in order. Some time ago a unique case was solved readily by a change in diet. A Christian lady, single and in her thirties, would become depressed and think about suicide only on the weekends. Each Friday night she would treat herself to a good meal at her favorite restaurant, where she ordered two glasses of sweetened tea and ended the meal with a giant piece of German chocolate cake. She would then consume a box of chocolates by Saturday noon. By omitting this excess and eating a well-balanced diet, she was able to balance her blood sugar and soon eliminated her weekend depression.

Aerobic Exercise: A third area of physical treatment relates to the need for exercise. An inactive person should begin exercising. He should begin slowly a regular aerobic exercise program of his choice, such as jogging, biking, brisk walking, or swimming. Even regular walking in God's outdoors can be uplifting to physical and mental health. If there are health problems, the person should check with his doctor before he begins any exercise program.

Physical exam: This should be part of the detective work for an ongoing mental problem.

If the church would take seriously its commission to heal as given in James 5:14-16, there would be much less need for the services of medical doctors, hospital stays, and the abundance of medications taken by many Christians. It is not only the elders who pray for the sick; James 5:16 commands all Christians to pray for each other "that you may be healed." If Christians would take God's commands in believing faith and also use preventive measures such as exercise, appropriate rest, and nutrition (I Cor. 10:31), we would see fewer physical and mental problems.

Spiritual

There are a number of general spiritual solutions that can be suggested.

1. Instruction on the appropriation of the Holy Spirit in one's life is the greatest tool a counselor has for the perfection of the saints for solving the multitude of problems that arise in their lives. Most Christians realize that the Holy Spirit indwells them at the time they receive Christ, and most experience the joy of the Holy Spirit at the time of salvation, but few Christians benefit from the fruit of the Holy Spirit or the power of the Holy Spirit in their daily lives. Most would like to be filled with the Holy Spirit and daily walk in the

Spirit, but they do not know how to go about it. (Table X shows three phases of the Holy Spirit in the Christian's life.)

a. *Receiving the Holy Spirit at salvation* (Rom. 8:9-14). For this to happen, the individual must first of all repent of his sins and believe. He must then receive Jesus Christ. At the same time he also surrenders his sin, the Holy Spirit then enters the person's life, and the believer experiences the joy of the Holy Spirit.

b. *The filling of the Holy Spirit at dedication* (Eph. 5:18-19; 2:4-7; Rom. 12:1). The individual must abandon self and yield his life for service. He does this by identifying with Christ (see Chapter 14) and surrendering his life to God. The Holy Spirit then takes full possession and gives the believer the fruit of the Holy Spirit, which is the manifestation of the Holy Spirit filling one's life. The Holy Spirit also gives various gifts of the Spirit as mentioned in I Corinthians 12:4-11.

c. *Walking in the Holy Spirit in daily action* (Gal. 5:16-25). For this to happen, the individual believer must confess his sin every day (I John 1:9), deny self (Luke 9:23), and obey the commandments of Christ (John 14:21). He does this by abiding in Christ (John 15) and surrendering self. The Holy Spirit then is renewed daily in a believer's life, and he has the power and guidance of the Holy Spirit for service. The reason that most Christians are so ineffective and burned-out with so many problems is that they do not have the knowledge about the Holy Spirit and what He can do in their lives.

2. Anyone suffering from guilt feelings needs to take heed to the three-point formula outlined in the book of Romans for getting rid of sin boils (long-standing moral sins) in the life. This formula is found in Romans 14:17: "For the kingdom of God is not meat and drink; but righteousness, and peace, and joy in the Holy Ghost." First, righteousness comes by taking full responsibility for the sin, instead of trying to blame another for it, and by confessing the sin before God (Isa. 1:18; Eph. 1:7; I John 1:9). Second, peace comes by forgetting the sin after it has been cleansed (Phil. 3:13; Isa. 43:18-19, 25).

TABLE X
THE HOLY SPIRIT

	Salvation *Receiving the Holy Spirit*	Dedication *Filling of the Holy Spirit*	Daily Action *Walking in the Holy Spirit*
The individual acts as a result of the Holy Spirit's conviction.	Repents and believes Receives Christ Surrenders sins	Abandons self and yields Identifies with Christ Surrenders life	Confesses, denies self, and obeys Abides in Christ Surrenders self
The Holy Spirit reacts as a result of God's grace.	Enters Gives joy	Takes full possession Produces fruit	Is renewed Gives power and guidance for service

Third, joy in the Holy Spirit comes by praising God for His forgiveness (Isa. 44:22-23; Ps. 107:8).

3. To allow the Holy Spirit to work in his life, a person should read appropriate passages of Scripture every day for thirty days. Each day he should underline the verse that speaks to him on that particular day. Usually these passages are selected chapters or even whole books suggested by the counselor, but it is best not to assign a total of more than five or six chapters. A few of these selected passages and the problems they deal with are listed below.

- Battling temptation—Romans 6, 7, and 8
- Bitterness, wrath, hatred—I John; Ephesians 4:30-32; Matthew 5:22-24; 18:15-18
- Depression—Psalms 42, 43, and 77
- Desire for vengeance—Romans 12:14-21; I Peter 2:18-25; 3:8-18
- Doubt—Psalm 119; Hebrews 13
- Discontentment and love of money and things—Matthew 6; I Timothy 6:6-13
- Marital problems—Ephesians 4–5; I Corinthians 7:1-6; I Peter 3:1-7
- Immorality—I Thessalonians 4:1-7; Proverbs 5–7

4. It is vital to start thinking positive faith thoughts (Phil. 4:8) and to discipline the mind against negative doubt thoughts (II Cor. 10:5). The Thinking Man diagram (Table IV) illustrates this idea.

5. To break a bad habit, a person should study Romans 6:11-13 and work through these six steps.

a. Confess the habit of sin.

b. Set a goal for victory (three days, then three weeks, then three months). After three months, a person usually has the bad habit pretty well under control and a good habit well established to replace the bad habit.

c. If backsliding should occur, confess, recover, and set a new goal.

d. Exercise whenever temptation strikes. This activity dissipates and rechannels the "demand-for-pleasure" energies that are a part of every sinful habit.

    e. Choose a verse, such as I Corinthians 10:13, that can be quoted every time the temptation threatens.

    f. Stay away from places, people, or situations associated with the temptation or habit.

6. Counselees can be directed to read books, listen to tapes, or view videos that not only deal with the problem but also save counseling time. Couples with marriage problems should read *Formula for Family Unity* by Walter and Trudy Fremont and view the six videos of his Family Seminar (Bob Jones University Press). Parents needing help in guiding and training children will find scriptural answers in *Training Your Children to Turn Out Right* by David Sorenson. Those beset with tragedy and suffering should read *The Prisoner in the Third Cell* by Gene Edwards or *More Precious than Gold* by John and Brenda Vaughn. Those who lack trust in God for needs and care should read Hannah Whitehall Smith's book *The Christian's Secret of a Happy Life.* For lack of discipline, *The Disciplined Life* by Richard Taylor may be beneficial. For pride and conceit problems, Paul Brownback's book *The Danger of Self-Love* can be highly recommended. Gary Inrig's *Quality Friendships* deals with relationship problems. Charles Solomon's book, *Handbook to Happiness,* gives help to those having rejection problems. For rigid, legalistic life-style problems, *Transforming Grace* and *The Discipline of Grace* by Jerry Bridges present some answers. *Your Finances in Changing Times* by Larry Burkett offers good advice to those with financial problems.

7. Those who are battling problems are often given a new focus by taking on life projects. A person with a discontented spirit may choose to work in the inner-city projects with a poor family or serve meals in a homeless shelter. A woman who has had an abortion and feels deep regret about it can often find great satisfaction in counseling at a pregnancy counseling center. A self-centered person might be encouraged to pick out a friend whom he can help or to make a working trip to a mission field.

8. Eliminate corrupt input (Ps. 101:3; Titus 2:11-14) by eliminating unwholesome fiction, television, and un-Christian activities. A good substitute is a one-hour-a-day program of

reading the Bible, Christian books, periodicals, or other good material.

9. Start a daily praise program as a part of devotions or at a separate time (Heb. 13:5; Ps. 9:1-2; 107:8; 119:164; 145:2-5; 150:1-6; I Chron. 16:8-36.)

10. Fast and pray one day a week or month regarding the solution to the problem or for the offending party that is supposedly causing the problem.

11. Understand the Three Classes of Men (Table XI; e.g., use with Problem 11 in Chapter 14) and take the steps to become the spiritual man walking in the Spirit.

12. For cases of immorality, use the Love-Sex diagram (Table XII; e.g., use with Problem 4 in Chapter 12).

13. For cases of rape, incest, and sexual abuse, use the Triune Man diagram (Table VI), pointing out that Christians will receive a new body. What has happened to the body does not matter if one chooses not to let it affect the soul and the spirit. This would also apply to deformity and handicap situations.

There is a tendency for untrained or beginning counselors to latch onto one root cause as a basis for most problems. Some would focus on materialism, since the Scripture says in I Timothy 6:10 that "the love of money is the root of all evil." Someone else may claim that rejection is the one main cause of most problems. There may be several root causes for one problem. Rarely is the problem related to just one root cause.

The same idea is often followed in suggesting solutions. Inexperienced counselors like to get a magic potion that cures all problems. They find one solution that seems to cure two or three cases, so they begin to use it as a "cure-all" for all the problems presented to them. There are no simple causes or pat cures. It is wise to be "open-minded" and flexible in the hands of the Holy Spirit's direction. The Holy Spirit discerns the thoughts and intents of the counselee's heart and can direct the counselor in the counseling sessions to find the correct cause(s) and the best solution(s).

Chapter 5 discusses diseases and physical conditions which may contribute to or cause some mental problems, necessitating a referral to a medical doctor.

TABLE XI
THREE CLASSES OF MEN

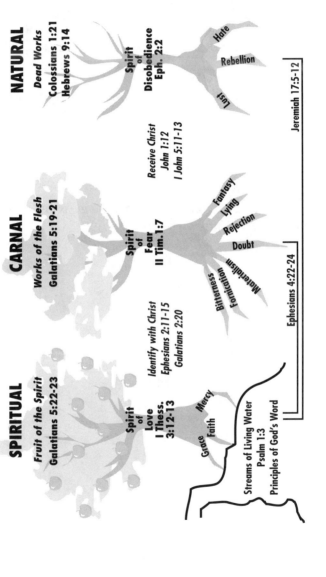

SPIRITUAL

Fruit of the Spirit
Galatians 5:22-23

Spirit of Love
I Thess. 3:12-13

Identify with Christ
Ephesians 2:11-15
Galatians 2:20

Grace
Faith
Mercy

Streams of Living Water
Psalm 1:3
Principles of God's Word

CARNAL

Works of the Flesh
Galatians 5:19-21

Spirit of Fear
II Tim. 1:7

Receive Christ
John 1:12
I John 5:11-13

Fantasy
Lying
Rejection
Doubt
Materialism
Bitterness
Fornication

Ephesians 4:22-24

NATURAL

Dead Works
Colossians 1:21
Hebrews 9:14

Spirit of Disobedience
Eph. 2:2

Hate
Rebellion
Lust

Jeremiah 17:5-12

Chapters 6 and 7 detail the function of the counselor in the process of counseling. It is twofold: the counselor is a detective and a teacher, as outlined below.

Chapter 6 Detecting	Chapter 7 Teaching
Discover Problem and Root Causes	Bring About Change
1. Listen .	1. Teach biblical beliefs
2. Determine cause(s)	2. Teach "How To" steps for change (Rom. 6:11-13)
3. Explain the problem	3. Teach how to appropriate the Holy Spirit's power (Mark. 9:23)
4. Confront	

A knowledge of the process of counseling is essential in becoming an effective Christian counselor.

TABLE XII
DEVELOPMENT OF LOVE-SEX DESIRE

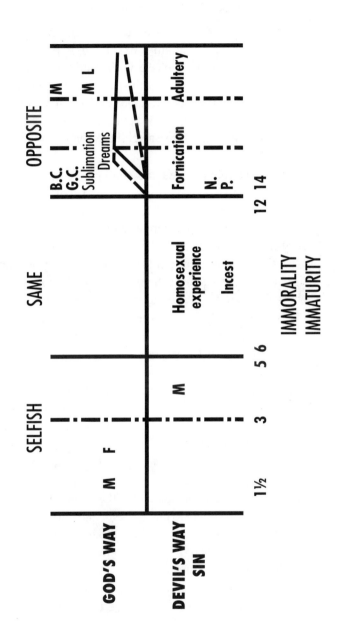

GOD'S WAY

DEVIL'S WAY
SIN

SELFISH

M   F

M

SAME

Homosexual
experience

Incest

OPPOSITE

B.C.
G.C.
Sublimation
Dreams

M

M   L

Fornication

N.
P.

Adultery

1½   3   5 6   12 14

IMMORALITY
IMMATURITY

Description of Table XII

The Love-Sex diagram is used to present the purity principle (I Thess. 4:1-7). The diagram is explained by presenting the three phases of love. The first phase is the self-centered phase, from infancy to six years of age. For the first year and a half, the baby's love is centered on the mother; it then expands to include the father, relatives, playmates, and finally the first-grade teacher. During this period the parent is teaching the child to share with and care about others.

Around six years of age, the child enters the second phase of love, that of the same sex. Boys have their best buddies and girls have their girlfriends. Those friendships should be encouraged, for both boys and girls are learning identification of their sex through their peers. This is an ideal time for fathers to befriend their sons and teach them masculine skills such as carpentry, mechanics, and lawn care; mothers should help their girls become feminine by teaching them cooking, sewing, and household duties.

At puberty (twelve years for girls and fourteen for boys), the child switches to the third phase, love of the opposite sex, introduced by the junior high boy-crazy and girl-crazy stages. With maturity, the person settles down to dating, going steady with, becoming engaged to, and finally marrying one member of the opposite sex. If love is understood as an unselfish, self-sacrificing desire to meet the other person's needs, then marriage can become the ultimate in mature love.

The sex desire is in three stages. In the first stage (the first three years of life), the sex desire is zero; from three years to six years there is a slight rise in desire, called the exploratory phase. At this time boys and girls begin to play "doctor and nurse" with each other, and masturbation may start. Mother, though perhaps alarmed when she discovers these activities, should not overreact but simply tell her children that they are not to do these things. She can begin giving very basic sex education at this time.

The second stage, from six to puberty, sex desire is back at zero again. Now parents can help children set goals and begin to channel their energy into work, study, sports, and creative activities such as painting or practicing a musical instrument. It is important that boys associate with other boys and girls with other girls during this period so that their sex identification is solidified.

In the third stage, starting at puberty, a boy's sexual desire (solid line) rises dramatically to its normal adult level. A girl's desire (dotted line) rises gradually to the age of twenty-five, when it reaches adult level. (About 20 percent of the girls experience a sharp rise in sexual desire much like the male's and hence have the same problems that boys have controlling it.)

God's way of handling these desires is for teenagers to sublimate them by channeling their energy into the activities begun in grade school. Men (and about 20 percent of women) also experience tension-releasing dreams. God has provided marriage as the legitimate outlet for sexual desire (I Cor. 7:2; Heb. 13:4). The purity principle of I Thessalonians 4:1-7 commands a Christian to maintain his sexuality in a blameless, God-honoring way. The Devil, on the other hand, wants a person to express his sexuality through masturbation, necking and petting, premarital sex, adultery, incest, and in any other way that defies God's design.

The diagram shows that immorality is also immaturity. A woman who commits adultery not only has decided to be immoral but also is immature in her love development. She is still back in the boy-crazy stage of junior high. A man who has decided to be a homosexual is immoral and is still in the love-of-the-same-sex stage of late childhood. People are not locked into immorality, whether adultery or homosexuality, by overactive glands. They must decide to quit sinning, choose God's way of morality, and take steps to mature in their love development.

Physical Causes of Mental Problems

Not all mental problems are caused by a person's sinful actions or reactions to the circumstances, people, and things in his life. Some problems come from within the body itself. A person should see his physician at some point in his counseling if problems do not seem related to his spiritual life. Even if they do seem related, the physical condition may be the underlying cause of a person's maladjustment. With correct physical diagnosis and treatment, some problems and behaviors will be corrected or at least minimized. The following discussion will give some idea of how physical problems can cause or add to mental and behavioral symptoms.

Predisposing Physical Diseases

The symptoms from physical diseases may themselves be a source of problems. For example, "a person with a duodenal ulcer may have pain that is high in his abdomen and even in the lower chest. This pain is partially due to spasms in the duodenum. Before the ulcer is found, he may become very concerned as a result of where he hurts. Because it is in his chest he may become worried about his heart. He thinks he is having a heart attack and thinks he might even die from it. This fear and worry produces an increase in the spasms already present in the duodenum and thus increases the pain."[1]

Brain injury and diseases

Brain injury and diseases which affect the function of the brain can cause serious mental and personality problems. Brain injury is usually a result of motor vehicle accidents or falls. Diseases such as encephalitis and meningitis may also diminish functions of the brain. Alzheimer's disease is another disease that affects the function of the brain and personality of the individual. There is some evidence that the accumulative effect of psychoactive drugs may produce symptoms much like Alzheimer's disease, another reason that all drugs being taken by a client should be reported to the doctor.[2]

"Brain injury and disease have predictable behavioral correlates. That is, if we know the degree of brain damage a person has suffered, we can estimate the social, familial, and vocational repercussions of the injury. . . . With severe brain injury there may be almost immediate physical well-being, but also persistent changes in personality and intellect that can have devastating consequences. . . . The greatest handicap associated with moderate to severe brain injury is the difficulties with self-regulation or self-control. . . . Impulsiveness is the key word. Emotionally it can look like childishness, moodiness, emotional lability (rapid emotional fluctuations), or depression. Cognitively and behaviorally, it can take the appearance of poor judgment, inattentiveness, or difficulty learning new behaviors. . . . Impulsiveness can look like impatience, irritability, or anger."[3]

Endocrine Diseases

Thyroid malfunctioning The underactive thyroid may produce symptoms that are vague but could be confused with mental problems. Some of these symptoms are fatigue, forgetfulness, decreasing mental stability, anorexia, and lethargy.[4]

Some of the symptoms of an overactive thyroid are nervousness, heat intolerance, weight loss in spite of increased appetite, sweating, diarrhea, tremors and palpitations, and emotional mood swings, ranging from occasional outbursts to losing touch with reality.[5] Various diagnostic procedures, such as a scan, TRHS (thyroid releasing hormone stimulating) test, and radioimmunoassay tests, may be ordered to help with a diagnosis.

It is not unusual to find thyroid, pituitary, and even some adrenal gland conditions having symptoms that affect the emotions. These could be irritability or emotional instability, ranging from euphoria to depression to losing touch with reality. Conversely, emotional stress may affect the endocrine system.[6]

Estrogen deficiency A deficiency in this hormone may cause mental problems. It is assumed that approximately 10 percent of menopausal women and 5 percent of teen girls can have an imbalance sufficient enough to affect behavior. Menopause usually occurs from 45 to 55 years of age; some experience menopause in their thirties. There is a gradual decrease of estrogen over a period of time until menopause occurs. Approximately 5 percent of the women experience severe mental problems affecting the emotions. Those who have ovaries removed will go through menopause suddenly rather than gradually. In either situation a doctor may order estrogen replacement therapy. Some of the typical symptoms of menopause are hot flashes, irritability, anxiety, depression, crying spells, fits of anger, and "compulsive, manic or schizoid behavior."[7]

"Married women whose sexual desire has decreased or disappeared and is affecting their relationship with their husbands can be helped in some cases by taking testosterone with estrogen."[8] Some women have an upsurge in sexual desire just before menopause; this may be a contributing factor for many of the late babies and adulterous affairs.

Premenstrual Syndrome The disturbances that accompany this syndrome are tension, anxiety, irritability, mood swings, crying spells, fatigue, unexplained anger, and feelings of loneliness and depression. Some have reported suicidal feelings. Behavioral changes may decrease work efficiency and increase risk of accidents during the course of daily activities.

Most often the women say they feel an uncontrollable misery and irritability. A few report they "feel they are going crazy." Some women report an increased desire (almost compulsive) for carbohydrates and salty foods. For some women, the problem is present from the moment of ovulation to menstruation and may be severe. In others, it begins at variable times in between but before the menses.

It is suggested that a calendar be kept for several months to decide whether this problem is, in fact, cyclic and probably PMS. Many doctors will suggest a good exercise program and a good diet. It is also suggested by some to cut back on salty foods, such as chips and condiments (e.g., mustard and catsup), and to control the craving for sweet foods. Others advise eliminating caffeine, including tea, chocolate, and carbonated beverages. If these suggestions do not work, the physician may suggest certain vitamins and/or hormones.[9]

Addison's disease The underfunctioning of the adrenal glands produces depression, weight and appetite loss, dizziness, fainting, increased skin pigmentation (rather bronze-looking skin), and sometimes extreme fatigue. Addison's disease must be diagnosed and treated by a physician.[10]

Cushing's Syndrome On the other side of the coin is the excessive production of ACTH, a hormone of the pituitary gland. This malfunction may lead to depression, fullness of the face, and fat accumulation on the back and trunk of the body. Anxiety often results. This condition must also be diagnosed and treated by a physician.[11]

Calcium Imbalance

There are a number of causes for calcium imbalance, one being inadequate intake of calcium and vitamin D. There are a number of other causes that might be examined if symptoms such as drowsiness, headaches, depression or apathy, irritability, and confusion appear. The parathyroid and thyroid glands regulate ionized blood calcium and determine its removal from and resorption into bone. Calcium is critical to healthy neurological function. Severe imbalance requires emergency treatment, since it can lead to seizures.[12]

Hypoglycemia

"Is It a Disease or Isn't It?" is a title of an article by John Langone. He states that hypoglycemia is a disease that many doctors say does not exist. Some of the symptoms mimic or cause mental problems. These symptoms include fatigue, nervousness, irritability, trembling, headaches, rapid heart rate, confusion, blurred vision, and dizziness.[13] Some of the mild forms of hypoglycemia may be the result of an imbalanced diet deficient in nutrition to keep the blood sugar level stable. If a person is not eating regularly and has these symptoms, he can adjust his own eating habits to include sufficient nutrition and regularity. Foods to include should be complex carbohydrates, protein, fiber, and fat. Sugars and alcohol should be avoided. But if the condition continues, a physician should be consulted and a well-planned diet and exercise program advised.

Allergies (Atopy)

There are many possible causes for allergies, including pollen, dust and dust mites, mold spores, drugs, chemicals, feathers, animal dander, foods, or insects. Allergies have been known to cause or contribute to a number of symptoms ranging from a runny nose to personality changes.[14] Some complain of fatigue and a general feeling of being ill.

"Allergy is an abnormal response or immunologic reaction to a foreign substance that produces detrimental consequences in the body."[15] A family history should be taken because allergies are thought to be inherited. Some children seem to be hyperactive concurrent with allergy symptoms. Dr. William Crook, a pediatrician, reported that a number of children had what he called allergic-tension-fatigue syndrome. The children become easily fatigued, irritable, or easily depressed. Many experienced insomnia, night sweats, nightmares, and muscle cramps.[16] A doctor should be consulted for the right diagnosis, therapy, and/or medication for the child and/or adult.[17]

Chronic Fatigue Syndrome

This condition is a collection of symptoms (syndrome). The cause is unknown and in the past years has been a source of frustration for those who have had it because it was not recognized as a physical disorder. It is now defined by the medical profession as a physical condition with some mental symptoms rather than as a mental condition.[18] The symptoms are varied. Some symptoms are sluggishness, sleep disorders, sore throat, swollen lymph glands, mild fever, headaches, sore muscles, aching joints, forgetfulness, irritability, and confusion. There are a number of specific criteria that doctors use to diagnose the syndrome. Some have thought it was a type of Epstein-Barr virus disease, but this theory has not been proved. The Canadians call it myalgic encephalomye-litis. It is not flu, polio, mononucleosis, Lyme's disease, or mental problems. There is no specific treatment, and it may last weeks to years. Diagnosis may take months to years.[19]

Welch lists nine "must-know" diseases about which the coun-selor should know. The counselor should be acquainted with the symptoms and implications of these diseases which Welch dis-cusses at length.[20] The diseases are as follows:

1. Alzheimer's disease and dementia
2. Multiple sclerosis
3. Parkinson's disease and related disorders
4. Seizures and epilepsy
5. Stroke, or cerebral vascular accident (cva)
6. Brain tumors
7. Head injury
8. Diabetes
9. Female hormonal changes

The above diseases "can impair understanding, pose limitations on the expression of the heart, provide occasions for temptation and sin, and raise unique problems for families. . . . Because they mimic spiritual problems of the heart, they are often misdiagnosed by counselors and physicians."[21]

Mental Problems Which May Have Physical Origins

Depression

There are conditions causing depression that are not a result of sin. They are assumed to have a biological cause. This does not mean the person will need no counseling. Congruent medical treatment and counseling will be more effective in most situations. The most widely accepted biological explanations of depression are the monoamine (neurotransmitters) depletion theories. The theories suggest a deficiency in the monoamines, generally a deficiency in norepinephrine or serotonin or both. When the transmitter sub-stance leaks into the cellular cytoplasm, it can be degraded by monoamine oxidase, and depression can occur.[22] Chemicals such as serotonin and norepinephrine transmit signals from one nerve cell to the next across a small junction called the synaptic gap. Some of these substances bind to receptors on the next nerve cell. Others are reabsorbed in a process called reuptake. Some of the drugs block the reuptake, allowing the nerve endings to be bathed by serotonin and norepinephrine for an extended period of time and helping the person to overcome the depression. Other drugs block the effect of monoamine oxidase. The person would need to have a medical doctor's diagnosis, prescription, and follow-up.[23]

These neurotransmitters and others have been implicated in mood disorders such as manic-depression (bipolar disorder or mood swings from an elated or irritable mood with erratic hyperactivity, to deep depression) and have responded to medical treatment.[24] Neurotransmitters originate from the brain to provide the means by which the brain changes and regulates mood, behavior, and virtually all bodily functions.[25]

Under the same umbrella of biological problems as the source of depression is seasonal affective disorder (SAD). It is characterized by recurrent depressions that occur typically in winter and may last as late as April. As many as 20 percent of people in the northern latitude of the United States experience winter doldrums. It is associated with increased feelings of listlessness, irritability, oversleep, fatigue, weight gain, and carbohydrate craving.[26] Children may pick fights without a valid reason. Symptoms of SAD occur every winter. The condition seems to be related to both season and latitude. The nearer to $40°$ north latitude, the more cases there are. The symptoms recede as spring and summer come. Some authorities place this condition as a subtype of bipolar disorder. When bright artificial light therapy is used, symptoms disappear within days.[27] It is thought to be caused by a "disturbance in the body's natural clock and an abnormal production of melatonin . . . and serotonin, a chemical that transmits nerve impulses."[28]

Another cause for depression has been related to altered sleep cycles. This has been shown by electroencephalograms (EEG).

Depression-Provoking Nutritional Deficiencies

These deficiencies are generally easily corrected once the physician finishes the physical exam. A deficiency of thiamin or vitamin B_1 can lead to depression, confusion, and memory impairment.

Riboflavin deficiency may also be implicated as a cause of depression as well as visual impairment. A deficit of pyridoxine or B_6 may also cause depression, fatigue, headaches, and blurred vision. Because treatment is so easily accessible, one must be careful not to use any to excess. They can be toxic. In addition, self-diagnosis may be incorrect, and something else may be seriously wrong.

Depression Related to the Elderly

This type of depression is usually related to a disease and/or too many medications that can cause confusion. Many elderly go to several doctors. Each doctor should have a list of *all* the medications that the person is taking. Many family members think that depression of the elderly is always the aging process. Not so. Insist on sufficient examination by the family doctor or select a specialist called a gerontologist, or "physician for the elderly." Report any undue depression to the doctor.

Drug-Related Depression

Any person using any type of drug that has depressive properties may have depression. These medications include prescription drugs and over-the-counter drugs as well as illegal drugs. The counselor probably should have a list of drugs that could cause depression or any other abnormal symptoms related to behavior and personality changes. Drugs that produce sleep or calmness and some antihistamines used for allergies are the more common ones causing depression. If these are used in excess or in combination with too many others, depression and confusion can occur. Some drugs have a cumulative effect in the body. Do not assume that because the doctor ordered it, it cannot be a problem. If the client is going to several doctors, give each doctor a list of *all* medications being taken and how they are taken. Report any unusual symptoms.

Compulsion

Once thought to be caused by feelings of aggression (or guilt), compulsion now appears, in some cases, to be firmly grounded in biochemistry. As many as five million people are unable to control the obsessive-compulsive behavior. Dopamine seems to be the engine and serotonin the brakes. The behavior in this disorder can be reduced by antidepressant drugs.[29]

Eating Disorders

Anorexia nervosa and bulimia nervosa are increasingly common disorders among young females. "Anorexia is a formidable disorder mainly affecting young women and is characterized by a determination to lose weight despite emaciation. Bulimia nervosa is characterized by recurrent eating binges, purging, and dieting."[30] There is a 5 to 8 percent mortality rate with anorexic persons. Limited research is available on the biochemical factors that may predispose individuals to these disorders. Some of these factors include the neurotransmitters such as dopamine and serotonin that increase or inhibit food intake. It is yet unknown whether these disturbances in the neurotransmitters reflect an underlying biologic pathology or are secondary to the eating disorders.[31]

Anorexics usually become emaciated, whereas bulimics usually maintain their normal weight. There are several other possible reasons for these conditions. These reasons will be discussed in Chapter 24.

It is important that a counselor does not jump to any conclusions until all the facts are in. Concluding simply that every problem is a spiritual problem may lead the counselee to further problems because of the frustration and discouragement that wrong diagnosis produces. Conversely, saying that the problem is only a physical problem, ignoring the spiritual implications, and not holding the counselee accountable for his sinful behavior could seriously hinder the search for a solution. There must be a realization that the causes of many problems are both physical and spiritual. Cooperation between the counselor and the medical doctor is vital. The counselor should take full advantage of the medical doctor's skills in helping to solve problems.

Chapter 6

Detecting: Discovering the Problem

Christlikeness, the goal of counseling, can be realized only in the life of a person rightly related to God. The sinner, following the dictates of his sinful nature, is maladjusted. He must be born again (John 3:6-17) and receive a new nature before he can be properly counseled, for the sinner does not understand the things of the Lord (I Cor. 2:14). However, the born-again Christian who is not obeying the principles of the Word of God and not being led of the Holy Spirit can also become maladjusted and have problems.

Immediate Goal: Change

The immediate goal in the biblical counseling process is to bring about change in the maladjusted Christian—change in his basic beliefs, in his attitudes, in his motives, in his decisions, and in his behavior. If the proper changes are made, right feelings will automatically follow. Because of the flesh, which is a part of every Christian until he dies, there is a tendency to glorify self instead of God (I Cor. 10:31). Such self-glory always brings about unbiblical, devilish beliefs, Devil-directed attitudes, motives, and decisions, which cause sinful behavior (James 1:13-15). As a result, wrong, stressful, upsetting, guilty feelings occur. The first part of the job of the counselor is to help the counselee make the proper changes in a biblical way by having him make up his mind to follow the steps in Romans 6:11-13. The counselee then needs exhortation to crucify self (Luke 9:23) so that the Holy Spirit, who is in every Christian, can be properly manifested and the needed change can come about.

The counselor has a two-fold role: he must be a detective and then a teacher.

Detecting

The process of counseling includes the counselor's detective role in discovering the problem. The counselor becomes a spiritual Sherlock Holmes in the pursuit of pertinent facts. He trusts the Holy Spirit to help him find the right clues and to lead him in asking additional questions. Through careful listening and proper questioning, he determines the real problem and the basic cause or causes of the problem. He then explains the problem to the counselee and confronts him with any sinful beliefs, attitudes, motives, decisions, and behavior. As the counselor discovers clues to the problem, he learns a great deal about the counselee.

Step 1: Active listening Proverbs 18:13 warns, "He that answereth a matter before he heareth it, it is folly and shame unto him"; active listening is essential in the counseling process. The keys to hearing a matter are as follows:

1. Giving undivided attention, not doing other things such as answering the phone or rifling through your folders or work on your desk
2. Using direct eye contact
3. Occasionally nodding positively or giving encouraging statements such as, "I understand what you are saying."
4. Briefly summing up and restating the counselee's ideas to let him know that you are fully aware of and understand exactly what he said and meant
5. Not showing shock or surprise when the counselee shares a corrupt story or an outrageous detail
6. Not correcting contradictory statements or misuse of words (These may be cleared up later; let him tell his story without interruption.)
7. Understanding and accepting his feelings about the problem (You do not have to condone bad feelings, but suspend judgment until the teaching phase of the interview.)

8. Avoiding the giving of solutions or your ideas about the problem too early in the interview because the counselee may feel misunderstood and rejected

The proper type of probing questions or statements will bring out useful information: "Tell me about . . . ." "If I were to ask you if you hated your mother, what would you say?" (The word "if" takes the accusation out of the question.) "How did you feel when that happened?" "What other action could you have taken?" "What was your response?" Rarely ask "why" questions or questions that demand a yes or no answer; the counselee is in your office to find out "why." Yes or no questions stifle a free-flowing response and usually put the counselee on the defensive.

Some of the questions that the counselor may ask to discover the problems and root causes mentioned in Chapter 4 are as follows:

1. How do you feel toward your mother, father, brothers, and sisters? coworkers, relatives, or authority?
2. What do you feel guilty about?
3. What is your greatest area of temptation?
4. What makes you very angry?
5. What is your biggest problem?
6. What would you change about your body or yourself?
7. What makes you fearful and afraid?
8. What are your goals in life?
9. What would you do or be if you had a choice?
10. What makes you feel rejected?
11. What do you think is your greatest need?

As he asks pertinent questions, the counselor listens until the Holy Spirit helps him discern the problem and its cause(s). A final question might be, "Is there anything else you want to tell me?" or "Are there any other facts you think I need to know?" or "Is there another problem you want to talk about?" Remember, the problem the counselee first presents, which makes him appear good, is not always the real problem. That is one of the reasons for probing questions. With good questions, the counselor is not only getting additional information but is also helping the counselee to identify and clarify his real problem and to desire a solution.

The counselor needs to collect whatever history, especially family history, about the counselee that will help them both understand the problem better. The more the counselee understands about the origin and nature of his fleshly behavior, the more he will desire to seek and implement a permanent solution. It is important for the counselee to realize that early trauma, an unwholesome environment, rejection, and an unsettling family situation are not the real problem. Rather, it is the counselee's habitual, ungodly, fleshly reactions that are contributing to his present problem. Throughout the detective phase, the counselor must always give hope by reassuring the counselee from the Word of God that there is a solution to or a way out of his problem.

Step 2: Explanation When the counselee has presented sufficient information for the counselor to understand the real problem, the counselor needs to explain the problem carefully and simply. Do not use psychological terms (e.g., "You are neurotically repressing incestual feelings") or theological jargon (e.g., "Your incomplete view of your hypostatic union with Christ leaves you vulnerable to demon obsession and a legalistic view"). Whenever possible, point out the influencing factors and the basic cause or causes as given in Chapter 4.

Step 3: Confrontation The next step in this process is to confront the person with any sinful behavior, pointing out from the Word of God the sinful beliefs, attitudes, motives, and decisions that are behind the sinful behavior. Gary Collins, in his book *How To Be a People Helper,* gives three additional types of confrontation.

> Confrontation involves the pointing out of sin in a helpee's life, but it is not limited to this. We can confront helpees with their inconsistent behavior ("You say you love your wife, but you are mean to her," "You claim to like sports, but you never play") or with their self-defeating behavior ("You want to succeed, but you set your standards so high that you are sure to fail") or with their tendency to evade issues ("You say you want to grow spiritually, but every time this issue comes up you change the subject").[1]

At this point in the counseling process, the counselor needs God's wisdom to make sure that he is looking at the problem from a truly scriptural viewpoint with a heart of love ready to help the counselee find restoration. The counselee may try to rationalize or excuse his behavior. The counselor should listen to his explanations and point out from Scripture how the counselee is wrong.

The detective phase of the counseling process is listening for clues to determine the cause or causes and then explaining the problem and confronting the person with any sin. After this phase occurs, the counselor is ready for the next phase of counseling—teaching.

Chapter 7

Teaching: Bringing About Change

In the process of counseling, the counselor then functions as a teacher, teaching Bible doctrines or Bible principles that relate to the problem and helping the counselee to solve his problem by making the needed changes. Being a good teacher is essential to becoming an effective Christian counselor. Those who are reaching people and seeing them change to do God's will are following certain teaching principles.

Great teachers teach Bible principles rather than just facts. Facts are important because they buttress, illustrate, and illuminate the truth; but facts are the medium and not the message. People tend to forget facts quickly, but principles become hooks in the mind upon which to hang facts. Principles are the categories under which facts can be filed. Though facts help a learner to understand truth, it is principles that determine behavior. Therefore, the counselor wants to help people learn to search out Bible principles in their devotions and apply them to their problems in daily life. The more the counselor knows about the Bible and the more Bible principles he has appropriated and applied in his own life, the better teacher he will be.

A superior teacher knows how to illustrate and simplify each truth that he presents. The purpose of the illustration is to capture the attention of the listener and to motivate him to accept the idea presented. The counselor can relate a real-life story or an example that gives a vivid picture of the practical way that Bible principles can be put into action in one's life. Charts and diagrams are excellent ways of simplifying profound Bible principles.

An outstanding teacher uses various techniques to get the counselee reacting mentally to the principles presented. He asks questions such as "How do you think this principle applies to your sin or problem?" Some use worksheets as assignments for application of a principle. Other counselors use audio tapes or booklets to stimulate the counselee's response to specific problems between sessions.

A motivating teacher is enthusiastically able to inspire the counselee to apply principles to his problem. A positive, cheerful attitude, always expressing hope, is part of this enthusiasm. It shows in the counselor's voice and facial expressions. Leaning toward the counselee connotes hope and interest. A counselor must not let his own daily problems, situations, and reactions affect his positive faith attitude.

A compassionate teacher uses positive reinforcement to build the counselee's confidence in succeeding at learning. Such approval helps to foster the counselee's desire for learning more about principles and applying them to his life. Positive reinforcement is not flattery: it is a figurative "pat on the back," "a word fitly spoken." It is praise for progress noted in the counselee's life. Flattery is for the benefit of the counselor; praise is for the benefit of the counselee. Reflecting the counselee's emotions, as the Bible directs, "Rejoice with them that do rejoice, and weep with them that weep," (Rom. 12:15), is part of positive reinforcement and compassion.

A spiritual teacher must be filled with the Spirit. The fruit of the Spirit should be daily evident in the counselor's life. He must be fervent in prayer, trusting God that the Holy Spirit will use the principles that are being taught from the Word of God to bring about a permanent change in the counselee.

The Goal and Four Steps of the Teaching Phase

The immediate goal of the teaching phase is to bring about change. The goal is expressed in II Timothy 3:17: "That the man of God may be perfect, throughly furnished unto all good works," and in Colossians 2:7, "Rooted and built up in him, and stablished in the faith, as ye have been taught, abounding therein with thanksgiving." This goal is best accomplished when a counselor follows the four steps given in II Timothy 3:16: "All Scripture is given by inspiration of God, and is profitable for doctrine, for reproof, for correction, for instruction in righteousness." Those who have experienced salvation can be confident that all of the Bible is the inspired Scripture and is useful and profitable for (1) doctrine or teaching Bible principles, (2) reproof or conviction, (3) correction or learning how to repent and apply Bible principles for change, and (4) instruction (discipline) in righteousness or making the change in habitual lifestyle and avoiding future temptation. Jay Adams, in his book *How to Help People Change*,[1] discusses these steps in detail.

Step 1—Doctrine

The counselee should be taught the Bible principle or principles that apply to his problem(s) so that the needed change can be accomplished. Donald Orthner has published a book of Bible principles found in Proverbs, covering seventy-nine topics grouped under seventeen categories.[2] A list of thirty-seven Bible principles that are useful in counseling are given in Appendix A. Chapter 4 of this book includes a list of Bible principles and the problems to which the principles relate.

The counselor must be careful that he does not teach extra-biblical convictions which are legitimately received and believed as a result of the Holy Spirit's convicting power in his own life. For example, consider that the counselor has been convicted by the Holy Spirit that his interest in professional sports and addiction to watching sports events on television are becoming a god and taking up valuable time. He decides that he will not attend any more professional games or watch professional sports on television. When he acts on his decision, his spiritual life improves tremendously, and he profitably uses his free time for family, church, soulwinning activities, Bible study, and prayer. Or perhaps another counselor decides not to play a particular musical instrument any longer because it reminds him too much of his lifestyle before he was saved. In both cases the counselors have been personally convinced of the problems of certain practices; however, if they insist that a counselee cannot be spiritual unless he adopts these personal convictions, the counselors are putting the counselee back under the law. The counselors destroy the working of the law of liberty in the counselee's life and thereby minimize the grace of God.

Proper teaching of Bible principles in counseling involves more than merely imparting Bible knowledge about how to solve an immediate problem. The counselor teaches principles that will help the counselee also solve future problems, avoid temptation, trust God, and become dependent on God instead of on man or self. It is no credit to the counselor if the counselee is calling the counselor two or three times a week for advice. The theme of counseling should constantly be as follows: trust God for the answers found in His Word and through prayer. Let the Holy Spirit guide you in all truth (John 14:26; 16:13) and give you the power to keep God's commandments (John 16:24; Rom.8:9-14). Doing the will of God is evidence that change is taking place (James 1:22; Matt. 7:24).

Step 2—Reproof

As Bible principles are taught in the power of the Holy Spirit, Hebrews 4:12 says that the second step will be conviction or reproof or rebuke: "For the word of God is quick, and powerful, and sharper than any twoedged sword, piercing even to the dividing asunder of soul and spirit, and of the joints and marrow, and is a discerner of the thoughts and intents of the heart."

To reprove in love because you care is to show the counselee his sin from the Word of God and urge him to repent. This is the pattern Jesus used with the Laodicean church in Revelation 3:19— "As many as I love, I rebuke and chasten: be zealous therefore, and repent." As Jay Adams states, "He sends counselors as modern-day Nathans to modern-day Davids."[3] It is up to the Holy Spirit to make the sinner feel guilty enough to turn to repentance and forgiveness. Since the Holy Spirit uses the Word of God to finish the work of conviction, the counselor must make sure he is led of the Holy Spirit in the Scripture he uses as the vehicle of conviction.

Step 3—Correction

After the second step of conviction takes place, the counselor is ready for the third. Correction is teaching the counselee how to genuinely repent. Repentance is turning from one's sin to God, requiring three steps: (1) confessing sin to God and to others, if needed (I John 1:9), (2) asking forgiveness from the wronged person (Matt. 5: 23-24; 18:15-17), and (3) forsaking sin and the contributing environment and following a new habit-pattern of behavior that is pleasing to God. Real repentance will result in godly sorrow, which may involve emotion but will always involve forsaking the old sin and adopting righteous behavior. Proverbs emphasizes this point: "He that covereth his sins shall not prosper: but whoso confesseth and forsaketh them shall have mercy" (28:13).

Step 4—Instruction in Righteousness

The fourth step given in II Timothy 3:16 is instruction in righteousness, or how to begin the new behavior of righteousness, how to continue that new habit pattern in one's life, and how to resist the Devil in future temptation. A permanent change is best accomplished when a Christian uses the three truths mentioned in Romans 6:11-13. The first truth is given in verse 11: "Likewise reckon ye also yourselves to be dead indeed unto sin, but alive unto God through Jesus Christ our Lord." Why? Because verses 6 and 7 of this chapter say that "our old man is crucified with him, that the body of sin might be destroyed, that henceforth we should not serve sin. For he that is dead is freed from sin." Therefore, sin does not have any power over the Christian. He is not helpless, and he is not a victim of his fleshly desires.

The second truth is found in verse 12: "Let not sin therefore reign in your mortal body, that ye should obey it in the lusts thereof." The Christian decides not to let sin have control. Sinful beliefs, attitudes, and motives must be purged from the mind by denying self (Luke 9:23) and learning how to praise God (Ps. 107:8; I Thess. 5:18).

The third truth is found in verse 13, which admonishes the counselee to decide that he is not going to "yield [his] members as instruments of unrighteousness unto sin: but yield [himself] unto God, as those that are alive from the dead, and [his] members as instruments of righteousness unto God." The counselor should give suggestions as to how this yielding can be done. What good and right actions could be substituted for the corrupt actions? The counselee must arm himself with the same mind that Christ has, who suffered every temptation yet did not sin (I Pet. 4:1-2).

The end result of the four-step teaching process is restoration: Galatians 6:1-3. How restoration is done is important. The counselor does not sit in judgment or act superior; but, as a forgiven sinner talking to his sinning brother, the counselor tries to help him. Restoring a brother should be done in a spirit of meekness, realizing that but for the grace of God, the counselor could be in the same position. If the counselee has been disciplined by the church, the counselor should work with the pastor to have the repentant brother publicly restored to full fellowship.

The Struggle

The counselee will be going through a struggle after he leaves the counselor's office. The law of sin working in his members will fight against the law of God which is within him. In Romans 7:14-25 Paul mentions the struggle he had, but then he tells the two ways to get victory (7:23-25 and 8:1-16). He mentions making up the mind. He sees another law in his members, warring against the law of his mind in verse 23. In verse 25 he says that with the mind one serves the law of God; therefore, the counselee must *make up his mind* in every situation to resist the Devil's temptations and to serve the law of God.

In Romans 8:1-16 Paul shows how the Holy Spirit can give one the power to make up one's mind to get victory over sin. Verses 18 through 25 mention the hope that we have of being delivered from this struggle. Verses 26 through 32 give the assurance that the Christian will have help in the struggle and eventual victory as he depends on the power of the Spirit. Great emphasis must be put on the counselee's making up his mind to live a righteous or sanctified life for God. This determining is done as the counselee identifies with Christ and becomes aware of the power of the Holy Spirit within him to give him victory (Eph. 3:20). The mind of man alone has a tendency to serve the law of sin. Being filled with the Holy Spirit simply means that one has confessed his sins and is dedicated to serving God. Although he may not live a perfect life, he is going to have victory over sin. He will have a strong desire to keep right with God by keeping sin out of his life. When sin does make inroads, he will be willing to confess and forsake his sin right away.

Other Types of Counseling

Some counseling situations involve merely giving information, giving help in decision-making, or giving encouragement; but when sin is involved in a person's life, the four-step process just explained should be followed. In information-giving sessions the counselor should have sources of accurate, up-to-date information such as the material in the book by Joe McIlhaney *1250 Health Questions Women Ask* [4] or J. Norman Wright's book *Questions Women Ask in Private*.[5] A list of service agencies in your community, such as the Muscular Dystrophy Association, Social Security Office, Salvation Army, and Veterans Administration, can be found through your public library or Chamber of Commerce.

To help people in decision-making, teach the Bible principles that apply to the situation. Then teach the six steps of solid decision making:

1. Determine what the choices are.
2. Find out when a decision must be made.
3. Obtain any needed additional information.
4. Identify the Bible principles that apply.
5. Pray for wisdom and for God to change the circumstance if it is His will.
6. Decide; then act on the decision.

Do not make the decision for the counselee, for he must learn to look to God for the right decision (Prov. 3:5-6; 16:3). Part of giving encouragement is being available in times of distress to pray with the person and direct him to appropriate passages of Scripture. Realize the power of the Word of God to comfort, encourage, and guide. The counselee may need to be directed to places where he can get his physical need supplied. A "Flying 20" may be in order, and you may be the one to put a twenty-dollar bill in the mail to the counselee without his knowing where it came from.

Assignments

It is good to give the counselee assignments (or "homework," as Jay Adams calls it) to be done before the next session with the counselee. These assignments should grow out of the counseling sessions, should reinforce the teaching that has been given, and should prepare the counselee for the next session. They should be for the purpose of continuing the change that was started in the previous counseling sessions. The assignments should be practical and simple to do, and there should be no more than three to do between sessions. Some examples of assignments are as follows: (1) Read I John every day and underline the important verse that God puts on your heart for that particular day. (2) Start an aerobic exercise program. (3) Write a love letter to a loved one, asking his forgiveness for things you have done to hurt him. (4) Take your mother or mother-in-law out to dinner and practice a right response to her outrageous accusations. (5) Sit down with your wife or husband and discuss a serious matter. Each time your spouse becomes angry, simply stand up until he or she cools down, then sit down and calmly finish the discussion. (6) List meaningful ways to spend time with your children. (7) Enroll in a local technical school, begin a program to finish a GED, or enroll in a Bible correspondence course. (8) Have a conference with your employer and get the conflict resolved that you have already resolved with the Lord. (9) Have a physical exam and tell the physician the problem that you have already shared with the counselor. (10) Leave your television set off for a week, read a good Christian book or the Bible, and pray or have family time during the time you would have watched TV.

The assignments would vary according to the counseling situation, and at the next session the counselor would check to see whether the assignment had been done. Willingness to do the assignments can be a clue to the seriousness of the counselee's intentions to bring about change in his life. It is important that the counselor pray for the counselee during the time between sessions.

After all, it is God's working in the life of the counselee that brings about the permanent change that only He can make.

Termination

Counseling can be terminated when the counselor believes that the counselee has made the change that is going to be a habitual part of his lifestyle. After termination it is best to have the counselee call you after a three- or four-week space of time and then after three months. Always leave the counselee with the feeling that he can renew the counseling at any time or call you when he needs words of encouragement. Throughout the counseling session, always give the counselee hope that his problem can be solved. It can be if the counselor will use the Word of God and trust in the Holy Spirit's working in the counselee's life. The counselee must always be encouraged to use the power of God within him to bring about the needed change or to solve present and future problems. As the Bible assures us, God "is able to do exceeding abundantly above all that we ask or think, according to the power that worketh in us" (Eph. 3:20).

Chapter 8

Foundational Counseling

Two things are eternal in this life, and all the rest shall pass away. One is the Word of God, which God assures us is eternal: "For ever, O Lord, Thy word is settled in heaven" (Ps. 119:89). "Heaven and earth shall pass away, but my words shall not pass away" (Matt. 24:35). Christians study it to find direction in their lives; to gain true knowledge about God, eternity, and salvation; and to learn of God's plan for their lives. Theological training is the ultimate in academic pursuits, and no man is truly educated until he thoroughly knows the Word of God.

The other thing that will last for eternity is people. Every man is going to live eternally somewhere, either in heaven or in hell (Rev. 21:1-8). Jesus said, "He that believeth on the Son hath everlasting life: and he that believeth not the Son shall not see life; but the wrath of God abideth on him" (John 3:36). A Christian must be vitally interested in people, not only in their eternal destinies by being an active soulwinner, but in their temporal lives by being a loving helper and edifier. Most of a counselor's time should be spent in contact with these two important and eternal things.

Real Christian counseling is using the Word of God to help people solve their problems and improve their planning. Since the goal of counseling is Christlikeness, the only way the counselee can be adequately counseled is to be properly related to God through a salvation experience. A relationship with Christ provides him with unique and indispensable resources for solving his own problems. Only after the counselee is properly related to God can the counselor satisfactorily help him to be adjusted in other areas of his life.

Sin, or going against the will of God as revealed in the Word of God, is the main cause of maladjustment. Confronting people with their sins and bringing them into loving conformity with the will of God will solve most of the problems that human beings encounter.

The most productive, effective, and permanent counseling that the counselor will ever do is the foundational counseling of soul-winning. Not only will he "save a soul from death," but he will also "hide a multitude of sins" (James 5:20). He will help the counselee get rid of man's greatest underlying fears, the fear of death and the fear of judgment (Heb. 9:27). He will be helping to cure many medical problems caused by guilt (Pss. 32 and 51). He will give the counselee the means of understanding the Bible (I Cor. 2:14) upon which the counselee's future adjustment depends. The counselor will also be doing the will of God by soulwinning. The Bible states that "the Lord is . . . not willing that any should perish, but that all should come to repentance" (II Pet. 3:9). God desires to "have all men to be saved, and to come unto the knowledge of the truth" (I Tim. 2:4).

The Challenge

God, in His Word, challenges all Christians to win souls, beginning with the great commission, which is mentioned four times: Matthew 28:19-20; Mark 16:15; John 15:16; and Acts 1:8. Other challenges follow.

The sowing and reaping principle in Psalm 126:6 contains a good parallel to the task of soulwinning: "He that goeth forth and weepeth, bearing precious seed, shall doubtless come again with rejoicing, bringing his sheaves with him." First, *he* indicates that it takes individual, born-again Christians to do the work of soulwinning. Second, *that goeth forth* is a charge to reach out—to go where people are. Third, *weepeth* refers to verse 5: "They that sow in tears shall reap in joy." A soulwinner will have a heart concern and a willingness to make sacrifices to try to reach people. That concern will make him go out into the cold on snowy days, and it will make him go out on wet days and hot days as the Holy Spirit leads him to certain places to talk to certain people. Christians need to say every day, "Lord, lead me to some soul today. I'm ready to win souls." Fourth, *bearing precious seed* reminds the soulwinner that he has to go forth with the Word of God. Romans 10:17 points out this truth: "Faith cometh by hearing, and hearing by the word of God." So as the Word of God is used, God's power begins to work in a life. It is not words, not stories, but the Word of God that cuts to the heart (Heb. 4:12). The final step is found in the last part of Psalm 126:6: "shall doubtless come, . . . bringing his sheaves with him." This portion indicates that the soulwinner will see fruit for his labor. Souls will be saved if he faithfully gives out the Word of God.

Romans 1:14-16 contains another challenge to evangelism. It delineates three steps to becoming a soulwinner. Paul says, "I am debtor both to the Greeks, and to the Barbarians; both to the wise, and to the unwise." When Paul received the gospel, he realized that he had a debt to others who had not received Jesus Christ as their Savior.

In verse 15 Paul says, "As much as in me is, I am ready to preach the gospel." Like Paul, born-again Christians must be ready to give out tracts, to write letters to friends and relatives, and to witness in the office, on the job, over the telephone, on business trips, on pleasure trips, or wherever they meet people. People they meet are either saved or lost. If they are saved, the soulwinner can edify them and have fellowship with them. If they are lost, they can be given the gospel. Paul was always ready.

And then in verse 16 Paul says, "For I am not ashamed of the gospel of Christ: for it is the power of God unto salvation to every one that believeth; to the Jew first, and also to the Greek." The main reason people do not declare the simple way of salvation is that they are ashamed of the gospel, ashamed mainly because of the persecution that they fear. Every Christian must realize that he is going to be persecuted if he declares the gospel of Jesus Christ.

Christians need to be warned that the minute they start living a life for Christ, separating themselves from the corruption of the world, and witnessing, they are going to have persecution. First Peter 4:2-4 says that when a Christian departs from the fleshly lusts of men to do the will of God, people are going to think it strange that he does not enjoy the same things they enjoy, and they are going to start speaking evil of him. At that point the Christian must ask himself if he has a sweet testimony of love or if he reflects the evil spirit of the persecutor. First Peter 4:12-16 tells a Christian not to be surprised at this persecution as if it were not supposed to happen. When a Christian begins to give out the gospel, he is going to be reproached for the name of Christ. He is going to suffer as a Christian—maybe not physically but at least mentally—and he should not be ashamed. John 15:16-20 indicates that when a Christian starts bearing fruit, the world is going to hate him. It hated Jesus Christ first, and Christ tells us that "the servant is not greater than his lord" (John 15:20). If the people persecuted Christ, they will also persecute the Christian, especially when he keeps Christ's sayings and follows His will by holding forth the Word of Life.

Christians will not be ashamed if they realize the tremendous power of the gospel. As the Scripture emphasizes, "It is the power of God unto salvation to every one that believeth; to the Jew first, and also to the Greek" (Rom. 1:16). This powerful gospel overcomes the two greatest fears of mankind. Hebrews 9:27 says, "It is appointed unto men once to die, but after this the judgment." All people have a basic fear of death and judgment, but the gospel and salvation take away that fear. Born-again Christians are no longer under the terrible wrath of God (II Thess. 1:7-9; Rom. 8:1). Instead of worrying about the little opposition and persecution that they may receive, they can boldly preach the gospel of Jesus Christ. People will become angry, but believers must keep on preaching the gospel to them, knowing that many will receive Jesus Christ as their personal Savior.

Another challenge for evangelism is found in II Corinthians 5:11-20. Verse 11 says, "Knowing therefore the terror of the Lord, we persuade men," and then verse 14 adds, "For the love of Christ constraineth us." These are two great motivations for the soulwinner. First, knowing the terror of the Lord against sinners, the soulwinner must present the gospel. Second, knowing Christ's love for sinners, he must witness about that love. If Christ were willing to die for all men, the Christian certainly ought to be willing to tell others about His sacrifice. Verse 14 continues, "If one died for all, then were all dead." Every Christian has the life-saving remedy that will cure people of this dread sin disease.

Verse 15 indicates that the Christian should not live for himself but rather for Christ. Verse 17 declares that the Christian is a new creature in Christ Jesus; the old selfish desires have passed away, and all things have become new. There are new attitudes and new visions. The Christian needs to see people as they really are—not as heroes to be emulated in lifestyle, dress, and worldly attitudes, but rather as condemned human beings who are going to an eternal hell and who need rescuing. Verse 18 indicates that God has given to the Christian the ministry of reconciling people to Christ. Verse 20 shows plainly that he is an ambassador for Christ and a representative of the heavenly King in this foreign land, holding forth the message of Jesus Christ and His shed blood that can make a sinner completely righteous before God.

The Elements

The three essential elements for foundational counseling are the same for all counseling. First is the Word of God. The counselor is trying to get a person to have saving faith by giving him the plan of salvation; then he is trying to increase the convert's faith by discipling him. The only way to increase faith is by the Word of God. The Bible affirms that "faith cometh by hearing, and hearing by the word of God" (Rom. 10:17). "So shall my word be that goeth forth out of my mouth: it shall not return unto me void, but it shall accomplish that which I please, and it shall prosper in the thing whereto I sent it" (Isa. 55:11). The second essential element is prayer. The counselor should be praying daily for his counselees as the Bible instructs: "Confess your faults one to another, and pray one for another, that ye may be healed. The effectual fervent prayer of a righteous man availeth much" (James 5:16). It is God's working in the individual that is going to make the difference in his being converted and his becoming adjusted. The counselor needs to pray every day that the Lord will bring needy ones across his path. The third element is the power and work of the Holy Spirit. The Bible says, "Then he answered and spake unto me, saying, This is the word of the Lord unto Zerubbabel, saying, Not by might, nor by power, but by my spirit, saith the Lord of hosts" (Zech. 4:6). God's Holy Spirit works during the counseling session and between sessions, and it is the Holy Spirit who finally convicts the person of his sin.

The Approach

The approach to the counselee in foundational counseling should always be two-fold as alluded to in Jude, verses 22 and 23:

"And of some have compassion [mercy], making a difference" (vs. 22). Some people respond better to the love of God and to a loving, tender approach. Others need a more confrontational approach, a warning of judgment and the wrath of God against sin that you are fully aware of from studying the Bible: "And others save with fear, pulling them out of the fire; hating even the garment spotted by the flesh" (vs. 23). Both approaches should be used with every counselee, but one will receive more emphasis than the other, depending on the person and his reaction.

The Techniques

The techniques of evangelism are many and varied, and the one the counselor uses will depend on his personality and the situation. There are many people who are hungry for the gospel. The counselor is always ready to give out the "gospel sandwich" to satisfy the hunger of lost sinners. The bottom piece of bread in this "gospel sandwich" is a friendly spirit, getting acquainted and being interested in the lost person. It would also include a question inquiring about his spiritual condition, such as "If you were to die right now, would you go to heaven or hell?" or "Could you tell me in a few words how a person could be sure of going to heaven?" The meat of the "gospel sandwich" is six to ten verses explaining salvation, such as Romans 3:23, Romans 6:23, Hebrews 9:27, II Thessalonians 1:7-9, Romans 5:8, Ephesians 2:8-9, John 1:12, Revelation 3:20, I John 5:11-13, and Romans 10:13. The word "sin" in Romans 3:23 and Romans 6:23 is best explained by the counselor's going through the Ten Commandments, explaining how the person has broken every one of the Ten Commandments. James 2:10 explains that if anyone has broken one of them, he has broken them all. This approach is important, "for by the Law is the knowledge of sin" (Rom. 3:19-20; Ps. 19:7-9). The Law becomes a teacher to bring us to Christ (Gal. 3:24). A person needs to become desperate for God's salvation. Some people use the Romans road; others use the third chapter of John. There are many ways to present the gospel, but always the Word of God must be used. The top piece of bread in the "gospel sandwich" is the offer of an opportunity to accept Christ as Savior. This offer is usually in the form of a question, such as "Would you like to accept Christ as your Savior now?" or "In the light of what the Word of God says, what would you like to do about this matter?"

Under no circumstances should a counselor promise a sinner an easier life or wealth or health, for even though he receives eternal life, there may be a life of persecution, suffering, and difficulties ahead for this particular individual. God does say that there will be persecution for all those who live godly in Christ Jesus (II Tim. 3:12). The counselor can promise the abundant life (John 10:10) with Christ supplying every need (Phil. 4:19), giving grace in every situation (II Cor. 8:9), and never leaving the person alone in any circumstance (Matt. 28:20; Heb. 13:5).

One of the most powerful techniques is the soulwinner's personal testimony of how God brought about his own changed life, including how he reacted, what he thought, and what he did about it. This personal testimony must be backed up by a lifestyle of love and holiness so that the counselee can see a truly changed life.

The Follow-up

If the person does receive Christ, then the counselor must become a discipler as Paul was to Timothy: "And the things that thou hast heard of me among many witnesses, the same commit thou to faithful men, who shall be able to teach others also" (II Tim. 2:2). He will have a regular Bible study with the convert, become a real friend, take him to church and out soulwinning, encourage him to read and memorize Scripture, and do everything he can to build him up in the faith. If he cannot do the discipling himself, he will make sure that the new convert is connected with someone who can.

The Basic Ideas

In foundational counseling, the counselor is declaring certain ideas. (1) Man is a sinner, has broken God's law, and needs a Savior because there is terrible judgment coming on sin. (2) Man cannot save himself by his own works or by "turning over a new leaf" or by joining some church. (3) Jesus Christ, God's Son, died on the cross for man's sin, shedding His precious blood as a payment for the sin. (4) Jesus Christ is the resurrected Savior, who has the power to save man from sin because of His resurrection. Sinners must not only believe these truths, but they must also repent, or turn from, their sin and receive Jesus Christ into their lives as a personal Savior.

The Unbeliever

If the person does not receive Jesus Christ as His Savior at the initial counseling session, as few do, then the counselor must in subsequent sessions reiterate this gospel message. The counselee must be converted before the counselor can carry on true biblical counseling and see any permanent solution to the counselee's present problems. The Bible predicts the response of the unconverted: "But the natural man receiveth not the things of the Spirit of God: for they are foolishness unto him: neither can he know them, because they are spiritually discerned" (I Cor. 2:14).

If the gospel has been presented and the person refuses to accept Christ, he is actually rebelling against God and His Word; therefore, any solution the counselor presents to him from the Word of God for his problems, he will reject, and the time will be wasted. If the person does accept Christ, many times salvation not only saves his soul but also clears up a multitude of problems in the person's life. The Bible details some rewards of successful foundational counseling: "Let him know, that he which converteth the sinner from the error of his way shall save a soul from death, and shall hide a multitude of sins" (James 5:20). "And the servant of the Lord must not strive; but be gentle unto all men, apt to teach, patient, in meekness instructing those that oppose themselves; if God peradventure will give them repentance to the acknowledging of the truth; and that they may recover themselves out of the snare of the devil, who are taken captive by him at his will" (II Tim. 2:24-26).

Chapter 9

Principles Related to the Counseling Process

There are certain principles related to the counseling process which, when followed, contribute to a successful helping situation.

Uphold the counselee's privacy and confidentiality. In the counseling session the counselee may reveal information that he has never revealed to another person. Therefore, the environment should be private enough so that there is no way the conversation can be overheard by anyone. The counselor must keep all crucial information private, revealing it to no one without the counselee's permission. The writer of Proverbs admonishes, "A talebearer revealeth secrets: but he that is of a faithful spirit concealeth the matter" (Prov. 11:13). For example, if the counselor decides to consult with the counselee's pastor, he should have the counselee's permission for the consultation. The case studies in this book are essentially true regarding the symptoms, diagnosis, solution, and outcome. However, to protect the counselees' privacy and confidentiality, names, gender, places, and details have been fictionalized.

Pay attention to the counselee during the counseling session, as well as to his problem. The counselee's gestures, his facial expressions, and his reactions all reveal a great deal about the person and may indicate deeper and more serious problems than those being discussed. Looking the counselee in the eye and responding make him feel understood. The best empathy and rapport arise from a simple and sincere effort to listen and hear accurately what the counselee has to say. The counselor can enhance rapport by being genuinely concerned about the counselee and not wondering whether the counselee likes him.

Work on understanding rather than giving sympathy or reassurances during the early stages of counseling. Understanding, which comes from listening carefully to the individual, helps the counselor to be fully aware of the counselee's feelings about the situation. Do not give sympathy, false reassurances, or condemnation. Comments such as "Oh, you poor thing" or "I do not see how you can stand it" or "Don't worry about it, it will be better tomorrow" or "A spiritual Christian should not have such feelings" are counterproductive. But statements like "The Word of God has the solution for your problem" or "We are going to pray and ask God to help you in a mighty way in this situation" or "Let's thank God for this, and let's trust Him to work these things together for good" offer hope for a troubled counselee.

Do not define success as completely solving every problem. The counselor is just an instrument in God's hands, helping people. Two Scriptures, "For we are his workmanship, created in Christ Jesus unto good works, which God hath before ordained that we should walk in them" (Eph. 2:10) and "For it is God which worketh in you both to will and to do of his good pleasure" (Phil. 2:13), indicate that God is continually working in the counselor and the counselee. He is using Spirit-led people and situations to bring the counselee to perfection, which is realized finally in Heaven. It is important that the counselor be led of the Holy Spirit. If the counselor has a deep need to rearrange people's lives and solve all their problems, he is taking on responsibility that should be left to God and the counselee. It is the counselee's responsibility to solve his own problems during the course of counseling. God is using the counselor, the preacher's sermons, the parents' ideas and suggestions, the comments of friends, the conviction of the Holy Spirit, and the prayers of many to bring that person to the solution of his problem. The counselee may come back a year later and say that his problem was completely solved six months after he terminated counseling with the counselor. If asked, "What was it that brought about the solution?" he may state, "Well, I finally got hold of a passage of Scripture that you gave" or "It was a sermon that I heard which reinforced everything you told me."

Do not become too emotionally involved with cases, either in the process or with the final outcome. The counselee may say unkind, cutting things or resist counsel or not follow suggestions. Remember that the counselee is the one with the problem. The counselor does not let the counselee's problem become his problem by wrong reactions in response to the counselee. If the counselor becomes distraught at every failure of the counselee or gets too emotionally involved, strain is going to wreak havoc in his life and he will not be the right kind of help to his counselees. Although the outcome may be that the couple will go ahead and get a divorce or the depressed person will commit suicide, the counselor is not responsible for the final behavior of the counselee; he is responsible for following the Holy Spirit's leading in giving all the help he can.

Sometimes the counselee misinterprets the counselor's interest in and understanding of his problem. He may desire a close friendship or have a romantic interest and even initiate behaviors to deepen the imagined relationship. If the counselor naively responds to these overtures, complications will arise.

Concentrate on the total adjustment. The counselor is trying to help people over time, not just solve a particular problem. The goal is to make the counselee dependent on God and independent of the counselor. The counselor tries to help the counselee solve his own problems in God's way. When the counselee begins calling about every decision he must make, he is becoming dependent upon the counselor. Teach the counselee to pray about every matter and trust God for answers from His Word, as the Bible directs: "Trust in the Lord with all thine heart, and lean not unto thine own understanding. In all thy ways acknowledge him, and he shall direct thy paths" (Prov. 3:5-6).

Laymen or nonprofessionals should not charge for counseling but use it as a ministry. When there is a fee for counseling, the counselor may tend to see the client as a source of income. Everyone likes a steady income, so the temptation is to line up clients at so much an hour once a week for a year to keep the checks coming. If your desire is to go into lay counseling as a full-time ministry, seek support from your church as a regular part of its ministry.

Realize that one counselor cannot counsel the whole world. One must be selective and follow the leadership of the Holy Spirit in choosing the number of people and the type of problems that he feels qualified to handle. Most counselors have specialties or areas in which they are proficient. A counselor who works with married couples or teenagers should refer to someone else a call concerning a child in need of counsel. Whenever possible, refer individuals with severe or complicated problems to your own pastor, a medical doctor, or a more qualified counselor.

Dispel the counseling myths that have been promoted by the secular and even the Christian media. Many of the myths are in direct opposition to God's Word.

Myth 1: Psychology is necessary to handle completely the problems of the Christian. On many Christian stations, Christian psychology programs are replacing Bible preaching.

Truth 1: The discipline of psychology is very theoretical, speculative, and unbiblical, denying that man is a created being with an eternal existence. The Word of God is sufficient for all nonmedical problems and will give the answers that are needed, as stated in II Timothy 3:16-17.

Myth 2: If one is a Christian with a proper kind of faith, he is going to be healthy and wealthy.

Truth 2: The Bible promises the born-again Christian persecution (II Tim. 3:12), God's protection (Ps. 91:11-12), grace (II Cor. 12:9), and guidance in his life (Prov. 3:5-6). It also promises that God will meet all of the Christian's needs (Phil. 4:19). But the scriptural emphasis is clearly not upon wealth and health. Such a focus is worldly, and Christians should not follow it. All people are going to die (Heb. 9:27). But born-again Christians are promised eternal life and a place prepared for them in heaven (John 3:36; John 14:1-3). Our riches are also to be in heaven rather than on this earth (Matt. 6:19-21).

Myth 3: Success and good adjustment in life are dependent upon one's positive feelings of personal worth or significance, popularly called "self-esteem" or "self-love." A related myth is that one cannot love others until he loves himself. These two myths form the basis for the sin of pride.

Truth 3: This type of "self-love" is on the *feeling level* and involves the self and the flesh. The Bible emphasizes the crucified self, "And they that are Christ's have crucified the flesh with the affections and lusts" (Gal. 5:24) with Jesus Christ increasing and self decreasing (John 3:30). The way down is the way up. Jesus said, "for every one that exalteth himself shall be abased; and he that humbleth himself shall be exalted" (Luke 18:14). And James says, "Humble yourselves in the sight of the Lord, and he shall lift you up" (James 4:10). People love themselves and are naturally selfish and self-centered. Christians have to work continually at loving others by denying self (Luke 9:23). They must also esteem others better than themselves (Phil. 2:3).

Christians do have an identity sometimes called self-awareness or self-evaluation on the *intellectual level,* which should be based on an accurate and realistic appraisal of their weaknesses, strengths, abilities, skills, performance, and gifts which God has given or allowed; but they must realize from whence these come and give the glory to God. As the Bible points out, "For who maketh thee to differ from another? And what hast thou that thou didst not receive? now if thou didst receive it, why dost thou glory, as if thou hadst not received it?" (I Cor. 4:7); and "But God forbid that I should glory, save in the cross of our Lord Jesus Christ, by whom the world is crucified unto me, and I unto the world" (Gal. 6:14). God resists the proud but gives grace to the humble (I Pet. 5:5; Luke 14:11).

Because of the fall (Gen. 3), man has an inborn desire to preserve, protect, and defend himself. This desire is controlled by the will, which is primarily on the *action level,* and involves action that is necessary to care for the self and preserve one's life. This desire, sometimes called self-preservation, must be subjugated to God's will. Saints down through the ages, rather than deny the faith, have been willing to suffer privation and torture, even death.

For a complete discussion of the three levels of self-love—feeling, intellectual, and action—see Paul Brownback's book, *The Danger of Self Love.*[1] The Christian's self-concept is in Christ, for we are "complete in him" (Col. 2:9-10), "partakers of the divine nature" (II Pet. 1:4), and "joint-heirs with Christ" (Rom. 8:17).

Myth 4: Myths about forgiveness.

Myth 4A: Forgive God for what He has done to you.

Truth 4A: Man does not forgive God. That would assume that God sins; He does not.

Myth 4B: Forgive yourself.

Truth 4B: God's forgiveness is sufficient. Only God can forgive sin, and His forgiveness is complete and final. Therefore, one must think forgiven and then act forgiven once he has repented and asked forgiveness (I John 1:9).

Myth 4C: Ask forgiveness from a dead spouse, parent, child, or aborted baby for how you treated him before he died.

Truth 4C: This myth is akin to spiritism and implies communing with dead spirits.

Myth 4D: One does not need to ask forgiveness for disobeying what one mistakenly thought was God's Word.

Truth 4D: If one deliberately violates a standard that he thought was God's, he is guilty and needs to ask forgiveness. "Therefore to him that knoweth to do good, and doeth it not, to him it is sin" (James 4:17); "whatsoever is not of faith is sin" (Rom. 14:23). For example, the Bible states that one should not sue another Christian, but it does not state that one should not sue a non-Christian. If a Christian believes that suing the non-Christian might hurt his testimony and sues anyway, he will rightfully feel guilty.

Although the world labels most guilt "false guilt," this term could be applied to some rigid, overly conscientious people who, tending toward perfectionism, never feel forgiven. They feel guilty about all kinds of minute things and usually feel guilty about an already-forgiven past. Although such guilt may be a cover-up of other, more serious sin, most just need good teaching on the grace of God.

Myth 4E: An offended person should forgive the offender even if the offender will not repent and ask for forgiveness.

Truth 4E: According to Luke 17:3 fellowship, forgiveness, and peace are conditional, dependent on the offender's repentance. This is also true of God's fellowship and forgiveness (I John 1:9). However, a spirit of forgiveness is maintained as the offended believer, through prayer, immediately releases the penalty of the offense (the desire to get even) to God (Mark 11:25; Rom. 12:19).

Myth 4F: Forgiving is forgetting.

Truth 4F: Man cannot and God does not forget an offense or sin at will. Man and God can choose to release the offender from the penalty of the offense after repentance. This is the true meaning of "not remember" in Jeremiah 31:34 and Isaiah 43:25. Wendell E. Miller, in his book *Forgiveness: The Power and the Puzzles,*[2] thoroughly discusses these ideas.

Myth 5: A person falls into sin accidentally or is coerced by some other influence.

Truth 5: No one accidentally falls into sin. People say, "The Devil made me do it" or "It's a demon in me that caused this." The truth is that they plot, scheme, plan, gamble, and finally make a deliberate decision to sin. The book of James makes this clear: "Let no man say when he is tempted, I am tempted of God: for God cannot be tempted with evil, neither tempteth he any man: but every man is tempted, when he is drawn away of his own lust, and enticed. Then when lust hath conceived, it bringeth forth sin: and sin, when it is finished, bringeth forth death" (James 1:13-15).

Myth 6: The homosexual, who makes up 10 percent of the American population according to Kinsey's invalid 1940 study, is not responsible for his sexual orientation, since he was born that way. Therefore, as a minority he has the right to freely practice and enjoy his alternate sexual lifestyle without any restrictions, discrimination, or condemnation from society, since there are no negative or harmful results or effects on persons or on society. This lie has been repeated so often on talk shows, sitcoms, and news broadcasts that the average citizen believes it.

Truth 6: The Bible says that homosexuality is a sin. It is a chosen and learned sinful unnatural behavior which the Bible and our laws refer to as sodomy (Deut. 23:17; I Kings 14:24; 15:12; II Kings 23:7; Rom. 1:25-29). (See Problem 4, Chapter 12.)

Myth 7: Morality cannot be legislated.

Truth 7: This myth is used when political conservatives are trying to outlaw gambling, pornography, or liquor. Lawmakers and those in authority do legislate morality. There are laws and rules against murder, rape, stealing, violence, drugs, and other types of sin.

Certainly there will always be a few people who will break the laws in spite of strict enforcement, but the laws and rules are still necessary. Actually, lawmakers legislate certain types of behavior, thereby creating a climate conducive to morality, but they cannot legislate moral character.

Myth 8: Alcoholism is a disease.

Truth 8: Several places in the Bible refer to alcoholism as a controllable behavior (Prov. 20:1; Rom. 13:13; Eph. 5:18). Herbert Fingarette, in his book *Heavy Drinking—The Myth of Alcoholism as a Disease,*[3] quotes G. A. Marlett as saying, "There's no adequate empirical support for the basic tenet of the classic disease concept of alcoholism."[4] Another expert, B. Kissin, "dismisses the classic disease concept of alcoholism as old and outmoded, whose propositions are invalid."[5] Fingarette states, "At any one time 20 percent of the U. S. population are so addicted to alcohol that they have alcohol-related problems."[6] He further states that an increase in taxes on all alcoholic beverages is the best way to reduce drinking, especially among the poor. The increase would also help pay for the sixty-billion-dollar cost to society per year as a result of heavy drinking.[7]

Myth 9: Because feelings are neither moral nor immoral, people are not responsible nor should they be concerned about them. Feelings just exist and are a part of normal lives.

Truth 9: The Bible deals specifically with the subject of feelings. Feelings are bodily reactions which stem from one's attitudes, motives, and beliefs. If these are sinful, the feelings will be sinful. Anger is an example of this. In Ephesians 4:26-27 one is told to deal with anger immediately or it becomes sin. If the attitude is sinful, then the angry reaction and behavior will be sinful. Anger may be righteous anger or indignation. Examples of righteous anger are found in I Kings 18:40 (Elijah at Mt. Carmel) and John 2:13-17 (Jesus cleansing the temple). Most anger, though, becomes sin and needs to be dealt with as sin.

A person is responsible for his feelings, and sinful ones will be judged and punished. A person needs to repent of the sinful ones and forsake them. When one has sinful feelings, he must change his motives, attitudes, and beliefs. The fruit of the Spirit is feelings that are a result of a person's deciding to be filled with the Spirit.

The works of the flesh given in Galatians 5:19-21 are feelings stemming from sinful motives, attitudes, and beliefs that are controlled by the flesh. A person is responsible for his feelings and can change them any time he decides they are sinfully wrong and need to be replaced by the right, Spirit-led feelings.

Myth 10: There is no significant difference between men and women; the differences that are evident are a result of cultural upbringing.

Truth 10: As human beings with a spiritual nature, men and women are the same; but physically and mentally they are different.

- Physically the woman is designed for a specific reproductive function, which involves menstruation, pregnancy, and nursing. The glands that control these functions act differently at different times; for example, the woman's thyroid is more active and is larger during pregnancy and menstruation than at other times. While it contributes to her immunity by giving her a layer of fat and to her beauty by giving her smooth skin and a lack of body hair, it also affects her emotions, making her more susceptible to depression and lack of emotional control.

- Since women have a lower metabolic rate, estrogen and the extra fat on their bodies serve as a protection against disease; women on the average outlive men by about 6.8 years (1990).

- The skeletal structure is different, with the woman having broader hips, a longer trunk, and shorter legs. Women have larger kidneys, liver, and stomach, and smaller lungs. Women have 21 percent fewer red cells in their blood. The red cells carry oxygen from these smaller lungs. Therefore, women tire and faint more easily than men, have lower long-term endurance, and need more sleep.

- Men are much more muscular than women with wider shoulders and narrower hips, giving them a mechanical advantage in strength and maneuverability. Men tend to be more aggressive as a result of a greater amount of testosterone.

- Women appear to have a higher level of verbal ability than men. These abilities develop at an earlier age than men's but become especially pronounced at adolescence. This verbal ability contributes to a woman's more fluent style of communication.

- Men generally do better on visual spatial ability tasks, such as recognition of block designs and figures. Men are often better at arithmetic and reasoning, skills that usually become apparent after puberty.

Counselors should be aware of these differences, especially when counseling engaged and married couples.

The general principles that have been discussed in this chapter can serve as a guide to make the counseling process more effective, even with the most difficult problems. The seven basic causes of problems and thirty-five common problems are examined in the next fifteen chapters. The general format that will be followed for these thirty-five problems is this: definition, Scripture, information, principles, solutions, and case studies. Competent and effective Christian counselors can be of great help to others and have lasting, even eternal, effects if Bible guidelines are followed.

Chapter 10

Bitterness

Bitterness resulting from unresolved anger is probably the most common root sin in the average Christian's life. Everyone is susceptible to it. Bitterness is a sin that interferes with a person's intimate relationship with God through Christ. It can destroy happiness and prevent a Christian from carrying out God's will in his daily life. Authority figures, especially parents, are the major targets of bitterness, followed by husbands or wives and brothers and sisters.

There are men who have bitterness and hatred against women in general and want to humiliate them, even to the point of physical violence, which can include rape. If such a man is married, all of his bitterness and hatred becomes directed at his wife and often his daughters. This problem will be discussed in Chapter 19.

Problem #1: Bitterness— Unresolved Anger

Definition:

Bitterness can be defined as a continual anger response coupled with an unforgiving spirit toward people who the bitter person believes have violated his rights. It is resentment based on discontentment, which leads to prolonged anger and a desire to get revenge, with no genuine reconciliation attempted.

Scripture:

Psalm 32:1-5; Proverbs 10:12; 14:17, 29; 15:1, 18; 16:32; 19:11, 19; 22:24-25; 25:28; 29:8, 22; Matthew 18:15-17; Romans 12:17-21; Ephesians 4:22-27, 30-32; Hebrews 12:15; James 1:19-20.

Information and Principles:

There are four types of anger.

1. **Protecting anger is a defense against an unjust aggressor or threatening situation.** This type of anger causes adrenaline to be released and helps a person to flee, fight, or to perform heroic deeds against the threat.

2. **Righteous indignation is anger that advances God's righteousness and, on behalf of others, is directed at unrighteousness or injustice.** A classic example of this anger is Jesus's cleansing of the temple (Mark 11:15-17). Jesus did not sin, but He was angry because the Pharisees were desecrating His Father's temple through their merchandising. He was also angry about their exploitation of the pilgrims who traveled long distances to worship and were met by unscrupulous temple merchants, or "thieves" as Jesus called them. He was angry enough to overturn their tables and flog them.

   Jesus was also angry with the Pharisees for condemning Him for healing on the Sabbath (Mark 3:1-5). They did not care that a suffering man was healed; they were looking only for an opportunity to attack Christ's ministry (vs. 2). He was angry with the Pharisees as well as with the scribes for false teaching, which was leading many to hell (Matt. 23:13-15).

   Another person who displayed righteous indignation was Martin Luther, who could not stand the religious abuses of the Catholic Church. He said, "I never work better than when I am inspired by anger. When I am angry I can write, pray, and preach well; for then my whole temperament is quickened, my understanding sharpened, and all mundane vexations and temptations depart." Luther's anger was directed at unrighteousness and injustice; he was not self-serving but was advancing God's righteousness.

A parallel in our day would be righteous indignation at the killing of a million and a half babies every year or the invasion of pornography on TV and into our communities.

3. **Unfocused anger is anger that occurs at the slightest provocation.** It is most often displayed by children in the form of temper tantrums or sulking from any kind of frustration. In adults, unfocused anger often results from unresolved anger against a mother or father and transfers to other people. Sometimes it is a result of accumulated anger at frustrations to which the person did not react properly, and one incident can break the dam (Prov. 17:14).

4. **Specific or focused anger is anger that results from the violation of one's rights, or imagined rights, and is directed at people, organizations, or even God.** This focused anger may be a result of injustice or humiliation of self, usually verbal.

Scripture says to be angry and sin not. Anger becomes a sin in three different ways: (1) when it is held overnight (Eph. 4:26-27); (2) if the immediate reaction is an ungodly response, such as physical violence or angry words (Prov. 29:22); and (3) if one gives place to the Devil by remembering hurts and storing them for future revenge (Rom. 12:17-21).

Signs That Anger Has Become Bitterness

1. Self-pity or a wounded spirit
2. Saying "It's not fair."
3. Not thanking God for a difficult situation
4. A caustic, critical, sarcastic attitude
5. Being easily offended
6. Holding a grudge or keeping a list of complaints against a person or organization over a long period of time
7. Wishing that someone would experience retribution or judgment
8. Being extremely negative about a person or organization every time the name is brought up in conversation
9. An unforgiving spirit, evidenced by remembering past hurts

There are several general principles that apply to the problem of bitterness.

God desires, honors, and blesses unity among the brethren; and bitterness destroys this unity. Christians should always work toward unity within the framework of Bible doctrine if they want to serve the Lord effectively and do God's will. Psalm 133:1 indicates that it is very pleasant "for brethren to dwell together in unity." And verse 3 says that the Lord will commend His blessing to those who dwell together in unity. To dwell in unity with others, one must first have a united heart to fear the Lord (Ps. 86:11). That means that he must not have sin in his life, especially the sins of bitterness, hatred, and malice. Sin shatters the unity and the fellowship of the saints and fellowship with God (I John 1:5-9). Love is a cohesive factor that binds Christians together in unity and fellowship. Christians are taught of God to love one another, as stated in I Thessalonians 4:9: "But as touching brotherly love ye need not that I write unto you: for ye yourselves are taught of God to love one another." As one increases in love, his heart is established "unblamable in holiness before God" (I Thess. 3:12-13). Anything that works against this love is sin.

First Corinthians 1:9-10 indicates that unity is God's desire for Christian brethren and the church. The same idea is given in Philippians 2:2-5. Christians should "be likeminded, having the same love, being of one accord, of one mind" (vs. 2). This is best accomplished by the admonition in verses 3-5: "Let nothing be done through strife or vainglory; but in lowliness of mind let each esteem others better than themselves. Look not every man on his own things, but every man also on the things of others. Let this mind be in you, which was also in Christ Jesus."

The book of Ephesians details God's desire for unity. Ephesians 1:10 says that eventually in the fullness of time God wants to "gather together in one all things in Christ." At salvation, He has "quickened us together with Christ . . . and hath raised us up together, and made us sit together in heavenly places" (Eph. 2:4-6), and the Christian can experience this full identification with Christ by daily living the crucified life (Luke 9:23). Christ has broken down the middle wall of partition between God and man through His blood so that man can be reconciled to God (Eph. 2:13-16). We are now made fellow citizens with the saints in the household of God (Eph. 2:19, 22). He then calls for Christians to forbear one another in love so that there will be a unity within the body of Christ (Eph. 4:2-6). In the unity of faith, the body is properly joined together and edifies itself in love (Eph. 4:13, 16). The ultimate example of human unity is the one-flesh unity between the husband and wife in marriage (Eph. 5:31-33).

Proper biblical unity in the body of Christ involves separation from unbelievers (II Cor. 6:14-17). To preserve in the church the holiness of God and the integrity of the Scriptures, Christians are not to be joined together with unbelievers in any union, either religious or secular, where the unbelievers can have control to affect the Christian's doctrine or testimony (II John 9-11). Separation from believers should occur only when the believers are disorderly (II Thess. 3:6, 14-15; I Tim. 6:3, 5), when they are disobedient, walking in the flesh (I Cor. 5:11), when they are disbelieving (Rom. 16:17), and when they transgress and refuse to be disciplined by the church (Matt. 18:15-17).

Bitterness is like a weak thread running through a beautiful tapestry of Christian unity. When it causes a break and our relationships begin to unravel, we then attempt to patch things up instead of repenting and eliminating the bitterness.

Ungodly anger which leads to bitterness can be learned through imitation. Proverbs gives this warning: "Make no friendship with an angry man; and with a furious man thou shalt not go: lest thou learn his ways, and get a snare to thy soul" (22:24-25). Be careful that an angry spouse, parent, or fellow workman does not influence you to sin because of his anger or bitterness.

The discipline of control is necessary to keep the natural anger that all possess and exhibit from becoming sinful bitterness. Control of one's spirit is essential for a Spirit-filled, stable Christian life (Prov. 14:29; 16:32; 19:11; 25:28; 29:11). Many people defend their outbursts by saying that they felt angry and did not want to hold the anger in because of the internal damage it might do to the body. However, the Scriptural instruction is to control feelings, not ventilate them: "Cease from anger, and forsake wrath: fret not thyself in any wise to do evil" (Ps. 37:8). Studies have concluded that ventilating anger is rarely beneficial.[1] It usually reinforces and increases present anger and serves as a rehearsal of future angry episodes.[2]

The Christian life can be compared to a train. God's power working in love in one's life is the engine. The decisions, actions, and friends that are made are the boxcars and passenger cars. The coupling between the cars is faith, and the caboose is feelings. Good feelings should follow and not determine right decisions, actions, and interpersonal relations.

A Christian is to be slow to anger and quick to get rid of the anger by handling it in a biblical way. James admonishes: "Wherefore, my beloved brethren, let every man be swift to hear, slow to speak, slow to wrath: for the wrath of man worketh not the righteousness of God" (James 1:19-20). Many problems between Christians, in families, and in churches would never occur if Christians were diligent in following this principle. Jesus gives four ways for resolving anger in Luke 6:27-28. (1) "Love your enemies." (2) "Do good to them which hate you." (3) "Bless them that curse you." (4) "Pray for them which despitefully use you." In verses 29-30 and 34-38, Christ gives some practical illustrations that teach just the opposite from how the world thinks and acts. He sums up the four points in verse 31: "As ye would that men would do to you, do ye also to them likewise." Two choice examples of how to handle unjust aggressors properly are Christ on the cross ("Then said Jesus, Father, forgive them; for they know not what they do." Luke 23:34) and Stephen being martyred ("And he kneeled down, and cried with a loud voice, Lord, lay not this sin to their charge." Acts 7:60).

Gossip is a means of exhibiting bitterness, expanding it, and transmitting it to others. Donna Eder at Indiana University did a study of preteens' and teenagers' conversation patterns and found that the second negative remark about a person seemed to set a nasty pattern of condemnation. Apparently a word of agreement is all it takes to give the impression of group consensus. She found that no one ever challenged an evaluation that had been seconded. However, if the second remark were a challenge to the initial negative evaluation, the pattern of the conversation changed.

A bitter person is the one who suffers the unhappiness, frustration, and misery of his own unresolved anger. The target of the bitterness usually is not aware of or has forgotten the incident that caused the hurt feelings. Bitterness handcuffs one negatively to a perceived enemy. Plotting and planning revenge keeps one from using the key of forgiveness, which would bring freedom.

Forgiveness must always be given no matter how often the offense occurs (Luke 17:3-4) or how weak the character of the

offending party. Although you may think the apology is insincere and the offense may occur again very soon, you still must forgive the person who asks for forgiveness. (See Myths of Forgiveness in Chapter 9.) Christians must forgive because they have been forgiven by God for extreme trespasses (Eph. 4:31-32) and because God will forgive them as they forgive others (Matt. 6:14-15).

Bitterness, fueled by an unforgiving spirit, is the chain that binds one to the post of past unpleasantness and sin. Every time someone rattles the chain by mentioning the person or situation, the imaginative memory adds to the chain. Forgiveness is the only way to break the chain and gain release.

Solutions:

1. Review the appropriate Scriptures and principles given in this chapter.
2. Go through the four steps for resolving anger that Jesus gave in Luke 6:27-28.
3. Have the couselee confess any offense to a wronged individual and handle any difficulty with another person in a biblical way (Matt. 18:15-17). The offended person should go to the offender and resolve the offensive situation or remark. If the offender will not get it resolved, the offended one needs to take it to the church. If a person has offended a brother or has been offended, that person needs to go to the brother and settle the matter before he worships (Matt. 5:23-24).
4. Since the angry or bitter person lacks love in his heart for people, have him read I John every day for thirty days, underlining one verse that is significant to him each day. Also have him perform a loving deed for someone each day.
5. Since Hebrews 12:15 says that bitterness defiles others, have him list the people that he has defiled and make it right with every one of them. Especially if children are involved, help him to stop provoking his children to wrath and to ask their forgiveness if the children are bitter toward him.

Case Study:

Gary and Madge came to the counselor with a big problem in their marriage. Gary had come reluctantly after Madge had threatened to leave him. Gary was forty-five, and Madge was forty-one.

They had two children: a girl, eighteen, and a boy, twenty-one. Madge said that ever since they'd been married, Gary had been sullen and would get upset at the least little thing that she did. He would ridicule her in front of other people and was always trying to pick a fight with her. She said, "I would do anything to please him, but I never could do it right. I never argued with him because he is very belligerent, and if he thinks he's lost the argument or cannot make me give in to him, he will sulk and pout for several days and not speak."

She said that they'd been in eight different churches in fifteen years since they had been saved. He was disciplined out of two churches for being a troublemaker and for being against the pastor. At each of the other churches, he had some type of altercation with one of the members and, after causing a ruckus, he left the church in a huff.

As Madge talked, Gary sat there with his arms folded and a scowl on his face. She said he was the most negative man about things of the Lord that she had ever known. Something was always wrong with the preacher, the deacons, the sermon, or the music. She said he supposedly had his devotions every day, but it did not seem to make any difference in his life. He was in partnership with his son, but his son had taken such verbal beatings from his dad in front of office and sales personnel that he was ready to pull out of the partnership.

When the counselor asked Gary to reply, his comment was, "That about sums it up. That's the way I am. That's what she married. I'm too old to change now." The counselor asked him, "How did you acquire such a gruff, obnoxious personality?" At this, his wife came to his defense and said that he was from a very combative family and he was just like his father and three brothers. Even his sisters were like that, although none of them were Christians. She said he'd been a sergeant in the marines and had done a tour of duty in Vietnam. He said that he had been a good sergeant: the meaner you were, the more the men respected you. Madge said, "When he was discharged, I married him, and he carried that meanness right into our marriage." She said she had thought it was a result of his being in combat and that he would get over it within a year, but instead it got worse.

Case Study Solution:

The counselor explained to Gary that his family background and his service in the marines had left him with a bitter spirit toward people. When he was saved, he was supposed to put off the old man, or old behavior, and put on the new man, or new behavior (Eph. 4:22-24). The counselor told Gary that verse 23 indicated that he had to make up his mind to do it. It was impossible to *put off* and *put on* without the Holy Spirit's power; and, although the Holy Spirit had come into his life at the time of his salvation, Gary had not been *filled* with the Holy Spirit (Eph. 5:19-20). Therefore, he was not manifesting the fruit of the Spirit (Gal. 5:22-23). The counselor requested that Gary read Romans 6–8 and Ephesians 4–5 every day for one month and underline one verse each day that had a special meaning to him.

When the couple came back a month later, Gary said that he had dedicated his life to the Lord and made some changes in his life. Madge said that after he had dedicated his life in church, he had come to her right away and apologized for the hard time he had given her all those years. He then went to his son and did the same thing and was reconciled to him also. She said that she could see a difference in his behavior, but, she added, he had "not arrived yet." The counselor had them both read every day for the next month all five chapters of I John. When they came back for a follow-up conference, Madge said that she had made some changes herself and that they now had a real Christian marriage.

Problem #2: Obsessions and Compulsions

Some obsessions and compulsions are a result of guilt feelings. A classic example in literature is Shakespeare's Lady Macbeth as she tries to wash the imaginary blood from her murderous hands. However, most obsessions and compulsions are a means of handling extreme anger and bitterness that the person is afraid to acknowledge or exhibit toward the hated person (most often a family member). Usually people who have these problems are of very high intelligence and seem to have their lives all together. They are secretive about their compulsions because they do not want anybody to think that they are weird or different. They rarely seek help until the compulsion becomes such a habit that it begins to interfere with their lives.

Definitions:

An obsession is a repetitive, disturbing, violent, or guilty thought that creates a continuing fear. This fear can be somewhat relieved by a time-consuming ritualistic behavior, called a compulsion. Compulsive behavior soon becomes an annoying habit pattern.

Scripture:

II Corinthians 10:5; Philippians 4:8; Ephesians 4:22-24

Information and Principles:

There are four categories of compulsions. The type of compulsion gives a clue as to the cause, whether it be guilt or bitterness.

1. *Fear of contamination,* such as excessive handwashing or cleaning of one's environment, is a result of guilt feelings about something that has a strong emotional content, such as incest, masturbation, or premarital sex.
2. *Hoarding* is mainly a result of guilt feelings and fear that God will take away all possessions as a punishment.
3. *Checking* of doors and windows to make sure that they are locked or *unusual concern* about the safety of others, such as being fearful of having run over someone is a result of bitterness which creates violent, aggressive, and vengeful obsessive thoughts.
4. *Order and control,* or constant, repetitive counting, touching, and arranging, or repeating things in a certain sequence or pattern, usually results from a fear of doing something which will result in evil consequences.

The compulsions in these last two categories help to control and contain these obsessive thoughts and to prevent them from becoming reality.

There are several general principles that apply to the problems of obsessions and compulsions.

1. **Compulsions are the end result of obsessive thoughts, and the concentration should be on eliminating those thoughts rather than on conquering the compulsion.** If

the counselor were to work on the compulsion without eliminating the obsession, the counselee would just substitute another compulsion for the one eliminated.

2. **Obsessive thoughts are one of the chief ways that the Devil attacks Christians.** The Devil cannot possess a Christian, but he can oppress the Christian through circumstances which bring depression, and he can attack the Christian with obsessive thoughts.

3. **Obsessive thoughts can be eliminated by casting out the devilish thoughts and imaginations (II Cor. 10:5) and substituting praise and thanksgiving and concentrating on the promises and works of God (Ps. 107:8).** A daily time of praise and sharing God's blessings with others can be very helpful.

Solutions:

1. Ask questions about the counselee's past or present relationships with others, looking for anger and bitterness against a mother or father or family member or some authority figure, such as a teacher or a boss.

2. If the obsessive thoughts are a result of guilt feelings, have the counselee repent and confess the sin that is disturbing him.

3. If the obsessive thoughts are a result of bitterness, have the person take steps of forgiveness and reconciliation.

4. Help him break the compulsive habit by taking the steps for breaking a habit given in Chapter 4.

Case Study:

Roy came to the counselor at the insistence of his wife. He was driving her crazy because he would get up ten or fifteen times a night and check the doors and windows to see if they were locked. Whenever he paid any bills by mail, he would not seal the envelope until he had checked the contents four or five times. He would ask his wife a dozen times if she had had the car serviced. It was the same thing at work: when he was supposed to lock up at night, he would go back to the plant several times to make sure he had locked everything. While driving, if he passed pedestrians or cyclists, he would wonder whether he had hit them. He would then retrace his route several times to make sure he had not.

Roy's wife had reported that he would get angry at home, especially toward her, whenever she did the least thing contrary to his wishes. She said he kept a loaded gun in their bedroom, and she was afraid for her own safety. Roy had been a Christian for fifteen years, but he did not like the church his wife and children went to, so he had stopped going. When asked about his Christian growth, Roy said that in his first year of being saved, he was an enthusiastic church member. But after the first year, he had gotten into an argument with a deacon, who was his wife's favorite brother, and had hated the man ever since. He also admitted that he hated his boss.

Case Study Solution:

The counselor, knowing that most obsessions and compulsions are a result of unresolved anger, zeroed in on Roy's hatred toward his brother-in-law, which had spilled over to his wife and toward his boss. The counselor explained to Roy that his anger and bitterness had become so strong that he was afraid he would kill someone. That was the reason for Roy's obsessions and compulsions. The counselor went over the Scriptures on bitterness and forgiveness and told Roy that until he made things right with the brother-in-law, his compulsions would get worse and his relationship with his wife would deteriorate. The counselor questioned Roy's salvation in light of I John, and Roy agreed to read the book of I John every day for a month and to underline the verse that the Lord impressed on his heart each day.

Two months later, in an evangelistic meeting, Roy ran down the aisle, crying. He headed straight for the deacon whom he hated and asked his forgiveness. Roy then went to his wife and asked her forgiveness. Then he stood before the whole congregation, confessed his hatred and bitterness, and told them that he had completely given his life to the Lord. Later that week he was reconciled to his boss.

In the following months, Roy was faithful in his attendance at church and grew spiritually. His home life improved, and his obsessions and compulsions completely disappeared. His wife was overjoyed at the drastic change that she observed.

Immorality

In the last forty years, and especially since the sexual revolution of the 1960s, America has become a very immoral nation. Consequently, a counselor will hear about many corrupt and outlandish practices from his supposedly Christian counselees. The flesh, which is in every Christian, is corrupt, and any Christian, no matter what his position in the church, is capable of being tempted by the Devil. Therefore, the counselor is not surprised or shocked by anything he hears during the counseling session. This fact should make the counselor painfully aware of the truth found in I Corinthians 10:11-13, that temptation is common to man. Although many Christians are tempted and do fall, God can and does give victory over every temptation.

This area of counseling is emotionally charged and can be a fertile field of temptation by the Devil for both the counselor and counselee. To avoid vulnerability in this area, certain cautions are in order.

1. The counselor should be careful where he counsels. Counseling with the opposite sex or with those under eighteen never should be done alone in an empty church or in a private home. A secretary or wife or husband should be nearby. A counselor should not put himself into a situation where he "can or can't" sin. He does not need to try to find out whether he is a David or a Joseph.

2. Be knowledgeable about definitions. The counselor who uses the teenage vernacular or street talk runs the risk of the

meanings changing. A counselor should always use the correct terms and make sure he is talking about the same thing as the counselee. For example, a naive junior high school girl might define heavy petting as a boy kissing her on the neck and blowing in her ear.

3. Be careful about going into details about a particular episode or sinful situation. Some people get a vicarious thrill from either telling or hearing about the specific details.

There is certain information that a counselor needs (such as the frequency of an occurrence) to determine whether it is a habit pattern. He also needs to know the situation that brought the problem about to determine the temptation pattern that the Devil used to get the counselee into the sin.

There are a few general principles that ought to be considered in this area of counseling.

Principle 1: How immoral people are counseled will depend on one's viewpoint of morality.

There are three types of morality: (1) God's morality, based on the Word of God. The Ten Commandments are the foundation of God's morality. These Ten Commandments are further elaborated on by Jesus Christ in the gospels and by the other New Testament writings. God's morality must be the basis for any type of Christian counseling. (2) A second type of morality is the goal morality, or "the end justifies the means," which is part of the new morality. This old Jesuit idea was revived and promoted in 1966 by Joseph F. Fletcher in his book *Situation Ethics: The New Morality.*[1] To the question "Was Robin Hood a hero or a criminal?" proponents of the new morality would answer, "He was a hero because he stole from the rich and gave to the poor." But the facts of the case are that he was a criminal and in rebellion against the society of his time. One woman purportedly asked another woman, "Would you cheat on your husband for a million dollars?" The second woman replied, "For a million dollars I would." The first woman then asked, "Would you cheat on your husband for one dollar?" The other woman replied, "No, what do you think I am?" The first woman said, "I already know what you are; I am just wondering what you would charge." In sexual matters, the basis for this type of morality is "Does it feel good?" "Does it give satisfaction?" "Are you in love?" or "Does it satisfy your need?" It rejects God's criterion of marriage as the only legitimate legal and moral use of the sex mechanism. (3) A third type of morality is group morality. This morality is based on what the majority of the people are doing. If most people are doing a certain thing, that practice must be normal. The so-called scientific basis for group morality is the publication of Alfred C. Kinsey's work in 1948 entitled *Sexual Behavior in the Human Male,*[2] followed by the 1953 publication of his second volume, *Sexual Behavior in the Human Female.*[3] These reports define what people supposedly do sexually, thereby establishing what is allegedly normal. These two reports exploded in the minds of the general population the traditional Judeo-Christian legal and moral codes of what is normal/abnormal and natural/unnatural in sex behavior. The purpose of the two reports was to demonstrate a wide divergence between actual sexual behavior and publicly espoused norms. The implication was that the moral and cultural values that society held so dear needed vast revision.

These two studies did more to break down the standards of morality that existed in 1950 than probably anything other than rock music, the legalization of abortion, and the orchestrated erosion of decency and morals in the TV and film industry. The Kinsey reports were widely accepted by the media and the public because they had the scientific backing of a team of scientists, including Kinsey, and were sponsored by the University of Indiana. After the publication of the two reports, there was a clamor by the media, including many articles in women's magazines, for a complete rethinking of the attitudes toward sexual matters. Many experts agree that the Kinsey reports served as the foundation for the sexual revolution of the '60s, the intense clamor by the media and educators for the sex education courses of the '70s and '80s, and the AIDS epidemic of the '80s and '90s. The Kinsey Institute for Research in Sex, Gender, and Reproduction, located on the University of Indiana campus, has carried on Kinsey's research and expanded its role by providing massive sex information resources to national and international organizations, including the Center for Disease Control in Atlanta and various sex education programs and curricula written in the last twenty years and used in the public schools.

The myth of scientific objectivity of Kinsey's research was revealed in the 1990 book entitled *Kinsey, Sex, and Fraud,* written by Dr. Judith A. Reisman and Edward W. Eichel.[4] They claim that the supposedly scientific studies' results were obtained by fraudulent methods and riddled with inherent bias. For example, Reisman, the main author, mentions that Kinsey used the accumulative incidents technique, which makes a person a statistic, if he has done a thing once in his life.[5] Of course, humans being what they are, a researcher can prove almost anything by this method. For example, according to the accumulative incidents technique, 100 percent of the people in America are liars, for everyone has told at least one lie in his life. One hundred percent of the population are thieves because everyone has stolen something in his life, even if it were just a cookie from his mother's cookie jar. Using the accumulative incidents technique, Kinsey established statistically common behavior by implying that behaviors that may occur only once have occurred throughout the lifetime of the individual. Kinsey did include with many of his statistics the active incidence (behavior done in the last six months), which gave a more accurate picture of prevailing behaviors.

Reisman also brings out the fact that Kinsey's sample of interviewees was not representative of society. A high percentage of male samples—approximately 25 percent—were prisoners and sex offenders.[6]

In the 1953 female study, the 7,789 females aged two to seventy years were wholly unrepresentative of women of the period. Seventy-five percent of the total female sample had attended college, and 19 percent had gone on to postgraduate work when in 1950 less than 15 percent of American women had attended college.[7]

Kinsey's use of volunteers further negates his research. Reisman recounts that Abraham H. Maslow had warned Kinsey about the probability of bias in the personality type and sexual behavior of his volunteers. Maslow concluded that "any study in which data is obtained from volunteers will always have a preponderance of aggressive, high-dominance people, and therefore will show a falsely high percentage of non-virginity, masturbation, promiscuity, homosexuality, etc., in the population."[8] Kinsey did a joint project with Maslow to test the degree of this volunteer bias in his own study. It was proved true that the bias was present in his study, but Kinsey suppressed the findings of the research.

Eichel and Reisman state that Kinsey provided a biased statistical base for the new morality that was in line with his goals and philosophy: (1) he viewed all sex activity as normal, including sexual contact with children and animals; (2) he wanted homosexuality to be accepted on the same par with heterosexuality; (3) he claimed that children were born with a full capability for sexual response; it was only the inhibitions and morality of the parents that prevented this capability from properly developing; (4) he was in favor of parent-child and adult-child sex relationships and believed that from a young age children did benefit from sexual interaction with adults.[9] These authors claim that Kinsey's philosophy and bias affected not only his methods of obtaining statistics but also the conclusions that he drew. Most of the sex research and sex education programs that have been developed in the last forty years are based on Kinsey's fraudulent research and his erroneous conclusions.

Under this the first and most important principle, the Christian counselor must base his counseling on God's Word and God's morality. It is to be expected that the unsaved counselor will base his counseling on goal morality and/or group morality, which make up the new morality of the world.

Principle 2: Sex sins tend to cause the most severe problems and most deeply offend God.

This principle is drawn from I Corinthians 6:18 and Romans 1:32. "Flee fornication. Every sin that a man doeth is without the body; but he that committeth fornication sinneth against his own body" (I Cor. 6:18). The word *fornication* here is the broad term referring to all types of sexual sin, including masturbation, incest, homosexuality, premarital sex, adultery, bestiality, voyeurism, exhibitionism, transvestitism, and other types of sexual perversion. The guilt feelings that result from these types of sins can have a devastating effect on the body, mind, and soul of a human being. Women seem to be more affected than men by these guilt feelings because they seem to have a more tender conscience than men. In addition, sex to a man is an act performed, but to a woman, sex is a part of her whole reproductive function which includes nursing and mothering a baby.

Principle 3: God has given each one a sex mechanism designed to be used for the glory of God in marriage only (I Cor. 7:1-5; Heb. 13:4).

First Thessalonians 4:1-7 gives clear direction concerning the sex mechanism. Verses 1 and 2 stress the necessity of keeping God's commandments if one wants to please God. Verse 3 says that God wills that if a person wants to be sanctified or set apart for the service of God, he needs to abstain from fornication. As found in this passage the word *fornication* covers the wide range of sex sins. Verse 4 says that every Christian "should know how to possess his vessel," or his body, or more specifically his sex mechanism, "in sanctification and honour." Verse 5 continues, "not in the lust of concupiscence," or illicit sexual desire, "even as the Gentiles," or the world, "which know not God." Verses 6 and 7 warn us not to defraud or harm a brother by fornication, for God has called us unto holiness. Everyone has to make up his mind to use his sex mechanism only as God intended.

Principle 4: Christians must take definite steps to guard themselves against committing immorality.

This need for guarding oneself is presented in Romans 13:14, "But put ye on the Lord Jesus Christ, and make not provision for the flesh, to fulfil the lusts thereof." Specific steps include the following: (1) shunning evil companions, who talk about immorality or suggest immoral activities (I Cor. 15:33; Prov. 14:7; 17:18); (2) staying away from situations where there are no safeguards against immorality; for example, a young man should never be in a girl's apartment alone and vice versa; (3) because Christians are not immune to visual stimuli such as pornography or X- or R-rated films and TV programs, they should take extreme care in planning and participating in video and TV viewing; and (4) avoiding activities and places such as dances, discos, and bars, which are known sources of extreme temptation. The Bible says, "Let not then your good be evil spoken of" (Rom. 14:16). First Thessalonians 5:22 gives the same idea of avoiding "all appearance of evil."

Christians have a testimony of holiness to uphold. The Devil is able to wreak havoc in the church through gossip and slander by the indiscreet actions of God's choice servants. Christian counselors must be especially aware of Satan's devices when counseling the opposite sex. Genuine heartfelt understanding is the foundation of good Christian counseling, but it also is the foundation for love between the sexes; therefore, counselors must guard their testimonies.

As a preliminary step to spiritual growth, Christians need to take certain vows before the Lord. One of the most important of these vows is never to commit immorality or allow oneself to be in the position where immorality can occur. A definite making up of one's mind and committing this matter to the Lord brings the Lord on the person's side. Only the Lord can give the power and grace to overcome any temptation (I Cor. 10:13).

Principle 5: Minimize or limit sex education in the schools for children and adolescents.

Studies in Sweden since 1956 and in Denmark since 1970 show that wherever compulsory sex education has been taught in the public schools from kindergarten through high school, it has been detrimental to morality and has contributed to a tremendous rise in sexually transmitted disease rates, children born out of wedlock, abortions, sex crimes, homosexuality, and intercourse at an earlier age. The facts from these studies are exactly opposite from the claims and promises made by Planned Parenthood, SIECUS, and sex educators across America in their promotion of sex education in the public schools.

Sex education for young children should occur in the home as the parents answer the simple questions that children ask about reproduction as they see animals and pets reproducing or the pregnancy of the mother resulting in a younger sibling.

Children and teens must be given warnings about what to do in case of sexual advances and attempted rape. They should be advised never to submit but to try to get away by running, screaming, kicking, biting, scratching, attracting attention by blowing the car horn, and so on. They should also be warned about the dangers of pornography.

Before puberty, parents should give their children complete instruction about the changes that are going to take place in their bodies to prepare them for adulthood and their role as future mothers or fathers. They must be warned about the immorality of necking and petting, premarital sex, homosexuality, and other perverted corruptions of God's great gift of sexuality. One or two months before marriage, couples should read several good books such as Tim LaHaye's *The Act of Marriage*[10] and Dr. Ed Wheat's *Intended for Pleasure.*[11] A premarital exam and follow-up consultation with a doctor or nurse and premarital counseling sessions with a knowledgeable pastor or counselor can be beneficial. Christian couples should go into marriage with all the knowledge that they need for a happy intimate life in marriage. All along, the parents must give a godly, biblical approach and develop godly attitudes toward sexuality. Before puberty, children have little interest in sexual matters and too much sex information at that time can disturb children's thinking and attitudes about Christian sexuality.

Principle 6: The First Pleasure Principle

It has been observed in counseling situations that many individuals later in life tend to revert to the behavior in which they received their first sex pleasure. The first emotional sex imprinting tends to make a lasting impression, especially if it is continued for any length of time. If a twelve-year-old boy molested a six-year-old girl and received his first sex pleasure from the act, later in life he may have a tendency to be a child molester, picking on girls six or seven years old. If he received his first pleasure in masturbation, there will be a tendency later in life, even though he is married, to revert to this behavior in which he received his first pleasure. Sometimes this principle coupled with pornography accounts for the bizarre behavior of some individuals in adulthood.

Principle 7: Because of man's sin nature, children can and do get involved voluntarily and involuntarily in all kinds of immoral and corrupt sex activity, especially when they are with other children.

Because of their natural curiosity, children will accept nearly any situation and action. They should be warned about this tendency. Some children whose sex desire has been awakened prematurely can experience full sexual pleasure. They face great temptation to indulge in sex play with brothers and sisters or cousins or with animals. Boys getting together at camps or in treehouses can get involved in pornography and sex acts. Even girls spending the night with other girls or attending unsupervised slumber parties can face sexual temptation. Parents should carefully supervise their children so that youngsters are not put into situations of temptation.

Unfortunately, happy occasions such as family vacations, holidays, and reunions can present problems for the unwary child. For example, when families get together, the adults often become so preoccupied with renewing old times and with their interests that the children are left relatively unsupervised. During such times sleeping conditions are usually crowded and children are thrown together at night. When the ages of the children vary over a span of four to eight years, the children are often placed in a compromising position. Parents must make sure that children are supervised during these times, and children should be warned to tell parents immediately when anything out of the ordinary occurs.

These general principles will apply to most of the problems of immorality given in the next chapter.

Moral and Sexual Problems

There are some common moral problems with which the counselor will have to deal frequently. These types of problems cause more severe guilt feelings than others because they involve the perversion of a basic God-given life function. This chapter gives Scripture, information, principles, suggested steps for solutions, and case studies on the problems of masturbation, homosexuality, incest, premarital sex, adultery, and the sexual problems of frigidity and impotence.

Problem #3: Masturbation

Definition:
Sexual stimulation of oneself leading to orgasm.

Scripture:
I Thessalonians 4:4-7; Romans 13:14; I Corinthians 10:13

Information and Principles:
There is no special Bible verse against this practice; however, the purity principle of I Thessalonians 4:4-7 does apply: "That every one of you should know how to possess his vessel in sanctification and honour; not in the lust of concupiscence. . . . For God hath not called us unto uncleanness, but unto holiness." Romans 13:14 also applies: "Make not provision for the flesh, to fulfil the lusts thereof." First Corinthians 10:13 guarantees that God gives the victory: "There hath no temptation taken you but such as is

common to man: but God is faithful, who will not suffer you to be tempted above that ye are able; but will with the temptation also make a way to escape, that ye may be able to bear it." The habit of masturbation is also wrong for the following reasons.

1. It is a perversion of God's natural plan that sexual satisfaction is to be found only in the marriage relationship.
2. It cannot be done to the honor and glory of the Lord (I Cor. 10:31).
3. Since it results in such extreme pleasure, it can become an addictive habit accompanied by unwholesome, corrupt thinking and imaginations.
4. It tends to lead to pornography and further illicit sexual behavior.
5. It is a self-centered act and later works against the normal marriage relationship of unity and giving pleasure to the marriage partner.

The practice of masturbation may start as early as three to six years of age during the exploratory phase that most children go through. Those who get into the habit at this age are usually introduced to it by older children or even adults. Since the children can experience sex pleasure at this age, masturbation tends to be repeated, and children easily get into the habit. Mothers, upon discovering their children masturbating, should not make a federal case of it but should treat it much like thumbsucking or hair pulling or any other habit that they do not want their children to form. The most common time for this habit to occur is in the preadolescent and the teenage years. Some children use it as a relaxation technique to go to sleep, and some teenage girls use it as a way to relieve cramps. Various studies indicate that 95 percent of boys and 65 percent of girls have practiced the habit at some time in their lives. Approximately 40 percent of teen boys and 20 percent of teen girls are currently practicing masturbation.

Solutions:

Since children and teenagers feel guilty about masturbation (I Cor. 6:18), the counselee must be helped to overcome the habit. As an occasional act of sin, masturbation does not become a problem, for the counselee can confess that and move on in his Christian life much as he does with the occasional sin of lying. But when it becomes a habit, other problems begin to occur. The steps in breaking a habit apply here.

1. Confess it as sin.
2. Set a goal for victory.
3. Exercise at every time of temptation.
4. Memorize a verse such as I Corinthians 10:31 to repeat through a rough time.
5. Redirect the buildup of sex energy into other channels such as work, sports, study, or creative activity.
6. Trust God to take care of tension in sex-releasing dreams, which is God's way of releasing sexual tension before marriage.
7. Do not continue to discuss, read, or view sex-related material.
8. Make a vow to God that immoral actions will be shunned for the remainder of life and look forward to a happy married life where the sex mechanism can be used to God's glory.

Case Study:

Jim came to the counselor feeling guilty and doubting his salvation. From infancy Jim had been in a good church with his family, and he had been saved at ten years of age in an evangelistic meeting. He was seventeen at the time of his visit and said he had doubted his salvation since he was about twelve. He also did not know what he felt guilty about. His relationship with his parents was good, and he said he had never been rebellious against them.

When questioned about any sinful habits, he admitted he had had the habit of masturbation since age twelve. He did not think the habit was wrong because he had read in psychology books that it was a healthful way to fulfill the sex desire. Jim masturbated every night to relax himself to the point at which he could go to sleep. He had a vivid imagination and would imagine all kinds of corruption while masturbating, even though he was not involved with pornography (except that he liked to look at bra ads in the newspaper and in magazines).

Case Study Solution:

The counselor explained that on the basis of I Corinthians 6:18 and I Thessalonians 4:1-8, masturbation was not only a sinful habit but also the reason for Jim's feeling guilty and doubting his salvation. After Jim's repentance, the counselor went over the three points of Romans 6:11-13 and then took him through the steps in breaking a habit. The counselor also suggested that he exercise regularly, and Jim agreed to start a jogging program. The counselor explained the necessity of letting God take care of sexual tension by sex-releasing dreams, which Jim never had experienced. The counselor encouraged him, if he had any more problems with doubting his salvation, to always look for sin and take care of it.

Problem #4: Homosexuality

Definition:

Sexual relations and sexual stimulation with the same sex.

Scriptures:

Genesis 19:1-11; Leviticus 18:22; 20:13; Deuteronomy 23:17; Judges 19:22-25; Romans 1:24-28; I Corinthians 6:9-10; I Timothy 1:9-10; II Peter 2:6; Jude 7.

Information and Principles:

The Bible says that homosexuality is a sin. It is a chosen and learned sinful, unnatural behavior, which the Bible and our laws refer to as "sodomy" (Deut. 23:17; I Kings 14:24; 15:12; II Kings 23:7). The word *sodomy* is derived from the city of Sodom where male prostitution was openly practiced. God called these men "wicked" and "sinners" (Gen. 13:13) and later God destroyed the cities of Sodom and Gomorrah because of their wickedness (Gen. 19). Leviticus 18:22 describes sodomy and calls it an "abomination." In Judges 19 God nearly destroyed one whole tribe of Israel because of the sin of sodomy. God gives clear description of sodomy in Romans 1:24, 26-28, where He calls it uncleanness, "unnatural," "dishonoring their bodies," "vile affection," and "unseemly behavior." Finally God gives this kind of person over to a reprobate mind. God warns of His judgment on people who commit sodomy (II Peter 2:6). Jude 7 describes God's hatred and judgment of sodomy, which is called "strange flesh."

The rate of homosexuality in America is about 1 percent, and in some studies that estimate is below 1 percent. Reisman, in her book *Kinsey, Sex, and Fraud,* said,

Certainly Kinsey's figures of four percent for exclusive life-time homosexuality and 10% for more or less exclusive homosexuality (for at least three years between 16 and 55) for 1940's males look extravagant even by comparison to data from 1970's and 1980's (post-sexual revolution) males. . . .

Late breaking news from the presentation of several sex surveys at the 1990 annual meeting of the American Association for the Advancement of Science in New Orleans seems to confirm a very low homosexuality rate in the U.S. population. . . .

In [Winnel] Smith's study entitled *Adult Sexual Behavior in 1989: Number of Partners, Frequency, and Risk,* conducted among a national full-probability sample of the adult household population of the United States, it was found that "overall . . . less than one percent (of the study population) has been exclusively homosexual."[1]

There is a variety of evidence to indicate that the percentage of homosexuals in the United States is only about 1 percent of the population. A study by Christian Financial Concepts found that 1 percent said that they definitely were or probably would be homosexual in the future. A survey by the National Opinion Science Research Center, conducted in 1989, and another study funded by the National Science Foundation in 1991 found the same percentage (1–1.5%). A 1987–88 study of 34,706 Minnesota junior and senior high school students, grades 7–12, found that 1.1 percent described themselves as bisexual or predominantly homosexual. By the time the students had reached age eighteen, this percentage had dropped to less than one percent (.8%). A 1993 nationwide study by the Battelle Human Affairs Research Centers found that only 1.1 percent of Americans claim to be homosexuals. *The London Daily Mail* released in January 1994 what it calls "the most exhaustive survey ever conducted into British sexual habits." The study found that only 1.1 percent of British men said that they were active homosexuals, a figure similar to the most recent American study.

These up-to-date statistics are very far from Kinsey's estimated 10 percent. One of the reasons that he got such a high figure was that over 25 percent of his sample population in his male report were prisoners and sex offenders.

There are several general principles that apply to this problem.

Homosexuality is a mental problem. For twenty-three years, the American Psychiatric Association in its diagnostic manual listed homosexuality as a mental disorder. In December 1973 the Board of Directors of the APA succumbed to the pressures of the gay groups and voted to remove homosexuality from the list of mental disorders. Homosexuals were in effect declared to be normal. Not all psychiatrists agreed with this declaration. According to a *Time* magazine report, New York psychiatrist Charles Socarides said, "It is flying in the face of the one fact that we know which is that male and female are programmed to mate with the opposite sex, and this is the story of . . . any society that hopes to survive." Dr. Socarides called the ruling "the medical hoax of the century."[2] Dr. Reisman stated in her book, "Four years after the APA decision, *The General Aspects of Human Sexuality,* November 1977, published the results of a survey taken among 2,500 psychiatrists on the subject *Current Thinking on Homosexuality.* By 69 percent to 18 percent—13 percent uncertain—respondents answered that homosexuality was usually a pathological adaptation as opposed to a normal variation. This result suggests that the political component of the APA decision process led that body to a position not supported by the majority of the psychiatric profession."[3]

The wrong choice causes a multitude of personal and mental problems. "Dr. Armand Nicholai, chief psychiatrist of the Medical School at Harvard University and editor of the Harvard Guide to Psychiatry, said: 'I have treated hundreds of homosexuals. None of them deep down thought he was normal.' "[4]

According to a 1989 Department of Health and Human Services report, 30 percent of youth suicides occur among gays and lesbians.[5] A study of 120 male anorexics done by Dr. Arnold Anderson, a psychiatrist at the University of Iowa, found that 22 percent were homosexual.[6] If the homosexual decides to get married, it spawns a host of additional problems, including perversion of the children, bringing sexually transmitted diseases into the marriage, and causing family disruption that usually ends in divorce. In the light of the above, one would have to say that there is nothing "gay" about being homosexual; "gap" (Guaranteed Awful Problems) might be a more accurate term.

Homosexuality as a tendency is a learned behavior rather than a part of the individual's biological inheritance. Homosexuality

is purely a matter of choice. It has nothing to do with genetics, physiology, or hormones. In the article reprinted in the *Journal of Nervous Mental Disease,* researcher John Money stated,

> "the assumption that homosexuality is a hormonal disorder; an assumption held in discredit by the majority of endocrine authorities today. . . . Failure to detect a hormonal anomaly in homosexuals has been paralleled by a failure to effect a cure with hormonal treatment. . . . The obverse of a lack of abnormal hormonal findings in homosexuality is the lack of increased incidence of homosexuality in sex-endocrine dysfunction."[7]

Even Kinsey agreed with this principle. Kinsey listed four factors that underlie the origin of homosexuality. They are as follows:

> 1) The basic physiological capacity of every mammal to respond to any sufficient stimuli. 2) The accident which leads an individual into his or her first sexual experience with a person of the same sex. 3) The conditioning effects of such experience. 4) The indirect, but powerful, conditioning, which the opinions of other persons and the social codes may have on an individual's decision to accept or reject this type of sexual contact. . . . There is no need of hypothesizing peculiar hormonal factors that make certain individuals especially liable to engage in homosexual activity, and we know of no data which proves the existence of such hormonal factors. There are no sufficient data indicating that specific hereditary factors are involved.[8]

Belliveau and Ritcher in their book *Understanding Human Sexual Inadequacy* reviewed a significant study.

> Masters and Johnson did a study of 213 men whom they treated for sexual dysfunction. Twenty-one had homosexual experiences as teenagers. Since none of these men had engaged in heterosexual relations before their homosexual experience, their first pleasurable sex experience seemed to be an important factor. The conclusion was the man whose first mature sexual experience is homosexual appears to be marked by it, even though he switches to heterosexual lovemaking. There may be some pattern implanted on his behavior that cannot be erased. Both primary and secondary impotent men who had homosexual experiences as teenagers continue to think of themselves as homosexually oriented in their adult lives, even though many are married.[9]

Homosexuality is a sinful choice. A person is born with a sexual orientation that is consistent with his gender, anatomy, and physiology. At some point in a homosexual's development—either before, during, or soon after puberty—he has made a wrong choice to go against the inborn, natural sexual orientation and has chosen a corrupt sexual lifestyle oriented toward the same sex. There is no scientific evidence that there is a hormonal, genetic, or heredity factor that is in any way related to homosexuality.

According to Cal Thomas, a Los Angeles syndicated columnist, there are some significant facts disqualifying the recently widely publicized reports about finding a supposed gene which may predetermine homosexuality. The two studies were done by a molecular biologist, Dean Hamer, at the National Cancer Institute. The first study was done in 1993 and is under investigation by the Federal Office of Research Integrity. The second study was reported in 1995 and is not strong enough statistically to stand on its own because, among other things, 22 percent of the nonhomosexual brothers had the same genetic markers. Incidentally the media forgot to mention that Hamer is a homosexual and therefore very biased. Hamer once told a meeting of parents and friends of lesbians and gays, "If you tell the press what to write about a scientific study, they'll write it." The gay-advocacy groups are very adept at using fraudulent science and the sympathetic, nonobjective media to deceive a gullible public.

There may be predisposing factors that contribute to homosexual behavior, but an individual still chooses his sexual orientation. Homosexuality is a decision by the individual to be immoral and to remain in the immature state of the same-sex love development. (See the Love-Sex chart, Table XII, Chapter 4.) Medical experts agree that homosexuality is not a physiological problem (i.e., due to genetic factor, hormone imbalance, or some other purely physical condition) except in very rare cases of hermaphroditism; rather, it is a decision problem (i.e., due to deliberate decisions by the individual).

Many ideas have been suggested as predisposing factors for these wrong decisions. Of course, continual remarks about a child's appearance, actions, or mannerisms being like those of the opposite sex can cause him to be confused about his sex orientation. But the most common factor in the background of homosexuals is a home that contains a domineering, overprotective mother and a weak, ineffectual, or absent father. A related problem is a home with no proper role model of the child's sex while the child is between the ages of three and fourteen. Divorced or widowed women must make sure that their boys have good father-substitutes during these years.

Another motivating factor is the "first pleasure" principle. A boy between the ages of six and fifteen who experiences extreme sex pleasure with another boy will tend to repeat this first sex pleasure experience in later years. Then he will begin to wonder if he is not destined to be locked into a homosexual lifestyle because of his strong desire for this kind of pleasure. With girls, who are touch-oriented, this tendency can start with other girls through innocent back massages that develop into sensuous erotic pleasure, bringing all kinds of doubts about their sex orientation. But regardless of what influences a person toward his wrong decisions, homosexuality is still a matter of sinful choices, not an inevitable destiny.

Isolated incidents of homosexual behavior do not necessarily indicate homosexual tendencies. John Drakeford in his book *A Christian's View of Homosexuality* says that "1/3 of girls and 2/3 of boys have engaged in some type of homosexual experimentation by age 15. These are efforts at understanding sexuality and do not indicate homosexual tendencies."[10] He goes on to say that

> during this time of an emerging, sometimes throbbing sexuality, the adolescent may be more self-conscious, more uncertain and anxious. Because of this factor, a group of peers frequently provides a safe milieu for sexual talk, comparison of sex organs, and sexual experimentation. . . . In the years of childhood and early adolescence the human is in a situation where sexuality is particularly pliable. Add to this the penchant of homosexuals to turn to younger sex objects and you are confronted with the heart of the problems. If gays are entitled to their sexual preferences, should not each individual have the same privilege? Biologically, the child is being prepared for heterosexual functioning—does anyone have the right to condition him into the imprisonment of homosexual reaction?[11]

Homosexuality seems to cause severe problems. Dr. Daniel Cappon, a Canadian psychiatrist at the University of Toronto, said in his book *Toward an Understanding of Homosexuality,*

> The homosexual person will die younger and suffer emotional, mental and physical illness more often than the normal person. The natural history of the homosexual person seems to be one of frigidity, impotence, broken personal relationships, psychosomatic disorders, alcoholism, paranoia, psychosis, and suicide.[12]

Homosexuality, which is against a person's very nature, causes more personality problems than any other sin.

The homosexual promotes devilish moral consequences. Morally, the homosexual becomes increasingly corrupt as he reaches out to new contacts and new means to satisfy his perverted appetite. Usually these new contacts are innocent young teens or children who have not yet developed their sexual orientation and are easier to introduce gradually and pervert to his corrupt lifestyle. One study by two homosexual authors states that "three-fourths of homosexuals had at some time had sex with boys sixteen to nineteen or younger."[13]

A survey reported in the official publication of the American Public Health Association, for example, said that over a lifetime the typical homosexual has forty-nine different sexual partners and that between 8 percent and 12 percent of homosexuals have more than five hundred partners during their lifetime.[14]

The homosexual lifestyle has disastrous physical consequences. Medically the homosexual lifestyle is unhealthful and an invitation to disaster and death. Homosexuals are responsible for the spread of AIDS, the most dangerous and fatal epidemic ever to hit America. When it was first detected in 1981, it was called GRID (Gay-Related Immune Deficiency) disease, and homosexuals continue to be the chief recipients and transmitters of the disease. A good slogan for AIDS Awareness Day would be "Prevent AIDS—Fight sodomy and promiscuity." The fatal disease of AIDS is beginning to spread to the general population because the hardy and transmuting AIDS virus is easily transmitted by coming in contact with homosexuals' infected blood and body fluids and with that of heterosexuals who have had sexual contact with infected homosexuals.

> Of course we now know that AIDS can be spread by conventional female-male relations. It happened in Africa. It also happens here. Needlesticks? Yes. Kissing? Yes. Transmission

through blood on intact skin? Yes. Aerosols? Probably. Contagion through perspiration? Big question mark. Water, soil, and public restroom toilet seats? Who knows? We just do not know because research is lacking. . . . As late as 1987 we were told that only ten to twenty percent of people who turn HIV positive would develop AIDS and die. We now know with virtual certainty that anybody carrying the virus is carrying his final script.[15]

Other diseases are common to homosexuals, such as given in the following quote: "Almost all gay males have or have had hepatitis B. Many gay males have ulcers and oozing blisters in or around the intestinal tract, including the mouth and rectum. More than half of all reported cases of syphilis in the United States occur in homosexual men."[16] It is estimated that today three out of four AIDS-stricken people on the American continent are male homosexuals.

The choice of the homosexual's lifestyle is condemned by God for a good reason, and His judgment of AIDS or other diseases and problems are a consequence of this wrong choice.

Solutions:

Counsel should include the following:

1. Explanation by the counselor using the Love-Sex chart (Table XII, Chapter 4), putting emphasis on immaturity and immorality
2. Complete repentance, confessing homosexuality as a sin that offends God and affects other people (I Thess. 4:6)
3. Encouragement to get rid of any gestures or mannerisms that would indicate having been part of this lifestyle. Young men should be helped to eliminate limp wrist gestures by doing pushups on their fists. They should sit with knees apart or with the ankle on the knee. When they walk, they should walk with large steps, putting the heel down first. They need to get a good short haircut and get rid of any feminine jewelry. Girls should learn how to sit properly and to walk with small steps. They should be taught how to appear feminine in dress and hairstyles.
4. Admonition to stay away from places where homosexuals normally congregate and to have no further contact with their homosexual former friends

5. Instruction to treat this lifestyel as a habit of sin and to take steps to break the habit as described in Chapter 4.

Case Study:

Ted came to see the counselor about his reluctance to get married. He was engaged to a nice girl whom he had met at college five years before. They had been engaged for three years, but he had kept putting off the wedding. When the counselor asked him why, he gave finances as a reason, although he had a good job, a home partially paid for, and thousands of dollars in investments.

Ted finally admitted that he was a homosexual and had been since high school. His first homosexual experience had been in eighth grade with a coach. Four or five other encounters followed when the coach had boys over to his house to spend the night. Ted's next experience was when he was a sophomore in high school. A college boy in the neighborhood had befriended him and invited him to his college for a football weekend at a fraternity house. Ted was also introduced to drinking then. That liaison lasted through Ted's high school years. By the time he enrolled at the state college, Ted had had several different partners from the local high school. His family and church friends did not know about his homosexuality, for he kept up appearances by dating the opposite sex regularly.

Ted was very fond of the girl to whom he was engaged, but the thought of sex with her repulsed him. He said he was a Christian, having made a profession as a sophomore in a Christian high school, but Amy, his fiancée, was not, although she was a church member. He said he did not think homosexuality was a sin and had read numerous psychology books on the subject.

He was from a middle-class, churchgoing family with a domineering mother and a weak, happy-go-lucky, overweight father who was always joking. His father was absorbed with TV sports and rarely interacted with his son. Ted had three older sisters. He said to the counselor, "I want to get this problem taken care of so I can feel like a normal human being."

Case Study Solution:

The counselor went over the Scriptures on homosexuality, emphasizing that the practice was a grievous sin that God abhorred and pointing out the extent of the immorality involved (i.e., even if he had been normally inclined toward women, he *still* would have been considered immoral, a "whoremonger," for his constant sexual activity outside of marriage). Ted repented of his sin and made a confession before the church without naming the sin.

The counselor next dealt with Ted about breaking the lifestyle habits he was presently following, such as hanging around with his two homosexual friends and going to the fast-food drive-in where teenagers hung out every Friday night after the high school ballgame. The counselor told Ted to tell his unsaved fiancée about his problem and give her time to decide whether she still wanted to marry him. Then the counselor took Ted through II Corinthians 6:14 and warned him not to marry Amy until she got saved. The counselor also discussed with him the idea of dedicating his life to the Lord for full-time service.

About three months later, Ted dedicated his life to the Lord and his fiancée was converted. She became a very zealous, soulwinning Christian. She eventually decided she wanted to marry Ted, but wanted to wait a year to help him overcome his problem. The counselor had them both read three books on marriage with an emphasis on a godly physical relationship. Ted also agreed to get together with his father for some shared activities.

A year later Ted and Amy were married. The counselor warned Ted that when he reached mid-life and his wife reached menopause, gained weight, and lost some of her sexual desire, he would be tempted to relapse into homosexuality. He could avoid this temptation by working with his wife to continually build their relationship and family unity. Ted would also have to discipline his thought life and never lapse into homosexual thinking.

Problem #5: Incest

Definition:
Any sexual contact between family members who could not be legally married.

Scriptures:
Leviticus 18:6-18; 20:11-12, 14, 17, 19-21. There are four cases mentioned in Scripture, all of which are condemned: Genesis 19:30-38; 35:22; II Samuel 13:6-22; I Corinthians 5:1.

Information and Principles:

In the past it has been difficult to estimate the extent of this problem because most of the cases are never reported; however, it seems that more and more cases are being referred to counselors. The most frequent case is incest between the father or stepfather and the daughter. The next most frequent case is the older brother with the younger sister. The least frequent (approximately 1 percent) of the reported cases is incest between mother and son. When children report sexual abuse, they should be taken seriously and an investigation instituted, no matter how bizarre the story sounds or who may be involved. An investigation and appropriate action should be instituted at the lowest level possible. Start by reporting it to the pastor. To be safe, check with local authorities in the community in which you serve to find the specifics of laws governing the reporting of such cases.

Solutions:

When confronted with cases of abuse, counselors should take these steps:

1. Let the victim tell the story fully.
2. Make sure that the blame is put where it belongs: on the older person who took advantage of the younger innocent person.
3. Use the Triune Man diagram (Table VI). Explain that the sin was done to the body and can hurt the soul and spirit only if the victim chooses to dwell on the Devil thoughts of shame, blame, fault, bitterness, and/or guilt. This diagram should also be used in cases of rape.
4. If the victim has deceived either parent or both parents, he needs to confess and repent of his own sin. One example would be the case of the teenage girl who takes a bath only when her mother is away from the home and leaves the bathroom door unlocked, inviting the father's corruptness. Use the three-step formula for eliminating the sin (Rom. 10:17) as described in Chapter 4.
5. Help the victim to deal with ingrained bitterness against God (and sometimes against the innocent parent) for not having prevented or stopped the incest by intervening. This bitterness may occur in rape victims as well. The bitterness problem must be properly handled as explained in Chapter 10.

6. Deal with the perpetrator of the sin by reporting the situation to the pastor, who will in turn contact the mother or the parents and handle the case in a scriptural manner. In some cases this may involve reporting the incident to civil authorities. (Again, check with local authorities in the community in which you serve to find the specifics of laws governing the reporting of such cases.)

Case Study:

Dorothy, age twenty-one, came to the counselor with a shyness problem. She was pretty and vivacious but socially withdrawn and self-centered. When the counselor asked her about her childhood and her family relationships, her eyes teared up and her lips started quivering. She said her father had had a drinking problem and, when she was fifteen years old, had run his car off the road. The car had hit the outside of a bridge abutment and spun into the river, killing him. Dorothy had been saved at a Christian camp soon after her father's death and had gotten into a good youth group.

When questioned further, Dorothy revealed that any time her father drank, he would get mean to her mother, who would then reject him physically. He would go into Dorothy's room and force her to do all kinds of things with him, including having intercourse. Dorothy told her mother, but the mother ignored the problem and the incest went on over an eight-year period.

She said her mother was very immoral and had affairs with several men while her husband was alive. Then, after he died, she had a succession of boyfriends with whom she was even more immoral. Dorothy used to come home from school and find her mother and her boyfriend having intercourse on the living room floor. Her mother's drinking also increased after the father's death, and she too became an alcoholic. One time, at the mother's urging, one of the boyfriends tried to rape Dorothy, but she screamed and fought the man, scratching and biting and kicking him until he finally left her alone.

She said she used to retreat to her room and, with her vivid imagination, create the ideal family in her mind. In high school Dorothy had read many books on marriage and was looking for the ideal Christian man to marry. However, she was afraid to be friendly to any man. She said she had been very bitter against her father but when she got saved, God took all the bitterness away. She still was disgusted with her mother, though, and did not want to have anything to do with her. When describing herself, Dorothy was very negative about her body and personality and felt that no one would ever marry her because of what had happened between her and her father and because of her mother's reputation.

Case Study Solution:

The counselor showed Dorothy the "Triune Man" diagram and discussed the difference between virginity and purity, explaining that what was done to her body need not affect her soul or spirit if she chose not to let it. Even though the personality and feelings are in the physical realm, they are controlled by a person's mental attitudes. The counselor pointed out that Dorothy had good reason to fear men after the experience with her father, since drinking men are prone to that sort of behavior with their daughters. As long as she stayed away from men who drank and were unsaved, she would have a better chance of the Lord's directing her to the man of her dreams.

The counselor then told Dorothy how to develop her personality not only to reach men in social situations but also to reach other people with the gospel. She agreed that thinking about other people and their needs instead of worrying about what they thought of her was the first ingredient in friendliness and Christian love. The counselor told her to ask God to find the right man for her and, instead of continually turning down dates, as was her custom, she should pick out five eligible Christian men that she felt comfortable with and be friendly to them. Then if they asked her out, she should date them at least several times, finding out all she could about them.

The counselor then took Dorothy to Psalm 139 and showed her that the Lord had directed her life even before she was born and had put her into that family for a specific reason. Now that she was saved, God probably wanted her to reach her mother by first forgiving and being reconciled to her. The counselor suggested that she make a list of all the attributes that God had given her and start thanking God for them instead of berating God for His stinginess in not giving her the attributes she imagined and wanted.

Over a period of three months, Dorothy was able to forgive her mother and be reconciled to her. She eventually found her ideal man and married him, becoming a pastor's wife in a very effective ministry.

Problem #6: Premarital Sex

Definition:

Any sexual intercourse before marriage.

Scripture:

I Corinthians 6:15-20; 7:1-2; I Thessalonians 4:1-7.

Information and Principles:

Although there are no comprehensive, conclusive studies on this sin, it is estimated that over three-fourths of all newlyweds are not virgins at the time of their wedding. Christian doctors say that the number is about one-fourth of the couples they examine and counsel. Since the 1960s, the media propaganda in movies, television, magazines, and rock music has conditioned the younger generation against morality and toward immorality. The propaganda seems to center on the fact that if one is in love or engaged, having sex is all right. The media propaganda goes so far as to indicate that premarital sex is a healthful step in the person's sexual development and the sooner that it is accomplished after puberty the better.

Counselors and parents need to reiterate and teach to Christian young people the five main reasons that premarital sex is wrong.

1. **Spiritual reasons**—It is a sin against God and a person's own body. It seems to produce more guilt feelings than other types of sin (I Cor. 6:18). There is also a fear of judgment and death (I Cor. 11:29-32), fear of reaping what is sown (Gal. 6:7-8), and the certainty of prayers not being answered (Isa. 1:15).

2. **Physical consequences**—The possibility of pregnancy is apparent, since no birth control is 100 percent effective. There are approximately fifteen different sexually transmitted diseases that could be contracted. There is no effective cure for herpes II, AIDS, and several other of these diseases.

3. **Marriage preparation**—If the relationship before marriage is physical, it produces a shallow relationship, and there is no real communication that builds a friendship and oneness before marriage. Premarital sex will wreck a good potential relationship and sustain and glamorize a bad one.

4. **Morality indicator**—If immorality occurs now, there is no guarantee that there will not be infidelity after marriage since premarital sex is a good indicator of a lack of moral standards and emotional control. The counselee may be in love now and even engaged, but he can never be sure that this is the one he will actually marry.

5. **Post-marriage problems**—Sex tends to be associated with fear of discovery and tainted memories. Especially for a woman, this sordid view of sex can destroy romance and may result in her becoming frigid. Parents find it much harder to teach morality to their children when they themselves did not follow God's plan. Josh McDowell has written a book for parents on teaching their teens on the subject. It is titled *How to Help Your Child Say No to Sexual Pressure.*[17]

Solutions:

1. Have the counselee repent and confess the sin to God.
2. Use the three-point formula found in Romans 14:17. (See Chapter 4.)
3. Have the counselee break off the relationship for a period of time to have a chance to analyze with the counselor the total relationship to see whether it was just a physical relationship or if there is genuine love, compatibility, and responsibility enough for a good marriage. If not, the break should be complete and final. Having intercourse does not mean that a couple was married in God's eyes. Marriage, spiritually and legally, is a commitment to each other for life before God and man. If the couple decides to go ahead and marry, they will need help in setting up guidelines to avoid temptation to further immorality before the wedding.

Case Study:

Marjorie came down the aisle at a revival meeting, and Brian, her fiancé, followed her about two minutes later. Both admitted having intimate relations with each other for the last two months. They'd been engaged for a year and were waiting to get married until the following June when they both would be graduated from college. They had been dating for three years and admitted that they had been doing a lot of necking and petting for several years. Two months before, the people for whom Marjorie had been baby-sitting had allowed her to have her boyfriend over after she put the kids to bed. Because of that evening and their subsequent intimacies, she did not know whether she was pregnant and wondered what to do if she were. The couple had discussed the idea of moving the wedding up and getting married at Christmastime instead of waiting until June.

Case Study Solution:

The counselor found that this was not a continuing immoral lifestyle that he was dealing with. Both Brian and Marjorie had previously had high moral standards in high school, and this was their first incident of immorality with anyone. The counselor had Marjorie take a pregnancy test, which showed that she was not pregnant. He pointed out that not only the intimate relations but also the necking and petting were a sin—even though they were getting married—since intimacy is an inevitable result of necking and petting. After asking the Lord to forgive them and asking forgiveness of each other, they both agreed to limit their affection to hand-holding and a good-night kiss. They also agreed never to be together alone in a house without a chaperon or a crowd. The couple was able to control themselves together physically until the wedding by substituting communication, board games, and group activities for physical affection.

Problem #7: Adultery in Marriage

Definition:

Sex relations outside the marriage.

Scripture:

Exodus 20:14; Leviticus 18:20; 19:29; Deuteronomy 5:18; 23:17; Job 31:1, 9-12; Proverbs 6:29-33; Matthew 5:27-28, 32;

19:18; Luke 18:20; Acts 15:20; Romans 13:9; I Corinthians 15:18; Hebrews 13:4; James 2:11.

Information and Principles:

Studies on the incidence of adultery in America are so varied that they are almost worthless. From the statistics of the 1993 General Social Survey conducted by Tom W. Smith of the National Opinion Research Center, it was estimated that 15 percent of married or previously married Americans have committed adultery. Three to four percent of husbands and wives have a sexual partner outside of their marriage in a given year. From the General Social Survey, Smith has concluded that the level of extramarital activity has changed little since 1988 when its first survey on the subject was conducted.[18] Women who tend to stray complain about no romance, such as no love talk, no compliments, no understanding, and no caresses. Men who commit adultery complain of not having their physical needs met and not being understood.

Solutions:

Talk to the husband and the wife together. Lead each one in the following steps:

1. Confess sin and seek forgiveness from God and the offended partner.
2. Reestablish an attitude of communication and love.
3. Set guidelines and signals for meeting each other's needs and avoiding future temptation (I Cor. 7:4-5).
4. Work on sixteen ways to restore family unity. (See Appendix B.)

Case Study:

Clint, a forty-year-old, debonair, athletic man, went alone to the counselor at the insistence of his wife. She had said he was a hypocrite, and she was upset about his drinking, worldly attitudes, and lack of interest in spiritual things. He was a deacon and a generous giver to his church but went to church only every other Sunday morning when he was home. When Clint talked with the counselor, he claimed his wife was too pious and legalistic and that she had no concept of Christian liberty. He also said she was expecting unrealistic standards from him and their three teens.

Clint was a supervisor over several high fashion stores in four large cities: Los Angeles, Chicago, New York, and Miami. He made a good salary and provided for his family a luxurious lifestyle and a large house on three acres on the northwest side of Chicago. Every month he spent three to five days in each of the cities where the stores were located. Clint said that in each city except Chicago, he had a beautiful, rich woman who stayed with him in a suite in a luxury hotel. They enjoyed fine meals served in the room, the best night clubs, and parties on yachts. The women paid all the bills in return for the love and affection they could receive from him on the days he spent in their cities. Clint's wife had suspected this behavior but had no proof.

Clint justified his actions by saying that he was human and he was like many of the Old Testament men who had more than one wife. He justified his drinking, saying that wine was used by New Testament Christians and Christ's first miracle turned water into wine. When questioned about his salvation, Clint said he had made a decision on Easter Sunday when he was twelve.

Case Study Solution:

The counselor told Clint that he was a gigolo, accepting the accommodations, fine meals, entertainment, and presents in payment for the sexual pleasure he gave each woman. He was committing adultery against his wife, and she had scriptural grounds for divorce. Clint responded that she would not get a divorce because of the nice home, lifestyle, and security he provided and her love and commitment to him.

The counselor took Clint to the Ten Commandments, showed him how he was violating all of them and then, from the New Testament, discussed what Christ had to say about each. He also went over the Scriptures about God's eternal judgment on sinners who do not know Christ. The counselor confronted Clint with the truth that he had never repented of his sin and believed in Jesus Christ as the Son of God. He challenged Clint to read I John every day for thirty days, which he agreed to do.

A month later Clint went back to the counselor. He told about not being able to sleep one night and listening at 2:00 A.M. to a gospel program on the radio in the den. He had become convicted and had cried for an hour. On his knees, he had finally repented and accepted Christ as his Lord. When he awoke his wife and told her, she began crying and praising the Lord. She told him that she had been praying for him and his salvation for years. Clint told the counselor that early in the morning, as the sun was coming up, was the happiest time of their nineteen years of marriage.

The change was dramatic. Clint quit his job and took over a business in a nearby town. He later became a lay preacher and a soulwinner.

Problem #8: Frigidity

The two sexual problems that are not immoral in and of themselves in marriage are frigidity on the part of the wife and impotence on the part of the husband.

Definition:

Wife's inability to achieve orgasm during intercourse.

Information and Principles:

Frigidity in the wife may be caused by one or more of ten factors: (1) lack of proper awareness of self, (2) lack of a submissive spirit, (3) lack of concentration on bodily feelings, (4) insecure feelings or hidden fears of loss and separation, (5) guilt feelings, especially about moral matters, (6) pain, (7) fatigue, (8) lack of mood stimulation, (9) the hormone cycle, and (10) lack of proper physical caressing and stimulation. (A discussion of these factors may be found in *Formula for Family Unity,* pp. 70-73.)

Solutions:

Encourage the wife to do the following:

1. See a doctor for a medical evaluation. Ask the doctor about hormones or medication for frigidity.
2. Start the Kegel exercises. (See Tim LeHaye's *The Act of Marriage.*)
3. Check for a rebellious and bitter spirit and study the Scriptures on submission.
4. Discuss the ten factors listed above.
5. Have her fantasize about her husband in various intimate situations.

Case Study:

Martha, who had been married for two years, came to the counselor saying that there was a big problem in her marriage: she had never had a sex response in her physical relationship with her husband. Her husband was an impulsive man who was not attentive to her feelings. He wanted what he wanted whenever it was convenient to him. She said she had grown to resent the physical relationship after the first month of marriage, and she avoided it through many ploys, such as headaches, sickness, and fatigue. Her husband had once threatened to leave her if she did not become more cooperative. She resented his wanting to be the boss and make all the final decisions. She said he was just like her father, trying to run everything.

She also had an uncle who, when she was about thirteen and had matured, had tried to hug and kiss her and put his hands all over her every time he came around. After about a year of resisting him, she had told her mother, and he had never bothered her after that.

Case Study Solution:

The counselor found that Martha had little knowledge of the physical relationship or of her own anatomy and physiology; therefore, she had no knowledge of what to expect in a good response. The counselor explained to her that the reason she rejected her husband was two-fold: (1) she was not obeying the submission principle, which the counselor later reviewed with her, because she resented her dad's control of the family and had determined that her husband was not going to control her; (2) she also equated her husband's sexual advances with those of her uncle. The counselor explained that a first sexual contact makes a profound impression, and hers with her uncle had been very negative. She admitted that, in high school, if a boy she was dating tried to kiss her, she would break up with him. She had met her husband at a Christian college and had fallen in love and gotten engaged during her senior year. They had gotten married in June. She said that they had kissed only one time before marriage and that was when they got engaged. He had tried to kiss her several times, such as on vacation at Christmastime, but she had rebuffed him by shaming him for not being spiritual.

The counselor had her read several good books on marriage, including Tim LaHaye's *The Act of Marriage,* chapter seven of *Formula for Family Unity,* Joseph Dillow's *Solomon on Sex,* and Dr. Ed Wheat's *Intended for Pleasure.* He encouraged her to get her husband to read them with her. Because she had a problem with bladder control whenever she laughed or sneezed, the counselor had her do the Kegel exercises, which also improves the sex response. The counselor also explained to her the steps of stimulation which could precede intercourse and encouraged her to make a list of different places, positions, and techniques with which she could feel comfortable. She was also to imagine her husband stimulating her in the ways that were mentioned in the books and on her list and, for a month, to try one new thing each time. The counselor also suggested that every time her husband came home, she was to meet him at the door and give him a big hug and kiss. Every evening she was to fix him something special that he liked to eat. The counselor went over with her the submission principle given in Ephesians 5:20-24 and I Peter 3:1-6.

Martha returned two months later and reported that she had had her first sex response and had been having them regularly. She said that her relationship with her husband had improved in other areas as well, and she was beginning to realize what a loving and caring husband she had. She said she was beginning to realize how much her bad attitudes had affected her marriage, and she was determined to make her marriage a supremely happy one.

Problem #9: Impotence

Definition:
Inability of the husband to have or maintain an erection to achieve satisfactory intercourse.

Information and Principles:
There are approximately ten million men in the United States who have this problem. Doctors used to believe that impotence in a man was mostly a mental problem, but now it is considered that 50 to 80 percent of the impotence problems are a result of physical reasons. Absence of night erections during dreaming sleep is an indication that it is a physical problem. The physical causes for

impotence could be diseases such as diabetes (50 percent of male diabetics have the problem of impotence), hardening of the arteries, chronic kidney failure, alcoholism, and medication for high blood pressure. Impotence could also be the result of surgery—either vascular surgery involving nerve damage, cancer surgery such as prostate removal, or bladder surgery and sometimes even rectal surgery. Accidents that cause injury to the spinal cord or to the pelvis could also be a cause of impotence.

Solutions:

Encourage the husband to do the following:

1. See a doctor for a medical evaluation and ask about medications for impotence and about the three types of surgical implants.

2. Contact Osbon Medical System (1-800-438-8592) for information. It has produced an external vacuum pump called the Erectaide, which claims 90 percent effectiveness. It requires a physician's prescription. Further information can be obtained by writing to Impotence Information Center, Dept. 1, C. T. P. O. Box 9, Minneapolis, MN 55440.

In 20 to 50 percent of men, impotence is caused by mental problems, such as fear, stress, worry, anger, and bitterness against the wife, or depression resulting from guilt feelings. Help the husband and/or the wife to deal appropriately with these problems.

Case Study:

Bob, a forty-five-year-old man, came to the counselor with the problem of impotence. He had not been able to perform sexually for the last year and a half. It did not bother his wife—she said that she preferred the cuddling without the sex—but it bothered him. He had been taking a high-blood-pressure medicine for the last two years and, when questioned, he said that at his last physical exam, his doctor had suspected diabetes, which ran in his family.

Case Study Solution:

The counselor immediately suggested that Bob see the doctor and tell him about his condition. Three months later, Bob came back and said the doctor had changed his medicine and put him on a strict diet for his diabetes, but it had not helped him at all with his impotence.

The counselor talked to Bob about bitterness toward his wife. Bob admitted that he had been bitter toward her because she had pushed him into buying a house that he felt was beyond their means. He said that he had taken on an extra job to balance the budget, but they still had problems balancing it every month. The counselor went over the Scriptures on bitterness and suggested that Bob deal with his bitterness problem by confessing it, and then handle the budget problem as a separate issue, which might mean selling the house or having his wife go back to work, at least for a time, to help balance the budget.

For immediate relief of his physical problem, the counselor suggested the Osbon system, which needed to be prescribed by a doctor. The counselor also suggested that Bob talk to his doctor about a new drug, Papaverine, which had to be prescribed and injected by a doctor. Bob chose the mechanical method rather than surgery or drugs. After using the mechanical method for a time, he no longer needed it because during that time, he had gotten over his bitterness and had completely regained his confidence.

Materialism

Materialism is a common root sin and the greatest enemy of a Christian ministry and personal holiness that a Christian has to face in America. Living in a land of affluence can have a devastating effect on even the most dedicated Christian. Materialism is based on the false notion that having more makes one happy, successful, and complete.

Luxuries that the previous generations in America dreamed about, this generation considers necessities. When a recession comes, people get very upset, not because they do not have basic needs such as food, housing, and clothing, but because they cannot live the luxurious lifestyles to which they have become accustomed.

Problem #10: Materialism

Definition:

Rejecting God's plan for acquiring, spending, and sharing wealth, and operating outside of God's rules in handling money and possessions. Setting one's heart on or being preoccupied or obsessed with acquiring more money, possessions, power, and prestige, commonly referred to as greed.

Scripture:

Proverbs 3:9-10; 11:28; 21:26; Matthew 6:1-4, 19-34; Luke 12:22-34; Romans 13:6-8; II Corinthians 9:6-8; I Timothy 6:6-11, 17-19; Hebrews 13:5

Information and Principles:

America is a land of things. This country has seventy telephones for every one hundred people; the average modern industrial nation has eighteen telephones for every one hundred people. Ninety-eight percent of American households have at least one TV set, and there is one automobile for every two Americans. Americans live in the top 1 percent of the world economic scale. To satisfy the covetous desire for acquiring more things, more money is necessary. Society has always associated wealth, evidenced by an abundance of possessions, with power and prestige. Therefore, in a person's quest for success, money can easily become the motivation and the goal of life.

Lewis Lapham, in his book *Money and Class in America: Notes and Observations on Our Civil Religion,* gives some startling statistics of money's evil influence on people and society. He says, "Among both men and women the incidence of marital infidelity rises in conjunction with an increase in income. Of the married men earning $20,000 a year, only 31 percent conduct [extramarital] love affairs; of the men earning more than $60,000, 70 percent."[1]

He also says, "Motives having to do with money or sex account for 99 percent of the crimes committed in the United States, but those with money as their object exceed sexual offenses by a ratio of 4 to 1."[2] Lapham describes money as a sacrament of America's civil religion which demands and gets our worship.

"Thou shalt not covet" is the tenth commandment, and the Bible says in I Timothy 6:10 that "the love of money is the root of all evil: which while some coveted after, they have erred from the faith, and pierced themselves through with many sorrows."

In many places in the New Testament, contentment is emphasized. Paul indicated in Philippians 4:11 that contentment is a learned trait. "I have learned in whatsoever state I am, therewith to be content." Paul also mentioned in I Timothy 6:6 that "godliness with contentment is great gain." A facet of the "deceitfulness of riches" (Matt. 13:22) is that money and things do not bring contentment.

Materialism grows out of selfishness, which is an inborn trait that is compounded from early childhood by television advertisements, catalogs, billboards, newspapers, and magazines. These media preach the message that one needs and deserves unnecessary things, and therefore it is all right to have them.

In 1992 Robert Wuthnow completed a three-year research project on Religion and Economic Values at Princeton University by using a nationally representative survey. Two thousand employed people participated, and he interviewed more than 150 people from various faiths and occupations. Their responses provided new insight into America's deepest obsession: money. In the survey 89 percent agreed that "our society is much too materialistic"; 74 percent said materialism is a serious problem; 90 percent agreed that "children today want too many material things"; and 75 percent agreed that "advertising is corrupting our basic values."

According to the American Academy of Pediatrics, the average child watches 20,000 television commercials each year. Sixty percent of these commercials promote products such as candy, cereals, and toys. Over six billion dollars is spent every year on toys, dolls, and games. Adults are just as susceptible as children to this materialistic influence. As someone has well said, "The difference between a man and a boy is the price of his toy."

There are certain characteristics of a person who is caught in the trap of materialism.

1. Worry over money and investments (Matt. 6:25)
2. Preoccupation with money and the things money buys instead of with the kingdom of God (Matt. 6:33)
3. Irritation at opportunities to give and giving grudgingly (Luke 6:38)
4. Letting overdue bills go unpaid while still buying unnecessary things (Rom. 13:8)
5. Comparing his financial status to others' (II Cor. 10:11-12)
6. Not being content and thankful for what he has (Phil. 4:11)

There are several general principles that apply to materialism.

Relinquish ownership of everything to God, for He, in truth, owns everything and just allows people to use it (Ps. 50:10). The Lord gives and the Lord takes away (Job 1:21-22). God is in control, and He sometimes turns Christians back to Himself through medical bills, car and house repairs, and even lost jobs.

Christians must learn to live simple, contented lives (I Tim. 6:6-10; Matt. 6:24-34). Enjoying and praising God for His great creation and for the wonders and workings of nature and reading good books for character-building or for entertainment is going in the right direction—away from materialism.

Think of wealth and possessions as a matter of biblical stewardship (Matt. 6:19-34). The material things of this world that come under a Christian's direction and control are to be used as tools in accomplishing the work of Christ and for advancing His kingdom (II Cor. 9).

Avoid greed, which is an excessive desire and motivation to gain more money, own more things, assume more control, or have more prestige (Luke 12:13-35). God says in Luke 12:16-21 that He will provide all of our needs and that we can die at any time and may not have any need for what we so desperately want. Greed is like drinking salt water; it makes you want more and eventually makes you sick. Jesus gives the cure for greed in Luke 12:34-35: we are to sell possessions, give away money, and provide for ourselves bags of heavenly treasures.

Avoid window-shopping, catalog-browsing, and hunting for "the bargain," for they arouse new wants and trigger impulse buying (Rom. 13:14). The old motto used in the Depression, "Use it up, wear it out, make it do, or do without," should be used in times of prosperity to avoid a materialistic emphasis.

Every Christian has a choice of changing his lifestyle of striving for ever-increasing possessions, money, status, and authority or living with a violated conscience outside the will of God (Matt. 6:24). Daniel purposed in his heart to deny himself the luxuries of the king's court (Dan. 1:8), and Moses also chose to go the right way (Heb. 11:25).

Solutions:

1. Review the applicable Scripture and principles given in this chapter, including the proverbs about material possessions and covetousness.

2. Give God the firstfruits (tithe) of all your income (Prov. 3:9-10). Do not rob God (Mal. 3:8-10).

3. Cultivate the grace of giving as the antidote for materialism (II Cor 9:7-9). This would include giving things, time, and talent as well as money. Develop the principle of never lending money. Instead, give it to the person who has a

legitimate need; that way, you are never disappointed by people's failure to pay back loans.

4. Eliminate all credit spending. Pay cash for needs, wants, and desires. Get out of debt and stay out. The Bible emphasizes "Owe no man anything but to love one another" (Rom. 13:8).

5. For a satisfying and God-ordained substitute for acquiring money, seek to acquire the character traits of I Timothy 6:11.

Case Study:

Ben and Eileen came to the counselor with a big problem in their marriage. Ben, who was a dedicated Christian, a deacon in the church, chairman of the missions committee, and a successful businessman, felt that he and his wife were going two different directions spiritually. He said that she was dedicated to spending money and acquiring things for herself and the house. She was interested in worldly things and had little spiritual interest. She went shopping four or five times a week at a nearby large city, which was her favorite shopping place.

Ben said that money was not the question but that Eileen made a god out of acquiring things. He said she had over 200 pairs of shoes. She had a collection of more than 300 stuffed animals. These animals were not the ordinary kind; they were collectors' items that cost $100 or more, and they were all over the house. In addition, she had started a Hummel figurine collection.

She also liked to go on several cruises each year. Ben said that he did not mind one or two cruises in a ten-year period, but two a year was just too much. They had been on one Christian cruise, which he liked, but she did not. The cruises that she enjoyed were the "glamorous" ones with gambling, drinking, and partying, although neither one of them drank alcohol or gambled, and he did not enjoy being around people who did. He said that, after a while, all the ports were the same, and it was the most boring thing he could do. He said that after two days, he was like a caged lion and the only redeeming feature was his early-morning three-mile jog around the deck.

Eileen told the counselor that Ben was very unromantic. He was an "old stick-in-the-mud" socially and never wanted to have any fun. She admitted that she had a love for shopping and that cruises gave her an opportunity to do that in exotic places. She said that she had been saved and had joined the church at an early age. Her family were regular churchgoers, but only on Sunday mornings. However, she said that her husband wanted to drag her off to church every time the doors were open. She also said that "the only reason he objects to my shopping is that he wants to give all of our money away to missions."

Ben interrupted to say that that was the key point right there. He had gone into partnership with God when he started in business and had promised God 30 percent. God had prospered him with that arrangement, but Eileen wanted to bite the hand that really fed her.

Case Study Solution:

The counselor had Eileen discuss her home background. She revealed that her father was a busy, successful businessman who never spent any time with his family. He always bought them things to show that he loved them and always gave them plenty of money to spend. She said that shopping and having things around her gave her a feeling of security and peace, which Ben never gave her because he was too practical and analytical. He always had a spiritual explanation for everything.

The counselor discussed with Ben and Eileen the Identity with Christ principle. He then took Eileen through the Scriptures on materialism and asked her if she would be willing to read the sixth chapters of Matthew and I Timothy and the third and fifteenth chapters of John every day for a month. She agreed to do it. She also agreed to limit her shopping trips to one a week for a period of three months.

Ben agreed to read Gary Smalley's book *If He Only Knew Her,* and they both agreed to read Smalley's other book *For Better and for Best,* as well as the authors' book *Formula for Family Unity.* The counselor also asked Ben to read the entire book of Ephesians every night for a month, which Ben agreed to do.

In subsequent sessions, the counselor talked to Ben about trying to understand his wife and not "beating her over the head" with spiritual sermonettes. He was admonished to take some leadership in creating family unity instead of spiritually dividing the family with his extreme interest in business and church activities to the neglect of his family. He was encouraged to allow the Holy Spirit to work instead of trying to do it himself.

Several months later, Eileen dedicated her life to the Lord, and her attitudes and interests suddenly changed. Ben commented that at last he felt that he and his wife were going down the same path together. She said that the books he had read had helped change him into a more understanding and compassionate person.

Rejection

A root cause of many problems is rejection and the ungodly feelings that it provokes. Rejection and rejection feelings started when Satan rebelled against God, rejected God, and tried to usurp His throne. Satan with a host of his angels was cast out of heaven. Satan passed rejection feelings on to man when he tried to get Adam and Eve to believe that God was not good and did not have their best interests at heart. Adam and Eve sinned by rejecting God and His Word and were cast out of the Garden of Eden. Cain rejected his brother, Abel, and slew him. Satan, appearing as an angel of light (II Cor. 11:14), is still working in the children of disobedience (Eph. 2:2) and leading them to reject God. They in turn feel as if they are rejected as they await God's righteous judgment (Heb. 9:27; II Thess. 1:7-9). They tend to pass this feeling on to their children and others.

Problem #11: Rejection

Definition:

Rejection is withholding love from another person when one is in a position to bestow that love. Rejection is a failure to fulfill the second commandment given in Matthew 22:39—"And the second is like unto it, Thou shalt love thy neighbour as thyself." It is a failure to fulfill the new commandment that Jesus gave in John 13:34-35—"A new commandment I give unto you, That ye love one another; as I have loved you, that ye also love one another. By this shall all men know that ye are my disciples, if ye have love one to another." It is also a failure to carry out the royal law of love given in James 2:8—"If ye fulfil the royal law according to the scripture, Thou shalt love thy neighbour as thyself, ye do well."

Scripture:

Luke 9:23; Romans 8:1; Galatians 2:20; Ephesians 1:6-7; 2:4-10; Philippians 3:7-10; Colossians 1:27; 2:9-10; 3:1-4; II Timothy 4:16-17; I John 3:1

Information and Principles:

Most people experience some rejection at some time. It is not the frequency or severity of the rejection but rather the person's perception of the rejection circumstance or situation and his ungodly feelings and responses that cause the problem.

A person feels rejection when he is not accepted because of his lack of money or unattractive appearance, like the poor man in James 2:1-7, or because of immaturity level, like the young children whom the disciples rejected in Matthew 19:13-15, or because of race, culture, religion, skills, accomplishments, or abilities. A person tends to find his identity and define himself and his acceptance in terms of people, places, possessions, and the power and prestige that he gets from his experiences. When identity and definition are lacking in his life, he becomes susceptible to rejection feelings.

Christians must be careful that they do not promote feelings of rejection by insensitive attitudes, words, and actions, even in joke or jest. Most people feel rejection in some area, and minorities and the handicapped are particularly vulnerable because of their past experiences. To minimize feelings of rejection in others, the Christian should:

1. Provoke others to love and good works (Heb. 10:24).
2. Communicate to edify (Eph. 4:29).
3. Avoid becoming easily provoked himself (I Cor. 13:5).
4. Avoid thinking more highly of himself than he ought (Rom. 12:3).
5. Take deliberate action to bring about understanding and reconciliation between races and cultural groups (Col. 3:11).

These activities can be open doors for the effective presentation of the gospel or the edification of believers.

Rejection feelings, which are a reaction to perceived rejection, arise when a person thinks he is not getting the love, attention, or recognition to which he is entitled. Rejection feelings arise in two stages. The first stage starts with self-pity, envy, feelings of inferiority, and sometimes anger. In the first stage a person will usually do anything to please others and God for the purpose of winning love and acceptance. For example, a grade school child may steal money and give it to his peers. Children and teens in this stage are very susceptible to peer pressure because of a fear of further rejection. Christians with rejection problems tend to work for God to gain God's approval instead of letting God work through them (Phil. 2:13).

These feelings of the first stage may persist throughout one's life and not cause any problems except unhappiness and depression. If the feelings intensify to the second stage, they may interfere with a person's normal adjustment and relationships with others.

The second stage of rejection feelings can start at any time in life but usually follows the first stage. It involves a mixture of feelings from the first stage with more intense feelings such as bitterness, hate, and revenge. Usually a dramatic incident or situation precedes the second stage of rejection feelings. For example, when the Valentine box was opened and the Valentines were distributed to his classmates, one second-grade boy did not receive any Valentines, not even from his teacher. Another example is a fifth-grade girl in a class Christmas gift exchange who received a beautifully wrapped cake of deodorant soap and deodorant for her gift. A particularly intense episode of sexual or physical abuse could also send a person into the second stage of rejection feelings.

These persons then begin to reject others, especially family members and the people they perceive as rejecting them. They will purposefully do things that invite rejection from others and increase the intensity of their feelings. This process, then, becomes a vicious circle of increasing intensity that solidifies the rejection feelings. The result may be a persecution complex.

Appearance, intelligence, physical abilities, and the family's socioeconomic status (in that order) have the greatest effect on a child's feelings of rejection. Physical handicaps and poor home life, including divorce or the death of a parent, can also have an adverse effect. About 30 percent of the young girls today feel so rejected that at some time in their childhood they imagine they are adopted.

Some general principles that apply to the root cause and problem of rejection are as follows.

Rejection feelings start in childhood and get progressively worse as the person moves toward adulthood. Most children at times feel unloved and rebuffed at home, at school, and later on in social and dating situations. Some react to these situations with rejection feelings. They become very sensitive to the cuts, slights, and snide remarks of their parents, friends, and authority figures. They begin to feel socially and emotionally rejected by others and react with varying degrees of rejection feelings. As these rejection feelings intensify, some children begin to set up their defenses and withdraw into a selfish, self-centered, introspective existence that results in personality abnormalities and disturbances that sometimes lead to suicide.

Since 1970, suicides of school-age children, especially teens, have increased at an alarming rate. (See Chapter 21.) Some experts believe that the primary cause of suicide is a lack of a meaningful relationship with at least one parent and the resultant rejection feelings. A Penn State study found that the average parent spends less than seven minutes per week in intense personal time with his child. Another complicating factor is that by 1990, 72 percent of the mothers of school-age children were working full time.

Kevin Leman, in his book *Making Children Mind Without Losing Yours,* gives some revealing statistics from a survey of 2,200 teens from Christian homes in which 79 percent claimed that they frequently felt a lack of love at home.

Parents unwittingly show rejection to their children by careless remarks such as, "How can you be so stupid as to do a thing like that?" or "Here, let me do it; you never seem to do anything right." Even negative facial expressions and gestures as a parent is changing a dirty diaper or carrying out other daily interactions are viewed by some infants and children as rejection. Rejection is also felt by many preschool children who are left for long periods of time in day care centers while Mother works full time.

Later on, when children are school age, peers and even older siblings can be rejecting, mean, and cruel by saying vicious things and taunting with nicknames or phrases such as "Fatty, fatty, two by four." When a junior-high boy asks for his first date and the girl replies, "I would not go with you if you were the last boy on earth," rejection has occurred. High school girls who sit by the telephone waiting for dates can feel very much rejected when they never get a single call. Even poor grades can be viewed as rejection. Some family situations, such as the death of a parent or divorce, are viewed by most children as rejection.

Positive parental love can prevent or minimize rejection feelings. Parents can do a great deal to minimize rejection feelings by maintaining a warm atmosphere of love in the home and by showing Christian love and forgiveness in everyday situations with their family and others. Daily communication between parents and children, with positive comments and words of encouragement, is especially effective at mealtime and at bedtime in promoting a feeling of love and acceptance. Regular physical expressions of affection such as pats, hugs, handholding, kisses, and cuddles are important in demonstrating love to children.

God has provided the cure for rejection feelings through salvation. God has made the Christian at salvation "accepted in the beloved" through Jesus Christ's blood (Eph. 1:6-7). God then does the following things to confirm that acceptance: He takes away all condemnation (Romans 8:1), holds the Christian in His hand (John 10:28-29), accepts the Christian into His family (I John 3:1-3), and makes him a new creature in Christ Jesus (II Cor. 5:17). If Christians are accepted by God, they should no longer need to be concerned about being accepted by people. To eliminate rejection feelings, a Christian needs to realize that he is identified with Christ at salvation.

Biblical Truth—
Identification with Christ

Second Corinthians 5:17: "Therefore if any man be in Christ, he is a new creature: old things are passed away; behold, all things are become new."

Galatians 2:20: "I am crucified with Christ: nevertheless I live; yet not I, but Christ liveth in me: and the life which I now live in the flesh I live by the faith of the Son of God, who loved me, and gave himself for me."

Ephesians 2:4-10: "But God, who is rich in mercy, for his great love wherewith he loved us, even when we were dead in sins, hath quickened us together with Christ, (by grace ye are saved;) and hath raised us up together, and made us sit together in heavenly places in Christ Jesus: that in the ages to come he might shew the exceeding riches of his grace in his kindness toward us through Christ Jesus. For by grace are ye saved through faith; and that not of yourselves: it is the gift of God: not of works, lest any man should boast. For we are his workmanship, created in Christ Jesus unto good works, which God hath before ordained that we should walk in them."

Philippians 3:7-10: "But what things were gain to me, those I counted loss for Christ. Yea doubtless, and I count all things but loss for the excellency of the knowledge of Christ Jesus my Lord: for whom I have suffered the loss of all things, and do count them but dung, that I may win Christ, and be found in him, not having mine own righteousness, which is of the law, but that which is through the faith of Christ, the righteousness which is of God by faith: that I may know him, and the power of his resurrection, and the fellowship of his sufferings, being made conformable unto his death."

Colossians 1:27: "To whom God would make known what is the riches of the glory of this mystery among the Gentiles; which is Christ in you, the hope of glory."

Colossians 2:9-10: "For in him dwelleth all the fulness of the Godhead bodily. And ye are complete in him, which is the head of all principality and power."

Colossians 3:1-4: "If ye then be risen with Christ, seek those things which are above, where Christ sitteth on the right hand of God. Set your affection on things above, not on things on the earth. For ye are dead, and your life is hid with Christ in God. When Christ, who is our life, shall appear, then shall ye also appear with him in glory."

This identification with Christ is fully realized by commitment or dedication of one's life to the Lord (Rom. 12:1-2) to be used, as the Lord directs, in spreading the gospel of the grace of God (Acts 20:24). Christ's purpose for dying becomes the dedicated Christian's purpose for living. It includes denying self or crucifying self daily (Luke 9:23). It is exchanging the self-centered life for the Christ-centered life, and this results in the Christian's being filled with the Holy Spirit (Eph. 5:18). The evidence of the filling is the fruit of the Spirit being manifested in the Christian's life (Gal. 5:22-23).

A good discipleship program for the new convert after salvation should point out God's complete acceptance and how to appropriate identification with Christ using the verses listed above.

Charles Solomon gives details on the idea of identification with Christ as the cure for rejection in his books *The Handbook to Happiness*[1] and *The Ins and Outs of Rejection.*[2]

Godly, witnessing Christians will suffer rejection and persecution even as Paul did from his own countrymen and from the heathen. "Of the Jews five times received I forty stripes save one. Thrice was I beaten with rods, once was I stoned, thrice I suffered shipwreck, a night and a day I have been in the deep; in journeyings often, in perils of waters, in perils of robbers, in perils by mine own countrymen, in perils by the heathen, in perils in the city, in perils in the wilderness, in perils in the sea, in perils among false brethren" (II Cor. 11:24-26). Paul also suffered rejection from fellow Christians when Demas forsook him (II Tim. 4:10, 16-18) and when all forsook him (vs. 16). However, he knew that God stood with him (vs. 17). Peter, who also knew rejection and persecution, gives instruction on how to handle these situations (I Pet. 4:12-19). The Christian is to rejoice, for later he will "be glad also with exceeding joy" (vs. 13) and be happy because Christ is glorified (vs. 14). He is not to be ashamed but is to glorify God (vs. 16) and is to commit the keeping of his soul to God (vs. 19).

God wants Christians to find their acceptance and identity in Jesus Christ as part of His free gift of salvation (Gal. 2:20; Eph. 2:9-10; Col. 3:3). Acceptance should be based on God's unconditional love and His complete acceptance at the time a person receives Christ as his Savior. Only as one completely identifies with Christ and His crucifixion, burial, resurrection, and ascension on high can that person gain freedom from rejection feelings (Eph. 2:4-7). Being dead to self is the best way to maintain that freedom (Col. 3:3). Our real identity is based not on what we do or accomplish but on who we are in Christ as a result of God's grace (II Cor. 5:17).

Solutions:

1. Review the appropriate principles and Scriptures in this chapter.
2. Explain that salvation is the first step in curing the problem of rejection (Eph. 1:6-7).
3. Urge the counselee to confess any known sin.
4. Review with the counselee all the times he thinks he was rejected, pointing out that the problem was not so much what was done as it was the counselee's ungodly reactions to the incident or situation and the attitudes he has retained about it.
5. Emphasize that the counselee must completely forgive the parents or persons who he feels were, or are now, involved in the rejection.
6. Teach the counselee about identification with Christ (II Cor. 5:17; Gal. 2:20; Eph. 2:4-10; Phil. 3:7-10; Col. 1:27; 2:9-10; 3:1-4). This truth will become a reality to the counselee as he commits or dedicates his life in full surrender to Christ (Rom. 12:1-2). It is exchanging the self-centered life for the Christ-centered life.
7. Point out that rejection feelings are purely self-centered feelings, and the counselee needs to crucify self daily (Luke 9:23).
8. Have the counselee read I John every day for thirty days and each day underline a verse that has real meaning for him.
9. Get the counselee started on a program of reaching out to others with deeds of love, performing one deed every day.
10. Have the counselee make a tangible plan for witnessing and showing people how they can obtain eternal life, for this is the ultimate in loving people.

Case Study:

Rebecca, a forty-year-old Jewish woman, was referred to the counselor by a woman who had led her to the Lord a month before. Rebecca had been divorced for a year and felt that she should be reconciled with Paul, her former husband, now that she was a Christian. She had initiated the divorce, not because of immorality but because they were "incompatible": their marriage was a continual series of arguments. They were still having intimate relations about once a week. Rebecca said she was frigid but enjoyed the cuddling and tender affection that went with the intimate relations. She said that Paul was a good man and a good provider and he still loved her and wanted her back. He was a Gentile, a church-going Baptist who claimed to be a born-again Christian. She said she could not stand his desire to control her and make all the final decisions, especially about financial matters. She claimed that she still loved him but that he would always end any argument by saying mean, cutting things that put her down and made her feel unloved.

The counselor got Paul and Rebecca together for some counseling sessions. Paul verified everything Rebecca had said, with the exception of her claim that he made cutting, vicious comments. On the contrary, he maintained that she would goad him until he finally blew up. Paul said that his wife strongly resisted his family leadership because she did not respect her father and always compared him to her father. Rebecca admitted that she was full of bitterness against her father and always thought of and referred to him negatively. Her father was a Marine officer and was away from the family for long periods of time. When he returned home, he would give everyone presents, take the family out to eat, and spend money on them. He would then "whip the family into shape" with a series of corrective edicts. These episodes would last for about a week, and then the mother would take control of the family again. The father was a very disciplined man, somewhat of an inventor. Eventually, he would retire to his study to work on projects that he was developing and would ignore the three children. Since Rebecca was the oldest, she seemed to feel his rejection the most.

The counselor noticed that Rebecca was very contentious, as Paul had claimed. She argued with everything Paul said and would bait him with comments about his lack of love, understanding, and leadership. At one of the sessions, she even verbally attacked the counselor, questioning his qualifications and abilities. The counselor noticed her attempts to court anger and rejection from him and showed Paul how a Christian should biblically respond to her attacks.

Rebecca admitted to the counselor that she had felt rejected in school, where she was the only Jewish girl, and took a lot of taunting and teasing. At home the mother was a strict disciplinarian and a meticulous housekeeper but rarely showed any affection or interest in the children's activities. The mother did not work outside the home, and in her spare time she was absorbed in reading romantic novels and practicing her voice and piano lessons. When Rebecca was fifteen, her parents sent her to live with relatives so that she could attend a fine private school for two years. She felt that her parents just wanted to get rid of her because they did not understand her independent spirit.

Case Study Solution:

The counselor recognized a classic case of rejection with first- and second-stage feelings of self-pity, inferiority, and anger that had grown into bitterness, hatred, and revenge. Rebecca's main object of these feelings was her dad, but she had also transferred the feelings to her husband. The counselor explained to her why she felt rejected, including her Jewish heritage, her father's absence and lack of concern for his children, and her mother's emotional neglect of the children because of her absorption in herself and her own interests. He then had Rebecca list all the times she had perceived rejection and encouraged her to forgive and make an attempt to be reconciled to all the people involved. He explained what Jesus Christ had done for her at salvation from Ephesians 1:6-7 and the twenty benefits of salvation, listed in Chapter 17, Problem 18. He then taught Rebecca the Identification with Christ principle and encouraged her to dedicate her life to the Lord, a step that she was not willing to take at that time.

About this time, the couple was remarried. The counselor found out that they still were having arguments and not demonstrating love toward each other, so he assigned both Paul and Rebecca the reading of I John every day for thirty days. At the end of the second week of reading I John, Rebecca said that early one morning, while she was reading the fourth chapter, it dawned on her that Jesus was God. She began to cry and dedicated her life completely to the Lord. She cried for several hours and said it seemed she was being bathed in waves of God's love. She said it changed her whole attitude toward her husband and others, and she was finally reconciled to her father through a long letter and an extended phone call.

The change in her life was so apparent to her husband that he wanted what she had. He also dedicated his life to the Lord. Paul said that the subsequent change in his life was so significant that he wondered if he had been saved prior to that time. He also said that a side result of the change in Rebecca was that her frigidity disappeared. Their relationship had improved one hundred percent and, according to him, it was like a continual honeymoon. They opened their home to a neighborhood Bible study that their pastor taught, and they were instrumental in seeing some of their neighbors accept Christ, including one Jewish couple.

Chapter 15

Lying

"A bedrock of honesty is fundamental to any society that expects to flourish. People cannot happily and sanely live together in a climate of distrust." This quote, which appeared in a national news magazine, depicts honesty and the trust it engenders as the glue which holds together any social unit or organization. Christians must have the virtue of honesty as a part of their Christian character if they expect to prosper and enjoy the favor of God.

All men have a tendency to lie occasionally, and this sin must be confessed. Oliver Wendell Holmes said, "Sin has many tools, but a lie is the handle that fits them all." The habit of lying is especially devastating to a life because it distorts reality and moves the person into a fantasy world of his own making. God is the God of truth, and lying is an offense against the very nature of God. Since lying can easily be done in any situation without immediate detection, it can become a very sinful habit that must be broken. This habit damages one's character and can easily become a lifestyle, affecting every action and situation. Lying is the beginning of a reprobate mind (Rom. 1:28), or what the world calls sociopathic behavior.

Problem #12: Lying

Definition:

Lying is deliberately distorting reality to deceive or mislead others by falsifying or concealing information.

Scripture:

Exodus 20:1-17; Numbers 32:23; Joshua 7:1-13; Psalm 5:6; Proverbs 6:16-17, 19; 10:18; 12:22; 13:5; 19:9; Ephesians 4:25; examples: Adam's distorting the truth to God (Gen. 3:12), Saul's lying to Samuel (I Sam. 15:13-15), Ananias and Sapphira's lying to the church (Acts 5:1-10)

Information and Principles:

As the sixth commandment prohibits killing except for three general reasons (capital punishment, self-defense, or national defensive war), so the ninth commandment prohibits lying with one possible exception: in a moral dilemma the biblical exception of protecting oneself or others from unjust aggressors would supersede the law of lying. The main scriptural examples of this exception are as follows.

1. The Hebrew midwives lied to Pharaoh by telling him that they could not kill the boys who were born too fast (Exod. 1:15-20).

2. Elijah deceived the army of Syria that sought to capture and kill him by leading them, with the help of God, into the hands of the king of Israel (II Kings 6:8-23).

3. Rahab is twice commended in the New Testament for her faith (Heb. 11:31 and James 2:25). She deceived the king's representatives by hiding the Israelite spies and saying that she did not know where they were (Josh. 2:1-24).

4. Joshua deceived the city of Ai by means of an ambush (Josh. 8:3-29).

5. Samuel, in order to save his own life, was instructed by God Himself to mislead others by creating the false impression that he was only offering sacrifices when in fact he was anointing the king-elect of Israel (I Sam. 16:1-5).

6. Jael was praised as "blessed above women" after she deceptively promised to protect Sisera, the wicked tyrant, and then killed him by driving a tent peg through his skull (Judges 4–5).

7. Michal, David's wife, substituted a fake body in his bed and lied after David had fled for his life from Saul's henchmen (I Sam. 19:12-17).

8. David himself feigned insanity to deceive the king of Gath (I Sam. 21:10-15; 22:1).

9. Jeremiah was commanded by King Zedekiah to lie so that Jeremiah would not die (Jer. 38:24-28).

A person is not guilty of lying under these circumstances:

1. He unintentionally makes a mistake in presenting facts.

2. An authority figure such as an administrator, teacher, or parent states he is going to do a certain thing and intends to do it; however, changing circumstances do not permit him to do what he said he would do or he completely changes plans. That appears to the followers as a lie. Authority figures need to explain to their followers the reason for the change in a course of action or the followers lose confidence in the authority.

3. He engages in games or situations in which deceit is expected and accepted, such as fake moves in sports, surprises, or rhetorical devices.

4. He tries to protect himself or others from unjust aggressors.

Daniel Reid, president of Reid Psychological Systems, a Chicago-based lie detector testing company, devised what he called "integrity tests." His tests, given nationwide, indicate that 75 percent of the people pass the tests; he classified them as honest Americans. Reid identified the one-fourth who failed the integrity tests as being self-centered and as needing self-gratification. This group included those who were addicts, alcoholics, phobics, and unstable personalities.

There are three general categories of lying.

1. **Lies to cause harm to others**—These kinds of lies are deliberate attempts to discredit someone or to destroy his reputation. Especially feared are lies that will mislead a person into doing something stupid or cause financial loss.

2. **Lies to protect others**—well-intended deception. Most social lies, called "white lies," such as flattery or protecting someone's feelings, fall into this category.

3. **Lies in the interest of the liar**—This is the most common category of lying. The types of lies in this category are usually caused by guilt or greed. The following are types of lies told in the interest of the liar.

a. The most common type in this category is the defensive lie. Faced with the possibility of punishment, of being put on the spot, of being found out, or of failure, a person will lie to get out of that situation.

b. People, to look good in other people's eyes, will exaggerate their exploits or abilities to make themselves look good.

c. Social lies are used to get one out of an awkward social situation such as, "I can't go tomorrow night because I have another appointment."

d. There is the distortion lie, which twists facts out of their true meaning or proportion. It is falsified reproduction.

e. Another type of lie is the omission lie in which certain facts are purposefully omitted.

f. A common lie in business is the profitable lie. In order to make the sale or swing the deal their way, some salesmen will say or do almost anything, especially if a big commission is involved.

Some perceived advantage prompts most lying. If there are no benefits in telling a lie, most people will not bother to make one up.

There are certain general principles that must be considered when dealing with the problem and root cause of lying.

God is truth (Ps. 31:5), and Jesus Christ is the Lord and revelation of truth (John 14:6; Deut. 32:4; Exod. 34:6), and the Holy Spirit is the spirit of truth (John 14:16-17). Jesus said in John 14:6, "I am the way, the truth, and the life: no man cometh unto the Father, but by me." In John 8:32 He said, "Ye shall know the truth, and the truth shall make you free." Interestingly, in the book of John, Jesus is quoted twenty-nine times as saying "I tell you the truth." Jesus Christ is identified as the revelation of truth (John 1:14).

The Devil is the author and father of lies. The source of lies is given in John 8:44: "Ye are of your father the devil, and the lusts of your father ye will do. He was a murderer from the beginning, and abode not in the truth, because there is no truth in him. When he speaketh a lie, he speaketh of his own: for he is a liar, and the father of it." He lied to Eve in the Garden of Eden and motivated her to start the sin cycle on earth.

Lying shows hatred toward God and will be punished (Prov. 14:2; Rev. 2:18). Lying is a sin and brings God's judgment.

Christians must always put away lying and "speak the truth in love" (Eph. 4:15, 25). The qualifying phrase "in love" indicates that one should not always blurt out the bold truth. Many times silence is the best course of action in a situation. The Scripture enjoins in Matthew 5:37 to "let your communication be, Yea, yea; Nay, nay." One must obey this command if he is going to put away lying (Eph. 4:25). Jesus said that He came into the world to "bear witness unto the truth" (John 18:37). If a person belongs to Christ, he will hear His voice and speak the truth.

Solutions:

1. Review the appropriate Scriptures and principles about lying and liars.
2. Review the person's childhood and have him recount what might have started his lying—what were the reasons that he lied the first time. Those same reasons are operating today in his life and keep his habit continuing.
3. Go through the steps of breaking a habit.
4. Explain that there should be full repentance, asking forgiveness for this horrible sin.
5. Every time he lies, tell him to correct himself immediately to the person to whom he told the lie, no matter how embarrassing it is.
6. Have him fine himself one dollar or even five dollars for every lie. The money is to be donated to missions.
7. Offer to give him a hypothetical reward of $10,000 if he can go one month without telling a single lie. In other words, set a real goal for victory to get out of the habit.

Case Study:

Monica, a forty-year-old woman, came to the counselor about her husband's sinful habit of lying. She said that before they were married, the one thing that had attracted her to Abe was that he used to tell such interesting stories about his life. After she was married, she found that his stories, although they had a grain of truth to them, were highly embellished and 90 percent fiction. She said that in everyday conversation, he said those things that people wanted to hear, whether they were true or not. She said she thought it was a result of his job as a salesman and businessman in an auto business. She knew he lied to customers, especially women, who he said were "naive suckers and would believe anything you told them." She said that in social situations he gave an embellished account of any travel experience that they had shared and she had to sit and listen to his lies. He told people he would do favors for them, and they knew it was just talk and overlooked it because he was a businessman. He had become a regular con man, cheating people out of money, all in the name of good business. However, he did help people in need with money and used cars, and he was a deacon in their church and did some lay preaching.

The wife agreed to tell Abe what she had told the counselor and to see if he would come in for counseling. Abe made an appointment with the counselor and showed up for three sessions with his wife. The counselor asked about his background, trying to find out when the lies started. He said it started very early, around five years of age, when he lied to his parents about his frequent escapades in the neighborhood. His parents always believed him and would take his side, claiming their boy was innocent of the broken windows, damaged property, and bullying activities with other children. He lied to teachers about homework and tests and cheated his way all through school. He said that even in elementary school, he would make his stories so interesting by lying that everyone would believe them. When he got into business as a salesman, he found that lying worked to his advantage, and he would get better commissions. He would tell the customers anything to make the sale. He said that as long as it did not hurt anyone, he did not feel bad about lying.

Case Study Solution:

The counselor dealt with Abe about his sin by taking him to a number of verses that showed what God thought about lying. He then discussed Romans 6:11-13 and how to overcome this sinful habit. The counselor suggested that if Abe meant business about getting rid of his sin, he would go forward at the invitation Sunday morning. He would admit his sin to the pastor and ask the church to pray for him that the Lord would help him to conquer the sinful habit. Abe was also to correct lies in his conversation immediately after he told them by telling the listener that it was a lie and by giving the correct version. The counselor also suggested that he enlist his wife as an ally in overcoming this sin: in the future she would list all the times she caught him in a lie and make him pay a one-dollar penalty to a fund that they would use for benevolent purposes.

The counselor suggested that in Abe's desire to gain attention and entertain people with interesting stories, he should collect funny stories like Jerry Clower tells and preface them with a statement such as, "I don't know whether this is true or not, but . . . ," and then go on to tell his story. He agreed to follow these steps, and six months later, he and his wife both said that he had overcome the sin. He said that at first, his sales in the business went down considerably, but he found that customers eventually appreciated his honesty, and his sales soon went up again.

Problem #13: A Reprobate Mind (sociopathic and strange-woman behavior)

Definition:

A mind with a seared conscience, which turns God's truth into a lie, becomes receptive to any type of sin and motivates the person to abandon himself to wickedness. A woman with a reprobate mind may exhibit "strange woman" behavior, i.e., using lying, deceit, and her sexual favors to exploit naive men for personal gain (Prov. 6–7).

Scripture:

Romans 1:21-32; Proverbs 2:16-17; 5:3-6; 6:24-25; 7:10-21; 9:13-18

Information and Principles:

This behavior is described in Romans 1:21-32. The key verse in this passage is verse 25: "Who changed the truth of God into a lie." Lying is the prevailing characteristic of persons with the reprobate mind. As they go this downward path, God's Word says that they do not like to retain God in their knowledge; therefore, God gives them over to a reprobate mind, and they do all of the things which are not convenient (vs. 28). In verses 29-31, they seem to have no conscience about these sins. They know they are doing wrong, but in verse 32 they seem to have pleasure in these wrong-doings. The Scripture says that this kind of person is without understanding. They do not seem to know how society works or how relationships among people operate. They also are without natural affection for their loved ones or for people in general. They are filthy and calloused and seem to have no loyalty to others.

Their lifestyle of lying is usually deeply rooted in their child-hood and usually results from a complete lack of moral training. They may come from homes where there has been either physical, sexual, or verbal abuse. Sometimes divorce in the home produces this kind of child, but the primary source is a home without a father and/or mother to lead, guide, train, and give the child the security and values that will stabilize his life. These characteristics are the child's way of coping with life. Other characteristics of this type of person are self-centeredness and immaturity. He is likable and even charming with few close personal relationships and has traits that make it easy for him to manipulate (con) people. He constantly seeks approval and affirmation. He has difficulty with intimate relationships. He is an impulsive person who wants instant gratifi-cation, which makes him susceptible to drugs (especially alcohol) and sex addiction. For the reprobate-minded person, or the "con man" and the "strange woman," other than a genuine conversion, there is little hope for a cure.

There is a general principle that applies to this problem: **repro-bate-minded (sociopathic) people are usually men.** Their char-acteristics are described in Romans 1:28-32. This behavior can go to the extreme and result in serial killers, Mafia hit men, or pimps.

"Strange woman" behavior is described in Proverbs 2:16-17; 5:3-6; 6:24-25; 7:10-21; 9:13-18. The strange woman has no char-acter, for her ways are movable (Prov. 5:6). She is manipulative (Prov. 2:16; 5:3, 7). She is known as "the other woman" in most adultery cases.

Solutions:

1. Go over the appropriate Scriptures.
2. Go over the plan of salvation, stressing the Ten Command-ments and the holiness of God. A weekly discipleship pro-gram is necessary after conversion.

3. Be ready to give help, counsel, and support to close associates affected by the person, usually a husband or wife.
4. Treat any addiction (Chapter 18) that may accompany the problem.

Case Study:

Joe, a church member, local politician, and businessman who had married into money, came to the counselor after his wife threatened him with divorce if he did not get his life straightened out. The incident that precipitated the blowup occurred when the wife came home early from her semiannual visit to her mother (after being tipped off by a neighbor) and found Joe, half-drunk, with a girlfriend living in their home while his wife was gone. Joe was very reluctant to talk to the counselor at first but finally opened up and revealed a long history of corruption, going back to junior high school.

He had done many wicked things in junior high and high school, including taking a girl with three other boys up to a cabin in the mountains for a weekend, getting her drunk at gunpoint, and having her do all kinds of debased things. Whenever she objected to anything they wanted, they threatened her again with the gun. The girl did not tell her parents because she had told them she was going to a girlfriend's house over the weekend. The girlfriend had planned to go with her but had backed out at the last moment.

He had started drinking in high school. After one party, he and two other sixteen-year-old boys had gotten a fifteen-year-old girl pregnant; but, since no one knew who the father was, nothing had been done about it. He finally admitted to the counselor that his having a girlfriend in had not happened just once as he had told his wife but had happened with different women every time his wife had gone to see her mother.

Before his present business, he had been in telemarketing, selling such things as oil stocks and land deals. He liked that kind of work, he said, because, with greed as their motive, people would believe anything; consequently, he always had a high percentage of sales.

He supposedly had been saved after he had graduated from high school, was a regular church attender, and took an active part in the men's sports fellowship at the church. In the middle of one counseling session, he lamented that his wife was not a good Christian because she would not forgive him, and he began to quote Scriptures on forgiveness. The counselor confronted him with the idea that he talked rather piously considering the freewheeling life that he had been living as a politician and businessman. His sorrow at his wife's reaction did not match the callous actions that he had recounted from his past.

Case Study Solution:

The counselor went through the Ten Commandments with him and the Scriptures on fornication, adultery, and lying, since he had been living a lie. Every corrupt thing that he had done since he had supposedly been saved was inconsistent with his front at church and at home as a Christian family man. The counselor stressed to him that his double life indicated that he was the "double-minded man" of James 1, was probably not saved, and was headed for hell. The counselor had him read the first chapter of Romans as well as verses on the judgment of God. In spite of these warnings, Joe left the counselor's office cocky and self-assured.

Five months later he was in a serious car wreck, which put him in the hospital for four months. Suddenly, Joe became willing to talk about his salvation. He realized he had not experienced the grace of God in his life and was ready to accept Christ. The pastor met with him for discipling once a week for two to three months after his salvation, and his wife, who had separated from him, finally forgave him and came back to him after he began to show the fruit of his salvation.

Chapter 16

Imagination and Fantasy

Everyone has an imagination, which can be either God-directed or Devil-directed. Imagination is the creation of mental images not present to the senses in reality. Fantasy is combining these images into a fictitious pattern. Imagination that is God-directed is goal-directed to glorify God and is useful in planning the future and in developing creative ideas. Creativity is imagination in action. Creativity that honors God is guided and disciplined by God's standard of form, beauty, contrast, repetition, tension and relaxation, order, and moral restraint. This kind of creativity is always in touch with God's reality and has as its goal "proving what is acceptable unto the Lord" (Eph. 5:10) and approving "things that are excellent" (Phil. 1:9-10). These are the criteria by which all creative works should be judged, whether art, drama, literature, or music. The modern generation has lost sight of these criteria because it does not desire to glorify God. Creative fantasy can also be used to plan ahead steps, procedures, or techniques for handling emergencies, resisting temptation, or reacting in unfamiliar situations.

Imagination that is Devil-directed creates fantasies that elevate man's base desires to legitimacy and can lead into all kinds of sin and corruption and eventually wreck a life. Devil-directed fantasizing is a root cause for many problems. All Christians, because of the flesh, have a tendency to use their imaginations to create evil fantasies. They conjure up pleasurable experiences by imagining situations that include all kinds of evil and companions of their own choosing. Men tend to fantasize about sex and aggression, which lead to lust and bitterness. Women tend to entertain romantic and rejection fantasies, which often result in discontentment and self-pity. Because no one else knows of this imaginative life, a person can continue his corrupt imagination without detection or without destroying the reputation that he enjoys. The only difficulty is that sooner or later, what one thinks about is going to come out as action. The Scripture says, "As [a man] thinketh in his heart, so is he" (Prov. 23:7). "Out of it [the heart] are the issues of life" (Prov. 4:23; Matt. 12:34-35; 15:19). The development of sin first starts with a thought, and then "every man is tempted when he is drawn away of his own lusts and enticed. Then when lust has conceived it brings forth sin; and sin, when it is finished, brings forth death" (James 1:14-15). The thought life is the source from which actions flow. Many people have used the acrostic HALT to avoid Devil-directed imagination, and they do not allow themselves to get too *h*ungry, *a*ngry, *l*onely, or *t*ired. When they are in these states, they realize they are very vulnerable to the wiles of the Devil and subject to temptation.

A Spirit-filled thought life is essential to a life of holiness that glorifies God in this corrupt, sin-cursed world. A Christian can have such a thought life only by "casting down imaginations, and every high thing that exalteth itself against the knowledge of God, and bringing into captivity every thought to the obedience of Christ" (II Cor. 10:5) and by directing his thinking toward godly thoughts (Phil. 4:8). If one's thought life is disciplined and controlled, his behavior will be disciplined and controlled.

Problem #14: Filthy Dreamers— Strange Women

Definition:

Filthy dreamers, called by the world *hysterical* (or, more recently, *histrionic*) *personalities,* use daydreaming and a vivid fantasy life to receive the love and attention they so desire.[1] They exaggerate and confuse fact with fantasy and, after a while, actually believe that things happen the way they imagined.

Scripture:

Psalms 34:1-3; 107:8; 119:164; 133; Proverbs 2:16-17; 4:23; 5:3, 6, 23; 6:24-25; 7:5, 10-21, 26; 9:13; 23:7; Matthew 12:34-35;

15:19; Romans 6:16; II Corinthians 10:5; Philippians 4:8; II Timothy 4:3-4; II Peter 3:6; Jude 8-19

Information and Principles:

In Jude the people who go the direction of Devil-directed fantasy are called "filthy dreamers" who despise righteous people in authority (vs. 8). They "speak evil of those things which they know not: but what they know naturally, as brute beasts, in those things they corrupt themselves" (vs. 10). They are greedy (vs. 11), unstable, and compared to clouds without waters, raging waves, and wandering stars (vv. 12-13). They are murmurers and complainers but very good talkers, especially to those who are rich or in high positions (vs. 16). They are sensual and walk after their ungodly lusts (vv. 18-19). They are further described in II Timothy 4:3-4, 10 as those who will not endure sound doctrine and who follow teachers with itching ears (vs. 3), turn from truth to fables (vs. 4), and love the present world (vs. 10). Women who go the direction of Devil-directed fantasy are also described in II Timothy 3:6 as susceptible to men of reprobate minds, who "creep into houses, and lead captive silly women laden with sins, led away with divers lusts."

Usually the "filthy-dreamer" personality has a longstanding bitterness toward the opposite-sex parent and an anger or hatred toward the opposite sex, even though they crave their attention. Men exhibit their hatred toward women by being controlling and even abusive (see Chapter 19), and their fantasies often lead to a reprobate mind (mentioned in Chapter 15). Women, because they tend to be more romantic and more often operate on a feeling level, have a tendency to go the direction of a "strange woman" as described in Proverbs. This type of woman has distinctive characteristics.

- She lies and is manipulative. She "flattereth with her words" (Prov. 2:16); her lips "drop as an honeycomb, and her mouth is smoother than oil" (5:3). God's Word promises "to keep thee from the evil woman, from the flattery of the tongue of a strange [evil] woman" (6:24); "from the stranger which flattereth with her words" (7:5); for "with her much fair speech she caused [the young man] to yield, with the flattering of her lips, she forced him" (7:21).

- She has no values or character. She forsakes the teaching of her youth and "forgetteth the covenant of her God" (2:17). "Her ways are movable" and she does not "ponder the path of life" (5:6).
- She is usually beautiful and knows how to use that beauty in a seductive manner. "Lust not after her beauty in thine heart; neither let her take thee with her eyelids" (6:25).
- She is seductive in her dress and actions, and she craves men's attention (7:10-21).
- She is dramatic, rebellious against authority, and, if married, rebellious against her husband (7:11).
- She basically hates men and desires their downfall, especially men of high position "for she hath cast down many wounded; yea, many strong men have been slain by her" (7:26).
- Although appearing worldly-wise, she is naive. "A foolish woman is clamorous: she is simple, and knoweth nothing" (9:13).

The counselor must be careful when counseling this type of person. She, through her actions and talk, is exciting and flattering and wants emotional and physical contact. The counselor should not be distracted or involved with this seductive behavior. He should be objective and should avoid touching her or doing anything that would suggest that he is responding to her sexual overtures or advances. If the counselor does respond, the person may use that to accuse him later and to bring about his downfall. Many a pastor, counselor, or youth worker has gotten himself into a difficult situation or has compromised his testimony and character by being unaware of this type of personality. He may not have responded by being immoral, but he may have responded by being indiscreet, by being alone with her, or by touching or hugging her in sympathy. The strange woman may use these indiscretions effectively to build a case against the Christian worker if she ever feels rejected by him.

The counselor can detect this type of woman because she usually feels inferior and reveals it by making devaluating remarks about herself, by dramatizing, by being helpless and dependent, and by looking for protective love. She is not looking for a lover but rather for a protective father.

"Filthy dreamer" personalities lack order in their lives and have no respect for order in other peoples' lives. They cannot put things off nor plan very well for tomorrow. They will not stick to a counseling schedule and will show up for appointments at the most inopportune times, demanding immediate attention. They try to interject themselves into the personal life of the counselor to get the love and attention of the father image they did not have in childhood. The counselor must not give in to these demands for attention because the demands will only increase. Certain rules, such as never calling the counselor at home and seeing the counselor only once a week for scheduled appointments, are necessary if this type of personality is to be helped. The presentation of the self as a dependent child needing protection is at the core of the "filthy dreamer" personality style.

There are several general principles that apply to this problem of Devil-directed imagination.

The fantasy life is enhanced by the stimulation that one receives from the environment. That is why the Scripture says in Psalm 101:3, "I will set no wicked thing before mine eyes. I hate the work of them that turn aside." Television, books, magazines, radio, music, newspapers, and real-life observations all contribute to one's fantasy life.

A fantasy life begins in early childhood and, in some children, can be a large part of their waking lives because of their desire to escape from reality. The reasons for this desire for escape may be (1) boredom or lack of a stimulating environment; (2) an environment that is too harsh or unpleasant, such as one that involves physical or sexual abuse; (3) a lack of goals and successes in reaching goals; (4) a flair for the dramatic; (5) creativity that is undirected and/or squelched; or (6) a pressure-filled life. Children should be encouraged to develop their imaginations, but they must be properly directed toward a godly standard of creativity; for the flesh can corrupt their imaginations and lead them into sin.

Parents must control the stimulation that their children receive. Parents should set up a quality reading program and provide good books and magazines. (See the Bob Jones University Press publication entitled *Best Books*.) A rich, fertile ground for a God-directed imagination is also provided by the parents' drastically curtailing or eliminating commercial television, replacing it with educational programs and videos, promoting good music in the home, censoring bad music, and creating rich learning experiences every day. Of importance also is a Christian education, including good training in the preschool years as well as home schooling or education in a Christian school during the school years up through college.

A regular program of Bible-reading and memorization establishes a superior foundation for a God-directed imagination and fantasy life (Ps. 119:11, 37). Establishing this as a habit early in life gives stability and peace and undergirds strong character.

Hypocrisy in a Christian parent or authority figure tends to produce in children or teens a fantasy life that is Devil-directed. The child or teen tends to reject the good that the parent or authority figure is teaching and gets in the habit of fantasizing about the alternate lifestyle that the parents seem to desire and follow. If Christianity does not seem to be of importance and value and to bring happiness to the adult, the child starts looking for something else.

Fantasy and denial are often substituted for reality when the person experiences an overwhelming traumatic situation. Seeing the violent death of a loved one or being in extremely abusive situations can cause a person to deny the situation in his mind. The next step is substituting a fantasy and imagining himself to be in circumstances in which the situation never occurs or where he feels happy and safe. Some people even take on separate identities in their imaginations, and this could lead to assuming two different personalities, which have separate identities.

In traumatic and abusive situations, denial and forgetting is very common. "In a recent study of 450 adults who'd been sexually abused in childhood, nearly 60 percent had at some point kept themselves from remembering the assaults. According to the study's author, the earlier the abuse, and the more violent it is, the more likely it is to result in massive forgetting."[2] According to Lenore Terr, a childhood trauma expert at the University of California at San Francisco, abused children may start counting or repeating phrases obsessively to keep the frightening thoughts at bay. They assume that they will die (possibly be murdered) before they grow up and may attempt suicide in their teenage years.[3] Usually, according to Terr, the recollections of the abuse begin to occur in the person's twenties, and they are almost always accurate. The counselor can usually tell the difference between a fantasy and a true memory because a true memory will be richly detailed, including even the sounds that occurred during the assault or traumatic situation. The counselor should accept the story as true in order to help the counselee but not to build a case against the abuser, especially if the abuse happened a long time before the counseling session. The counselor must realize that any story is subject to memory lapses or fantasy and could be colored by the emotional content of the situation or a desire for revenge.

Solutions:

1. Review the appropriate Scripture and principles with the counselee.

2. Teach the counselee these steps of a controlled thought life: (a) Confess and forsake all known sin (Prov. 28:13); (b) Read and obey the Bible (Ps. 119:15-18); (c) Eliminate negative, Devil thoughts (II Cor. 10:5); (d) Substitute godly thoughts (Phil. 4:8); (e) Order the environment to eliminate corrupt stimulation, perhaps cutting out television entirely and changing reading habits, music standards, friends, and the places one frequents (Rom. 13:14).

3. Have the counselee make a list of good things that have happened or that he can plan and do. Then, when the bad thoughts come, he can pull out his list and have some definite things to praise the Lord for, to think about, or to do. Negative fantasy thinking will return if not replaced with positive, God-directed thinking, such as thinking about Jesus Christ, His character, or His works. The Bible gives right direction for thinking: "But we all, with open face beholding as in a glass the glory of the Lord, are changed into the same image from glory to glory, even as by the Spirit of the Lord" (II Cor. 3:18). A Spirit-filled imagination sees even in nature and natural things a vision of spiritual, eternal things.

4. Deal with the root of bitterness toward the parents (usually the opposite-sex parent) or siblings, which probably started in childhood or the early teen years. Biblical steps of reconciliation must be instituted (Matt. 5:23-24; 18:15-17; Eph. 4:30-32).

5. Start the counselee on a regular daily program of Bible-reading, study, and memorization.
6. Have the counselee work toward transformation (Rom. 12:2) by having him take charge of his mind (I Pet. 1:13) and submit to the sanctifying power of the Holy Spirit (I Pet. 1:2).
7. Have the counselee start a daily praise program (Ps. 34:1-3; 107:8; 119:164).

Case Study:

Marian and Fred, a married couple with no children, came to see the counselor when they were on the verge of divorce after four years of marriage. She had committed adultery with two different men. The first time, six months after their wedding, Fred had forgiven her; the second time he thought she was hopeless, and, unless she could be cured of this infidelity, he did not want to go on with the marriage. She immediately countered with the accusation that she had caught him looking at video and cable TV pornography. In addition, because she had caught him looking at numerous pretty women that passed, she claimed that he had committed adultery himself a number of times, according to Matthew 5:28. She said that he was a lousy lover because they made love only about once a week, and, in the last three and a half years, he had not given her any real love and affection. According to her, all he was interested in was television and his job as an engineer. After supper he would start watching HBO, Showtime, or the sports channel until one or two o'clock in the morning. She explained that she went to bed every night at 10:30 because she needed eight hours of sleep in order to feel fresh on her job as the chief loan officer at a bank.

At this point, Fred said, "Tell the counselor what you told me six months after we were married." She, an only child from a middle-class, church-going family, then recounted a tale of corruption, which went back to masturbation before five years of age and incest with her father. The incest began with backrubs when she was eight years old and progressed at her urging to intercourse at eleven. (She had matured at ten.)

The mother caught them in the act of intercourse when Marian was twelve and threatened the husband that if it ever happened again, she would turn him in to the police. From then on, it happened only when the mother was away from the home at work. Marian remembered that even when she was a little girl, she and her mother were always in conflict, which increased during her teens. She said her mother's jealousy of her was the problem.

By the age of fifteen, Marian had started dating and turned against her father because he was too jealous and overprotective. He had started picking her up after school every day and would be upset if he saw her talking to a boy. She was in a Christian high school and having intimate relations with two football players that she was dating. When she walked across the stage to graduate, she was pregnant, and three days later she had an abortion without her parents' knowledge.

Marian went to a Christian college and worked at a bank in the summer, during which time she had a succession of affairs with older married men, including the bank president. The college she attended was very strict, and nothing went on during the school year. She met her husband in her senior year, and they were married upon graduation. He thought she was a pure girl and did not find out about her escapades until six months after the wedding. He admitted he lost interest in her and turned bitter after he caught her in the first affair.

She said that she would like to go back to church, but her husband would not let her. The husband said that he would not let her go back to the church that they had been attending because she had admitted to him that she was in love with the preacher. The preacher was innocent in the matter, but she thought every time the preacher looked at her or said certain things, even from the pulpit, he was making overtures to her. She had tried to be alone with the preacher numerous times by offering to take him to the airport or baby-sitting his children, and she had made a pest of herself to him by calling him frequently about inconsequential matters.

Case Study Solution:

The counselor first dealt with the husband about his bitterness toward his wife and the fact that he had not really forgiven her for her life before their marriage or for the first affair. The counselor also confronted Fred with the fact that he had not shown Marian the love and affection she was seeking in her marriage. She had stated that she liked to be cuddled every night; her sex demands, which Fred feared he could not meet, were a way of getting the tender love and affection she desired. The counselor suggested that Fred spend time every night cuddling her and relaxing her with means other than intercourse that Marian suggested. The counselor explained that TV pornography caused adultery in the mind, and they both agreed to give up all TV with the exception of five programs on educational TV that they both enjoyed.

The counselor then dealt with Marian by explaining that she had been in competition with her mother for the love and affection of her father and found that sex was the ideal weapon. She had repeated this pattern in her affairs, which were always with older married men. He took her through the Ten Commandments and Proverbs, chapters 5 through 7 and 9 which pertain to the strange woman. He also went through I Thessalonians 4:1-8 and explained to her the body-temple principle of I Corinthians 6:14-18. The counselor also discussed the danger of her bringing a disease into the marriage, including herpes and AIDS. He finished with the idea of her repenting of her sin and letting Christ have complete control of her life.

Marian agreed to start going to another good church on the other side of town with her husband and said she would have to think about the future direction of her life. She agreed to read everyday the Scriptures that the counselor had shown her.

Two months later, she was attending a revival meeting and "broke out crying during the invitation and ran down the aisle and repented of [her] sins and got saved," as she stated. She asked her mother for forgiveness and was reconciled to her. She forgave her father for leading her into corruption, and she asked for and received forgiveness from him for tempting him. Her life changed drastically after that; and, with the changes the husband had made, their marriage was restored; and they both became zealous workers in their new church.

Chapter 17

Doubt—Spirit of Fear

Doubt, a problem common to all Christians, is the opposite of faith. Doubt takes the Christian away from God, and faith brings him closer to God. A basic root cause of fear-related problems is doubt. Doubt creates a spirit of fear, which becomes more intense the further a person gets from God. Jesus Christ had no doubt or fear because He had no sin and had perfect love.

Every person, early in life, is given the choice of believing in or rejecting God. God reveals Himself to man in nature (Rom. 1:19-20; Ps. 19:1-3), in conscience (Rom. 2:1-3, 14-15), and through His Word (Ps. 119:89). Most men tend to reject God and His wonderful works (Rom. 1:21), and in their intellect they bring God down to a human level (vv. 22-23). God honors those who recognize Him in faith (Heb. 11). After recounting the faith exploits of the Old Testament saints in the first fifteen verses of Hebrews 11, the Scripture says in verse 16 that "God is not ashamed to be called their God: for He hath prepared for them a city." He gives up on people who continually reject Him and turns them over to their sin (Rom. 1:24). For the people who believe in and seek God and follow the faith way, He sets about to bless them and give them His eternal salvation (I Cor. 2:8, 10; Jer. 29:11-13).

Problem #15: Doubt

Definition:
Doubt is rejecting God as He reveals Himself to man.

Scripture:
Romans 1:18-32; Hebrews 11:1-46; James 1:6-8

Information and Principles:
There are several general principles that apply to doubt.

Because of God's love for man, He chooses to get the gospel to those who seek and believe in Him (Matt. 7:7-8; John 4:23). When a person is eventually presented with the gospel, he can either accept it or reject it. If he accepts it, he will have eternal life; but if he doubts and rejects God's plan of salvation, he will end up as any unbeliever under God's eternal judgment.

At the root of every doubt is a sin. When people doubt God, their doubt is a result of their sin. In Deuteronomy 28, God told the Israelites that because of their sin (vv. 45 and 47), they would have extreme doubt and fear (vv. 65-67). Every believer, because of the flesh, has a tendency to rationalize, excuse, and dismiss sin in his life. He must always be willing to ask God to search his heart and thoughts (Ps. 139:23-24), repent, and ask forgiveness (I John 1:9).

The doubt of some Christians may stem from their rejection of the Lord's conviction about dedication of their lives (Rom. 12:1). If a person does not dedicate his life at the time of salvation, the Lord will deal with him about the matter within a short time after salvation. God desires that every born-again Christian be a disciple of Christ, and Jesus said that no one could be His disciple unless there was complete dedication (Luke 14:26-27).

A dedication decision is important and should follow very close to the salvation decision. A few people make this decision at salvation, but most Christians make it a short time afterward. God very quickly convicts a born-again Christian of the necessity of presenting his body as a living sacrifice that is holy and acceptable to Him (Rom. 12:1-2). Dedication is a decision to commit one's life completely, unreservedly to the Lord. From this time on, the Christian decides to do everything to the glory of God (I Cor. 10:31). He decides to use his life in advancing God's kingdom by getting the gospel to every person. Dedication is a lifelong decision of complete commitment to the cause of Christ.

Doubt brings a spirit of fear and results in many fear-related problems (I John 4:18). Doubt blocks the manifestation of God's love in one's life and thereby creates fear. But God's love is stronger than fear, and perfect love drives out fear. Love is perfected in one's life by faith and negated by doubt (Gal. 5:6).

Doubt causes a double-mindedness which results in instability (James 1:6-8). Goal-directed action results from definite decisions. Doubt causes indecisiveness, which results in confusion and purposeless action. Doubters tend to be unstable in all areas of life.

Trusting God brings freedom from fear (Isa. 12:2; Ps. 56:3-4), brings peace (Isa. 26:3), and brings direction and guidance for life (Prov. 3:5-6).

Solutions:

1. Review the appropriate Scriptures and principles on doubt in this section.
2. Urge the counselee to confess to God any known sin.
3. Help the counselee to recognize that doubt is the root cause of most fears.
4. To increase the counselee's faith, have him read Hebrews 11 every day for thirty days. Instruct him to read once a week in the Old Testament chapters connected to four of the outstanding men of faith mentioned in Hebrews 11.
5. Have the counselee memorize some of the promises of God, such as I Samuel 17:47; Ephesians 3:20; Philippians 4:19; and II Timothy 1:7.
6. Have the counselee trust God in a particular life situation and pray with him about it until God works it out.

Case Study:

Dick came to the counselor with all kinds of doubts about God and religion. He was brought up in a Christian home and had gone to a Christian school from kindergarten through the twelfth grade, but now, as a freshman in a state school, he had begun to doubt everything he had learned. He was a straight-A student and an avid reader. He said that as a freshman in high school, he had read Aldous

Huxley's *Brave New World* and *Walden II* by B. F. Skinner and that these two books had prompted some serious doubts. When asked about his devotional life, he said he had read the Bible through in the seventh grade and had not read it since, except for assignments in high school Bible classes. He said that he quit praying in the ninth grade because he could not see that his prayers were ever answered. He had supposedly been saved at five years of age. He said that recently he had been having dreams of hell, which disturbed him. One of Dick's friends had died recently in an auto wreck, and Dick had been thinking a lot about eternity, and this was why he had come to the counselor.

Case Study Solution:

The counselor took Dick through the first chapter of Romans and showed him that doubt is the beginning of a corrupt lifestyle. Dick admitted that in junior high and high school he had done some wicked things but did not elaborate on them. The counselor, sensing that he was not saved, went through many salvation verses. He then discussed the true meaning of faith and had Dick read Hebrews 11 and I John every day for a month. Dick was to write out the evidences of salvation from I John. The counselor also had him read Josh McDowell's book *Evidence That Demands a Verdict* and C. S. Lewis's *Mere Christianity.* Dick came back a month later ready to accept Christ as his Savior, which he did in the counselor's office. He joined a Bible study group on campus and became a fervent soulwinner. He later transferred to a Christian college, took ministerial classes, and eventually became a missionary.

Problem #16: Anxiety

Definition:

Anxiety is fear created by continually thinking about (worrying) and trying to solve seemingly unsolvable problems. Because a person can do nothing about such problems, his dynamic energies, being thwarted, are turned inward and can cause mental and physical problems. Anxiety is doubt to the second degree. If continued over a period of time, anxiety can cause physical distress, panic attacks, depression, and even suicide. It is a result of focusing on self rather than on God's promises.

Scripture:

Exodus 14:13-14; I Samuel 17:47; Psalms 55:22; 94:19; 131:1; 138:8; Isaiah 41:10; Matthew 6:24-27; Romans 8:28-32; 11:33; Philippians 4:6-9, 19; I Peter 5:7.

Information and Principles:

Everybody worries, and the extent of the worrying depends on the lack of faith. People who have strong faith do little worrying and, conversely, people who have weak faith do a great deal of worrying every day. Worry is a sin because of the following facts:

1. We are commanded in Scripture not to worry (Phil. 4:6).
2. Worry is doubting the sovereignty of God, who cares for His children (I Pet. 5:7).
3. Worry is doubting the promises of God given in His Word (II Pet. 1:4; Heb. 4:2).

There are several general principles that apply to anxiety.

There is a difference between anxiety and planning for future things. Scripture states that before one builds a tower, he should consider the cost (Luke 14:28-30) and that a wise man foresees evil (Prov. 27:12). It is prudent to make plans, have fire drills, take out insurance, learn first aid and CPR, and have some savings "for a rainy day." In planning, the Christian should commend his work to the Lord and let Him establish his thoughts (Prov. 16:3). The next step is to set goals and let God direct the steps (Prov. 16:9). Planning is redirecting one's concern to the immediate and future matters which can be controlled and leaving uncontrollable matters in God's hands.

To eliminate anxiety, recognize God's sovereignty by appropriating the four P's.

1. God's **Power.** The same Lord who designed and made the universe, who multiplied the loaves and fishes and fed five thousand, who made man from the dust of the ground, and who willingly redeemed him can also bring all of His power to bear on man's problems. The Christian appropriates this power through faith, and the promises of God provide the rationale for this faith (Heb. 4:2). God wants Christians to pray, trusting Him to work out the problem to His honor and glory. He is all-powerful and always willing to work in a life to bring about His perfect plan. Finite man may not always

conceive of how things are to be, but God knows the end from the beginning, and He knows exactly when and how to use His power for man's benefit.

2. God's **Promises.** A promise is no greater than the person who makes it, no greater than the ability of that person to fulfill it. What comfort it is to know that the God of the universe has a promise for every problem. Every Christian would benefit from memorizing a backlog of these promises so that the Holy Spirit may easily bring them to mind when they are needed. God's promises will give divine perspective in every situation and peace in tragic times.

3. God's **Past Performance.** Many can remember the last time God worked a miracle, the time He answered a desperate prayer, the day He provided needed funds, the moment His hand protected a child from some catastrophe. But it is easy to forget God's daily blessings. Accustomed to benefiting from God's grace and protection, many Christians no longer seem awed by His power. They sometimes forget that the conception, growth, and birth of a baby, the wonders of nature's cycles, and God's provision for their very daily existence are all regular demonstrations of His daily performance in their lives. God's performance does not depend on who or what man is but on who and what God is. This is pure grace.

4. God's **Prophecy.** A knowledge of prophecy eliminates worry about future events in the world. From the moment of salvation, the Christian has perfect peace with Christ, knowing that He is completely in charge of all future things, which must turn out according to His plan (Ps. 131:1). The Christian who wants to have peace about future events must take God at His word regarding them. (See Bob Shelton's book, *God's Prophetic Blueprint.*[1])

Solutions:

1. Review the appropriate Scripture and principles, especially Matthew 6:25-31, where Jesus discusses Christian thinking about provision for food or drink (vv. 25-27) or clothing (vv. 28-31).

2. Urge the counselee to confess to God any known sin.

3. Teach the counselee to use the five-step formula given in Philippians 4:6-9:
    a. "Be careful for nothing" (vs. 6). Stop trying to solve future problems over which you have no control. Turn those problems over to God and work on today's problems, redirecting energies from worry to action.
    b. "In every thing by prayer and supplication" (vs. 6). Pray for God's solution (I Cor. 10:13). God has a solution for every problem.
    c. "With thanksgiving let your requests be made known unto God" (vs. 6). Thanksgiving is based on a promise as well as on the fulfillment of a request. It is thanking God for what He will do as well as what He has done. Thanking God for the answer before it is received, based on a promise of God, is a demonstration of real faith (Heb. 11:1).
    d. "Think on these things" (vs. 8). Think right. Focus on solutions and not on problems. Acquire God's viewpoint on every situation. Eliminate the Devil's viewpoint (II Cor. 10:5).
    e. "And the peace of God, which passeth all understanding, shall keep your hearts and minds through Christ Jesus" (vs. 7). In verse 9, Paul challenges Christians to heed "those things, which ye have both learned, and received, and heard, and seen in me . . . and the God of peace shall be with you." This challenge refers to the "faith way" that Paul taught and lived throughout his Christian life, no matter what occurred.
4. Encourage the counselee to thank God in everything, in little matters as well as in major tragedies (I Thess. 5:18). A sovereign God is working "all things . . . together for good to them that love God, to them who are the called according to his purpose" (Rom. 8:28). God is working out His perfect will in His timing in every Christian's life (Phil. 2:13).
5. Explain the three-point formula found in I Peter 5:6-10.
    a. "Humble yourselves therefore under the mighty hand of God" (vs. 6). Recognize that the God you serve is omnipotent. If He can make the heavens and the earth just by His Word (Ps. 33:6-7), He can certainly handle any

problem that man has. Realize that you cannot do anything in your own strength (John 15:5).

b. "Casting all your care upon him; for he careth for you" (vs. 7). *Praying* about every problem and then *trusting* God to take care of it is the way to eliminate anxiety. This approach brings the peace that Jesus promised. "Peace I leave with you, my peace I give unto you: not as the world giveth, give I unto you. Let not your heart be troubled, neither let it be afraid "(John 14:27). Make a list of all your concerns, go over each problem in prayer, commit the problems to the Lord, and then tear up the list. If God can save your soul from hell, He can take care of any problem.

c. "Be sober, be vigilant; because your adversary the devil, as a roaring lion, walketh about, seeking whom he may devour" (vv. 8-10). Getting a Christian mired down in his problems and doubting God's ability to solve them is the Devil's chief tool to defeat Christians. Resist the Devil (vs. 9), and let "the God of all grace . . . stablish, strengthen, [and] settle you" (vs. 10).

6. Instruct the anxious person to list his problems and goals in order of importance along with the steps he needs to take to solve the problems or accomplish the goals. Each day some action should be taken (on at least one item) and the item checked off on the list. The two main cures for anxiety are trust and action (work).

7. Point out the necessity of the counselee's using the God-given power of choice every day. He can choose to trust God in every situation rather than be anxious (Phil. 4:6), have faith instead of doubt (Heb. 11:6), think the best instead of the worst (Phil. 4:8), thank God rather than complain (I Thess. 5:18), cast his cares upon the Lord rather than bearing them (I Pet. 5:7), look to God's grace rather than to his own strength (II Cor. 12:9), do better instead of being bitter (Eph. 4:29-30), and love instead of fear (I John 4:18).

8. Help the counselee acquire additional information about the problem by directing him to the right sources. Inadequate information is the source of much anxiety.

9. Encourage the counselee to stop watching evening news programs. Studies have shown that people who regularly watch these programs are more fearful and anxious than those who do not. These programs bring all the crucial problems of the world right into one's living room in a dramatic fashion, and there is nothing that can be done about them. Instead, have him read a weekly news magazine that is objective, less threatening, and gives a more accurate view of world events. Make the counselee aware that "reality" police and emergency programs have much the same effect as news programs.

Case Study:

Patricia was taken to the hospital by her mother after a breakdown at home where she had started crying uncontrollably and screaming, "I can't take it any more!" The Christian family doctor gave her a sleeping pill, and she slept for twenty-four hours. Rather than referring her to a psychiatrist, Patricia's doctor called in a Christian counselor who was a friend of the family and had known Patricia since she was a little girl. When the counselor arrived, she was crying and babbling, "I can't take it" over and over. The counselor kept calling her name and demanded that she stop her crying and babbling and writhing on the hospital bed. He urged her to talk to him about her problem. After assurance from the counselor that he would not reveal the information to her parents or pastor, Patricia related what she had been hiding. She was from a Christian home, had been in church all her life, was saved at age six, and in her teen years was vice president of her youth group. However, at age fifteen, she started having sex with her boyfriend, who was nineteen and a student at the city college. Two years later she became pregnant, in spite of the fact that she had been on the pill to regulate her periods. Her boyfriend insisted that she have an abortion and tell no one, not even her parents. He would pay for it. She did not want to have an abortion and cried as the clinic staff dealt with her and had her sign the consent form. She said it was the worst thing that had ever happened to her. The procedure was very painful, and she bled for at least a week afterward; but she was afraid to go to the doctor for fear that he would tell her parents about the abortion. A month after the abortion, Patricia went to a Christian college, where a teacher showed an anti-abortion film in her science class. Feeling upset and guilty, she ran from the room sick and crying. She later told the instructor that the gory film had made her sick. Patricia consequently had stomach problems and dizzy spells, could not go to sleep until the wee hours of the morning, and was anxious and upset for two months afterward. While Patricia was at home for Christmas vacation, she had her breakdown.

Case Study Solution:

The counselor reviewed Patricia's three main sins of immorality, hypocrisy, and murder. He then reviewed the steps of forgiveness and the three-point formula from I Peter 5:6-10 and Romans 14:17 for getting rid of anxiety and sin. (See the last part of Chapter 4.) She accepted full responsibility for the abortion and other sins, quit blaming her former boyfriend, and confessed her sins to God. She agreed not to think about her sin any more, since it was under the blood, and decided to start praising the Lord every time the Devil tried to accuse her. When Patricia asked whether she should ever get married and have children, the counselor reassured her that there was no reason not to. They agreed that she did not need to tell her parents, but the counselor advised her to tell her future husband before they got engaged. Three years later, Patricia married a fine Christian young man whom she had met at college. Ironically, she could not get pregnant. After four years of effort that included help from a fertility clinic, the couple adopted two children. Patricia later became a volunteer counselor at a pregnancy counseling center.

Problem #17: Phobias

Phobias are not mentioned in Scripture, for they are a specialized degree of fear. Phobias are a protective fear and need only to be eliminated if they are interfering with a person's life adjustment or his doing God's will.

Definition:

A phobia is a highly intensified fear of a particular object, place, or situation. This problem usually stems from some traumatic experience during childhood. There are approximately one hundred common phobias. To describe them, attach the Latin term for the feared thing to the word "phobia." For example, fear of open spaces is "agoraphobia" and fear of confined spaces is "claustrophobia."

Scripture:

Psalms 56:3-4; 112:7; 118:6; Isaiah 12:2; 41:10, 13; 43:1-2, 11; Matthew 10:28; II Timothy 1:7; I John 4:15

Information and Principles:

Phobias are common. One study indicates that the average man has two phobias and the average woman has three. Phobias are benign problems except when they interfere with God's will for one's life or the normal functioning of life. The fear then becomes a sin problem and needs to be overcome. For example, a person might have a phobia of snakes; but if, during his lifetime, he has no contact with them because he lives in the city, the phobia of snakes would not be a problem to him. If he will not go to the mission field to which God has called him because of his phobia, then it becomes a sin. He can trust God for the grace and courage to overcome any feared situation or thing—even if it is life-threatening—that prevents him from doing God's will.

Solutions:

1. Refer the counselee to the Scripture on fear.
2. Try to pinpoint when the fear first occurred, and help the counselee to think through how it was later reinforced.
3. Give facts and information that will help to relieve the fear.
4. Help the counselee acquire skills for coping with the feared object, such as learning to swim or learning water safety as one means of handling a fear of water.
5. Help the counselee see that the phobia may be a mask for a deeper problem, usually extreme guilt. The thing a person is afraid of usually gives the clue to the underlying problem. For example, a woman who has a phobia of babies, fearful she will drop them and hurt them, might feel guilty about an abortion that she has never resolved.

Case Study:

Terry, a college student, came to the counselor with an unusual fear. She said that anytime she was in a balcony, whether it was in church, at a concert, or a sports arena, she had a terrible fear of a urinary accident. She would leave four or five times during a church service, or anytime she was in a balcony, to go to the bathroom. She said that she had had this fear as long as she could remember but that it had gotten worse since she had started dating her boyfriend, with whom she was very much in love.

Case Study Solution:

The counselor explained to Terry that she had a phobia and went over the principles on phobias and the Scriptures on fear. Since phobias usually start with a crucial childhood incident, the counselor had her tell about the earliest memories she had of having a urinary accident. She told about three significant ones.

The first was when she was visiting her favorite cousin at a Midwestern farm when she was five years old and he was six. They were up in the hay loft doing some "bodily exploration" when his dad and a hired hand came in and caught them. She said that his dad had spanked them both and had given them a stern warning never to be up there again together. She said that the wrath of his father had scared her so badly that she had had an accident.

The second incident had happened when she was seven years old and her family was living in San Diego. They used to go down to the docks and tour the warships. Her dad had warned the children about getting too close to the edge, saying that if they fell overboard, they could be crushed between the ship and the dock. She remembered that her dad was angry at her mother for making them arrive late and that he was carrying her on his shoulders up the gangplank when she looked down; it seemed like a mile to the water, and she had had an accident on her dad's shoulders.

The third incident occurred in the balcony of a department store. She and two other fifth-grade girls had skipped school after an afternoon recess and had gone downtown. There was no place to go to the bathroom, and she had had an accident.

The counselor explained to Terry that the first incident had set up the fear and caused her to feel guilty because she had been doing something she knew she was not supposed to do. The subsequent incidents had reinforced her fear. The counselor then asked her about sin that she was presently committing with her boyfriend, and she admitted the sin of necking and petting. She began to see the cause of her problem. The counselor had her repent of her sin, and she got her boyfriend to agree that they would keep their relationship on a Christian basis of morality from that point on.

The counselor had her practice Kegel exercises to strengthen her bladder control and also had her begin sitting in the church balcony with her boyfriend for all services for as long a time as she could while wearing adult undergarment protection. She agreed to go over the verses on fear, memorize them, and pick one that would be her life verse. She chose II Timothy 1:7. She called the counselor several months later and said that her problem was completely cured.

Problem #18: Salvation Doubt

Definition:
Doubting salvation is a person's wondering, after receiving Christ, if he is ever going to reach heaven after he dies. The problem usually results from a fear of judgment for some sin in which he is involved.

Scripture:
John 3:1-17, 36; 10:28-29; Ephesians 2:8-9; I John 5:11-13.

Information and Principles:
Having doubt about one's salvation experience is a problem common to the majority of Christians. It occurs most frequently among those from Christian homes who made a salvation decision at a very young age or who have rarely seen Christianity demonstrated by their parents in daily family living. Doubters often come from churches that lack teaching on grace, "blessed assurance," and communion with Christ. Activity is substituted for worship and communion. The doubts are most prevalent during the teen years and are usually resolved by the doubter's making another decision which often includes a dedication decision.

There are several general principles that apply to doubting salvation.

The Devil is the great accuser of the brethren (Rev. 12:10-11) and has been using the following standard questions for years to get people to doubt their salvation:

   a. Have I blasphemed the Holy Spirit, thereby making it impossible for me to be saved?

   b. When I made the decision for salvation, did I really repent?

   c. Did I make a head decision or a heart decision?

   d. When I made that decision, did I make Christ the Lord of my life or was it just a superficial decision?

   e. Had I come to the end of myself and my works before I made that decision?

   f. Was the decision made in the flesh or in the Spirit?

When one begins to intellectualize these doubts from the Devil, he finds intellectual theological substance for them. The more a person reads about and discusses these matters, the more confused he gets.

God made salvation very simple so that a simple, uneducated individual or a young child can be saved. A person does not have to have a theological education or seminary training to be saved and to serve the Lord. When a person realizes that he is a sinner and has broken every one of God's Ten Commandments (James 2:10) and when he sees no way to remedy the situation on his own, he is ready for God's saving grace. He must believe that Jesus Christ is God and that Jesus Christ paid the penalty for his sin by shedding His blood on the cross of Calvary as a full payment for his sins and for the sins of the whole world (Eph. 1:7). That person must also believe that Jesus was buried, that He arose from the dead the third day, ascended to heaven, and is waiting for an invitation to come into the person's life (Rev. 3:20). There must be repentance and a definite decision by the individual to receive Christ and to confess Him to others (John 1:12; Rom.10:9-11).

There is usually some habit of sin that made the person doubt his salvation. This sin needs to be confessed and forgiven. The Christian needs to have ways to overcome the temptation of this sin (Rom. 6:11-13). He also needs to know that all Christians sin, but this fact does not jeopardize their eternal salvation. Fully explain the procedure of confession found in I John 1:7-9.

Salvation is based on God's promise given in the Word of God. A person who does not believe that the Bible is the Word of God has a hard time accepting God's promise of salvation. That person needs to have the words of Jesus Christ about salvation, such as found in John 3, renewed in his mind.

Some people are doubters because they faced many broken promises in their early childhood. Their confidence in God and His Word must be strengthened. The counselor must make sure that he never breaks a promise to the doubting counselee.

Solutions:

1. Review the appropriate Scripture and principles.
2. Go over the plan of salvation, putting the stress on the Ten Commandments and the judgment to follow from breaking those commandments (Heb. 9:27; II Thess. 1:7-9; Rom. 1:18).
3. Have the counselee read, study, and thank God for each of the twenty objective truths that apply to a person the minute he receives Christ as his Savior. Encourage him to review and thank God for these periodically. Real assurance comes as the new believer thanks God for what has already been accomplished in his life at salvation rather than praying for God to do what he imagines God ought to do. One's assurance is based on the promises of God given in His Word (I John 5:11-13) and not on how one feels.

Twenty Objective Truths

- I became a child of God (John 1:12-13).
- I started living forever (John 3:16).
- I'm held in God's and Christ's hand (John 10:28-29).
- I have a place prepared for me (John 14:1-3).
- I am justified forever (Rom. 5:1).
- I am forever joined to Christ (Rom. 6:5).
- I have no condemnation (Rom. 8:1).
- I am vitally linked to the Father (Rom. 8:16).
- I am set apart to God (I Cor. 6:11).
- I am united to all believers (I Cor. 12:12-13).
- I am declared righteous (II Cor. 5:21).
- I am adopted and made acceptable to God (Eph. 1:4-6).

- I am identified with Christ (Eph. 2:5-7).
- I am His workmanship (Eph. 2:10).
- I have God's power within me (Eph. 3:20).
- I am sealed and empowered by the Spirit (Eph. 4:30; 5:18).
- I am a citizen of heaven (Phil. 3:20).
- I am complete in Christ (Col. 2:9-10).
- I am in God's kingdom (I Thess. 2:12).
- I have an inheritance reserved for me (I Pet. 1:4).

4. Pair him with a veteran soulwinner to go out on weekly soulwinning visitation. Seeing God perform the miracle of the new birth helps to increase anyone's faith, especially if it is a friend or relative who is the recipient. Have him give his salvation testimony on these visits.
5. Make sure he is regularly attending a good, Bible-preaching, soulwinning church (Rom. 10:17).

Case Study:

Randy came to the counselor because he was doubting his salvation. He'd been saved in an evangelistic meeting when he was fourteen, but he had doubted his salvation off and on ever since. When the counselor asked him about his home background, Randy said that his mother and father were church-going Christians, but his mother worked full-time all the years he was growing up, and his father was a businessman who virtually lived at his business and never had time for the family.

When Randy was eleven, his father ran off with another woman. The mother was very bitter against Randy's father. The father had visiting rights with Randy and his two younger sisters, but he had rarely taken them to his house and was very sporadic in his financial support. He would promise the children that he was going to take them somewhere but would not. Randy said that he and his two sisters would wait in anticipation but were usually disappointed because their father rarely showed up as he had promised.

Randy said that he had gradually turned bitter against his father, who was still maintaining a semblance of a Christian life by going to another church with his girlfriend. He had been doing this ever since he had left the family, even though the mother had not divorced him until five years later.

Case Study Solution:

The counselor explained to Randy that his childhood environment set him up for rejection feelings and doubting God because a child acquires his concept of God from his father. Randy's father was very unloving, inconsistent, and did not keep his promises, so that is the way Randy viewed God. Bitterness against his father was identified as Randy's main sin problem, which he readily confessed. The counselor suggested that Randy read I John every day for thirty days and underline what he found in the book about Jesus Christ. The counselor went over the verses on assurance of salvation and asked Randy to memorize five of them. He then went over the Identity with Christ principle with Randy and urged him to dedicate his life to the Lord.

Two months later Randy finally committed his life to the Lord at a Christian camp. Believing that God had called him to the mission field, Randy changed his college major from business to pastoral studies.

Problem #19: Shyness

Shyness stems from a root cause of doubt that develops into a fear of people. God has made most people very simple creatures, and He best uses simple things and simple people. This concept is explained in I Corinthians 1:25-31. Verses 25-27 mention that "not many mighty, not many noble, are called: but God hath chosen the foolish things of the world to confound the wise; and God hath chosen the weak things of the world to confound the things which are mighty." God has chosen weak and foolish things so that "no flesh should glory in his presence" (vs. 29). Verse 30 reveals that Christians' power—which is wisdom, righteousness, sanctification, and redemption—comes from being in Christ Jesus. Therefore, any glory should go to the Lord. With this God-confidence instead of self-confidence, one can interact with the world and people without fear.

Definition:

A fear of what people will think of what one says or does in social situations. Shy people fear they will blunder socially and suffer embarrassment. As a consequence, they are hesitant about getting into any social situation in which they will have to interact with others.

Scripture:

Luke 9:23; I Corinthians 1:26-31; 10:24; Philippians 2:3-4, 21; I John 3-4

Information and Principles:

Twenty-five percent of Americans consider themselves shy, according to research by Dr. Philip Zimbardo. They admit to the pounding heart, the clammy hands, and the blushing face of shyness in most social situations. In his book *Shyness: What It Is, What To Do About It,* Dr. Zimbardo explains that most shy people "feel intimidated and awkward in certain situations with certain types of people" and the "discomfort is strong enough to disturb their social lives and inhibit their functioning, making it difficult or impossible to say what they think or do what they'd like to do."[2] Most shy people tend to be self-centered, selfish individuals. They are always thinking about themselves and imagining what people are saying and thinking about them. It can even develop to the extreme of a persecution complex: they wonder if people are plotting to harm them in some way.

There are several general principles that apply to this problem of shyness.

A person who expects people to be friendly to him must first be friendly. When coming into contact with people at school, at work, or in social situations, one should always give a greeting first, using the person's name if he knows it. When meeting someone for the first time, one should walk up to him, greet him, introduce oneself, and ask the person's name. Even looking a person in the eyes and smiling helps break the social ice. As a person continues this approach, he finds that other people will respond in a friendly manner.

Social interaction is based on conversational ability—the ability to ask appropriate questions and to give appropriate answers to others' questions. One should ask questions that have to do with the other person's life, interests, and feelings. The questions should be open-ended and not ones that can be answered by a yes or a no. One can ask factual questions to get information about the individual and then follow with questions such as "How do you feel about this?" or "What do you think about this?" The good conversationalist listens carefully to the answer given and asks another question related to the answer. When the conversation begins to lag, the person should ask another question, perhaps on a different topic, to keep the conversation going. Since women generally have better verbal ability than men, it usually falls their lot to keep the conversation going. A good conversationalist frequently has a series of questions in mind to ask when meeting new people or when on a date.

Developing the love principle in one's life is the best cure for shyness. Constantly thinking about how one can serve others as he becomes aware of needs in others' lives is an important step. Looking for ways to be helpful is a good habit to develop.

Solutions:

1. Review the appropriate Scriptures and principles.

2. Urge the counselee to confess to God any known sin.

3. Have the counselee pick one person a day with whom he is going to interact and for whom he will develop a plan of love, conversation, and helpful deeds.

4. When the counselee knows he is going to be in a new situation, have him determine ahead of time to meet three different people with whom he will converse and ask his series of questions, if appropriate.

5. Have the counselee pick out one person a week in his church, school, or work place with whom he is going to be friendly.

6. Teach the counselee that deep, slow, diaphragmatic breathing helps calm the physical manifestations of fear that accompany shyness.

7. Have the counselee eliminate from his thinking negative-devilish thoughts and statements about himself such as "I'm hopeless" or "I'm not smart or creative" or "I'm a naturally shy person."

8. Tell the counselee not to allow others to criticize him as a person but to graciously accept criticism for specific actions and to seek to make improvement.

9. See Chapter 14 for suggestions on how to help the counselee overcome feelings of rejection, for this is usually one of the root problems causing shyness.

Case Study:

Sam, a thirty-seven-year-old engineer, came to the counselor with the problem of shyness. He said he had been shy all throughout his childhood and teenage years. As he gained success in college and got a job, he had not noticed his shyness too much, but he said that now it was interfering with his job. He said he had to make project presentations as a group leader, and he would get "tied up in knots." He would mumble because his mouth would get so dry, he was starting to have stomach problems, and he was even shaking before presentations. Sam had achieved success in his career, but his shyness was hurting his chances for advancement.

In talking about his home background, he said that he was the only black boy in a white elementary school where some of the children used to call him Little Black Sambo. He said he always took it good-naturedly, but it hurt him deeply. Coming from a professional family—his father was a doctor—he always prided himself in making top grades in elementary school, but other kids seemed to be jealous and would increase their taunts.

When he got to high school, there were ten to fifteen blacks in the school, and he got along very well, especially with the better students. He did not associate with many of the other blacks because they were all good athletes and he never cared much for sports. He never dated in high school but met a lovely young lady in college whom he married upon graduation. His son in elementary school was starting to receive the same type of teasing that he himself had taken.

Sam was from a good Christian family, attended a Fundamentalist church, and had been saved at an early age. He and his wife held a Bible study taught by their pastor in their home. Sam was a deacon in their church.

Case Study Solution:

The counselor explained that Sam's shyness was a result of his early rejection in elementary school and his continued rejection by the blacks in high school because he was not an athlete. His son's being teased in elementary school brought back in full force the memories of his own ordeal at the hands of his insensitive classmates. Behind the smiles of his coworkers, to whom he was a competitor, he perceived rejection.

The counselor went over the verses on fear and emphasized the idea of Christ as his strength (II Tim. 1:7; Eph. 3:20; Phil. 4:13). Sam did not understand how to use that strength to help him on the job, so the counselor went through the Identity with Christ principle and all the verses and asked him whether he had ever given his life completely to the Lord. Sam replied that he had not; he was afraid that if he did, it would hurt his career. The counselor asked him whether he wanted God's will for his life or a career. Sam said he would have to think about it.

At the next session two weeks later, Sam said that he had struggled with that question for a solid week. Then, the Sunday before the session, he had dedicated his life to the Lord and now knew he was filled with the Holy Spirit. The counselor went over the verses again on identification with Christ and the implications of Sam's decision. He suggested that, with Sam's Bible knowledge and intelligence, Sam should start teaching a Sunday school class. Sam said that the preacher had already approached him two weeks before with the offer of a class, but Sam had turned it down.

The counselor also suggested that Sam sign up for a speech class in a technical school, since he had never taken speech in college and would benefit from practicing speech techniques for a class. Because Sam had a tendency to hold himself aloof from people, presenting a superior air, the counselor suggested he also sign up for a Dale Carnegie course to be held in their city.

Six months later Sam reported that his problem had cleared up and he had received an advancement at work. He was also teaching a boys' Sunday school class and had taught the Bible study in his home a few times in the absence of the pastor.

Problem #20: Panic Attacks

Extreme anxiety and panic attacks usually indicate a serious and longstanding unconfessed sin.

Definition:

Extreme anxiety is an intense fear or a vague apprehension of impending doom without any known cause. It may also take the form of unfounded concern about loved ones, finances, or some other area of life when there is no real threat. Panic attacks are intense times of fear, dread, and apprehension without any apparent causes other than stress. The attacks are always accompanied by extreme physical symptoms of fear.

Scripture:

Psalms 27:13-14; 37:1-9; 43:5; Isaiah 26:3; Matthew 6:25-34; John 14:1, 27; I John 3:19-21; 4:18; II Timothy 1:7; II Corinthians 10:5

Information and Principles:

Extreme anxiety has certain physical symptoms that persist for six months or more. These include general nervousness, tenseness, increased irritability, problems with concentration, lightheadedness, dry mouth, sweaty palms, heart palpitations, and shortness of breath. There may be heartburn, nausea, diarrhea, and frequent urination.

Panic attacks usually develop suddenly with some of the same symptoms as extreme anxiety, increasing in intensity in the first ten minutes of the attack. During an attack, the person frequently feels numbness, a tingling sensation in the hands, feet, and face, some chest pain, trembling, sweating, a sense of choking, a sensation of smothering, and rapid heartbeat. The person has a fear of dying or of losing his mind and is afraid that he has some strange disease. Sometimes these symptoms are mistaken for a heart attack or a stroke. There is a heart condition known as mitral valve prolapse, usually benign, which may be associated with the development of panic disorders. Panic attacks can occur once or twice a day but generally occur on a weekly or monthly basis.

There are several general principles that apply to the problems of extreme anxiety and panic attacks.

Agoraphobia, a fear of open spaces or of places where an individual feels vulnerable or somehow exposed, usually accompanies extreme anxiety and panic attacks. Although estimates vary, from two to ten million Americans suffer from agoraphobia. About 75 percent are women who are bright, energetic, and sociable but usually dependent. Such women may suffer from the attacks because they had overprotective or overly critical parents and, as a result, did not learn adequate coping skills. Many felt extreme anxiety in their teenage years, usually following some very stressful event. Agoraphobia usually occurs when the victim is between the ages of twenty-four and thirty, but it may continue into the forties. In severe cases the person becomes a lifetime recluse. The victim retreats to a safe place and becomes a prisoner in her own home and even her own room.

Agoraphobics typically engage in catastrophic thinking, imagining the worst possible things happening in situations. For example, as an agoraphobic crosses a bridge, she is certain it will collapse and she will drown because she will be unable to get out of the car after it falls into the water. The situation is always a "worst case" scenario.

Some counselors have found that a few people who experience extreme anxiety or panic attacks have confused feelings and memories about some early sex experience (before the age of sixteen) in which there has been no threat or force. (Premarital sex, especially if it resulted in an abortion or forced marriage, can also be a cause.) These early sex experiences in which the person was a willing but reluctant participant bring up contradictory feelings and memories: acceptance and apprehension, concern and contempt, desire and dread, fascination and fear, longing and lingering regret, and pleasure and pain. Such contradictory feelings and memories can also occur when the person has experienced some types of physical and sexual abuse. The worst thing about such early sex experiences is the awakening of powerful, overwhelming feelings under frightening, guilt-inducing situations. The experiences tend to result in a mental dichotomy and doublemindedness, creating anxiety.

A betrayal of love and trust in childhood or teen years may later bring on anxiety and even panic attacks. The betrayal can be a result of any traumatic event, such as divorce, the death of a parent or sibling, a childhood or premarital-sex experience, or sexual or physical abuse. The victim's unanswered question is "If you really loved me, how could you have done this to me?" Actually, the experience is viewed as rejection. To solve the dilemma in her mind, the person may deny that the situation ever happened, lie about it, or rationalize it by giving reasons to justify her actions or by blaming her parents or God for having allowed it to happen. The person must be brought face-to-face with any sinful reaction to the experience, such as willingness to participate, being the initiator, or bitterness or hate toward the perpetrator or the one believed to have allowed the situation to happen.

Children tend to take the blame and responsibility for situations over which they had no control, such as accidents, death, divorce, and abuse. This blame and shame must be separated from true guilt, for which the child is responsible. In incidents of abuse, the child is almost always innocent and is the victim.

Solutions:

1. Review the appropriate Scripture and principles.
2. Help the counselee find the cause by obtaining a full childhood background, especially the events leading up to any traumatic situation. Look for childhood incidents, like an early sex experience, physical or sexual abuse, or the accidental death of another, about which the person feels guilty and blames himself for carelessness which he feels contributed to the severity of the incident.
3. Help the person to understand the situation, and get him to acknowledge his sin if any exists. Help him to eliminate any sinful, negative thoughts and attitudes, such as bitterness, anger, or fear, and to acquire biblical attitudes and feelings about the situation, including confession if necessary. Proper feelings will follow right, biblical attitudes (II Cor. 10:5; Phil. 4:8). If the person has been full of extreme insecurity as a result of constant criticism, failure, and guilt, help him readjust his thinking by getting him to concentrate on the promises of God and on the approval of God instead of on man (Eph. 6:5-8).
4. Urge full confession of any sin, especially hatred and bitterness, involved with the situation, including confession to a

wronged individual. Make sure that the blame is placed where it belongs—on the perpetrator and not on the victim.

5. To handle the physical symptoms of extreme anxiety and panic attacks, advise deep, diaphragmatic breathing when the symptoms begin to occur. Unintended hyperventilation has long been known to be a prominent feature of fear episodes. Such overbreathing drives carbon dioxide out of the lungs too rapidly, setting off a series of chemical changes in the body, causing the typical physical symptoms of extreme anxiety and panic attacks. British researchers have observed that the overbreathing is not just a response to fright but, in turn, is a direct cause of the worst symptoms attributed to fright. In diaphragmatic breathing, one should breathe with the diaphragm, keeping the chest wall as immobile as possible.

6. Physicians have been aware that a high intake of caffeine increases the frequency and severity of panic attacks. Eliminating the ten cups of coffee, tea, soda pop, and also chocolate can work wonders and can be a major factor in helping to alleviate the physical symptoms of this problem.

7. Doctors at the Duke University Medical Center believe that many panic attacks are chemically induced and can be controlled by medication. They use the drug Alprazolam to counteract an inherited sensitivity to lactate, a lactic acid, which is chemically produced naturally in the body. Therefore, the counselee might benefit from a medical exam and treatment.

Case Study:

Mary, a twenty-five-year-old woman married to a professional man, came to the counselor with a problem, dating back to her teen years, of doubting her salvation. Upon questioning, the counselor uncovered the real problem: Mary was afraid to go out of her house because she experienced panic attacks at least once a week just before going to church. She sometimes experienced the attacks on long trips or whenever she wanted to go downtown. Mary was also afraid to have children because she was afraid she would die in childbirth. She revealed that she and her younger brother had had frequent arguments during teen years and had been estranged since she left home at eighteen years of age to get married. When questioned about longstanding, serious sin, Mary revealed that she had started the habit of masturbation at about age eight and had continued until she was married. She had also engaged in premarital sex with her fiancé for about a year. Further questioning revealed that Mary had started incest with her younger brother when she was seven and he was five and had continued until he reached puberty, at which time she stopped the incest because she was afraid of getting pregnant. She was saved about that time.

Case Study Solution:

Mary was cured of her panic attacks after she applied the three-point formula (righteousness and peace and joy) found in I Peter 5:6-10 and Romans 14:17. (See last part of Chapter 4.) When she asked forgiveness of God for her sins and put them under the blood, she received full assurance of forgiveness. Mary was then reconciled with her brother after she asked his forgiveness for involving him in the sin of incest. She agreed not to think about the past, since it was under the blood. She also agreed to praise the Lord every time the Devil tried to accuse her about the past. Mary was instructed about diaphragmatic breathing and used it whenever she felt panicky. She reluctantly gave up her ten-cups-a-day coffee habit. After going over the twenty verses mentioned in Problem 18, Mary received full assurance of her salvation. She also dedicated her life to the Lord and became actively involved in her church missions program.

Chapter 18

Addiction—Bondage of Sin

Addiction, according to the world, is a disease and must be treated as a disease. Some of the popular views of the causes of addiction that make a person lose control and become a helpless victim who is not responsible for his addiction are as follows: it is genetic; it is a physical dependency caused by a chemical in the abused substance; it is a result of a codependent (i.e., a family member or friend) who cooperates with and supplies the addict; or it is a result of chemicals that are released within the body and cause pleasure feelings that reinforce the addiction. The adrenalin high or the jogger's high, which releases catecholamine hormones in the brain, are examples of the latter. Addicts and society are constantly looking to science, doctors, and psychiatrists to furnish some sort of medicine or treatment that will cure the disease of addiction.

The Christian, looking at addiction from a biblical standpoint, views it as being in the bondage of sin, which has a sure cure. Second Peter 2:19 calls addicts "servants of corruption" who are "brought in bondage." They are also referred to as "servants of sin" (John 8:34) who yield their members as "servants to uncleanness and to iniquity" (Rom. 6:19). Proverbs 5:22-23 describes the addict as being "holden with the cords of his sins." In times past, addiction was commonly referred to as a besetting sin (Heb. 12:1). A cure can be effected when an addict repents of his sin and decides to go God's way by receiving Christ and then trusting His power to help him put off the old habit of addiction and put on new habits of godly behavior (John 8:36; Rom. 6:22; Eph. 4:22-24).

Problem #21: Addiction

Definition:

Addiction is a habitual, obsessive overdependence on a thing, substance, or situation to meet a craving for love, pleasure, or satisfaction. Dr. Franklin Payne defines it as "a repetitive pleasure-seeking behavior that is habitual in spite of moral or physical reasons that should rationally preclude its practice and that displaces spiritual obligation."

The addiction becomes a physical dependence and/or a mental dependence. The addicted one feels that he cannot function normally without the needs being fulfilled. When the need is not satisfied, panic ensues, and all energies are concentrated on fulfilling the need.

Scripture:

Proverbs 5:22-23; John 8:34-36; Romans 6-8; I Corinthians 6:12; 9:27; Galatians 4:3, 9, 24; Ephesians 4:22-24; Hebrews 11:25; II Peter 2:18-19

Information and Principles:

Addiction is not a disease but a chosen, habitual way of living. Paul alluded to addiction as being a choice when he said "I will not be brought under the power of any" (I Cor. 6:12). He also said, "I will keep my body under, and bring it into subjection" (I Cor. 9:27). In a similar verse Moses chose to suffer affliction with the people of God rather than to enjoy the pleasures of sin for a season (Heb. 11:25). Historically, because addiction is a matter of choice, it has implied a weakness of character, a loss of control over one's life, and a desperate life of deception. All humans are creatures of habit. The Lord has programmed this method of operating within man so that he can perform learned tasks, like driving a car, without having to think through each step every time. Certain habits should be cultivated, for they make life more efficient. However, sinful habits should be eliminated.

The core of a sinful addiction is an intense preoccupation with a habit that brings pleasure. This habit could be ingesting a substance or performing an activity. Substance addictions are destructive and sinful, whereas activity addictions may be sinful but not destructive, depending on the goal and the effect on self and others. Some activities carried to the extreme, such as hard work, making money, and giving, are looked upon as virtues because society puts a premium on them (I Cor. 16:15). But when an activity—no matter how laudable—is done for self and not to the glory of God, it becomes sin (I Cor. 10:31). When it begins to adversely affect one's loved ones, life, or service for the Lord and others, it becomes destructive.

The most common addiction, and the one that has received the most attention, is addiction to drugs, which include alcohol (the most abused drug) and caffeine, as well as over-the-counter, pre-scription, and illegal drugs. Other addictions are to television, pornography, work, computers, sports, gambling, vacation travel, or spending money. When the substance or activity starts control-ling a person's behavior and lifestyle and destructively affects his actions and reactions in daily life, he is in the bondage of sin, or full-blown addiction.

Sinful addictions in the life of a Christian always hurt his productivity, service, and testimony for the Lord. Certain addic-tions, such as voyeurism, pornography, or sexual immorality, might eventually drive a Christian out of his ministry. Others, such as gambling, hobbies, or shopping, could become so expensive that the person could not afford to stay in the service of the Lord. Self reigns during an addiction, and the Holy Spirit cannot lead, direct, or control the life.

There are certain symptoms that indicate the progress of an addiction and its degree of severity.

1. Disregarding the feelings and inconveniences of loved ones
2. Rationalizing and excusing the selfish behavior and denying that there is an addiction
3. Through arguments, threats, anger, and irrational outbursts, drawing loved ones into supporting the addiction, who will comply just to keep peace
4. Feeling driven to have the desire satisfied no matter what the cost in money, time, and energy or no matter how irrational and sinful the action to satisfy the addiction may be

There are several principles that apply to the problem of addiction.

A factor that may predispose a person to addictive behavior is the root problem of sinful rejection feelings from childhood. The idea has been proposed that an addict feels that he has not been given all the love and nourishment that he desired and deserved, either in his childhood or in his present home life. Most people are rejected at various times by parents and others in the formative childhood years. The death or absence of a parent, divorce, inadequate mothering, a working mother, personal handicaps or disfigurements, and other disadvantages sometimes result in sinful feelings of rejection, self-pity, and even bitterness in some people. Some people are affected more than others, and they may react in several different ways.

1. Some withdraw from close emotional ties and contact with people and become cold and calculating. They like to work with things rather than people. The more detailed, tedious, and detached the work, the more satisfaction they get.

2. Some become angry and bitter against the mother or father who rejected them and turn against any woman or man who loves them. A wife or daughter may become the object of a man's bitterness against women; a husband or son may become the object of a woman's bitterness against men. These angry, bitter people may become spouse and/or child abusers.

3. Some rejected people, trying to get the missing love and affection from things, substances, or situations, become addicted.

Loving self predisposes a person to sinful rejection feelings and addictive behavior. Loving God first, which results in reaching out to others, is the chief way to overcome an addiction. Conquering self gets rid of selfishness which is the chief character trait of addiction.

Overcoming an addiction is always a matter of choice. People must choose between loving God and others and loving self. When one chooses to love God and others more than the pleasures of sin, he can break the addictive habit. Moses chose to love God, rather than addictive pleasures (Heb.11:25). Joshua's challenge to his people, "Choose you this day whom ye will serve" (Josh. 24:15), should be the recurring admonition to the counselee who is addicted: *Make up your mind.*

Personal responsibility and discipline are the prevention and part of the cure for an addiction. Preoccupation with pleasurable pursuits can lead to addiction. Therefore, Christians must be aware of the Devil's method of using the flesh to ensnare them in addictions to things that may be good in themselves. First Thessalonians 4:3-4 indicates that a Christian should have control of his body at all times and not be trapped in any kind of addiction. Paul admonishes every Christian "For this is the will of God, even your sanctification, . . . that every one of you should know how to possess his vessel (body) in sanctification and honor." Discipline is a key to godliness: "Exercise thyself rather unto godliness" (I Tim. 4:7).

Everyone should be aware that there can be a point of no return with each sinful addiction (Rom. 1:24, 26, 28): (a) God gave them up to uncleanness (v. 24); (b) God gave them up unto vile affections (v. 26); (c) God gave them over to a reprobate mind (v. 28). For the Christian the point of no return might be death, but the addiction would not affect his eternal destiny (I Cor. 11:29-30).

The way to break an addiction is to "put off" and "put on" (Eph. 4:22-24). It is not enough to get rid of a sinful habit. The Christian must reprogram his brain for a new way of operating; otherwise, there is a tendency to slip back into the old way. Habitual actions and reactions are programmed into our brains through practice and remain in our brains until we die. The Christian must consciously choose to practice the new way until it becomes a habitual way of responding.

Certain changes in the environment may be necessary for conquering an addiction (Ps. 101:3). Meeting together regularly with business associates at a popular local restaurant may be the stimulus to an alcohol addiction or even a pornography addiction if the place serves liquor and has live entertainment. Instead the believer must seek Christian fellowship and/or a restaurant without the harmful influences.

The reaction of the addicted Christian should be joy as he faces the severe and continual temptations of his sinful habit (James 1:2-3, 12). He should be aware that by enduring as he conquers the temptation, he shall receive the immediate reward of patience (v. 2) and the future reward of the crown of life (v. 12).

A confrontation by family members or friends is generally necessary before the addict recognizes that there is a problem.

In substance addiction, especially liquor, the addict usually does not recognize his problem. By rationalizing his abuse and forgetting the unpleasant behavior and effects that accompany the addiction, he deludes himself into thinking that he is in control and everything is all right. The family tends to shield the addict, making excuses and bailing the addict out of jams. The confrontation must be made by two or more family members or friends. If just one person confronts him, the addict construes it as nagging, creating a feeling of self-loathing and hopelessness, and he continues rationalizing his behavior, perpetuating the desire. These confrontations need to be well prepared even to each person's writing out in detail the effects on others, the embarrassing incidents, and traumatic scenes. When he is sober, all those involved with the addict need to sit down with him and present orally in loving but unsparing detail all that has happened. When he recognizes his problem, they need to insist on immediate counseling and complete abstinence. In acute cases, commitment to a Christian recovery center is necessary. If there is a relapse, the confrontation should be repeated and eventually it should work.

Solutions:
1. Review the appropriate principles and Scripture that apply to the problem.
2. Have the counselee acknowledge the addiction as a sin and repent and confess it to God.
3. Have the counselee confess the addiction to spouse, family member, or friend and become accountable to that person in monitoring his progress as he is changing his habits and defeating the addiction.
4. Have the counselee make up his mind to quit feeding the addiction by substituting new behavior habit patterns, such as the places he goes and the things he does. Since an addiction is largely a longstanding habit, he must use his mind to attack every facet of his addiction.
5. Have the counselee list definite conscious steps he is going to take every time he is tempted.
6. Show the counselee how to have a close relationship and identification with Jesus Christ, letting Christ supply the closeness, love, approval, and satisfaction that he needs.

7. Help the counselee replace the addiction with some definite steps toward reaching others, including family members, and unselfishly meeting their needs. These steps should involve his money, time, and activity.

8. Have the counselee practice conscious manipulation of normal habit patterns to learn mental control of his life actions. For example, ask the counselee to forego for two weeks the before-bedtime snack or to put the right shoe on first instead of the left or vice versa.

Case Study:

Brenda came to the counselor about her husband, Walt, who was addicted to alcohol. They had been married twenty-three years and had three teenage children. She said that her husband had started drinking beer in high school and had continued in college. It was not until he was recalled into the army and sent to Vietnam that he starting drinking hard liquor at the officers' club every night. She said that after he came home, he kept up his drinking and during the last year it had gotten much worse. Brenda said that she had tried to keep Walt's drinking from the children, but they were now aware of it. She had tried everything to make him stop, from pouring out every bottle she found to threatening a divorce. She said she must have poured out fifty bottles that she had found hidden all over the house. She had even found bottles hidden in his boots. The counselor suggested a confrontation. The wife, a brother, and an older son held the confrontation, and Walt agreed to come in for counseling, so an appointment was set up.

Case Study Solution:

Walt related to the counselor that he had accepted Christ in junior high school, but he had gotten in with the wrong crowd. When he went to college, he was in ROTC (Reserve Officers Training Corps), and he and his buddies were in a drinking fraternity. He had been called back into army duty and was sent overseas. He admitted to living with two different women while overseas and perhaps having made one of them pregnant.

After a long discussion with the counselor, he admitted his serious doubts about his own Christianity. After confessing his sin, he accepted the Lord in the counselor's office and dedicated his life to the Lord at the same time. The counselor then went over Romans 6:11-13 with Walt, explaining the steps to conquering a habitual sin. Walt still had the desire for alcohol but agreed to give it up. He also decided to give up smoking after the counselor told him that people who gave up drinking but continued to smoke usually went back to drinking after a short time. He also agreed to give up his Saturday-night outings with "the boys," which were usually drinking and poker-playing parties, now that he was a dedicated Christian. He agreed to attend an exercise program three times a week at a local health spa. He also agreed that, whenever he was tempted to drink, he would call the counselor, who would come with a deacon from the church to pray with him. The counselor had to go to his house three different times at his request, but Walt conquered the addiction without any relapses.

Chapter 19

Cruel and Irresponsible Men Who Become Wife Abusers

The worst cases of bitterness are the cruel men who abuse their wives and/or children. Abuse, a growing problem in our society, has recently come to light in Christian circles. "More American women—rich and poor alike—are injured by the men in their lives than by car accidents, muggings and rape combined. . . . Last year the A.M.A., backed by the Surgeon General, declared that violent men constitute a major threat to women's health."[1]

This problem is almost always brought to the counselor by the wife, rather than by the man himself. This type of man resists going for counseling; therefore, the counselor will be dealing primarily with the wife. Sometimes the wife is discontented and dissatisfied with her husband's insensitivity and irresponsibility, and the incidents she mentions cannot be classed as abuse but rather points of irritation that must be dealt with accordingly. Actual cases of mental, verbal, and physical abuse, to be handled properly, require that the husband be counseled to bring about a resolution of the problem.

Problem #22: Abusive Men

Definition:

Men who are abusers hate women and feel a need to control the women in their lives by aggressively abusing them mentally, verbally, and/or physically. They are angry in their contact with women. They use angry moods, words, and actions to gain the control to which they feel they are entitled as a man and/or as a husband. Susan Forward, in her book *Men Who Hate Women and the Women Who Love Them,* calls such a man a misogynist and defines him as follows: "A man who needs to control women. He does this in an aggressive way, by using intimidation and criticism, by demeaning her, by breaking down her confidence in herself, and by keeping her off balance with unpredictable switches from charm to rage."[2] "Abuse is defined as any behavior that is designed to control and subjugate another human being through the use of fear, humiliation, and verbal or physical assaults."[3]

Scripture:

Romans 12:9-21; Ephesians 5:25-30; Colossians 3:19; I Peter 3:8-18

Information and Principles:

Abusive husbands generally come from abusive homes, and less than one-quarter of them have what can be called good relationships with their parents. Studies in 1974 cited in Richard J. Gelles's book, *The Violent Home: A Study of Aggression Between Husbands and Wives,*[4] show that 85 percent of these cruel men grew up in violent homes and identified with their fathers in the teenage years, 30 percent of abused wives grew up in violent homes and identified with their mothers in the teenage years. "In 1991, when some 4 million women were beaten and 1,320 murdered in domestic attacks, 622 women killed their husbands or boyfriends. . . . Anywhere from one-third to as many as half of all female murder victims are killed by their spouses or lovers, compared with 4% of male victims."[5] Alcohol and drugs are a factor in over 50 percent of the domestic violence cases reported to the police.

Many Christian men hate women in general and are bitter against them. These men tend to hate their wives and make life miserable for them throughout their married lives. Most cases are a carryover from the man's bitterness and rebellion against his mother, begun in early childhood. The reasons for the bitterness may be fourfold.

1. A domineering mother with an absent or noninvolved father who gave no leadership to the family

2. An overprotective mother who never let her son become independent and self-sufficient and whose son resented this smothering

3. An absent mother whose working full-time or being completely absorbed in her career was interpreted by the son as rejection

4. An inadequate mother, such as an alcoholic or immoral mother, of whom the son was ashamed or at whom he was angry

If the man and/or woman comes from a violent home, this also contributes to the problem.

Anger is the only feeling that abusive men have developed and know how to express adequately in their relationships with women. With their wives, the anger is uncontrolled, and the men seem unable to bring it under the discipline of rational control. Most wife abusers are difficult to treat because of their stereotype of women as slaves to men and as existing to be used physically and controlled by charm, verbal abuse, and, if necessary, physical force instead of love. They are jealous and possessive and want complete control of their wives and their family situations. They are defensive because they are covering up their own weaknesses and insecurities. Most wife abusers deny or minimize the violent results of their anger. They do not try to understand their behavior because it makes them anxious and uncomfortable. The only thing that starts an abusive man on the road to a cure is a wife's separating from him and staying away until he gets counseling help. He will promise the moon to get his wife back but will renege on these grandiose promises within a week of her return. In acute cases, calling the police and having the husband jailed is the only thing that will relieve the situation. "In 1981 the Duluth Police Department in Minnesota became the first in the nation to make arrest mandatory for domestic violence—which means the police officer, not the victim, presses charges. . . . In a survey of women who had used the system [overnight jailing and six months of mandatory counseling or 30 days in jail], 87 percent were living without violence two years later. Among the rest, the violence was far less severe and less frequent."[6]

There are three stages to wife abuse, according to Kay Marshall Strom in her book *In the Name of Submission*. (1) The tension of anger begins and builds progressively no matter what the wife does. The least little thing can trigger this response. (2) The attack, an explosion of undiluted anger and rage directed at the wife, results in the husband's verbally or physically abusing the wife and possibly even tearing up furniture or anything the wife holds dear. (3) The aftermath of remorse and kindness when the husband first rationalizes his violence by blaming it on the wife or on being tired or frustrated. Then follows the loving respite part of the third stage when he may ask forgiveness and promise that the attack will never happen again. He then tries to make up to her by being loving, which rekindles her hope. Usually, there follows a long period of calm when the husband is sweet and loving.[7] He is still suspicious of his wife's fidelity and excuses his rigid control, rationalizing that he is trying to protect her by preventing her from running off with another man. When the wife is pregnant, the abuse increases, for the husband feels that his needs are being neglected and he is not going to get her full love and attention.

There are several general principles that apply to the problem of abusive or irresponsible husbands.

The typical wife abuser is selfish and self-centered, expecting his wife to be an unending source of love, adoration, concern, and approval. The abusive husband expects his wife to know what he is thinking and feeling. Though he demands that she anticipate his every need, he never gives any signals as to what those needs are. "You should have known what I wanted" is his favorite accusation. No matter how trivial the incident, it becomes the springboard of his anger, and he starts by blaming the wife. In an effort to appease him and placate his anger, the wife tends to accept the blame until she eventually believes that she is at fault.

Marriage is "until death do you part" (Matt. 19:3-9; Mark 10:2-12). Adultery or fornication is the only situation in which divorce is allowed, according to Scripture. Abuse is not grounds for divorce; however, separation without divorce may be in order in certain cases of physical abuse of the wife or children, sexual abuse of the children, and addiction to pornography, drugs, or alcohol. The wife should remain separated from the husband until he gets knowledgeable help from a pastor or Christian counselor. When husbands are completely corrupt in homosexuality or promiscuity, divorce may need to be considered. The long-term effect on the wife's health and on the children must be taken into account. Sexually transmitted diseases (STDs) can put the wife in danger if the husband is promiscuous.

The wife must work to make the best of a difficult situation (I Pet. 3:8-18). Very few marriages are ideal. In the first years of marriage, many adjustments need to be made by both the husband and the wife. Many men have trouble making these necessary adjustments because of their home backgrounds or their personality problems in relating to women. Some independent-minded wives misinterpret their husband's efforts to be the leader and head of the family and label it mental or verbal abuse. The wife, however, should be committed to the marriage "for better or for worse" and must finally accept her husband as he is. First Peter 3:9 indicates that she should not render evil for evil or railing for railing but instead should make herself a blessing to her husband. She might have a life of suffering, but her spiritual testimony through it all will be a blessing to her husband and will possibly effect a change in him. Her testimony of how a Christian should react to adverse circumstances will certainly be a blessing and a guide to her children as well as to others who know about her situation. If the husband, although not abusive, is irresponsible, backslidden, and lacking in leadership, the wife, as a team member, must take up the slack. She must accept his shortcomings, expecting nothing from him (Ps. 62:5), and give him a consistent double dose of devotion, love, and affection.

The wife should do her best to make her husband happy and let God make him holy (I Cor. 1:10). Wives tend to experience feelings of rejection when married to an immature and irresponsible husband. In turn, they unconsciously reject their partners by nagging them and by trying to change their various immature habits. Instead of rejection, this kind of husband needs a double dose of love and emotional support. He is truly an immature little boy in a man's body. He wants to be mothered even in the physical relationship with his wife (he is very breast-oriented) without the wife's making him feel as if she is his mother. The wife should strive to make the home a pleasant, nonconfrontational place, trying to meet her husband's needs for food and love, no matter how inappropriate or inconvenient it is. When he is hungry, she should fix him the things he likes best at the time he requests. He will want love and affection at the most inconvenient times, but the wife should always eagerly oblige.

Since the wife's expectations are from the Lord (Ps. 62:5), she should not expect anything from her husband. Wives have a tendency to dwell on one or two negative qualities or experiences and can become dissatisfied with their husbands by magnifying these things out of proportion in their minds. Instead, a wife needs to think on the qualities for which she can praise her husband.

The wife should not constantly go over her problems with a friend or confidante. This rehashing only magnifies the problem and makes her more discontented. Her unhappiness will be reflected in her relationship with her husband, causing him to feel rejected and to increase his demands for love and attention. The wife may want to take her problem to a competent counselor who can make an attempt to deal with the husband as well as the wife.

To get the abusive husband in for counseling, a "confrontation" (explained in Chapter 18, Principle 9) may be necessary.

Solutions:

1. Review the appropriate Scripture and principles with the wife and, if possible, with the husband.
2. If the husband's problem is irresponsibility, a backslidden condition, and lack of leadership, the wife must be counseled to compensate by taking over many of the responsibilities as well as the spiritual guidance of any children in the home.
3. If the husband is verbally abusive, the wife must be helped to step outside herself and become an observer of his behavior rather than a recipient of it. She can do this by refusing to respond to his attacks. Since the abusive comments do not apply to her and are just a means of his venting his anger, the wife should decide beforehand how she is going to react rather than automatically accept the blame in the situation. She must learn to look at her husband's actual behavior instead of expecting the idealistic, romantic behavior of her dream husband.
4. Help the wife to take control of certain areas of her life that do not interfere with the husband's schedule. She can grow

spiritually by having a regular time of Bible reading, memorization, and prayer. She can improve her intellectual life by starting a reading program or by learning a new skill such as word processing.

5. Help the wife to realize who has the real problem. In most cases, even with verbal abuse, it is the husband's problem.

6. Get the husband into counseling if at all possible on the strength of the fact that counseling will help the wife. Deal with him about his sins of selfishness, lying, uncontrolled anger, bitterness, and failure to love his wife (Eph. 4:25-32; 5:25-33; I Pet. 3:7).

7. In most cases the husband's present thoughts and feelings did not begin with his relationship to his wife. Try to locate the source of his anger and bitterness in his childhood and/or teen relationship with his mother.

8. Assist the abusive husband to become aware of his selfish dependent behavior. Help him to understand and appropriate the Identification with Christ truth given in Chapter 14.

9. If the husband is physically abusive to the wife or the children, encourage the wife to warn him that she is going to leave him the next time the abuse happens. She should also work out a plan of leaving: where she is going, how she is going to get there, and so on. She should not plan to return until he gets counseling. She should let her pastor and counselor know the full extent of the abuse so that they will know how to counsel the husband properly. The abusive husband will make all kinds of promises to get her back within a short time, but the wife must stay away until the pastor or counselor thinks that the husband has truly changed his behavior. Until the husband learns to handle his anger, gets rid of his sin of bitterness, and makes a dramatic change in his actions, there is no profit in trying to get the couple back together. Going back too soon will bring about a repetition of the abuse. Even after they are reunited, there must be continued counseling with the husband and wife together.

Case Study:

The counselor received a long-distance phone call in November from Betty, who had been married five years and had two children. She said that during the previous summer her husband, Ivan, had started abusing her physically. He would hit her with his fist whenever he was angry or frustrated. She said he never hit her where it would show; it was always on the back, upper arm, stomach, or chest. The verbal abuse had gotten worse each time she had been pregnant, and the physical abuse had started a month after their second child was born in June.

Betty said that Ivan had become verbally abusive on their honeymoon and would get upset at the slightest thing that displeased him, especially when she tried to correct him, even on minor matters. She said that he was also possessive and jealous if she talked to any man near her age and had accused her many times of infidelity. He would always check the car mileage when she went to a missionary meeting or the grocery store. He controlled all the money and never gave her any to spend unless he received an accounting of every penny. It had gotten to the point in the last year at which he would not let her go out of the house unless he was with her. She said that many times, if everything was not perfect at mealtimes, he would throw the contents of his plate on the floor and go to his room. If he got especially irritated with her, he would not speak to her for days. He also ridiculed her in front of their friends at church.

Ivan had a gun collection and once threatened to use a gun on a neighbor who had irritated him. Betty said that she was afraid he would use a gun on her or the children. After a beating, he would be very charming and loving and would apologize and say it would never happen again. She said that she was so afraid of him, she was going to take the two children and leave him. When the counselor asked whether he would get counseling, she said no, he was too proud.

Betty and Ivan both came from Christian families and had gone to a Christian high school. However, Ivan's father was an indulgent, permissive father and a passive Christian with a domineering wife. His father also had had three affairs, and the mother had divorced him when Ivan was fifteen.

The counselor knew Ivan and Betty because the couple had attended the counselor's church before they married and moved out of state. Ivan was a short, slightly built man, and the counselor's impression of him was that he was a spoiled brat grown up. Ivan had a job as a salesman and, because of his high intelligence and good social skills, seemed to be doing well. He had provided a nice house for his family.

The counselor advised Betty that if she were to leave Ivan, she should go to a safe place and not let him know where she was until he had received counseling. A month later the counselor heard from Betty that she had left her husband and was at a friend's house in another city. She had left a note for Ivan, saying that if he would get counseling, she would consider coming back. Her mother was supplying her with money to live on while she was separated. Four days after Betty's second phone call, Ivan called the counselor, told him about his wife's leaving, and said he would do anything to get her back. He set up an appointment with the counselor and agreed to commute one hundred miles once a week to see him.

Case Study Solution:

The counselor assured Ivan that his wife and children were safe and well taken care of and told him not to try to contact his wife until his problem was resolved. Ivan complained that his wife often refused to have sex with him and would serve him food that she knew he did not like because she said it was better for him than what he wanted. He had often come in from his sales trips at odd hours and asked for a meal, which she had refused to fix.

The counselor found that Ivan was bitter against his mother's control over his father and him when he was growing up. He said that he always felt like a weakling in any interaction with his mother and had even gotten to the point in his rebellion where he hated his mother. She used to whip him with a switch and rant and rave for an hour or two about his behavior. His dad would always side with Ivan and ridicule the mother. By his teenage years, Ivan would avoid a whipping or a tongue-lashing by running away from her. His basic problem was his bitterness and hatred toward his mother, which he transferred to his wife.

Ivan wrote a long letter to his mother, asking her forgiveness. He arranged a visit with her a week later at her home in California.

At the fourth session, after he'd been reconciled to his mother, he brought the counselor a copy of a five-page letter he had written to his wife, which he asked the counselor to send to his wife. In it he detailed all of the mean, hateful things he had done to her, some of which Betty did not know about, such as his burning several highly prized dolls from her childhood that she thought had been lost when they moved.

In the letter, Ivan agreed to several things the counselor had suggested: to give Betty an allowance and to let her have her own checking account. He also agreed never to check the car's mileage. She even got to have her own car, which he would not control except for the maintenance. He also agreed to sell his gun collection, to help more around the house, and to write her little love notes. He also said in the letter that he would like to have at least two sessions with her and the counselor before they were reconciled.

At their first joint session, Ivan asked his wife's forgiveness for his sorry treatment of her. After a discussion of I Corinthians 7:1-6, Ephesians 5:20-33, and I Peter 4:1-7, Betty then agreed to have an enthusiastic approach to his frequent sex demands and to make their marriage more sensual and affectionate by doing things such as greeting him with a hug and a kiss when he came home, taking showers with him, and wearing the delicate lingerie he frequently bought for her. She also agreed to fix him some of the food he liked instead of always insisting on her health-food menus. In addition, she agreed to keep in the freezer several special meals that he liked, which she could heat up no matter what time he came home.

About a year later, the counselor found that Ivan and Betty were getting along well, although there had been several relapses on Ivan's part regarding the verbal abuse and sulking. However, Betty realized that she had been partly at fault, and both had taken steps for immediate correction.

Chapter 20

Suffering and Grief

The human existence from birth to death is filled with hardship, suffering, and grief. Everyone experiences these things to some degree at some period in his life. The suffering and grief are particularly acute when they affect the innocent, such as a little child who had leukemia as well as other physical problems over a period of four years requiring several operations. Suffering is difficult to understand even for people who have lived a full life and for whom tragedy strikes just before retirement. In the case of one couple in their early sixties, the wife developed Alzheimer's disease, then within two years the husband contracted Parkinson's disease, and three years later, both had to be put in a nursing home.

The question that arises with the saved and the unsaved alike is "Why does God permit suffering?" Unbelievers, and oftentimes Christians, find it difficult to reconcile the love, mercy, and justice of God with the suffering of humanity. When suffering invades a life, a person is either drawn closer to God and profits from the experience by having his faith strengthened and his testimony for Christ enhanced, or he is devastated and defeated. As someone has said, "They either become better or bitter."

For the Christian, certain promises in the Word of God help in dealing with suffering, in gaining victory over hardships, and in counteracting the natural bent toward self-pity and bitterness. For example, Romans 8:28 says, "And we know that all things work together for good to them that love God, to them who are the called according to his purpose"; Hebrews 13:5 states, "I will never leave thee, nor forsake thee"; John 14:18 states, "I will not leave you comfortless: I will come to you"; and Joshua 1:5 states, "I will not fail thee, nor forsake thee."

God's Word recounts a great deal of suffering among the Israelites, God's chosen people. Brought on by their sin, this suffering was an understandable consequence because God promised them blessing if they would serve Him and misery and suffering if they turned from Him to idols (Deut. 30:15-20).

What is difficult to understand is the suffering of the innocent and the righteous. Righteous Job suffered, and God gave us the entire book of Job as a rational explanation. During Job's intense suffering, in view of his moral, righteous life and his love of God, he wondered, "For what purpose did this happen to me?" Job never did receive an answer but had to console himself by just trusting God. In the midst of suffering, by faith, he was able to verbalize the victory, "I shall come forth as gold" (Job 23:10). Job saw God through the suffering, because in faith he was listening to and seeing God: "I have heard of thee by the hearing of the ear: but now mine eye seeth thee" (Job 42:5).

God uses the fires of affliction and suffering to refine and purify every Christian by melting out the dross of self and the flesh. The refiner (God) is tending the fire, making sure it accomplishes His purpose as stated in the Old Testament: "And he shall sit as a refiner and purifier of silver . . . and purge them as gold and silver, that they might offer unto the Lord an offering of righteousness" (Mal. 3:3).

Habakkuk experienced suffering and received from the Lord the method of handling it: "And the Lord answered me, and said, . . . the just shall live by his faith" (Hab. 2:2, 4). Christians also view this faith as "an anchor of the soul, both sure and stedfast" (Heb. 6:19). This faith, which God gives to the penitent soul, is not natural optimism, a feeling of surety, or reasoned conclusions based on evidence received through the senses; it is a confidence in God which results in changed behavior and an obedience to God's Word.

The prophet Isaiah, seven hundred years before the suffering of Christ, predicted the crucifixion ("a man of sorrows, and acquainted with grief," Isa. 53:3). The New Testament indicates that Christ's suffering was an example for the Christian. "Christ also suffered for us, leaving us an example, that ye should follow his steps" (I Pet. 2:21).

Christians should rejoice in suffering because they are partakers of Christ's suffering (I Pet. 4:13). Most dedicated Christians share Paul's desire to "know him and the power of his resurrection," but they are not eager to share in "the fellowship of his sufferings" (Phil. 3:10). Yet sharing in the suffering is the thing that will magnify one's union with Christ. God has promised that the godly will suffer persecution (II Tim. 3:12). The godly Christian should not be surprised when persecution comes in its many forms. He is not hunted down by soldiers and fed to the lions as the Christians were in New Testament times; but persecution may take other forms, such as unjust accusation, loss of job and opportunity, and the sneering contempt of the world. "For unto you it is given in the behalf of Christ, not only to believe on him, but also to suffer for his sake" (Phil. 1:29).

Problem #23: Suffering and Grief

Definition:

Suffering is the state of being in pain, mental and/or physical, as a result of any one of or a combination of the following: tragedy to or the death of loved ones; sickness, injury, disability, or handicap; damage to or loss of property, career, character, or reputation; and rejection or persecution.

Scripture:

Job 1:21; 2:10; 42:5; Psalms 34:15-22; 119:67, 71, 75, 92; Isaiah 53:3-4, 7; Habakkuk 2:2, 4; Romans 8:18, 28; II Corinthians 9:8; 12:9; Philippians 3:10; II Timothy 2:12; Hebrews 12:5-13; I Peter 2:21; 4:13.

Information and Principles:

There are three types of grief:

1. **Tragedy grief**—The biggest tragedy in the minds of most people is death. The death of a child is probably the most traumatic. Fifty percent of marriages that suffer the death of a child break up within three years after that death because of the unconscious blame of one spouse toward the other. The second most traumatic is receiving the diagnosis of and enduring a terminal disease. Then come accidents, such as a

car wreck, and losing possessions, home, and irreplaceable keepsakes through fire, earthquake, tornado, hurricane, flood, or theft.

2. **Shame grief**—This type of grief might result from a family member's being jailed, being diagnosed with AIDS, committing suicide, or getting a divorce; a child's going wrong by running away, being addicted to drugs, or living in immorality; or a parent's being addicted to drugs or immorality.

3. **Neglected grief**—This type of grief is present but is usually not recognized as grief. It occurs after a woman has a miscarriage, especially in the last five months of pregnancy. After she has felt the movement of the baby, the baby is as alive to her as if it were born, and she will grieve to the same extent that she would for the death of a one- or two-month-old baby. She will also grieve the same way if the baby is stillborn, mentally retarded, or deformed. A man tends to suffer this type of grief when he loses his job or experiences failure in his career or foreclosure on a farm, business, or home.

The counselor must distinguish between real grief and self-pity. There's a natural sorrow over various situations, heartaches, and tragedies; but when the sorrow is prolonged over a period of many months and the counselee keeps talking about hurting inside, he is probably indulging in self-pity. It grows out of the sinful attitudes of discontentment and envy. Unless the counselee takes charge of his own mental state and ends the self-pity syndrome, he could lapse into severe depression. Self-pity can be a cover-up for bitterness against a person who he thinks caused or allowed the tragedy. Evidences of self-pity are as follows:

1. Repeated crying jags
2. Repeated questioning about why the tragedy happened
3. Lack of goals
4. Angry or bitter remarks
5. Depression

Healthy grief may last from several weeks up to three or four months. The person asks, "What is God trying to accomplish in my life?" He praises the Lord and thanks God for every situation. He sets goals and goes on with life, experiencing the joy of the Lord.

The counselor must use sensitivity in making the distinction between self-pity and healthy grief. The Bible encourages a sympathetic spirit: "Rejoice with them that do rejoice, and weep with them that weep" (Rom. 12:15).

There are several general principles that apply to the problem of suffering and grief.

God's love for the Christian is certain and eternal (I John 4:8-10, 16; John 3:16; Jer. 31:3). The evidence that God loves us is the sacrifice of His only Son to save us from hell. No matter what happens, nothing can separate us from the eternal love of God, which existed before the creation of the world (Rom. 8:35-39).

The extent of a person's grief and sorrow is the result of his choices. When tragedy and grief happen, there is natural sorrow and maybe tears with most people. There are also questions: "Is there anything that could have been done to prevent it?" "Was I to blame?" Then comes the choice to handle the grief God's way or the fleshly way. The sooner the right choice is made, the less the magnitude of the grief. God's way is first to thank God immediately for the situation (I Thess. 5:18; Eph. 5:20). The second step is to ask, "What is God trying to accomplish in my life?" (Prov. 3:5-6). It might be God's dealing with the individual about a particular sin or God's working out some future purpose so that His will might be done. In the case of death, the best thing that can happen to a Christian is to die and go to heaven to be with the Lord. The third step is to trust God to work good from the situation (Ps. 118:8; Rom. 8:28; Phil. 4:6). The fourth step is to set goals (Phil. 3:13). The fifth step is to have an attitude of praise (Ps. 107:8).

David's response to the announcement of his baby's death in II Samuel 12:19-23 was a godly response, which his aides could not understand because they were not accustomed to seeing anyone respond this way. David's response was based on his trust in God, knowing that his baby was in heaven and someday he would see the child again.

The fleshly choice is to ask the question "Why me?" as if it would be better if the tragedy had happened to somebody else, or "Why now?" as if it would be better if it had happened at another time. "Why" questions insult the intelligence of God. The second fleshly step is self-pity and envy of those who are not suffering. The third step is anger and trying to find someone to blame, such as the doctor, the one responsible for the accident, or even God. The fourth step is bitterness, and the fifth is depression.

SITUATION ↓	
GRIEF AND TEARS ↓	
↓ **GODLY STEPS**	↓ **FLESHLY STEPS**
1. Thanking God immediately for the situation	1. Asking "Why me?" or "Why now?"
2. Asking "What is God trying to accomplish in my life?"	2. Self-pity and envy of those who are not suffering
3. Trusting God to work good from the situation	3. Anger and attempted blame
4. Setting goals	4. Bitterness
5. An attitude of praise	5. Depression

The Christian thanks and praises God for everything that happens to him (Eph. 5:20; I Thess. 5:18). There may be tears, there may be heartache; but the Christian is inwardly rejoicing with a thankful spirit, knowing that God is working out His eternal will and purpose in the Christian's life. This attitude of thankfulness and praise in every situation becomes a habitual response as a Christian learns to focus on the sovereignty of God and His permissive will as well as on the positive eternal gain as Paul did instead of on the personal temporary pain (Phil. 1:12-25).

God allows problems, adverse circumstances, sickness, tragedy, suffering, and death for various reasons.

1. To conform a Christian to the image of Christ (Rom. 8:29; I Pet. 4:13; Phil. 3:10)
2. As a form of discipline (Heb. 12:5-13)
3. As a natural consequence of sin in the world (Rom. 5:12)
4. As a result of taking communion with unconfessed sin in the heart (I Cor. 11:29-30)
5. To purge out the dross and purify the Christian's life (Mal. 3:3)
6. In order that the glory of God might be revealed through supernatural healing, resolution of impossible circumstances, or the Spirit-led response of a Christian under pressure (Luke 7:16; Phil. 1:20; I Pet. 4:11-19)

When it rains, it usually pours. There is an idea, often called Murphy's Law, that if something can go wrong, it will and at the worst possible time. Sometimes one tragedy complicates or sets in motion additional tragedies. For example, a woman gets a telephone call at home that her husband has had a heart attack on the job and he's in the emergency room of the hospital. She grabs her two-year-old and her purse, leaves a pot boiling on the stove, and jumps into the car without buckling her child with the seat belt. In her hurry she runs a stoplight, gets hit by a car, and the child is injured. When the ambulance arrives, she jumps into the ambulance to accompany her child, leaving her purse in the wrecked car. The purse is stolen; and the pot boils dry on the stove, causing a fire that burns part of the kitchen and causes smoke damage to the rest of the house before the fire department can put it out. This example may sound exaggerated, but some people could tell us similar stories that are true. In cases like this, Christians can take consolation in the facts that this kind of situation happens to many people at some time in their lives, that God is fully aware of it and allows it to happen for a purpose, and that God will give the needed grace and will work all things together for good.

Solutions:
1. Review the appropriate principles and Scripture.
2. Help the counselee distinguish between real grief and self-pity.
3. Review the godly steps to handling grief listed in Principle 2.
4. Emphasize God's grace (II Cor. 9:8; 12:9-10).
5. Help the counselee see the situation from God's viewpoint, especially in the case of a loved one's death, by reviewing the promises of God, such as those found in II Samuel 12:23; Psalm 116:15; John 14:1-3; II Corinthians 5:1-9; and II Timothy 4:6-8.
6. Remind the counselee of how Paul handled adverse circumstances. He focused on Christ, on the sovereignty of God and His permissive will, and on the positive gain of the gospel of Christ rather than on the personal pain of his own circumstances (Phil. 1:12-24).
7. Suggest that the counselee to start or participate in some ministry of helping others.

8. Have the counselee set some daily, weekly, and monthly goals with specific steps for accomplishing them.

Case Study:

Betty, a well-educated, fifty-eight-year-old woman, was referred to the counselor by her daughter. She had accepted Christ at eight years of age and had been involved in church work all her life. When Betty was 55, her mother and father, both in their eighties, died within four months of each other. Two years later, Betty's husband died from a heart attack; and, although she thought she had adjusted to his death fairly well, a month after the funeral she went into depression. As a result of her depression, Betty became negligent in her housekeeping, had insomnia, and awoke very early every morning. She refused to go out socially and stopped attending church. When anyone visited, Betty would bring up her husband's death, crying as she spoke of it. Betty was financially well situated, her house was paid for, and she had investments that brought in a comfortable income. For the last two months, she had gotten to the point of not dressing during the day. She was extremely tired and usually slept half of the daytime hours.

Case Study Solution:

The counselor had Betty receive a physical examination. The doctor determined that she had an estrogen deficiency and put her on estrogen replacement therapy. He also found her anemic and prescribed iron tablets.

The counselor discovered that Betty and her husband had planned to buy a travel trailer and tour the United States and Canada. Their retirement plans had also included several trips to Europe and the Far East. Betty admitted that she was bitter against God for taking her husband and making it impossible for them to enjoy together the travel that they had dreamed of and for which they had made extensive plans.

The counselor talked to Betty about the sovereignty of God and the Identification with Christ truth (see Problem 11) and reviewed the steps of self-pity. Betty dedicated her life to Christ and became willing to do the Lord's will with her life and money. She volunteered as a supervisor at a nearby Christian college.

The counselor prescribed a daily walking program, continued volunteer work, and motivated Betty to begin teaching a women's Bible study class. She also took on a project of assisting an elderly widow in her church.

After a month of counseling, Betty's grief and self-pity with the resulting depression diminished to a point at which it was no longer a problem. She resumed the vibrant, rejoicing lifestyle that had been characteristic of her before her husband's death.

Depression

The most common problem the counselor will deal with in his ministry is depression. Depression, if not physical, is usually a result of the root sin of fornication or bitterness. Almost everyone experiences depression in varying degrees during his life. Unfortunately, Christians are not immune to this problem. Pastors verify that depression frequently saps the spiritual strength of God's people. Often, even those who know the Lord cry out as the psalmist David, "I looked on my right hand, and beheld, but there was no man that would know me: refuge failed me; no man cared for my soul" (Ps. 142:4). In such a state, one may begin to doubt his salvation, the Bible, and even the existence of God.

The Bible records some of the best-known Bible characters as being depressed: Moses (Num. 11:10-16; Exod. 18:12-22); David (II Sam. 12:1-17; Ps. 51:17); Elijah (I Kings 19:1-18); and Jonah (Jonah 4). Psalm 77 lists some of David's depression symptoms (vv. 2-9) and the steps he took to cure the depression (vv. 1, 10-20).

- He turned to the Lord instead of turning to some addiction or recreation to relieve his depression (vs. 1).
- He was weeping and refused to be comforted (vs. 2).
- He felt guilty because of his sin and added the sin of complaining. This is especially important because "Selah" is put after every notable sentence (vs. 3).
- He was so depressed that he could not sleep or even talk and had physical complaints (Ps. 32:3-4) (vs. 4).
- He was dwelling on past sins (vs. 5).

- He was especially depressed at nighttime and increased his introspection (vs. 6).
- He was worried about being cast away from the Lord forever (vs. 7).
- He did not feel that God's promises, mercy, and grace would ever again be applied to him (vv. 8-9).
- He started on the solution to his depression by recognizing it and its cause. He then confessed his sin (Ps. 32:1-5; 51) (vs. 10).
- He remembered the works, salvation, holiness, and majestic power of God. He started meditating on and talking about them (vv. 11-20).

Problem #24: Depression

Definition:

Depression is a sustained chronic mood of sadness, despondency, and discouragement resulting in difficulty in concentrating, slowing of thought, memory impairment, irritability, and an excessive response to small annoyances. There may be preoccupation with accompanying physical problems such as back pain, muscle pain, fatigue, weight loss or gain, loss of appetite and sexual interest, and sleep problems, which usually means waking early and not being able to go back to sleep.

Scripture:

Exodus 18:12-22; Numbers 11:10-16; II Samuel 12:1-17; I Kings 19:1-18; Psalms 23, 51, 77; Psalm 51:17; and Jonah 4

Information and Principles:

According to the National Institute of Mental Health, 15 percent of American adults ages 18 to 74 (20 million people) suffer from significant depressive illnesses every year, with twice as many women as men being affected. It is estimated that one-third of all adult women have been depressed to the point of considering suicide, and about one of every ten people will, at some time, need professional help for this problem. Teenage suicide attempts have increased dramatically, and depression is an underlying cause.

There are three main types of depression.

1. **Anxiety depression**—Usually this anxiety is caused by fear of being found out and punished by the world, by God, or by both for sin committed. Anxiety also results from double-mindedness or from not knowing what decision to make or from fear of bodily or mental harm, such as terminal disease or financial collapse. David is a good example of someone affected by anxiety depression. He was fearful of God's wrath and judgment, and his fear caused all kinds of physical problems (Ps. 77:1-9; 32:3-4). Another sufferer of anxiety depression was Moses (Num. 11:10-16). He was anxious and concerned about the burden of counseling and judging all the people of Israel (vv. 11-14). In verse 14 he said, "I'm not able to bear all this people alone, because it is too heavy for me." And then, in his depression, he said in verse 15, "And if thou deal thus with me, kill me I pray thee, out of hand, if I have found favor in thy sight; and let me not see my wretchedness."

2. **Anger depression**—Anger that cannot be vented on a victim often turns to bitterness and then is directed inward on the self as frustration and depression. A person affected by this type of depression might be angry at someone who was bringing pressure to bear on him. If that someone were a boss or some other authority to which the person could not exhibit his anger, he would turn the anger inward and become depressed. Jonah is an example of a person who experienced anger depression. In the fourth chapter of Jonah, verses 6 through 9, Jonah sat under a gourd, wishing that he would die. When God caused the gourd to wither (vs. 7), Jonah said, "I do well to be angry, even unto death."

3. **Withdrawal depression**—This is the most serious kind of depression and may result in suicide. In withdrawal depression, which can result from anxiety or anger depression, there is a complete sense of helplessness and hopelessness. An example of a man in these depths of depression is Elijah. After his victory at Mount Carmel, he fled from Jezebel, who had threatened to kill him the next day (I Kings 19:1-4). In verse 4 he sat under a juniper tree and finally became so depressed that he said, "It is enough; now, O Lord, take away my life; for I am not better than my fathers."

Manic, or bipolar, depression is likely an extreme swing in moods from anxiety depression to anger depression, or it may be the body's reaction to extreme depression to restore the balance necessary for good adjustment. Saul is an example of a manic depressive person (I Sam. 18:8-12). His depressed state began with anger depression (vs. 8) and swung to anxiety depression: "And Saul was afraid of David because the Lord was with him, and was departed from Saul" (vs. 12). The manic phase of the cycle opposite the depressive phase is evident in verse 11: "And Saul cast the javelin; for he said, I will smite David even to the wall with it."

There are several general principles that apply to the problem of depression.

Finding and eliminating the cause is the key to curing depression. The contributing causes of depression are either physical, environmental, mental, or a combination of all three. If one can identify the cause of the problem, he has a good chance of successfully alleviating it. Merely treating symptoms with pills and other superficial remedies may bring temporary relief, but recognizing the cause and taking steps to minimize it will help bring about a permanent cure. The causes can be grouped under the following three categories: physical, environmental, and mental. These are listed below with some nonmedical remedies.

Physical Causes (see also Chapter 5)

1. *Cycles* (regular periodic changes in the body)—The human body experiences certain basic cycles. Women are particularly affected by their hormonal cycles, which are probably the cause of frequent depression. Women can almost plot their three to four up-and-down cycles each month. Men may also notice such an up-and-down cycle, but they usually have only one low point during a thirty- to forty-day period of time. By plotting depressed times, one can anticipate the lows and take action to prevent depressing situations or events from occurring. Scheduling things to do, such as tasks or social events, will help keep one from slipping into despondency.

2. *Anemia* (a lack of iron)—Women are more susceptible to anemia than men. Two symptoms of anemia are fuzzy thinking and depression. A sample blood test during a regular physical checkup can determine whether additional iron is

needed. Good nutrition and extra vitamins and minerals are also helpful for anemia.

3. *Low blood sugar* (hypoglycemia)—A low blood sugar level is often caused by poor eating habits. The solution is to eat a balanced diet with adequate protein, rather than eating more sugar or carbohydrates. Eating nuts or cheese between meals, drinking fruit juices without added sugar, drinking milk for snacks, and eating a well-balanced breakfast are important factors. A person should not let more than four or five hours pass without eating something. Many find that a midnight snack of protein is helpful in preventing severe depression in the morning.

4. *Childbirth*—Following childbirth, some women tend to have a depressed period called post-partum blues, which can last from three days to six months. Advocates of natural birth and breast feeding have suggested that those who use a technique such as the Lamaze method or who breast-feed their babies are not so susceptible to this type of depression. Helen Wessel, in her book *Natural Childbirth and the Christian Family,*[1] gives some good ideas along these lines. A husband who is understanding, gives his wife security, and helps with the new duties and responsibilities will do much to alleviate her depressed feelings at this time.

5. *Hormone upset*—For some women there is a link between menopause and depression. When a woman susceptible to depression reaches menopause, the problem may be aggravated. To stabilize this upset hormone level, some doctors recommend estrogen therapy. A pap smear can determine whether estrogen therapy is necessary. Although not all doctors agree concerning the advisability of this therapy, it does seem to help in some cases. There may also be other endocrine problems, such as thyroid deficiency, that result in depression. Problems such as these require a doctor's diagnosis and treatment.

6. *Fatigue*—Both men and women may find that fatigue brings on depression. In a recent survey of Christian married women, it was found that, of those having marital problems and depression, most listed fatigue as a major cause of their difficulties. On the average, women seem to need approximately

one hour more sleep than do men. This finding is especially true of mothers with preschool children. Those mothers who fail to get enough rest are more disposed to depression.

The counselor must be careful that he does not make any medical diagnoses or give medical remedies. Such recommendations should be made by a qualified physician after a thorough medical exam.

Environmental Causes

1. *Seasons*—Periods of depression tend to recur for most people, and some of these periods may be more intense in the spring or fall. Other seasonal times may also be influential, such as Christmas, New Years, and post-vacation time.

2. *Color and music*—Many people may not be aware that both color and music can also affect their moods. Dull, dark colors in the home have a depressive effect on some people, while the use of primary colors may have an uplifting effect. In the kitchen, bright colors, especially yellows, usually have a positive effect on women. Certain types of music may also govern moods. For example, plaintive, nostalgic music associated with sad or unpleasant past experiences may cause depression. Saul called for David to play on the harp when he was troubled by "an evil spirit from God" (I Sam. 16:14-23). Listening to good and uplifting music such as marches and hymns of rejoicing and praise can help in overcoming depression.

3. *Lack of light*—Research has found that a lack of light is also a major factor in many people's depression. Studies indicate that depression is prevalent in the North during the months of January and February, when daylight hours are minimal. Also gaining attention is seasonal affective disorder (SAD), a syndrome characterized by seasonal mood swings in which people become depressed in wintertime and, as spring approaches, return to normal behavior. People affected by SAD are at their best during the long days of July and August. Researchers at the National Institute of Mental Health defined this syndrome in the early 1980s: "Latitude appears to be as important as season: the incidence and severity of SAD increase with distance from the equator, peaking at around

40° north. . . . Experts say the syndrome, which afflicts about four times as many women as men, usually appears in the early 20s." Researchers believe that there is a genetic factor involved "because more than two-thirds of those with the syndrome have a close relative with a mood disorder."[2]

Other theories are that SAD is "a disturbance in the body's natural clock and abnormal production of melatonin, a hormone manufactured in the brain, and serotonin, a chemical that helps transmit nerve impulses." Observers have found that light therapy relieves the SAD symptoms—the more sunlight, the better. If artificial light is used, it must be supplied by special fluorescent tubes that emit the full spectrum of natural light.[3]

Mental Causes

The following are some of the mental causes of depression.

1. *Guilt*—The greatest single cause of depression for the Christian is a feeling of guilt about either past sins or present sin habits. Many people have a "sin boil" in their lives—some past sin (usually immorality) for which they have never taken full responsibility and which they have never confessed. They need to use the three-point formula for getting rid of "sin boils" found in Romans 14:17: "For the kingdom of God is not meat and drink; but righteousness, and peace, and joy in the Holy Ghost." First, righteousness comes by taking full responsibility for the sin instead of trying to blame another for it, and confessing it before God (Isa. 1:18; Eph. 1:7; I John 1:7). Second, peace comes by refusing to think about the sin after it has been cleansed (Phil. 3:13; Isa. 43:18-19, 25). Third, joy in the Holy Spirit comes by praising God for His forgiveness (Isa. 44:22, 23; Ps. 107:8).

A present sin habit may also be a cause of depression. In this case many have used the following four-step formula. First, admit it as sin and confess it to the Lord. Second, set a goal for conquering the problem; for example, decide that for three days you will refrain from your particular sin habit. Concentrate on the goal rather than the sin. If you reach the goal, set new goals for victory. If you fail, confess it and set new goals. Third, when you are tempted with the sin you are trying to overcome, try to engage in some physical activity. A daily routine of exercise will help rechannel energies. Fourth, meditate on a verse of Scripture in times of temptation. This formula has helped many overcome such sinful habits as smoking, overeating, drinking, and various sex sins.

2. *Bitterness and hatred*—The connection between bitterness and hatred and depression is especially clear if the hatred is directed toward a basic love object such as mother, father, or God. Many people have blamed God for tragic events or the death of a loved one. Such bitterness is extremely harmful. God promises, however, that confession of bitterness (or hatred) will restore a Christian to His loving fellowship. One solution to this type of problem is to read I John every day for thirty days, underlining the important verses, since I John is the book that states what love is and what it accomplishes in the life. The Word of God will have a powerful effect in changing sinful attitudes. One must also take steps to right the wronged love relationship by making amends or by asking and giving forgiveness. Definite actions of love toward the formerly hated individual—a loving letter, a phone call, or an act of kindness—will tend to break completely the pattern of hate.

3. *Negative thinking*—People have a tendency to get into habits of negative, flesh-controlled thinking (self-deprecation), which have a bad effect on both the mind and body. Women are especially susceptible to this attitude while doing repetitious, nonthinking tasks such as ironing or washing dishes. To break this negative pattern, one woman pinned Bible verses on the curtains and used dishwashing time for memorization.

4. *Self-pity*—Comparing oneself to others may often lead to a private "pity party" and prohibit the attitude of praise that should fill every Christian's life. These sinful thoughts are described in II Corinthians 10:5 as wicked "imaginations . . . against the knowledge of God."

5. *Upsetting life events*—In a study, Dr. T. H. Holmes listed the top six events that produce depression: death of a spouse, divorce, marital separation, jail term, death of a close family member, and personal illness or injury. Circumstances such

as these cause a dramatic change in lifestyle and can result in depression. Other causes may be job loss, forced retirement, and loneliness. To avoid depression, one must set as his goal the restoration of normality to his life. Hard work and helping others are two positive steps in combatting the problem.

6. *Lack of goals*—Many people have found that setting and accomplishing daily and weekly goals gives them a feeling of satisfaction and success. The Scripture states, "Hope deferred maketh the heart sick: but when the desire cometh, it is a tree of life. . . . The desire accomplished is sweet to the soul" (Prov. 13:12, 19).

7. *Success letdown*—The natural letdown that follows success may be another cause of depression. After his triumph over the prophets of Baal, Elijah suffered from this problem. After his victory on Mount Carmel, we find him under a juniper tree asking God to let him die (I Kings 19:4). The natural letdown after the thrill of accomplishment is the body's way of readjusting to a normal status—and the bigger the success, the bigger the letdown. This letdown occurs because of the greater output of adrenalin in the circulatory system in times of emergency, following which the body must once again recover to a normal state. Listing future goals and planning the details are good exercises to overcome times of letdown.

Starting in early childhood, people fall into several habits of thinking that predispose them to depression.

1. *Learned helplessness*—When a person fails repeatedly, he is subject to repeated and undeserved criticism in some area of his life, is overprotected and never allowed to do things on his own, or comes up against many situations that he feels unable to control, he often gives up, quits trying, becomes dependent, and gives in to self-pity and finally depression.

2. *Ambivalent thinking or double-mindedness about decisions, people, or situations (James 1:8)*—A person who experiences ambivalent thinking vacillates between accepting or rejecting people or situations completely instead of viewing them as complex and taking a more objective view. Dependent people tend to be double-minded toward the person upon

whom they depend. They vacillate between feelings of reliance or appreciation for needs supplied and feelings of anger or hatred toward the supplier for making them dependent. Humans, because of the flesh, tend to bite the hand that feeds them.

3. *Blaming others for the present situation*—This habit of blaming usually starts in childhood with the person's blaming his parents for any adverse circumstances or attitudes.

The personality traits of a perfectionist, carried to the extreme, may lead to depression. The Bible does encourage perfection and excellence as a goal: "Be ye therefore perfect, even as your Father which is in heaven is perfect" (Matt. 5:48; Phil. 1:10). But every Christian realizes that this perfection, found in Christ, is finally achieved after death when the body and spirit are completely changed. When one fails in this life, he can be restored through confession and/or can recover with the attitude of "Do your best; let God do the rest." The wrong view is feeling upset, discouraged, and depressed when one cannot be perfect in every situation. Unrealistic perfectionism can take three forms.

1. *Extreme competitiveness*—These people always have to win, no matter what the cost, in any athletic, academic, business, or social situation. When a person does not win, he experiences envy, resentment, and bitterness, all of which may lead to depression.

2. *Extreme orderliness and frustration with people who disturb that order*—Usually these people feel insecure, and their slavish dedication to order helps them to feel that they are in control.

3. *Jot-and-tittle Christians*—These people feel compelled to keep every jot and tittle of the law, no matter what the circumstances, out of a fear of losing their salvation. They do not realize the liberty that, under grace, a Christian has in Christ (II Cor. 3:17; Gal. 5:1,13). They keep every rule, no matter how minute. For example, if during an emergency the jot-and-tittle Christian had to cross the grass in violation of a "Keep off the grass" sign, he would feel guilt-stricken for doing so. If the same Christian had to go down an "Up only" staircase to escape a fire, he would feel guilty in that case

also. Such Christians become slaves to rules and regulations (Eccl. 7:16).

Solutions:

1. Review the appropriate principles and Scripture.
2. Have the counselee confess any known sin, including anger and bitterness, and be reconciled to a hated one if necessary.
3. Review the steps in Psalms 51 and 77 that David took in conquering his depression.
4. Have the counselee see his physician or family doctor for a complete physical exam. Encourage the counselee to tell his doctor about the physical symptoms he has described to you.
5. Help the counselee follow a sensible diet, cutting down on sweets and increasing his protein intake.
6. Have the counselee start on a progressive aerobic exercise program within his capabilities. Some people cannot jog because of leg problems, but they could swim or engage in water aerobics.
7. Start the counselee on a program of helping others, starting with his family and expanding to fellow church members and neighbors.
8. If his environment is depressing, have the counselee change it as much as possible. For example, he could repaint a room in a brighter or lighter color, let in more light, or change the type of music he listens to.
9. In severe cases a doctor can prescribe an antidepressant drug that will not cure the problem but will relieve the symptoms and enable the person to respond to counseling through which he will try to find and eliminate the cause.

Case Study:

Tammy, a beautiful forty-two-year-old woman, came to see the counselor about terrible depression. Her husband, Don, had been very worried about her. He had told the counselor that she used to have a good sense of well-being and was very energetic and willing to serve the Lord in any church activity. In the last three months, she had lost her appetite and about fifteen pounds. She was waking up at 2:00 in the morning and could not go back to sleep. Consequently, she was tired all the time. Don said that Tammy used to be a very alert person but now she could not seem to think or concentrate on anything. She used to be a great lover and a very caring wife, but now she had begun to feel worthless as a wife and a Christian.

Don had convinced Tammy to go to a doctor for a complete physical four weeks prior to their visit with the counselor because he was afraid that she had cancer or some other disease that was causing her depression. However, the doctor had given her a clean bill of health. Rather than trying antidepressants that would treat only the symptoms, Tammy agreed to see a Christian counselor.

Don wondered whether Tammy's problem could be the "empty-nest syndrome" that he had read about. Their two children, a boy and a girl, were both away at college. Tammy did not work outside the home because her husband had a good job as an auto parts store manager, a job that kept him at work fifty to sixty hours a week.

Case Study Solution:

The counselor questioned Tammy about all kinds of matters but came up with nothing significant until finally she started talking about her "dilemma." She finally revealed that she was in love with another man. She said that a divorced Christian man, whose wife had left him, had moved in next door. He was working the evening shift and had gotten acquainted with her last spring when she was working in her garden. She would talk to him in the morning as she worked in her garden and wave to him as he left for work.

She said that she had gotten up one night, gone to the kitchen, and seen his kitchen light on across her driveway. She could see him standing at his sink. They had waved at each other and this had started what had seemed to be a harmless flirtation. After that she had started getting up about 2 A.M. and going to the kitchen.

One beautiful moonlit spring night with the smell of honeysuckle in the air, she had taken a walk with him, which had ended in sexual relations in a nearby woods. This was repeated several times in the following week. However, her husband had questioned her the last time she went for a walk in the middle of the night, so she had stopped.

She said she was in love with this man and had thought once about leaving her husband and marrying this man but had realized how wicked it was. She said her depression had hit her suddenly a few weeks after her immorality. If she told her husband, he would probably want a divorce and that would wreck her life. Or, if she left her husband and married this divorced man, it would wreck her life spiritually because it would go against all she had ever been taught and believed all these years.

She asked the counselor if she could get right with the Lord and not tell her husband. The counselor went over the Scripture on adultery with her and told her that she would have to tell her husband if she wanted to be right with God and get rid of the depression. The counselor also told her that she would have to abandon the romantic love for the divorced man and start building a real relationship with her husband. Tammy had focused all of her time and affection on the children because her husband worked so much and was never around. The children's leaving for college had revealed her lack of a good relationship with her husband.

Tammy said she wanted to get right with the Lord no matter what her husband would do; so the counselor called Don in, and Tammy told him the whole story. After a tearful time, he forgave her and agreed to start rebuilding their marriage, which they both had allowed to disintegrate through neglect. Don said he would sell the house to a friend who wanted to buy it and move to the other side of town closer to their church and his business.

Tammy got right with the Lord, called the divorced man with Don on the telephone line, and broke off the affair completely, saying that she never intended to see him again. She agreed to give up reading romance novels and watching daytime soap operas, which she felt had contributed to her sin. Don agreed to cut down on his working hours and to spend time rebuilding their relationship. The counselor met with the couple for four more sessions, giving them ideas to help them rebuild their marriage, including sixteen ways to build family unity and Gary Smalley's two books.

At the six-month follow-up visit, they reported a new unity and love which they had never before experienced. Tammy had no more problems with depression and was volunteering twenty hours a week at her church as the compassion ministries coordinator.

Problem #25: Suicide

Suicide is the ultimate step in depression, especially the with-drawal type, when the feelings of helplessness and hopelessness take over. According to the National Center for Disease Control, suicide is the tenth leading cause of death among all age groups, the third (following accidents and homicides) among teenagers and young adults ages fifteen to twenty-four and the second leading cause of death among teenagers ages thirteen to nineteen. Suicide is becoming a serious public health problem.

The Bible records six incidents of suicide in the Old Testament and one in the New Testament: Abimelech (Judges 9:53-54); Saul (I Sam. 31:4-5; I Chron. 10:4-5); Saul's armorbearer (I Sam. 31:5; I Chron. 10:5); Ahithophel (II Sam. 17:23); Zimri (I Kings 16:18); and Judas (Matt. 27:5; Acts 1:18). Nowhere in the Bible is suicide condoned.

Some would claim that Samson's death was a suicide (Judges 16:25-30), but a careful reading shows that his purpose in verse 28 is to commit an act of war against God's enemies (comparable to a marine who charges a machine-gun nest to help defeat an enemy), and he asked God to help him do so. In verse 30 he said, "Let me die with the Philistines," but it is separated from the prayer in verse 28 and may or may not be a plea to God to let him die; however, his own death was not his primary purpose. The destruction of thousands of Philistines was his goal.

A related but more controversial point concerns whether a true Christian can commit suicide; not just consider it, but do it. Romans 1:17 says, "the just shall live by faith." Faith is the basis of the Christian life, and suicide is the ultimate act of lack of faith. It is saying to God, "I do not trust You to handle my problem. I'll seek my own solution. I'll do it my way."

Definition:

Suicide is the taking of one's own life, voluntarily losing the will to live and taking action that will bring about death. The potential suicide appears to perceive his life as so hopeless or complex that he feels a great need to escape.

Scripture:

Judges 9:53-54; 16:25-30; I Samuel 31:4-5; II Samuel 17:23; I Kings 16:18; I Chronicles 10:4-5; Matthew 27:5; Acts 1:18

Information and Principles:

There are 30,000 successful suicides each year in America. Three times as many women as men attempt suicide, but men are three times more likely to succeed. The men who attempt suicide are usually professionals. The ratio of dentists and doctors (primarily psychiatrists) who commit suicide to other people who commit suicide is 6.5 to 1. Suicides occur more often in cities than in rural areas with the fewest number of incidents among farm workers. More college students commit suicide than nonstudents. There are more suicides among Protestants than Catholics and more among Catholics than Jews.[4] According to the American Association of Suicidology, the suicide rate in the last fifty years has remained fairly stable for all Americans, varying between ten and twelve suicides per 100,000 people. In the sixty-five and older age group, there was a dramatic decrease in one year from 30 per 100,000 people in 1930 to 17.1 in 1980. Then during the 1980s, it jumped to 21.7 by 1990, and no one seems to know the reason. In the teenage population, suicides have more than doubled in the last three decades. This increase has been attributed to many things.

1. A change in moral values since the 1960s, brought about by the media, particularly by movies and television
2. The teens' music with lyrics containing a theme of hopelessness and suicide
3. The lack of love and family unity, occasioned by the increase of mothers' working outside the home and fathers' lack of leadership and presence in the home
4. The rapid increase in divorce in the last forty years
5. Lack of extended family network and roots in the community

A national study in 1987 by the Division of Adolescent and School Health of the Centers for Disease Control found that, of 11,419 eighth- and tenth-grade students in 217 schools in twenty states, 25 percent of the boys and 42 percent of the girls had seriously considered suicide and 15 percent had attempted it.[5]

There are several general principles that apply to the problem of suicide.

Take all suicide threats seriously. A suicide threat should be viewed as a call for help and an opportunity for suicide prevention.

The following are some of the warning signs of potential suicide.

- Preoccupation with themes of death or expressing suicidal thoughts
- Giving away prized possessions, making a will, or other "final arrangements"
- Changes in sleeping patterns; getting too much or too little sleep
- Sudden and extreme changes in eating habits, such as loss of appetite, overeating, anorexia, or bulimia
- Withdrawal from friends and family or other major behavioral changes, such as promiscuity, speeding, or smoking
- Changes in school performance, such as lowered grades, cutting classes, dropping out of activities
- Personality changes, such as nervousness, outbursts of anger, or apathy about appearance and health
- Use of drugs or alcohol
- Previous suicide attempts

People who commit suicide usually do not have a close relationship with a supportive individual, such as a spouse, parent, or other relative. It is necessary for the counselor or other significant adult to be supportive in order to give them the warmth, interest, and love that they are lacking. This is especially true with children and teenagers.

Sins, situations, or habits which they feel helpless to correct bring about a feeling of despair and hopelessness. Sins such as abortion and murder, situations like personal or business bankruptcy, or habits such as the use of alcohol and other drugs set the stage for suicidal thinking.

People who threaten to commit or attempt suicide need a great amount of hope. Hope is a joyous expectation that faith will be rewarded and that the promises and power of God will be realized at some point in time. The counselor can introduce them to the hope of salvation (Col. 1:5, 29), the blessed hope of His appearing (Titus 2:13), and problem-solving hope (Rom. 15:4, 13). Hope can also be given through specific Scriptures, such as

I Corinthians 10:13, Philippians 4:13 and 19, Ephesians 3:20, and I Peter 5:7.

Solutions:

1. Review the appropriate Scripture and principles.
2. Through counseling the person, try to find the source of his feelings of hopelessness and helplessness and offer a solution to the problem. Usually there is a major sin problem that needs to be resolved. If it is abuse, take steps to correct the environment or to remove the person from the environment.
3. Depression is at the root of almost all suicide attempts, so follow the steps given to relieve depression. Be aware that there are many causes of depression, although guilt is the primary cause.
4. Make sure that there is a nurturing, concerned person with whom the victim can talk on a daily basis and from whom he can gain support.
5. Help the counselee set achievable goals and start a program aimed toward achieving them.

Case Study:

Candy, a fifteen-year-old, was referred to the counselor by her mother after having tried to kill herself by slitting her wrists. While Candy was in the hospital, the doctor had insisted she see a psychiatrist, but the mother got him to agree that if Candy could see a Christian counselor, a psychiatrist would not be necessary. Candy was a sweet girl who looked and acted like her mother. She supposedly had been saved at five years of age and had a good Christian family. She was somewhat overshadowed by two talented, beautiful older sisters and a younger brother who was becoming a star athlete.

The counselor questioned Candy about some sin in her life, including moral sin, but she seemed completely innocent and naive about anything sexual. When questioned about her reasons for attempting suicide, she said she got discouraged about herself, her looks, her lack of success, and her inability to make any friends. Candy's father was a busy professional man, and she felt that he was a poor father who did not care about his family, especially her, because he never talked with them or spent any time with them. She felt that her mother was incompetent as a mother and was nothing but a dumb blonde who gave all her attentions to the father and the other children. Her mother, realizing that the father neglected Candy, tried to be a friend to her, but Candy refused to have anything to do with her because of her seeming partiality to the other children.

Case Study Solution:

The counselor talked to Candy about her growth as a Christian. She admitted that she never read the Bible or prayed except when she had to. She said that although she went to a Christian school, she had never shared the gospel with anyone and had no desire to do so. The counselor talked to Candy about her salvation. Since she was not sure that she had been saved, the counselor went through the salvation verses, including the Ten Commandments. Candy accepted the Lord in the counselor's office and agreed to start reading the Bible and praying every day. The counselor also started her on a discipleship program and got her interested in the youth group's soulwinning program. At a Sunday service, Candy went to the front of the church, told the congregation about her salvation experience, and was rebaptized.

The counselor went through Psalm 139 with her, and she agreed to start thanking God for all the positive attributes that He had given her. She also agreed to start a program of praising God five minutes each day (Ps. 107:8). She determined to stop thinking negative Devil thoughts about herself and her family (II Cor. 10:5). Candy had a long talk with her mother, admitting a bitter spirit and asking her mother's forgiveness. She agreed to spend fifteen minutes a day walking and talking with her mother, who was gaining a little weight and needed the exercise.

The counselor met with the father and got him to agree to spend time each day talking to Candy in a noncritical fashion and to take her on a "date" at least once a month. With Candy's salvation and the attention of her parents, she blossomed into a wholesome Christian girl who went on to a Christian college, married a Christian school teacher, and taught in the same school as her husband.

Chapter 22

Husband and Wife Relationships

The American home is in trouble. In 1960, 27 percent of marriages ended in divorce. By 1980 the percentage had reached 50 percent. In 1985 the figure had dropped to 49 percent and in 1990 to 48 percent. Statistics show that 40 percent of first-time marriages end in divorce and one-half of these divorces occur during the first three years of marriage. According to one study, 85 percent of those still together have little or no intimacy, physical or otherwise. They are just living together. That could mean that only 15 percent of those remaining together have really happy marriages.

Predicting Happy Marriages

Termen's study of happy marriages in the 1930s indicated three main factors that contributed to a happy marriage.

1. *There was a role model of a happy marriage in childhood.* If a person has a role model of divorce or separation or unhappiness, he needs to seek out a positive role model in his community, such as a pastor or youth director or teacher.
2. *There was childhood happiness.* Adults who remember their childhoods as being happy seem to have happy marriages.
3. *There was a lack of conflict with the mother.* If children got along with their mother, they did pretty well in a marriage.

David H. Olsen at the University of Minnesota in the 1980s developed a questionnaire listing eleven areas that were necessary for a happy marriage. He has tested 30,000 couples and has found in a three-year follow-up study of 164 couples[1] that his *Prepare* questionnaire[2] can predict with 80 to 90 percent accuracy the ones that are going to have a happy marriage. Eight of the eleven areas of positive couple agreement scores that have predictive values (from the highest to the lowest) of happiness for married couples compared to divorced or separated couples in the first three years of marriage are as follows.

1. *Religious values* Both partners need to agree on religious values, what faith they will embrace, how they will rear their children religiously, and how devout they should be.

2. *Conflict resolution* Conflicts naturally occur, even in the engagement period, but the ability to work them out is a good indication of future success in marriage. A temperament that goes with the flow is a factor for success. A rigid temperament that is opinionated and nonconciliatory can wreak havoc in a marriage.

3. *Communication* The ability to communicate is essential in a happy marriage. There are standard rules of communication that must be followed.

4. *Family and friends* A child who has a good relationship with his mother seems to have a happy marriage. The way the man treats his mother is a good indication of how he will treat his wife. What a girl thinks of her father indicates the amount of respect and affection she will have for her husband. Getting along with the in-laws is as important as getting along with one's parents. Both partners also need to have an appreciation for and enjoy the same type of friends.

5. *Realistic expectations* Each spouse must have a realistic appreciation of the needs of the other partner and personally not expect too much. As someone said, it is best to have your eyes wide open before marriage and half closed after marriage. Each spouse must adjust to the weaknesses and failures of the other, and this adjustment takes a period of time and close association. Deuteronomy 24:5 implies that it takes about a year to make good adjustments. During the first year of marriage, the husband should not do such time-consuming activities as going off to war, starting a business, starting on

his doctoral studies, or taking on extra activities at the church or in recreation. The couple should spend the first year in an ordinary, nonpressured schedule, allowing themselves time to make the necessary adjustments.

6. *Personality issues* Positive personality traits are crucial. Negative personality traits such as jealousy, temper, tardiness, or messiness, which irritate before marriage, are going to be magnified after marriage.

7. *Leisure activity* The couple's leisure activities and interests should be similar. A homebody married to a social butterfly, an avid sports/fitness fan married to a couch potato, or a folk music enthusiast married to a Bach and opera buff are all going to have problems adjusting to each other.

8. *Sexual relationship* Both partners must agree about attitudes, purity, tone, frequency, and technique. Lack of flexibility, disgust, fear, and prudishness can cause problems.

The other three scores, which have lower predicting effect, are financial management, equalitarian roles, and views about children.

Premarital Counseling

Research seems to indicate that good premarital counseling is important for future happiness in marriage and for the prevention of divorce.

At the U.S. Air Force Academy in Colorado, a premarital course is required for all Air Force Academy seniors who are engaged and intend to marry right after graduation. Follow-up studies ten years after graduation indicated that there was less than a 1 percent divorce rate among these graduates whose premarital counseling included both husband and wife. For fifteen years, Bob Jones University offered a premarital counseling seminar for all engaged couples. The divorce rate among those couples was less than 1 percent. The standard topics included in regular premarital counseling courses are finances, communication (including methods of conflict resolution), physical relationships, in-laws, religion, goals, expectations, leisure time, and children and their training. The best Christian counseling includes a thorough discussion of additional Bible principles that apply to marriage. Among these are the agreement principle emphasizing spiritual agreement; the friendship principle, which is based on good communication; the heritage principle, which involves in-laws; and the purity principle, which involves morality before and after marriage.

Reasons for the Increased Divorce Rate

The reasons for the tremendous increase in the divorce rate in the last thirty years are many. Some of the more important are as follows.

1. Teenagers are coming from homes and schools that have seen a tremendous breakdown in moral standards because of a lack of moral training. The Supreme Court decisions in 1963 and 1964 taking prayer, Bible reading, and anything "relig- ious" out of the school have been partly responsible for the breakdown. Neglectful fathers and overburdened mothers have eliminated most of the moral and spiritual training in the home.

2. The Supreme Court decision of 1973 legalizing abortion has resulted in a million and a half abortions yearly, most of these performed on unmarried women. This legalization breeds a climate of immorality and corruption that is promoted by the media as a normal lifestyle.

3. In 1991, 72 percent of the mothers with children under eighteen years of age were working full-time outside the home, and 52 percent of the mothers of preschool children were working. (See the article in Appendix B for a full discussion of the disadvantages of this factor.) Letting moth- ers stay at home and letting fathers be the sole support of the home will help greatly to eliminate this negative factor.

4. Television is more responsible for a decline in morals and values than probably any other factor. The average adult watches twenty-seven hours per week, and the television set is on for forty-five hours per week in the average home. More and more television programs are actually anti-family, anti- moral, and anti-religious. Cutting down on television view- ing in the home and carefully selecting programs, especially

informative programs as found on educational television, might be alternatives to eliminating television from the home. Another substitute to promote happy family times might be games, traditions, projects, hiking, camping, and storytelling or reading times.

5. Since its inception, rock music has promoted a spiral of breakdown in morals. Rock musicians stay on the leading edge of shock in order to sell more records. In the late '50s, the lyrics of rock songs emphasized rebelling against authority, resulting in the rebellious '60s. In the '60s, rock music emphasized promiscuity and drugs, ushering in a wave of these sins ten years later. The rock hits in the '70s promoted sexual perversions, including incest, masturbation, homosexuality, and bestiality. It is no wonder that the '80s heralded the onslaught of AIDS. The songs of the '80s emphasized hopelessness, futility, and suicide, resulting in a tremendous rise in suicide among the teen population in particular. So far in the '90s, vulgarity and violence, especially against women and police, seem to be the dominant theme. Eliminating all rock music and substituting good Christian music and classical music would help eliminate this negative factor.

6. Other factors affecting the divorce rate are hypocritical Christianity and bitterness between husband and wife and children.

All of the above factors also create a barrier in the minds of young singles and married couples to permanence in marriage.

General Principles of the Husband and Wife Relationship

There are certain general principles that apply to all marriages if there is to be happiness, stability, and permanence.

Make a genuine commitment to marriage and to each other "till death do you part." This commitment is not only a legal contract but it is also an agreement with God that the couple is going to carry out His marriage plan. It must be larger than any problem that ever could arise and must involve a determination to make the marriage work and continue, no matter what occurs.

Expect a number of daily, weekly, and monthly problems that must be handled and solved in a proper way. These problems range all the way from what to do about the burned roast with company coming in thirty minutes to how to take care of the three children home with the mumps while the mother is hospitalized for emergency surgery. The husband and wife must agree to help each other find a solution to every problem, no matter how trivial or how disastrous.

Believe that God has a solution to every problem. Every problem that can arise is addressed in Scripture, at least in principle. The couple should start out by thanking God for every problem. When they have strong faith, they accept the fact that every problem is a part of God's plan and that God works "all things together for good" (Rom. 8:28). They then pray and ask God's wisdom in finding His solution. Problems may not always be solved immediately, but the couple who trusts God is willing to wait on the Lord and His timing for the right solution.

Be united as one, spiritually, emotionally, and physically, as taught in Ephesians 5:31. Open communication helps develop unity. To bring this unity about, couples must be willing to take appropriate steps, including a regular romantic, intimate relationship. See Appendix C for ideas on developing family unity.

Work toward making every day a happy day (Ps. 118:24; 67:1-7). Create family memories on a daily basis. Happiness is up to the individual husband and wife, and each one must work to make every day a happy day for the other. Success necessitates an unselfish, giving spirit in the marriage. It is not the individual's needs that count, but the needs and wishes of the other partner. Real love is all about giving instead of taking. And, of course, when one gives, he receives. The Bible says, "Give and it shall be given unto you" (Luke 6:38).

The husband and wife should never think or talk divorce, even when adultery is present in the marriage. God hates divorce, as indicated in Malachi 2:13-16 and forbids it in Matthew 19:3-11. A couple may have every scriptural right to get a divorce in the case of adultery, but they should be thinking instead, "How can this marriage be repaired so that the adultery never happens again?"

Understanding and trust are the core ingredients for love, a happy marriage, and family unity. Men and women are different beings, and, in marriage, both need a great deal of understanding to accept and make provision for the differences. Trust is built during the engagement period and early years of marriage by complete honesty and fidelity being practiced during the relationship. Any violation of trust can be a serious blow to the marriage, and the rebuilding of trust takes a long time.

Close friendship is an essential part of a long-lasting marriage. Shared interests, ideas, personal lifestyle, leisure time, and social activities weld the friendship closer with each passing year. When a husband and wife are true friends, they like each other as people and would rather be with each other than with anyone else.

The Main Problems of Marriages

In one recent four-year study, hundreds of marriage counselors were asked to list the main causes of marriage troubles in people they counseled. The counselors listed the inability to communicate as the number one cause in 86 percent of troubled marriages. Second on the list was the unrealistic expectations of the spouse. In 35 percent of the troubled marriages, the conflicts involved sex, money, leisure time, and infidelity. When asked which were the most difficult problems with which they had to deal, 54 percent of the counselors said the most difficult problem was alcoholism, number two was lack of loving feelings, number three was serious individual problems, and number four was power struggles.

In a study of happily married couples, partners listed sex as the major problem. In unhappily married couples, communication was the biggest problem. A study of retirees indicated that 70 percent of retired couples who stay together do so in mutual hostility. The silence barrier is the greatest problem.

There are six main problems that most marriage counselors deal with in the course of marriage counseling: (1) communication, (2) finances, (3) physical relationships, (4) in-laws, (5) the marriage rut, and (6) the training of children. The last problem will be taken up in Chapter 23.

Problem #26: Communication

Definition:

A two-way process by which a message, either verbal or non-verbal is transmitted from one person to another, and the receiver responds in some manner.

Scripture:

Proverbs 10:19; 12:17, 22, 25; 15:1, 23; 16:27-28; 17:27-28; 18:13; 21:23; 25:11, 23; 26:20, 26, 28; 29:5, 11, 20; Ephesians 4:15, 22-32; James 1:19

Information and Principles:

The average husband and wife get so busy in everyday family living that they do not take time to talk to each other. One research study found that the average husband and wife spend only twenty-three minutes a week communicating with each other. There are a number of general principles that apply to the problem of communication in marriage.

There is a difference in the communication styles of husbands and wives. The average wife is very verbal and enjoys talking, but there is a tendency for the husband to be nonverbal and action-oriented. Women talk to express their feelings, whereas most men believe that feelings are irrelevant and unproductive. Women tend to want eye contact, whereas men can do other things while listening and, consequently, seem uninterested. Women like to go into detail, talking about who was there, what was said, how everyone looked, and other minute details, whereas men want only the main facts. When discussing problems, women expect a response, whereas men tend to keep silent, listening and thinking toward a solution. Women can talk about a problem for hours and explore all the ramifications of it, whereas men are impatient and want to find a solution quickly. Women will bring up a difficult problem over and over again until it is solved, and men interpret this repetition as nagging. Men tend to be satisfied to wait with the problem unsolved until they can come up with a convenient solution.

Couples should know and follow the steps of problem solving.

1. List the possible choices.
2. Determine how much time can be taken in reaching a solution.
3. Find what God's Word says about the problem.
4. Decide what further information is necessary.
5. Reach a solution and then act on that solution.

Once the decision has been reached or the solution arrived at, the couple should take action with no further discussion. If a wrong decision has been made, it should be rescinded without either partner's blaming the other one. Work at solving the problem should then begin again.

Work toward finding a solution instead of trying to place blame. It is easier to get into a blame-placing discussion than into a solution discussion. Each partner should be willing to talk about general rules that could prevent a problem from recurring.

Develop the skill of active listening (James 1:19). Active listeners look the speaker in the eye, respond to what is being said by a nod, a smile, a touch, or encouraging words, restate briefly what is being said, and ask pertinent questions.

Attack the problem, not the person. Most confrontations between husbands and wives center on the personalities, rather than on a problem. This approach results in anger and bitterness.

Follow the rules of fair Christian confrontation. Such confrontation focuses on the real issue, deals only with the current problem, does not bring up the past, negotiates and is willing to make compromises, and includes praying together about the problem. Very often the trouble is not the problem itself but rather the couple's method of communication and confrontation. Christian communication should edify and build up as Ephesians 4:29 instructs: "Let no corrupt communication proceed out of your mouth, but that which is good to the use of edifying, that it may minister grace unto the hearers." Christians should never engage in the art of "put-downs," which can be devastating to their marriage and to their testimony. A loving husband will not make his spouse the butt of jokes or interrupt her to finish the story or correct some unimportant point. A caring wife will not put her husband in an unfavorable light or use phrases such as "shut up" or "stupid" or make fun of his past or present bad habits and weaknesses.

Principles of Communication from Proverbs

1. **Listening is better than speaking.** "In the multitude of words there wanteth not sin: but he that refraineth his lips is wise" (Prov. 10:19). "He that hath knowledge spareth his words: and a man of understanding is of an excellent spirit" (Prov. 17:27). "Even a fool, when he holdeth his peace, is counted wise; and he that shutteth his lips is esteemed a man of understanding" (Prov. 17:28). "He that answereth a matter before he heareth it, it is folly and shame unto him" (Prov. 18:13). "Seest thou a man that is hasty in his words? There is more hope of a fool than of him" (Prov. 29:20). "Whoso keepeth his mouth and his tongue keepeth his soul from troubles" (Prov. 21:23). "A fool uttereth all his mind: but a wise man keepeth it in till afterwards" (Prov. 29:11).

2. **Communicate only the truth.** "Lying lips are abomination to the Lord: but they that deal truly are his delight" (Prov. 12:22). "He that speaketh truth sheweth forth righteousness: but a false witness deceit" (Prov. 12:17).

3. **The communication should be positive speech that daily encourages others.** "Heaviness in the heart of man maketh it stoop: but a good word maketh it glad" (Prov. 12:25). "A man hath joy by the answer of his mouth: and a word spoken in due season, how good is it" (Prov. 15:23). "A word fitly spoken is like apples of gold in pictures of silver" (Prov. 25:11).

4. **Evil speaking should not be a part of communication.** "An ungodly man diggeth up evil: and in his lips there is as a burning fire" (Prov. 16:27). "The north wind driveth away rain: so doth an angry countenance a backbiting tongue" (Prov. 25:23). "A soft answer turneth away wrath: but grievous words stir up anger" (Prov. 15:1).

5. **Eliminate gossip from communication.** The Bible admonishes, "Where no wood is, there the fire goeth out: so where there is no talebearer, the strife ceaseth" (Prov. 26:20). "A froward man soweth strife: and a whisperer separateth chief friends" (Prov. 16:28).

6. **Flattery should not be a part of communication.** Proverbs declares, "A man that flattereth his neighbour spreadeth a net for his feet" (Prov. 29:5). "A lying tongue hateth those that are afflicted by it; and a flattering mouth worketh ruin" (Prov. 26:28).

The principles listed above are the keys to effective communication in all relationships as well as in marriage and family interaction.

Solutions:

1. Emphasize the five rules of good communication found in Ephesians 4:22-32.

   - Don't lie, but always "[speak] the truth in love" to each other (Eph. 4:15) (vs. 25).
   - Don't blow up or clam up, but rather "talk up" (vv. 26-27).
   - Don't steal each other's time. Take your share of responsibility in marriage and in the home. The husband in particular tends to let the wife do all the work, even when she is working full time. One study found that the husbands of wives who work forty hours a week and have an additional twenty-seven hours of housework to do per week help their wives only two hours a week (vs. 28).
   - Be careful what you say, how you say it, and how you gesture so that communication will be edifying. The husband and wife should try to edify and minister grace to each other and not damage each other (vs. 29).
   - There must be a spirit of forgiveness, even as Christ forgives the sinner. Husbands and wives say and do all kinds of hurtful things to each other, some purposefully, some unwittingly. However, they both must be ready to ask and give forgiveness at any time. They must be helped to get rid of the root of bitterness, which may go back many years (vv. 30-32).

2. Go over the appropriate scripture and principles that apply to the problem.

3. Urge the couple to agree to have a minimum of fifteen minutes per day to discuss various problems and events of the day, always including a positive thought or idea in this fifteen minutes. Remind them not to let it turn into a negative complaint session. This discussion is most effective after a meal or over a beverage. It should be an uninterrupted time at a place where the couple cannot be overheard, especially when they are talking about the children. If one person gets too upset or angry, the other one should stand up or raise a hand until the person cools down and then should sit back down (or lower the hand) and resume the discussion.

4. Admonish the couple to agree to submit highly charged emotional issues and problems to a competent third party who can give objective, wise, godly counsel about the matter.

5. Help the couple to agree not to ventilate ungodly feelings about each other. Several research studies have shown that ventilation of ungodly feelings complicates a problem, does not help in the solution, and may damage the marriage relationship.

6. Urge the couple to agree to pray for each other daily and to pray together before making any decision that will affect the family.

Case Study:

Dan and Becky both were Christians who had a Sunday school class of teenagers. He was an auditor, and she was a nursing supervisor at the local hospital. They came to the counselor about the main problem in their marriage. She said that he would never talk to her about problems, and whenever she tried to resolve even minor problems, he would retreat into the den to read or watch sports on the television. He said that she always tried to run everything and what he said did not really matter because she always insisted on having things her way. He said she had been like that the whole fifteen years of their marriage. He said that whenever he had tried to assert himself and solve a problem, there would be a big blow-up and she would not calm down until she got her way. He said that he had given up trying to control the family and had refused to discuss any problem with her, knowing that she would handle it.

Case Study Solution:

The counselor went over the Scripture on leadership in the home, the submission principle, and the Scriptures in Ephesians 4:25-32 on communication. He explained that, as a nursing supervisor, she was used to making life-and-death decisions and directing the personnel under her. Conversely, he, being an auditor, was used to figuring things out on paper and had never learned to solve problems verbally. In addition, he was from a home where the mother "ruled the roost."

The counselor had them both agree to sit down once a week for an hour and discuss all the current problems. Becky was to give her opinions and solutions, and Dan was to give his ideas. He was then to write down all of the solutions presented and make a final decision by the next day, and Becky was to abide by his decision. They both agreed to this. Every time she became overbearing or angry, he was to raise his hand. Whenever she perceived that he was clamming up, she was to raise her hand. Raising their hands would serve as a reminder that one of them was not following scriptural principles.

In a follow-up session several months later, they reported that the husband was in charge of the home. They said that during the first four weeks, there had been a lot of hand-raising; but they had learned how to communicate, and their marriage had consequently improved in other areas as well.

Problem #27: Finances

Definition:

Management of money, credit, investments, and liquid assets, best accomplished by use of a budget.

Scripture:

God has control of money: Exodus 19:5; Deuteronomy 10:14; Job 1:21; 41:11; Psalms 8:6; 24:1-2; 50:10-12; Haggai 2:8; I Corinthians 10:26; Philippians 4:19; *Giving:* Proverbs 3:9-10; Malachi 3:8-10; Luke 6:35; II Corinthians 9:6; *Right viewpoint:*

Matthew 6:19-34; I Timothy 6:6-10; *Warning against cosigning:* Proverbs 11:15; 22:26

Information and Principles:

Finances are a constantly recurring problem in most marriages. In one study of divorced couples, 80 percent listed finances as the main problem. The biggest and initial hurdle is deciding who should control money and its spending. Absence of a budget and huge credit debt are just two of the typical financial problems that plague most marriages. A few general principles apply to the area of finances.

Keep a proper view about money. All money belongs to God; in fact the earth and everything in it are His. Psalm 24:1-2 says, "The earth is the Lord's, and the fulness thereof; the world, and they that dwell therein. For he hath founded it upon the seas, and established it upon the floods." These inspired words are repeated in I Corinthians 10:26. The same idea is found in Job 41:11, Deuteronomy 10:14, Exodus 19:5, Psalm 50:10-12, and Haggai 2:8. God has allowed Christians to be stewards of His money and the things He has provided (Ps. 8:6). The Lord gives and the Lord takes away (Job 1:21). All of a Christian's money and property should be used with eternal values in view (Matt. 6:19-34). A sure sign that a person has the right view of money is his willingness to tithe the first part of all of his increase and then go beyond that to give offerings and to help the poor.

Couples need to develop a regular giving program (II Cor. 9:6) which includes both money and time. They also need to resist advertisements and indiscriminate shopping, which bring about a spirit of discontentment and tend to foster a materialistic attitude (I Tim. 6:6-10). The spirit of discontentment inflames a desire for (1) more money, possessions, and power, leading to the sin of greed; (2) bigger houses, cars, and boats, feeding the sin of self-indulgence; (3) furnishings, fashion, and luxuries better than others, increasing the sin of pride.

Avoid debt. Whenever possible a Christian should not go into debt for anything except for appreciating items. Such items could include a home or an investment, like a rental property from which the return more than pays off the debt. It is best never to cosign a note, for it can easily become the debt of the one who cosigns

(Prov. 11:15; 22:26). The wise person makes out a budget and keeps his accounts balanced every month. He also guards against confusing needs with wants (Phil. 4:19).

Have a regular savings program. A penny saved is worth much more than a penny earned because the saver does not have to pay income tax or Social Security or tithe on the penny saved. The average family can save large amounts of money at the grocery store. Among the most common ways to cut down on the food budget are looking for weekly bargains, taking advantage of introductory bargains, and clipping coupons for needed items. The thrifty shopper refuses to buy junk food and never shops at a grocery store on an empty stomach. "Big-ticket" items, such as furniture, appliances, tires, and clothing should be bought in August and January during seasonal sales. In fact, the best approach to purchasing wisely is to wait for the sales, if possible, for things that you need.

Avoid budget-busters. Typical American budget-busters are eating out, buying new cars, unrestrained long-distance telephoning, taking extravagant vacations (including time-share deals), impulse buying, and running up bills on high-interest charge cards.

Solutions:

1. Have the counselees submit to you a list of their yearly expenses.
2. Make sure that the counselees are tithing because only then can God really bless them (Prov. 3:9-10).
3. Help the counselees make out a budget, cutting out unnecessary purchases and budget-busters until their budget is in line with their yearly income.
4. Discuss ways for the counselees to earn extra money for the luxury items that they desire.
5. Review the scripture and principles in this section and encourage the counselees to apply them.
6. Have the counselees attend Larry Burkett's seminar or read his book *Your Finances in Changing Times.* Call 1-800-722-1976 for information about his materials and seminars, or write to Christian Financial Concepts, 601 Broad Street, SE, Gainesville, GA 30501-3729.

Case Study:

Bill and Audrey, married fifteen years with three children, decided to see the counselor about their family finances. They owed $25,000, not counting their mortgage, and were going deeper into debt every year. They both worked, had a combined salary of $50,000, and owned their own home. The wife had taken over the finances, but their financial situation had not improved because the husband's spending habits were unchanged. He loved to look extravagant by taking friends out to eat and paying the bill and by taking his family on expensive vacations. He liked to travel, and in the last four years would often go alone on special trips that he had planned, including a seven-day cruise. The couple had had many arguments over financial matters, and a rift in their marriage had developed.

Case Study Solution:

The counselor first asked Bill and Audrey about a budget, which they did not have. In making out a budget, they found that they were spending $55,000 a year on just their bills. The counselor dealt with the husband about his compulsion to impress others by spending money on them.

Bill had been brought up in a poor family and remembered times when there had not been enough food in the house for a wholesome meal. He could remember standing outside restaurants and dreaming about going in and ordering a big meal. When he was eighteen he worked for a rich man, who would take him out to eat several times a week to fancy restaurants. In trying to emulate this man, Bill was sinking his family finances. The counselor went through the Scriptures, dealing with Bill's selfish, materialistic attitude.

The counselor helped the couple cut their budget down to $42,000 a year by having them cancel all their credit cards and the cable TV, which cost them $80 a month, stop eating out three times a week, and eliminate other unnecessary expenditures. They also refinanced their home to pay their credit card bills and car payments.

Bill and Audrey had not been tithing, but they agreed to start tithing the "firstfruits" of all their income. They started an IRA savings account as their investment for the future. This budget left them with several thousand dollars a year that they decided to put in a savings account to pay for the children's college expenses or to use as an emergency fund. They both agreed on renting a beach condominium two hundred miles away for their family vacation as a substitute for expensive family vacations. The wife agreed to start using coupons at the local supermarket, and the savings she would realize would be hers to spend.

They both reported later to the counselor that their revamped finances had eliminated the family tension.

Problem #28: Physical Relationships

Definition:

Any type of touching, caressing, and sexual intimacy that belongs in the marriage.

Scripture:

Proverbs 5:15-19; Song of Solomon; Matthew 19:1-9; Romans 13:14; I Corinthians 7:1-6; Ephesians 5:31-33; Hebrews 13:4

Information and Principles:

Put an emphasis on unity and affection, as the Bible indicates, rather than on technique and the ultimate response. An interesting study on women and sex was conducted by Ann Landers and reported in *The Family Circle* magazine.[3] Miss Landers asked the question in her column, "Would you be content to be held close and treated tenderly and forget about the sex?" Respondents were requested to answer yes or no and then add whether they were over or under forty years of age. Of 100,000 replies, 72 percent of the respondents said that they would be content just to be held close and treated tenderly and to forget about the sex act. Of this 72 percent, 40 percent were under forty years of age. For women under forty, exhaustion could be the reason for the lack of sexual desire, especially if they have several young children and/or are working full time. For women over forty, the decrease in hormones and menopause are probably the main reasons for the lack of sexual desire. Sexual desire decreases drastically in most postmenopausal women in their fifties and sixties. Men's desire, though somewhat diminished, continues into the seventies, although some degree of impotence may be a recurring problem (see Chapter 12). The Bible emphasizes oneness and unity in the physical relationship, and if intimacy is not taking place regularly, something is wrong with the relationship. Lack of intimacy may indicate problems in other areas of the marriage.

The Christian married couple is obligated to have intimate relations regularly, meeting each other's needs as indicated in I Corinthians 7:1-6. Good communication between the husband and wife, indicating their regular and immediate needs, is essential. Every couple should establish signals to indicate an urgent need. Every loving husband and wife will take care of each other some-way, somehow, and never leave a need unmet, especially in times of physical difficulty, such as heart problems, the birth of a baby, or vaginal or bladder infections. (A 1994 study by a Harvard research group found that a cup a day of cranberry juice significantly reduced bladder infections in women.)[4] Such caring for each other is good insurance against infidelity (I Cor. 7:5). Men as well as women like affection, closeness, and cuddling. A husband needs to realize that these three manifestations of love are especially important to a wife in a private romantic atmosphere.

Avoid Devil-directed fantasy and use God-directed fantasy to improve the physical response and unity (Song of Solomon). Devil-directed fantasy concentrates on the spouse negatively, on another person (lust), and on an expected response, which is always disappointing. God-directed fantasy concentrates on the spouse positively and on what one can do to show love and give pleasure to the spouse.

Some wives are able to fantasize to a complete sex release, especially if accompanied by the Kegel exercises (rhythmic contraction of the PC muscle which controls the flow of urine. Strengthening this muscle helps to cure problems of frigidity and incontinence). A 1991 study by Beverly Whipple at the University of Rochester School of Nursing found that fantasized responses were equal physiologically to responses obtained by other means.

Some women expel a fluid from the urethra during an intense sex response and may be concerned that they are becoming incontinent. However, a 1980 study by Belzer Jr., Perry, and Whipple found that sample fluids collected from volunteers were chemically different from urine, resembling male prostatic fluid. They speculated that it came from the woman's Skenes glands, which are located in the woman's urethra.

Wives have found the most satisfying response comes from positions which elevate the hips and allow for stimulation of the top part of the vagina along the urethra, including the Grafenberg spot (two inches behind the pubic bone at the neck of the bladder). Strengthening the PC muscle by regular Kegel exercises also helps to improve the response.

A couple should agree together that they will avoid any physical contact, action, or talk with others that might cause jealousy in their spouse or contribute to a climate of infidelity (Rom. 13:14). Infidelity, or seeking sex and affection outside of the marriage bonds, more than any other sin, can destroy a good marriage. Trust, which is so essential to a happy, permanent marriage, is shattered by infidelity, and it is most difficult to put the pieces back together. In Christian marriages, infidelity culminating in adultery is scriptural grounds for divorce (Matthew 19:1-9).

Solutions:

1. Review the principles and Scriptures in this section and help the counselees to apply the appropriate one(s).

2. Go over I Corinthians 7:1-6 and have the couple determine, as they communicate together about their needs, whether the needs of the partner are being satisfactorily met. Since the average husband wants to have sex two or three times a week and the average wife wants to have sex two or three times a month, it might be appropriate to suggest to the wife that she be romantically and physically available every day to the husband and let him control the frequency and be the one to suggest another day or time.

3. Have the couple read (at least once a year) a good book on the physical relationship, such as Tim LaHaye's book *The Act of Marriage,* or Dr. Ed Wheat's *Intended for Pleasure,* or Joseph Dillow's *Solomon on Sex.* Also read Chapter 8 of Walter and Trudy Fremont's *Formula for Family Unity.*

4. If there are frigidity or impotence problems, follow the steps in the last part of Chapter 12.

Case Study:

Mack and his wife, Cindy, came to the counselor with a problem in the area of their sex relationship, which centered on three different points: frequency, foreplay, and the wife's response. Mack's complaint was that Cindy was interested in having relations only two or three times a month and that the other times she was too tired. He also said she was rigid in the things she would do with him and where they would do it; sex was always confined to the bed with the lights out and always had to be before 10:00.

Cindy said that Mack wanted to make love every other day and in the most outrageous places and positions. According to her, he had little or no knowledge of what a wife wanted and needed regarding romance or stimulation. He wanted to disregard all the preliminaries and proceed to "the main event." She also said that he would ridicule her for her lack of a sex response every time. She also maintained that she was always worn out because she had to take care of three preschoolers with very little help from her husband.

Case Study Solution:

The counselor had Mack read several books on the physical relationship—Tim LaHaye's *The Act of Marriage,* the seventh chapter of *Formula for Family Unity,* Dr. Ed Wheat's *Intended for Pleasure,* and Joseph Dillow's *Solomon on Sex*—and discuss them with his wife. The counselor went over the Scriptures on the physical relationship and had the couple read The Song of Solomon every day for a month. He also explained to Mack the woman's normal hormone cycle: during the times when she has a high hormone release, she can have a sex response; but when she has a low hormone release, it is almost impossible for a woman to have a response. Cindy determined that her best responses came about eight days apart and at other times, she had no feeling. She agreed to eagerly meet her husband's needs, and he agreed to give more attention to the romance and cuddling that she desired. He also agreed to help her with their children so that she could get more rest. He was a late-night person, and she was an early-morning person; so he agreed to go to bed with her at 9:30 and do his reading after she was asleep. After two months, they both reported a very satisfying and pleasure-enhanced relationship.

Problem #29: In-laws

Definition:

Any immediate family members related to the spouse.

Scripture:

Book of Ruth—Ruth got along very well with her mother-in-law. Exodus 18:14-27—Moses got along with his father-in-law very well and took advice from him.

Information and Principles:

There are several general principles that apply to the problem of in-laws.

Leave the parents and cleave to your partner (Matt. 19:5). Wisdom dictates that the couple not live with the in-laws, especially with the husband's mother and father. In this kind of an environment, it is a rare case in which some jealousy does not occur between the wife and the husband's mother, for both women are in love with the same man. The mother may feel that she is the only one who really knows her son after twenty-plus years and that she is the one who can best take care of him and meet his needs.

Be willing to take advice from the in-laws, but never give them advice, even if they ask for it. A son- or daughter-in-law might refer the in-laws to books that contain the needed information. However, they will tend to resent any advice coming from the spouse of their child.

Never criticize the in-laws, and do not allow them to criticize your spouse. Loyalty to one's spouse is paramount to loyalty to parents.

If living at a distance from one another, arrange for at least once-a-year visits to the in-laws' house, and have them visit you at least once a year. The wife may want one or two additional short visits a year alone with her parents, especially after the first baby arrives. It is suggested that if you live in the same town, you have contact with them no more than once a week. More frequent contact brings up the potential problems of parents' interference in your marriage. The couple should faithfully attend all family reunions on both sides of the family.

In-laws (parents) should be the first to know any important news, such as the wife's becoming pregnant or the decision to buy a house. They are vitally interested in their children's lives and usually are ready to offer tangible help.

Do not take marriage problems, especially financial problems, to the in-laws. Never try to borrow money from in-laws unless the loan is set up on a regular payment basis, such as a loan for a down payment for a house.

Do not try to change parents' lifestyles. If either parent is not a Christian, explain the gospel just once, and then live the Christian life before them. It is reasonable to insist that they not smoke or drink alcoholic beverages while in your home.

The daughter from a good home background will love her daddy no matter how much she loves her husband. In sickness, operations, or death in her family—the daughter wants to be with her parents in those times of stress.

Solutions:

1. Review the appropriate principles in this section.
2. Help the couple set up a reasonable visiting schedule and phone-call schedule with the in-laws.
3. If necessary, have the in-laws meet with the couple to work out any big differences or problems.

Case Study:

Gloria and Norm came to the counselor with a marriage problem involving both in-laws. Norm said that Gloria was tied to her parents and would spend a minimum of $200—sometimes as much as $300—a month on the phone long-distance, talking to her mother. Any big decision that came up had to be checked with her mother to see if she approved. Gloria's father pretty much stayed in the background. She admired her father but said that her mother made most of the family decisions, and her father took charge only in crises. Norm said that the mother had overprotected Gloria in childhood and had made Gloria very dependent.

Gloria said that Norm's father had interfered with their marriage ever since it began eight years ago. He had paid for their honeymoon in the Caribbean, had lent them the down payment for their new house a year after they were married, and had tried to control their budget by telling Norm how much and where to invest. Norm looked to him for every financial decision. Norm's father was always telling him how to develop the three acres that went with the house. Norm had followed his father's advice and had sold two lots and invested the money without consulting his wife. At least once a week, on his way home from work, Norm would stop at his parents' house for supper and not tell his wife until he got home around eight.

Norm kept Gloria on a very strict budget because he always had to have enough money for the investments his father recommended. She said that in the last four years, they had not been able to buy another car, she had not been able to buy any clothes, and they had not been able to take any vacation, except for a week at the beach with his family, which his dad paid for. Norm said that she would have plenty of money to spend if she would write letters to her mother instead of spending money on phone bills.

Gloria said they were not tithing because Norm's father was not a Christian and did not think it was necessary. She also said that Norm did not like her parents to visit; he was bitter against them because they had paid only $1000 toward their wedding, which cost $4000. Norm said his father had paid the other $3000 and was very annoyed with Gloria's father for setting a $1000-limit on the wedding. Gloria said that she had originally planned a very simple church wedding; it was his parents who insisted on a formal wedding.

Case Study Solution:

The counselor first discussed with Gloria and Norm their dependence on their parents and the "leave-and-cleave" principle found in Genesis; he also went over the Scriptures on family unity and bitterness. Gloria agreed to write letters to her mother instead of using the telephone and to trust her husband instead of rebelling against every decision he made simply because the decision was made under the direction of his father. Gloria agreed to limit her calls to fifteen minutes and to make them only one day a week when the rates were low. Norm agreed to stop at his parents' house only if the visits were prearranged and included Gloria.

The counselor then talked to Norm about making out a budget with his wife and, since they were both Christians, including tithe as the first item in the budget. He would not use over 10 percent on investments, including their IRA. Norm was also to include a set amount every week for his wife to spend on her own and was to consult with his wife on every investment decision. Gloria was to recognize that her father-in-law's advice on investment was sound, since he was a successful investor himself.

The counselor then discussed with Norm the idea of keeping their day-by-day finances private and not bringing his father into the details of their budget. Norm began to realize that his father was using money as a means of controlling their marriage. The counselor then dealt with Norm about his bitterness toward Gloria's parents. The $1000-limit that they said they would pay on the wedding had been set ahead of time within her father's budget; Norm and his parents were the ones who had wanted to have the bigger wedding. Norm admitted that the wedding finances had started his bitterness but maintained that quite a few other incidents had fed it. However, he agreed to apologize to Gloria's father and be reconciled to him, which he did within the week.

Three months later in a follow-up conference, the counselor found that Norm and Gloria had solved their in-law problems.

Problem #30: The Marriage Rut

Definition:
The marriage tends to get into a routine of the commonplace and hurried, and the husband and wife begin to take each other for granted.

Scripture:
Ephesians 5:25-29; I Peter 3:7

Information and Principles:
Usually the wife becomes dissatisfied first in a marriage that has fallen into a rut. The husband is usually too busy with his job or business to even notice that things are not right. This problem is revealed in statements such as "There is no time for fun in our marriage anymore," "I just don't love him anymore," "We have no shared goals. He goes his way and I go mine," or "We are just two people who happen to be living in the same house." The main reason

for the problem is that neither participant is continually working at building a unity in the marriage or trying to make each day a happy day. In some cases, the husband has refused to take the kind of leadership that he should in building a happy marriage and keeping romance alive. The couple's daily schedule may be so packed that it is causing pressure, fatigue, and short tempers. In such a hectic schedule, there is rarely time for activities that build a happy marriage and family unity.

Solutions:

1. Look for and deal with a root of bitterness that may be present.
2. Help the couple relax their schedule by eliminating activities that are not building the marriage and unity. Have them become involved with a church ministry that they can do together, such as building a Sunday school class or bus route or teaching a home Bible study.
3. Refer the counselees to the list of sixteen ways to create family unity (Appendix C).
4. Have the husband read Chapter 7 of the book *Formula for Family Unity.* Have the wife read Chapter 6.
5. Have them both read Gary Smalley's two books entitled *For Better or for Best* and *If He Only Knew Her* and Norman Wright's book *Holding On to Romance.*
6. Have the couple schedule a date once a week. The husband should choose what they will do one week and the wife should make the choice for the next week.
7. Have the husband and wife each list ten ways to make their marriage more romantic. Since each person differs in what he feels is romantic, this list will give each partner some good suggestions for enhancing romance in the marriage.
8. Encourage the husband and wife to agree that they are going to give one genuine compliment to each other every day.

Case Study:

Sally and Hal came to the counselor because Sally was bored in their marriage of twenty-one years. Sally said that at the beginning of their marriage they had "had a ball" because they were very much in love and always did interesting things together. She said that after four children, their lives had gotten into a boring rut. They never spent time together on the weekends because they were too busy, and he was too tired in the evenings to do anything with her.

Actually, Sally had come to the counselor the previous week, saying that she was strongly and sensually attracted to the man she car-pooled to work with. She had said that when she married, she had had a hard time choosing between Hal and another man she had been dating. She said that at that time she was not sure which one she loved, but she had married Hal and had felt it was the will of the Lord since they had such a good time together. After going over the Scripture on adultery and the strange woman, the counselor had then talked to her about her commitment to Hal, which she had made before the Lord "until death do us part." Sally was advised to start improving her marriage by bringing Hal with her to the next session so that both could work on the problem together. She had then agreed to quit her adulterous thinking and to work on improving the physical relationship in her marriage by following the suggestions of the counselor.

Hal said that he worked fifty hours a week at a very stressful job and just wanted to relax when he came home. Sally said that he was so tired because he watched cable television until midnight (she went to bed at 10:30 every night) and then got up at 6 A.M. Hal said that she did not realize that they were both in their forties and needed to settle down instead of going places and socializing all the time.

Case Study Solution:

The counselor suggested that Hal limit his TV-viewing to six hours a week of programs they could watch together. Hal agreed to start an exercise program, since he was overweight, and to take vitamins, since he seemed to lack energy and frequently had colds. The counselor also suggested that they start having regular family devotions after supper and that they adopt several suggestions on the list of sixteen ways to have family unity.

Hal agreed to let Sally entertain once a week, even if it meant just having a couple over after church on Sunday night. He also agreed to take Sally on a date once a month. The date would include more than merely eating out; they were to go to concerts and do other things they had enjoyed when they were first married. They both decided that they would start working together with the teen

Sunday school class that the pastor had asked Hal to take. (They already had an interest in teens, since their own children were in junior high and high school.)

The counselor also asked them to read together The Song of Solomon, Ephesians 4 and 5, Gary Smalley's two books *If He Only Knew Her* and *For Better or for Best,* and Norman Wright's book *Holding On to Romance.* These steps seemed to solve Sally's problem of boredom in her marriage.

Summary

The above five problems are the typical problems of most marriages. Because they are ongoing problems, they must be continually addressed by committed couples. Superior premarital counseling will warn couples of these pitfalls and help them acquire techniques to prevent and/or properly handle them.

There are other crucial problems between husband and wife that do not come up so frequently, but they can be as serious and can wreck the marriage. The first problem is addiction, which is discussed in Chapter 18. The most common addiction in marriage is to television, the men to sports and the women to soap operas. Another common addiction is pornography. This addiction usually involves the husband, who often introduces it into the marriage. Addiction to alcohol or substance abuse—even to prescription drugs—can become a disruptive influence. Addiction to gambling has become more of a problem as various states make gambling, especially lotteries, legal and legitimate. The best cure for the problem of addiction is "cold turkey" withdrawal. Counseling is usually needed for an addiction problem in a marriage.

Another problem is unrealistic expectations. The problem is most common among people who marry in their teenage years. They have a romanticized view of each other and expect the partner to be a Princess or Prince Charming as she or he was on special dates. The pitfall of unrealistic expectations can be avoided by a couple's waiting to get married until each one has lived on his own for a while. During the engagement period, they should spend time together in all kinds of situations. Being on mission teams together or counseling all summer long in a camp can help couples to get a more realistic view of each other.

The lingering effects of an abortion can cause devastating consequences in a marriage. Any woman with a conscience, knowing that she has murdered a living being, suffers severe depression and other mental problems. Every year a million and half women, as well as others involved in the abortion decision, are affected by the mental anguish of abortion. Good teaching during the teen years about the horrible consequences of abortion will help prevent the sin from occurring.

Another problem is selfishness on one or both partners' parts. People generally tend to be givers or takers. When you have two givers, you have a happy marriage. When you have two takers, you usually have an unhappy marriage. People who are right with God and Spirit-filled are givers and not takers. The cure is both partners being Spirit-filled.

Another problem is fatigue. This is usually the wife's problem and comes from overcommitment. The overcommitted wife often works full-time and has a husband who doesn't help out at home. She is frequently heavily involved in Sunday school and church work. Before too long, she is exhausted day in and day out, she has difficulty in her physical relationship with her husband, and the marriage is headed for problems. The counselor should make sure the husband and wife get into a reasonable schedule that both can comfortably handle. Setting priorities in the right order and seeing a doctor to detect any physical problems will also help.

Chapter 23

Family Problems Involving Children and Teenagers

A child is born without any philosophy, values, social concepts, or attitudes about anything. He has no knowledge of God, right and wrong, no sense of property rights, no understanding of respect for authority, justice, cooperation, or altruism. Everything must be learned, and according to the Bible, these ideas are best learned within the context of the home from two good parents, a mother and a father. The Bible has commissioned parents to do this training in Proverbs 22:6: "Train up a child in the way he should go: and when he is old, he will not depart from it." Deuteronomy 6:1-9 specifically tells parents to train their children morning, noon, and night. Ephesians 6:1-4 tells children to take this learning with obedience and gives fathers the responsibility for directing the training program.

Because of their sin nature, children tend to be selfish, ruthless, crude, unmannerly, inconsiderate, wicked, rebellious, and destructive at times. They go their sinful way naturally and must be trained with good Bible training to go God's way. God has no alternative to His plan. All the ills of society can be traced to the abandonment or perversion of His perfect plan for the family and the training of children.

Starting in the preschool years, children should receive training in the Faith Way. If children are going to be responsible Christian adults, they must be introduced early to the path of faith, which can be entered only by a person's receiving Christ as personal Savior, or experiencing salvation. See Table XIII at the end of the chapter for a complete description of this path of faith.

Parental Training

Proverbs warns that a child left to himself will bring his mother to shame. If the parents neglect their God-given training responsibility, some other influences such as the media and peers will give the child corrupt training. The devil will make sure that this bad seed that has been sown sprouts into reeds blowing in the wind of humanistic thinking, brambles of sensual behavior, and weeds of materialistic desires.

Godly Christian parents, however, can have a powerful influence on their children, especially in the preschool years, according to the promises of God, if they seize every opportunity to plant and water the seeds of the Gospel and Bible principles in the fertile soil of their minds and hearts. As this good seed is sown, God is responsible for the harvest of mighty trees of righteousness and character, sweet fruits of truth and virtue, and fragrant flowers of love and grace.

A foundational principle of this training is getting children, as early as is possible, to memorize, read, meditate on, and study the Word of God both day and night (Josh. 1:8; Ps. 1:1-3). Early morning (Bible before breakfast) seems to be the best time for devotions because it encourages the child to depend on God throughout the day. The time before going to bed (Psalms before bedtime) motivates the child to glorify God by thanking and praising Him for His mighty works and blessings that occurred during the day. This daily Bible reading habit is the key to developing self-discipline, which is "doing what God wants you to do at the appropriate time whether you feel like it or not."

There are certain general principles that should be followed by every parent if he is going to train his children properly in the Christian faith. These principles also lead to a happy, productive life that honors the Lord.

Children learn as much from watching the lives of the mother and father as they do from listening to their teaching. Children must see a genuine Christianity if the Bible teaching is going to have any effect on them. Children tend to be much like their parents, reflecting the parents' real lifestyle and not the life-style they claim to embrace.

This training and lifestyle must be nurtured in an atmosphere of genuine love. The right kind of love cuddles, kisses, hugs, appreciates, accepts, praises, and allows for mistakes. It also corrects, rebukes, spanks, and is just. Children respond well to authoritative discipline if it is accompanied by a good measure of love. The love between the husband and wife must be openly evident to the children. A child learns how husbands and wives are treated from the daily interaction of his parents. The love of the parents for their children and others is communicated in the daily incidents of normal family life. The atmosphere should be free from bitterness, wrath, anger, clamor, evil speaking, and malice. If any of these evils do occur, the child sees them handled in a loving, kind, forgiving way.

There must be a respect for each person in the family. Family members show this respect by recognizing that every person in the family has his own eccentricities and individual problems from time to time. These problems should be recognized by the parents and dealt with in a proper way without making a federal case of the minor things. This respect is also shown in the conversations and discussions that go on in every family. The individual's opinions and verbal contributions are recognized and taken into consideration with full awareness of the age and maturity level of the person.

Family members also show respect by being considerate of the privacy of each person and his property. Children should feel that their belongings and their rooms are private property. One well-known father used to knock on the door even when the door was open before ever entering his children's room, just out of respect for their privacy. Even little children need to feel ownership of certain things, and they expect that others must ask permission to use those things. Children should not be allowed to lock themselves in their rooms, live in a mess, and isolate themselves from the family. Nor is the room free from parental searches or jurisdiction; the parents own the house.

There must be a recognition that children go through many stages as they grow. Manifestation of certain behaviors at certain ages does not mean that a child is abnormal. For example, a mother expects crying, clinging behavior from a one-year-old as he fears to be separated from mother to go into a Sunday school class. The same type of behavior from an eight-year-old may be a sign of rebelliousness or some abnormality.

There are four crucial times in a child's day when the parents can have the greatest influence. The most important time is bedtime. Children should not be sent to bed but rather taken to bed with a fifteen-minute warning time. At bedtime children are most susceptible to spiritual, character, and family-value training from at least one parent, preferably the father. The second crucial time is upon awakening in the morning. This should be a positive, happy time ("There's a great day coming," Ps. 118:24). Mealtime is the third vital time. If parents will take the initiative, it can be a time of discussion and learning. The child can air his problems and ideas in the warm, friendly family circle without fear of rejection. The fourth important time is when the child comes home from school. Mother should be there with snacks and questions about the events of the day.

Children need a well-ordered system and environment with firm boundary lines. These boundary lines are tight in the pre-school years, but they gradually are expanded as the child becomes more mature and accepts more responsibility for his life. By the age of eighteen, a young person ought to be operating within the expanded boundary lines of normal Christian society. Consistent boundary lines in the child's life, within the family structure, give the child a sense of security.

A spiritual training program, which includes regular family devotions, should be a part of the overall training program in the home. This training is just as important as the academic training. The program will emphasize the seven spiritual decisions (see Chapter 2) that children need to make along the way. It will encourage the learning of Bible principles, which can be applied to life situations (see Appendix A). It will also include training in how to praise the Lord and appreciate the wonders of God as manifested in His creation. A good way to start appreciating God's wonders is to encourage bird watching (which is the number two hobby in America) and nature walks, pointing out the sights, sounds, and smells. Parents should be aware of spiritual "moments of opportunity," rather than depending on a good Sunday school, church, or youth group program, although those are very helpful. Teachable moments occur every day, and the mother, who is home with the children, should focus on these moments to enhance the education program in the home. Children need to be actively engaged in Christian service, such as missionary teams, regular soulwinning, visitation, and Christian projects in the community.

Parents need to do their best each day and then relax, instead of trying to do everything perfectly. All parents make mistakes or errors in judgment; they are inconsistent and they overreact. The best thing for a child is a happy parent. A parent who feels guilty because of not measuring up to some impossible standard creates a tense environment and makes a child feel insecure. An expert once said that happy parents live in the present; they do not look back except to learn; they do not look ahead except to plan. A touch of humor along the way also tends to relax failure situations.

Parents should provide Christian education for their children from kindergarten through college. If adequate Christian schools are not available, the parents should home school their children (see Appendix F). A college fund should be established when the children are born. Gifts from relatives and part of the children's and adolescents' earnings from paper routes, part-time jobs, and home businesses can help build the fund.

With the above general principles in mind, the counselor is better equipped to give counsel on some of the typical problems that parents face.

Problem #31: Discipline

Discipline is vexing to anyone who deals with children, and new parents feel particularly insecure in this area. Effective discipline is based on certain principles.

Definition:

Discipline is the effort of parents to *train, control,* and *remedy* the actions of their children so that they can make the proper adjustments in life.

Scripture:

Training: Deuteronomy 6:1-9; Psalm 78:4-7; Proverbs 3:1-2; 4:1-4; 10:21; 13:1; 14:16; 16:21; 22:6; 23:26; *control:* Proverbs

12:18, 25; 15:1, 23; 16:24; 18:13; 24:3-4; 25:11, 15; Ephesians 6:4; *correction and punishment:* Proverbs 3:11-12; 13:24; 19:18; 22:15; 23:13-14; 29:15; *results:* Proverbs 2:12; 3:1-2; 4:20-22; 6:20, 22; 10:1; 15:16, 20; 17:6; 19:26; 20:7, 11; 23:24-25; 30:11, 14

Information and Principles:

Most people think of discipline as punishment. However, the Bible teaches that it is threefold: training, control, and correction (see Scriptures). If training and control are properly administered, the need for correction and punishment will be minimal. *Training* children is the most important part of discipline, for children must be trained very early to acquire moral standards and to learn society's boundary lines. Training children is teaching them to recognize and respect the boundary lines of any situation. This training eventually becomes self-discipline and is the ultimate goal of discipline. *Controlling* children is providing the right conditions for right actions. Children generally will act right when they have the right conditions for right actions. Their sin nature, however, predisposes them to uncontrolled behavior, evil, and rebellion. If, when all has been done to train children and provide the right conditions for right actions, they still go beyond the boundary lines, the *remedial* measures must be applied. These measures often involve punishment. Because behavior is caused, the parent must always try to determine the cause and decide on the remedial action. Sometimes children's actions are merely accidents or are due to a lack of training and knowledge. However, rebellion or disobedience in children should result in a spanking as punishment. Parents must always follow through and make children accountable.

Children gain security when they have a good knowledge of where they stand and what they can and cannot expect of the world. They must learn to recognize and observe the rights and privileges of others. They must learn what their own rights and privileges are and the limits or boundary lines within which they must operate. They will test the boundary lines in every direction repeatedly until at last they determine how far they can go. If they are not restrained, they naturally recognize no limits. If they can encroach on the rights and privileges of others without hindrance, they have reason to believe that they are entitled to do so. Children must learn that because of the flesh and their lack of experience, they are not likely to make good decisions about what they may and may not do and what they should and should not do. These decisions must be made for the young child. Gradually, the privilege of making these decisions for himself will be transferred to him in accordance with his maturity as evidenced by his discrimination, judgment, and experience in various situations.

Children must learn to accept direction from the parents with immediate obedience. Children may need an explanation, but only one. Make sure the child hears your command and do not repeat it. With every repetition, the order, statement, or threat loses force. Any command, threat, or promise made by the parent must be implemented. Only in that way will children learn that their parents or authorities mean what they say. A child will whine or sulk and refuse to comply with the command, threat, or promise. If the child gains the victory by being allowed to act this way, he is encouraged to do the same the next time. Parents must always win the battle of wills.

The authors believe that most behavior that is diagnosed by psychologists as Attention Deficit Disorder and Hyperactivity, if not caused by too much sugar, caffeine, TV viewing, or possible allergic reactions, is due to a lack of training in self-discipline.

The following general principles will help to ensure good discipline in the home.

Parents should make general rules and decisions ahead of time concerning the child's life. Preset rules give the child security and eliminate much hassle, temptation, and peer pressure. Each home should have rules about television—what programs Dad will choose for the children to watch, what general principles apply to television watching, how many hours the children will be allowed to watch a week, and when they can watch. Young children need simple, general rules that apply in most situations around the house, rules such as "put it back," "turn it off," "clean it up," "shut the door." These rules need to be explained carefully and enforced.

Mother and Father must be in agreement on the rules and regulations and present a united front. Both parents must establish and agree on the standard operating procedures. This unity makes a child's world orderly and secure. The chores and extra jobs need to be organized and delegated. For children the chores can be very simple, like watering the flowers, sweeping the floor, cleaning the bathroom sinks, and vacuuming.

Mothers and fathers should rarely make instant decisions. Both parents should always talk a problem over and then give the child the agreed-upon decision the next day. Most instant decisions should be *no*. Children need to learn to make decisions so that by the age of eighteen they are ready for the adult world of decision making. They should be allowed to make simple decisions in the early years, such as "Would you like hamburgers or hot dogs at our picnic?" "Would you like to go to the park or the zoo?" "What dress or shirt would you like to wear today?"

There must be follow-through. If you tell your child about a particular rule or regulation or command, you should make sure you follow through and see that it is accomplished the way you want it accomplished. Flexibility may come on special occasions at the whim of the parents. For example, you might have a general principle about no television on Sunday, but when a special historical event is occurring on Sunday, then you might be flexible and watch television. (The Super Bowl is not a historical event.)

You can give rewards for accomplishing difficult tasks or chores. Do not ever dock the allowance because a child did not do something. However, if he did not do his chore, you might require him to pay mother for doing the chore, for which she charges so much an hour. There must be accountability. You as a parent must decide what you will do so that the child's actions will have consequences. For example, toys left around in the room and not picked up go into the Saturday box. The child must wait until Saturday to redeem them. The parent might say, "When you put away your art supplies from your last project, then you may start constructing your model airplane."

Do not overprotect your child by always coming to his defense in life situations. Life is not always fair. People are not always sweet and kind and consistent. If possible, let your children handle these situations. In a school situation, the child should be the one who goes to the teacher or principal and gets the matter resolved. Let the child handle as many situations as possible.

Balance positive compliments and encouragement against negative rebuke and correction. Both are necessary but ought to be weighted heavily in favor of a positive response in words, tone of voice, and gestures.

The parent should be a real counselor to the child every day. If a child gets used to talking to his parents about all matters, by the time he is eighteen years old, his parents will have become counselors rather than controllers. To be the right kind of counselor to children, a parent must look them in the eye and respond as they speak, giving them your full attention. Sometimes this counseling can be done while a parent is doing chores with them.

Teach children how to counteract peer pressure. Peer pressure starts in about the second grade, reaches its peak in the sixth grade, and remains high into adulthood. Peer pressure starts first of all with toys and playthings that children see on television. The pressure is increased by fashion. Children think that they must have the same clothes as other children. Next, children feel pressure about the places they go and those with whom they are seen. They put great stock in being at the right malls or restaurants or drive-ins or even parties. This "place pressure" can be very costly, demanding a lot of spending money in the teenage years. Another pressure results in their mimicking the "in" crowd in the neighborhood or at school in what they say and do. Young people must learn that they are uniquely created individuals and must continually let Christ work in them to develop His grace in their lives (Titus 2:11-14). One who experiences this maturity can take his stand against the world, daring to be a Daniel, a Joseph, or a Shadrach, Meshach, or Abednego.

Solutions:

1. With the counselee, go over the appropriate Scriptures and principles which apply to the problem.
2. Have the counselee confess any known sin, especially bitterness or provoking his children to wrath.
3. Have the parents read Chapters 9-15 in *Formula for Family Unity,*[1] John Stormer's book *Growing up God's Way,*[2] and David Sorenson's book *Training Your Children to Turn Out Right.*[3]
4. Find information about any specialized problems that the parents bring up, such as bed-wetting, poor sleep habits, or eating problems, in the book *The Complete Book of Baby and Child Care for Christian Parents* by Dr. Grace H. Ketterman.[4]

Case Study:

Craig and Debbie had four children, ages two, four, seven, and nine. They had been married twelve years, and Debbie did not work outside the home. Craig had a good job, they had a budget, and although money was tight, they had no financial problems. Craig said that their problem was with the children, who were completely undisciplined. He said their house was always messy and things were usually "in an uproar," with bickering and fighting among the children. The situation had gotten so bad that he dreaded going home at night.

Debbie said that she could not control the children and her husband ignored them because he was always glued to the television. He would go to the master bedroom to read and watch TV after supper every night and would never help with the children. She said it was all she could do to get meals on the table, pick up after the children, and get the laundry done, much less have time to clean.

When asked about her schedule, Debbie said that after breakfast and getting the two older children off to school, she and the two preschoolers would watch television for over two hours, and then the children would play while she fixed lunch. After lunch the two-year-old would take a nap while she and the four-year-old watched television. She then fixed supper and made the beds. After supper she cleaned up the kitchen. Then she and the children all watched television in the den. After she got the four youngsters into bed and picked up after them, she went to bed herself.

When the counselor asked about punishment for the children, Craig said that Debbie did not believe in spanking and strongly objected whenever he tried to spank them. He said that the reason he would not help with the children was that he felt that since Debbie did not work outside the home, she could at least handle the children. He thought that rearing children was a mother's job.

Case Study Solution:

The counselor admonished both Craig and Debbie for their disobedience to God in failing to discipline their children in a biblical fashion and in neglecting to train them properly as the Bible commands. He discussed with them some simple house rules that would apply to everyone, such as "pick up messes you've made," "put it back or turn it off when you're done with it," "shut doors that you open," and "follow through on what you start." He also suggested that the parents make a list of daily and weekly chores for each child, have regular family devotions together after supper, and follow the list of sixteen ways to have family unity. He told them they needed to agree on how and when punishment would be applied.

Debbie agreed to begin a regular schedule of housekeeping with the children instead of watching television. They eliminated television altogether and substituted story time, reading, and family activities. Craig agreed to take an active part in the evening and weekend activities of the family, to enforce the discipline, and to start setting some goals for the family. The two also agreed to read together *Formula for Family Unity.* It took them about three months to bring about proper discipline and training in their family, but they both had to admit that the resulting tranquility was worth the struggle.

Problem #32: Teenage Adjustments

Definition:

The many changes that an adolescent must make as he goes from childhood dependence upon the parents to mature independence of adulthood.

Scripture:

I Corinthians 13:11; II Timothy 2:15-23; I Peter 2:1-3.

Information and Principles:

Teenagers' biggest adjustment involves family relationships as they move from being a dependent child to becoming a responsible, independent adult. Teenage behavior is thought to begin at thirteen, but it actually begins at the onset of puberty (time of sexual maturity), which may begin as early as age nine in some girls and as late as age sixteen in some boys. A definite change in behavior takes place at this time because of the change of hormones, the adjustment of the teen to a changing body and appearance, and the teen's efforts to be an independent adult. As someone has quipped, "The teenage years are the terrible two's repeated with a driver's license and the telephone thrown in to complicate matters." This stereotype can be avoided if the proper principles are implemented.

Teen behavior will be the result of their early childhood training. If children have been trained in biblical and proper values and standards, the children may be slightly modified, but they will not drastically be changed during the teen years.

Teenagers need the chance to make as many decisions on their own as possible and to take increasing responsibility. Parents should adjust their rules and regulations to minimize protection and control in order to accommodate the young person's growing independence and responsible behavior. By the time the teen is eighteen, parents should be counselors to him instead of controllers. Responsibility is further developed as teens go on summer mission teams, counsel at Christian camps, and work at part-time jobs. Setting up their own bank accounts and being responsible for their own savings, purchases, and budgets help young people adjust to the adult world in a responsible way.

Teenagers should feel a responsibility toward family functioning, unity, and happiness. Teenagers must have a regular part in the chores that need to be done, beyond keeping their rooms neat and clean. These chores could include things such as washing the car; cutting the grass; cleaning out the garage, carport, or attic; or regular housecleaning and cooking duties. Young people can become responsible for happy times by helping to plan traditions, family nights, and family vacations.

Teenagers need a regular time with their parents during which the parents listen and give minimal advice. When a parent listens at an appointed time once a week and after dates, special events, and even after school, the maturing teenager will use the adult as a sounding board.

Teenagers need techniques for resisting peer pressure. Rehearsing beforehand what a teen should do and say in certain ticklish situations is a big help. Teach young people to call home when they see trouble developing. Let them know that they can call at any time of the night or day and you will come and get them without making a big scene.

A teenager must know that while he is living in your home, he is under your authority and must obey the house rules. These rules might include curfew, activities conducted in your home, and performance of chores and other responsibilities.

Plan to control the typical bickering between siblings and with parents that normally begins at puberty. Creative techniques, other than just punishment, can be very effective. One family had the brother and sister hug and kiss each other every time the bickering got annoying. One father had two siblings of the same sex put on boxing gloves and slug it out. Have them wash both sides of the *same* window to dissipate their energy. Have some rules that will minimize conflict between teens, for example, asking permission to enter each other's room or borrow clothes. Some of the bickering should be ignored because it is an attention-getting technique.

Discipline for a teenager should consist of withholding privileges and other alternatives, rather than physical punishment. Privileges could include television, attendance at certain functions, and use of the car or telephone. Alternative scenarios could be similar to this one: "Either pay the $800 damage bill you caused to our car, or take $1200 from your car fund and put it in your college fund, or give me three weeks free labor as we paint the house during my vacation."

Prepare your children in late childhood for the adolescent period by discussing the rules they will be expected to follow. Rules might include the following: start group dating at fourteen, double dating at sixteen, single dating at eighteen; require a potential date to meet Dad and ask whether he can date the daughter; or get your driver's license only after age sixteen and after passing Driver's Education.

Solutions:

1. Go over the appropriate principles and Scriptures in this section with the parents.
2. Have the parents and the teen read Chapters 4 ("The Junior High Years") and 5 ("The Senior High Years") of *Forming a New Generation*[5] and Chapter 14 ("The Generation Gap") of *Formula for Family Unity.*
3. Have the parents read Josh McDowell's book *Why Wait? Helping Teens Say No to Sexual Involvement,*[6] and Charles Stanley's book *How to Keep Your Kids on Your Team.*[7]

4. Get the teenager and parents together in a counseling session. Make sure the teenager gets to tell his side of the story without interruption.

5. Check for a root of bitterness in the parents or the teenager and urge them to confess any known sin.

6. Get the parents to arrange for the teen to work on an independent project or experience in which he will be under another authority. Such projects might be taking a job, counseling at a camp, being an AWANA leader, or going on a mission trip.

7. Have the parents work out a family project for the teenager in which all three can work to accomplish a family goal, such as building a barbecue or deck (see Appendix C for sixteen ways to have family unity).

Other common problems of teens are rejection (Chapter 14), sexual and moral problems (Chapter 12), depression (Chapter 21), bitterness (Chapter 10), and addiction (Chapter 18). Unique problems like anorexia or bulimia are discussed in Chapter 24. An understanding mother and father providing a rich home life full of love and unity can handle, solve, or at least minimize most of a teen's problems.

Case Study:

Joel and Nancy came to the counselor because of their fifteen-year-old son, Rick. Joel said that his wife hovered over Rick "like a mother hen" and that Rick was rebelling against his mother's smothering interest and becoming rebellious toward spiritual things. He was running around with two boys who smoked and were very likely into drugs.

On several occasions Rick had told off-color jokes to neighborhood girls. He had also walked in on each of his two younger sisters, ages ten and twelve, when each was taking a bath. (Both of the sisters had reached puberty at ten years of age. Rick had reached puberty at thirteen.) He had also become surly and antagonistic lately toward his mother.

Nancy complained that Joel had never taken an interest in his son and never did anything with him. Joel complained that Rick was "her boy" and she gave all of her affection, time, and interest to him, neglecting her husband and two daughters. He said frankly that he was jealous of the attention that Rick received.

Case Study Solution:

The counselor went over the principles on teenagers and their strong desire for independence to become mature adults. The mother had been smothering Rick and was controlling him in his teenage years as she had during his childhood. In his effort to be a man, he was turning to his peers and their bad habits, which he thought were the marks of manhood. The counselor told them both to read Chapters 4, 5, and 16 of the authors' book *Forming a New Generation.*

The counselor urged the father to start spending time with his son once a week and suggested several activities they could start with. The father was also urged to have a father-son talk with Rick about sexual development and its implications. He was also to discuss dating and the conduct of a boy toward his sisters and other girls.

The mother was to start calling him "Rick" instead of "Ricky" or "Ricky-boy," as she often did, and was to start turning her attention toward her two daughters to prevent future problems with them.

The parents both agreed that Rick would get a paper route so that he would learn how to work and manage money on his own. They also agreed to have him work the following summer at a Christian camp to help him in his spiritual development. They decided to encourage him to go to the youth activities of a nearby Fundamentalist church since their small church did not have a youth group.

A year later, the father contacted the counselor and said that Rick's rebellion problem was nonexistent since he had dedicated his life to the Lord at the summer camp. They had also gotten their daughters into the youth group of the nearby church, and both were growing spiritually.

TABLE XIII
THE FAITH WAY

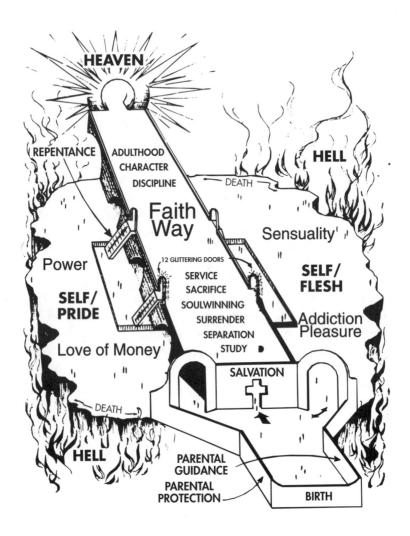

Description of Table XIII

A child is under the parental training and parental protection in his early years. After the age of accountability, which varies with each child, he must make the salvation decision to enter the Faith Way. He could decide to go to the right into sensuality and serving the flesh or to the left into the love of money and things that money will buy, serving the pride and power of materialism.

After the person enters the Faith Way by the way of the cross, he must then make six other decisions if he is going to have a faith walk with the Lord, resulting in godly character and a disciplined Christian life (Heb. 11:16). These six decisions (explained in Chapter 2) after the salvation decision are the following: (1) study the Word, (2) separate to God's holiness, (3) surrender one's life to God, (4) win souls to Christ, (5) make the sacrifice of praise, and (6) render the service of love. Being on the Faith Way assures a person of going to heaven no matter how far he has progressed toward maturity.

The Devil has many glittering one-way doors leading off the Faith Way. Beside each glittering door is a one-way door of repentance provided by God's grace for Christians to return to the Faith Way. Sinners can enter on the Faith Way only through the door of salvation.

There are twelve glittering doors of temptation on the left side of the Faith Way and twelve on the right represented in the diagram by one door on each side. The twelve on the left leading to the love of money are rebellion, lying, selfishness, hate, bitterness, discontentment, envy, peer pressure, credit overspending, loving fancy vehicles, serving the god of sports, and complete devotion of time and energy to work. The twelve on the right leading to sensuality and addiction are television, rock music, pornography, masturbation habits, sexual abuse of others, homosexuality, petting, premarital sex and/or adultery, eating abuse, alcohol, smoking, and other drugs.

Parents and mature Christians can do a great deal to minimize the temptation of these glittering doors by setting a good example, giving biblical warnings about the dangers, teaching the necessity of a disciplined life, ordering a right environment (e.g., television), sending children and teens to Christian schools and camps, and urging the making of decisions for God concerning a holy life (e.g., a purity decision; Titus 2:11-14).

Chapter 24

Special Family Problems

There are special problems that arise as a result of faulty family interaction. The three most common are divorce, pride, and food-related problems—anorexia, bulimia, and obesity. These problems originate in the family relationships, especially between the husband and the wife. Parents are usually unaware of these problems until they are serious. A good marriage relationship is the best insurance against the development of these problems.

Problem #33: Divorce

In the last fifty years, the divorce rate has increased alarmingly in Christian circles as well as in society as a whole. In the face of this increase, the church needs to uphold biblical standards on divorce and acceptable family life and must graciously discipline those members who violate the standards. Members would take Bible standards more seriously if the churches were committed to the biblical pattern of church discipline.

The counselor will be faced with many problems related to impending divorce. He will counsel people who have been divorced and want to be remarried, singles who want to marry divorced people, and even people contemplating second and third marriages. One of the basic facts that the counselor must understand is that divorce grows out of the root problems of bitterness, immorality, and lying.

Definition:

Divorce is legally dissolving a marriage and violating a sacred vow. The family, as established by God in Genesis 1 and 2, is a man and woman joined together before God and the law. The couple may or may not have natural or adopted children. A family is "broken" when one or both parents die or when there is divorce or separation. One parent's being absent for a period of time for military duty or out-of-town work, or a parent's neglect of responsibilities would not be considered a broken home, although the absence might hurt the family unity.

Scripture:

Genesis 1–2; Deuteronomy 6:1-10; 24:1-2; Malachi 2:16; Matthew 5:31-32; 18:15-17; 19:4-6, 8-9; Mark 10:2-12; Luke 16:18; Romans 7:1-3; I Corinthians 7:15, 32-33; Ephesians 4:25-29; 5:25; I Peter 3:8-17

Information and Principles:

Divorce creates broken families, and broken families are the source of most social ills. The absence of the father in a home can bring about serious consequences in the lives of the children involved. According to the 1985 U. S. Department of Commerce statistics, 22 percent of American children, ages six to fourteen, live in single-parent households, and as many as 40 percent of children will live in single-parent households some time in their lives. Sixty-five percent of single-parent families are a result of divorce or separation, and 24 percent are headed by unwed mothers. Most of these children are being brought up in homes where the father is absent. Most daughters of unwed teen mothers become unwed teen mothers themselves. The children are living in broken homes. The percentages of children under eighteen living in single-parent households by ethnic group were as follows: 17.2 percent were white, 26.8 percent were hispanic; and 53.1 percent were black.

The effects of divorce and broken homes on children According to 1988 data from the National Center for Health Statistics, children from divorced families are two to three times more likely to suffer emotional and behavioral problems as those in intact families. A 1991 University of Maryland study by Blasio of 1,500 adolescents found that a teen was more likely to engage in sexual activity if he or she were from a broken home. A 1991 study done by Arland Thornton at the University of Michigan found that there was a remarkably higher rate of premarital sex among young adults whose parents had divorced: 73 percent compared to 50 percent. Another study by Bernadette Melnyk at the University of Rochester found that after parents divorce, children's relationships with their parents deteriorate markedly. The mother-child bond especially deteriorates after divorce. A 1991 study at Case Western Reserve University found that the rate for illegitimate births was highly correlated with a predominance of the female-headed household. Another study by Edward Beal at Georgetown University Medical School followed 300 families from the time of divorce until up to twenty years later. He found that the children from these families had earlier and more frequent premarital sex. They married earlier and were more likely to divorce. The rates were 64 percent higher for women and 33 percent higher for men.

A recent study by Belsay and Eggebeen at Pennsylvania State University of 1,200 children ages four through six revealed that children whose mothers were employed full-time, beginning in the child's first or second year of life, scored more poorly on a composite measure of adjustment than did children whose mothers were not employed during the child's first three years. They also found that these children were much more disobedient to authority. A 1990 study at the University of Southern California found that young men whose parents divorced during the men's teen years were far more likely to commit crimes. A 1990 study of 45,000 Canadians between the ages of eighteen and thirty-four found that children from one-parent homes had significantly lower occupational and educational attainments. A nationwide study in 1988 by the National Center for Health Statistics found a high incidence of emotional and academic problems among children living in single-parent families and stepfamilies. They also had two to three times more emotional or behavioral problems than those whose biological parents were both present in the home. A study in 1992 at Columbia University and New York State Psychiatric Institute revealed that the risk for developing a substance abuse disorder was seven times greater among adolescents from divorced homes. A study reported in 1990 by Jane Mauldon at the University of California at Berkeley of the health histories of 6,000 children found that children from divorced families run a greater risk of developing health problems than those not from. The health risk for these children is above average in the first four years after a separation; it increases after that even if the mother has remarried.

A counselor must decide what he believes is the scriptural position on divorce. Theologians disagree on some points about divorce, and the Scripture is not specific about some of the ramifications and life applications. Some biblical truths that all can agree on follow.

1. *The family is God's first and foremost institution to nurture, train, and develop an individual to the point at which he can independently accept salvation and live a life that glorifies God (Gen. 1–2; Deut. 6:1-10; Prov. 22:6; Eph. 6:4).* When family unity breaks down, the training and nurturing of the children is drastically affected, and a multitude of problems results.

2. *God is against divorce (Mal. 2:16; Matt. 19:4-6).* Divorce nullifies the living illustration of Christ's relationship with the church (Eph. 5:25). Divorce damages a Christian's testimony that Christ is all-sufficient for every problem of life (II Cor. 9:8). Divorce indicates that the person initiating it is practicing the sins of self-centered pride (Prov. 13:10; 15:25) and unforgiveness (Eph. 4:30-32) as well as a lack of endurance, compassion, and understanding (I Pet. 3:8-17).

3. *The exception to the injunction against divorce is fornication (Matt. 19:9).* Some would also include the exception of desertion by an unbeliever (I Cor. 7:15).

The historic Protestant views on divorce would agree on these first three points. However, a controversy arises on the following points.

1. *The Bible states that divorce implies remarriage (Deut. 24:1-2:* "And when she is departed, . . . she may go and be another man's wife." Guy Duty, in his book *Divorce and Remarriage,*[1] makes a good case for remarriage after divorce. See his summary of evidence.[2] The opposing view forbidding remarriage says that this permission was given in the Mosaic Law to the Jews because of the hardness of their hearts (Matt. 19:8). Those who oppose remarriage also use Romans 7:1-3,

in which Paul, giving an illustration concerning law and grace, restates the idea that marriage is until death and only after the death of a spouse is the person free to remarry. They also use I Corinthians 7:10-11 and 39, in which plain instruction is given against remarriage until the spouse dies. They interpret the phrase in verse 15, "not under bondage," to mean "not responsible for care, support, debts, physical intimacy." They also use Mark 10:2-12 and Luke 16:18, which state that remarriage after divorce is the sin of adultery. Some believe that the innocent party would be free to remarry only if the former spouse remarries. Only then could it be accurately stated that adultery was committed (Matt. 19:9) and that there was no hope of reconciliation.

If a counselor determines that the Bible does allow divorce and remarriage, it might be wise to counsel against remarriage of a divorced believer while the divorced partner is still unmarried. This delay would leave open the possibility of reconciliation if one or both parties should get right with God and decide to remarry. The authors know of a Jewish man and a Protestant woman who had divorced and remarried and then divorced again. Then they both accepted Christ and married for the third time, this time successfully.

2. *Some believe that if a couple were divorced before they were saved and one person has been saved since, that person ought to be free to remarry since he is now under grace.* The opposing view holds that being saved does not nullify the plain teaching of Scripture. Also the person still probably retains the same personality traits that contributed to the breakup of the first marriage and would be a marriage risk.

3. *Some believe that divorce is not allowed for a Christian couple because, to get the divorce, they would have to go to law before unbelievers, which would be a violation of the principle forbidding this (I Cor. 6:1-8).* John Murray, in his book on divorce,[3] claims that the man (or woman) should be disciplined by the church only after the wife (or husband) has followed Matthew 18:15-17. If the husband (or wife) refuses to make the sin right and be reconciled, the church should put him (or her) out of the fellowship. He (or she) would then be treated "as a heathen and a publican" (Matt. 18:17). The wife

(or husband) would then be allowed to go to civil law and divorce him (or her) without violating the principle.

The counselor's decisions and beliefs on the points listed above will determine the counsel that he will give to couples considering divorce. There are several general principles that apply.

The counselor is always aiming for reconciliation and, therefore, should never counsel divorce. In the case of abuse of the wife or children or fear of disease from the partner's promiscuous sex behavior, the counselor might advise separation until the abusive partner receives counseling and turns from his violation of Ephesians 5:25-29 or his immorality. In the case of immorality, the innocent party should insist on a physical examination, including tests for sexually transmitted diseases, before reconciliation.

Since the remarriage of a divorced person prevents any reconciliation of the divorced parties and ties the nondivorced person to a potential problem person, the counselor would do well never to counsel remarriage of a divorced person. The question that often occurs to the supposedly innocent person in a divorce is "Is it fair that I should have to live single the rest of my life because of the sin of someone else?" This very statement implies that God wants everyone to be married. One can be happy as a single, serving the Lord—as I Corinthians 7:32-33 points out and as many never-married singles will attest. The counselor should counsel, encourage, and assist the divorced person in his adjustment to single life instead of encouraging and giving the hope of finding happiness in a second marriage. A second marriage can bring about a multitude of problems, especially if children are involved.

Divorce is the worst kind of rejection that an adult can experience. The longer the marriage, the more severe the rejection. The innocent one feels betrayed and conned because the initiator has broken a sacred vow and a legal contract. (Some children in a divorce are even more affected by the feelings of rejection and abandonment than the rejected parent.) A person who has shared the most intimate experiences and secrets of life finds it difficult not to harbor hate and bitterness when the spouse wants to abandon the marriage. The counselee with these sinful feelings needs to be encouraged to repent.

The counselor must use extreme sensitivity and discernment when counseling the divorced one because divorced people perceive prejudice against their position. Couples who have gone through a divorce expect rejection from other Christians, and many times they interpret normal behavior as prejudice against them. However, the sin in their lives must be dealt with forthrightly even though the divorced one feels misunderstood.

If the divorced spouse has remarried another and divorced a second time, he is defiled (Deut. 24:3-4). There should not be a remarriage to the first partner, for that second marriage would be an abomination to the Lord.

To preserve the marriage and family unity, the offended spouse should be encouraged to persevere in difficult circumstances instead of considering separation or divorce (I Pet. 2:19-23; 3:8-18). The exception to such perseverance would be physical or sexual abuse (see Chapter 19) for which separation would be in order. Christian spouses should be counseled against suing for divorce, for they would be violating the Bible principle of I Corinthians 6:1-8.

The counselor should help the single parent to counteract the effect of a broken home by trying to arrange for a substitute parent for the children. Especially if the children do not have the adequate attention of the one remaining parent because the parent is working full-time, it is vital that they have some available adult to turn to. The best substitute parent would be a grandparent, followed by an aunt or an uncle, then a pastor, youth leader, or deacon in the church, and then possibly a neighbor.

Solutions:

1. Review the appropriate Scripture and principles.
2. Review the various steps of reconciliation, including church discipline if necessary, that you would use with any disagreement between believers (Matt. 5:23-24; 18:15-17). Dr. Jay Adams has a good chapter on church discipline in *The Christian Counselor's Manual.*[4]
3. Deal with the specific area of difficulty, such as communication, finances, the physical relationship, in-laws, and so on mentioned in Chapter 22.

4. Help the couple to rebuild their relationship and communication skills. Help them take steps to rebuild family unity (see Appendix C) and thereby "divorce-proof" their marriage.

5. Have the couple agree that they will never talk of divorce again but will instead take the biblical steps of problem-solving, reconciliation, and forgiveness.

6. Try to arrange for a parent substitute for the children, especially in the case of boys who are separated from their fathers.

Case Study:

Doug and Sue came to the counselor about their marriage, which was beginning to break up after twenty-one years. They had three teenagers: a boy, 13, and two girls, 16 and 19. Sue did all the talking during the first session and had a long list of complaints, all of which seemed to center on her feeling that Doug had never met her needs.

Sue said Doug was tightfisted with money and questioned and objected to every expenditure she made. Four years before, they had moved into a new home in a nice section of town. Doug did not want Sue to spend anything on the house and never let her spend the money that she earned. She was an executive secretary and made a good salary; he was a salesman and earned about twice what she did.

Sue said that Doug never paid attention to the children and never helped out at home because he was always too busy working on his books and orders. She said he was not affectionate, even in their physical relationship. She said the children had no love or respect for their father because he was so distant.

Sue said that at the end of their first year of marriage, she had caught her husband in an affair, and things had started to go downhill from there. At the end of the second session, she finished her list of Doug's deficiencies and then let Doug tell his side of the story, with frequent interruptions from her.

Doug said that Sue's catching him in an affair was nothing more than finding three letters that his old girlfriend had written him during their first year of marriage. In the third letter his old girlfriend, who was single, had suggested meeting for dinner in a hotel dining room in another town. He said he had written her only one letter after they were married and had requested that she not write him anymore.

The wife interrupted to ask why the girlfriend kept writing him and why she wanted to meet him in a *hotel* dining room if they did not have further plans to stay in the hotel. Doug said that his wife had been bitter against him since that day and he was completely innocent of any wrongdoing, although he admitted he should never have kept the three letters.

Doug said he had been very insecure financially, since he came from a poor family, and he always liked to have a savings account for emergencies. He said that Sue wanted to spend money any time they got ahead to redecorate and buy new clothes. She said that because she earned the money, she had a right to spend her portion any way she wanted. Doug said her spending had gotten so bad that they had gotten about $8,000 in debt and had had to refinance the house to pay off the debt. He said that Sue did not seem to understand that by doing so, they merely shifted the debt from high-interest credit cards to a low-interest equity loan, because she kept right on spending and put them further into debt.

When the counselor asked about a budget, Doug said that he had a budget for the family, but she refused to stick with it. This statement prompted Sue to complain vehemently about Doug's lack of sensitivity to her needs. At this point she refused to see the counselor anymore, accusing him of being on Doug's side. She said that, if Doug did not change, she was going to divorce him.

Two weeks later Sue served Doug with divorce papers. A month later, she moved out. The son stayed with Doug, and the younger girl stayed with Sue. The older girl was in college and tended to be on the father's side.

A year later Doug and Sue were divorced. Doug, who did not believe in divorce or remarriage after divorce and still loved his wife, continued to see the counselor and prayed that he and Sue would get back together.

Case Study Solution:

About a year and a half after the divorce, Sue came back to the counselor a totally changed person. She had attended a Christian seminar and realized that she had been bitter against her husband since their first year of marriage. She had also dedicated her life to the Lord. The counselor found that her attitudes were completely changed and that she manifested the fruit of the Spirit in her life. She said she still loved her husband and wanted to get back with him again. The counselor suggested that Doug start dating her again at least once a week and both started coming together for counseling once a week.

The counselor went over the Scriptures on forgiveness and Christian marriage and suggested that Doug and Sue read Gary Smalley's two books *If He Only Knew Her* and *For Better or Best,* the Fremonts' book *Formula for Family Unity,* and H. Norman Wright's book *Holding On to Romance.* The counselor discussed with Sue the necessity of sticking to a budget and spending only what was allotted to her in the budget, which she agreed to do. The counselor had previously been working with Doug on his insensitivity to people in general and his lack of compassion.

Three months later Doug and Sue remarried and, with the changes both made, they seemed to have a happy marriage. The counselor also suggested that in their new marriage they institute the sixteen ways to have family unity.

Problem #34: Pride—Rebellion

According to theologians of the past, the utmost evil is pride. It was through pride that Satan rebelled against God and was cast out of heaven to begin his reign as the enemy of the human race. Pride is the antithesis of humility and is the result and fruit of the root sin of doubt. It is an indication of a rebellion against God. Pride keeps man from acknowledging God and His perfect plan of salvation. Pride is a work of the flesh and is motivated by the Devil (Gal. 5:19-21; I John 2:16). It is his chief weapon in his spiritual warfare against the saints. Pride sets a man up for a fall and destruction (Prov. 18:12; 29:23). Proverbs 16:18 says that "Pride goeth before destruction, and an haughty spirit before a fall."

Pride is essentially a comparison with others. It brings a feeling of power when one thinks that he is better than others. Pride is competing with others and imagining oneself to be superior. A proud man is always looking down on people, authority, and things. Pride is the basis of prejudice and rebellion. The Bible says in James 4:16, "But now ye rejoice in your boastings: all such rejoicing is evil."

Pride begins in childhood when a child rebels against his parents (Prov. 30:11-13). If not properly disciplined at one and two years of age, the child gets into the habit of thinking that authority does not matter and that his own ideas and way of doing things are more important than the authority's ideas and way of doing things. If parents reinforce this thinking by coddling the child and giving in to his every whim, they strengthen his belief that he is superior to any authority.

A child like this is likely to reject the authority of God and His Word. If he should become a Christian, he will still feel that he knows best how to direct his life and behavior. Therefore, the Bible stresses the proper discipline of a child to bring about obedience and honor toward parental authority (Exod. 20:12; 21:15; I Sam. 15:22-23; Eph. 6:1-2). This kind of teaching sets the stage for humble obedience to all adult authority and, eventually, obedience to God and His Word (I Tim. 6:1-5). When this teaching is neglected, a proud spirit is the result.

Pride has wrecked lives and caused the downfall of many Christians and Christian works. C. S. Lewis said, "Pride leads to every other vice: it is the complete anti-God state of mind. . . . Pride is spiritual cancer; it eats the very possibility of love, or contentment, or even common sense."[5]

Definition:

Pride is thinking of self more highly than one ought to think, comparing oneself with others, and feeling superior in some area of life such as intelligence, physical appearance, abilities, or talents. It is a faulty idea of one's own worth (II Cor. 10:12).

Scripture:

Psalms 40:4; 119:78; 123:4; Proverbs 6:16-17; 8:13; 11:2; 13:10; 16:5, 18; 18:12; 21:4; 26:12; 30:11-13; Isaiah 5:21; Romans 12:3, 16; I Corinthians 8:2; II Corinthians 10:12; Galatians 6:14; I Timothy 6:1-5; II Timothy 3:1-2; I Peter 5:5-6; I John 2:16

Information and Principles:

Most people have a tendency to be proud and to think highly of themselves. In a survey of nearly a million high school seniors in the 1980s, 70 percent rated their leadership ability above average, and only 2 percent rated it below average. In the category of getting along with others, nobody rated himself below average, and 25 percent rated themselves in the top 1 percent. People tend to be unreasonably optimistic in various areas of their lives. Certainly, people do not need to be encouraged in the Pollyanna attitude embodied in the teaching of the self-esteem approach, for their self-esteem is naturally too positive (Rom. 12:3). Christians should be working on improving their God concept and minimizing their self-concept (John 3:30). God did not attempt to build up Moses' low self-confidence when He called Moses to lead the Israelites out of Egypt. Instead God just declared Himself and His power (Exod. 3:11-15).

There are several general principles that are related to the problem of pride.

In the American culture, the extreme emphasis on competition can become the spawning ground for pride. Pride is most evident in sports. However, it is also evident in academics, music, and finances. If everyone else were superior in sports or made the same grade or had the same level of musical talent or had an equal amount of money, there would be nothing to be proud about. It is the comparison that makes one proud and gives the pleasurable feeling of superiority. Pride is competitive by its very nature; pride feeds competition, and competition feeds pride.

Parents must be careful that they do not encourage pride in their children when the children excel. The children should receive praise for doing their best and depending on and thanking God for His intervention in bringing about the success or victory. The pleasurable feeling children get from trying and succeeding or winning is not pride if they give God the glory and if the feeling is based on the accomplishment rather than on what they are (Gal. 6:14). The delight should not be in what one is but on what has been done with God's help.

The person who feels inferior is just as much affected by pride as the one who feels superior. The inferior one believes that others do not see his potential. He feels that the treatment he receives from others is inconsistent with his superior view of himself. He has a faulty idea of his own worth. This feeling of inferiority can be a result of and fostered by excessively harsh criticism from parents, teachers, and coaches.

Self-abasement is a different form of pride rather than the opposite of pride. The person who is bitter about his limitations and is unwilling to accept himself with the minimal abilities and meager talents that God has given him reveals an inner pride. The self-abasing person feels inferior, but in addition he will exaggerate his faults and make degrading comments about himself to obtain pity and compliments.

Every asset is bestowed by God and could just as easily be taken away if not used to glorify God. The Bible says, "Every good gift and every perfect gift is from above, and cometh down from the Father of lights, with whom is no variableness, neither shadow of turning" (James 1:17). "For who maketh thee to differ from another? and what hast thou that thou didst not receive? now if thou didst receive it, why dost thou glory, as if thou hadst not received it?" (I Cor. 4:7).

Christians should be encouraged to develop humility before God and man (James 4:10; Matt. 18:4; I Pet. 5:6). God resists the proud and gives grace to the humble (James 4:6). When people do not give honor and glory to the Lord but take the glory themselves, God cannot use them or bless them. A humble spirit is basic to serving God and having an effective ministry with others.

Solutions:

1. Review the appropriate principles and Scripture.
2. Help the counselee to understand that God needs to receive the glory (Gal. 6:14).
3. Help the counselee to understand that whatever he does should be done to the glory of God (I Cor. 10:31).
4. Teach the counselee to accept praise for his accomplishments and to put off the natural feeling of superiority that results from pride.
5. Teach the counselee to deny self and to find his worth in identifying with Christ (Luke 9:23; Rom. 8:17; Eph. 2:4-10; II Pet. 1:4; also Chapters 9 and 14 of this book).

Case Study:

A mother and a father came to the counselor about their daughter, Angela, who was eighteen. She was a freshman at the nearby technical college and was employed at the nearby fast-food restaurant. They said she had been a dedicated Christian girl, but in her senior year of high school, she had become proud and rebellious. After she had started working part-time at the fast-food restaurant and earning her own money, she had become clothes-conscious and had spent all of her money on the latest fashions. They said she had been dating an unsaved fellow worker and several times, after getting off work at 11:00 P.M., had come in at 2 or 3 A.M. She would not tell her parents where she had been or what she had been doing.

Case Study Solution:

The counselor asked the parents if Angela used either alcohol or drugs. They said that they had found no evidence of either but suspected she had been drinking. The counselor talked to Angela about the submission-to-authority and materialism principles found in I Timothy 6:1-11. She realized that her parents had jurisdiction over her as long as she was living in their house and taking their tuition money for college, but she was still very rebellious and complained bitterly to the counselor that her parents made all her decisions for her and would not let her have any freedom.

The counselor asked her if she would consider going away to college to get away from their day-by-day authority. She said that she had wanted to do that in the first place, but her parents had insisted she go to the local technical college so she would be at home under their watchful eyes. The counselor recommended to the parents that they enroll her right away in a small Christian college a thousand miles from home, since a new semester was to begin in two weeks. Angela readily agreed to this, so the parents had her transcripts sent to the college and flew her there.

In the middle of the second semester, they got a long letter from Angela, saying that she had dedicated her life to the Lord, apologizing to them for the grief she had caused them, and asking their forgiveness. For three summers she worked at a Christian camp. Upon graduation she married a fine Christian young man she had met at college.

Problem # 35: Anorexia Nervosa, Bulimia, and Obesity

America is a food-rich culture. Americans are overly concerned with appearance and health and put great emphasis on diet and exercise, contributing to the problems of anorexia nervosa, bulimia, and obesity. These problems are not found in underdeveloped countries. Adolescent girls in our culture use weight and appearance as manipulative tools in interactions with their parents because most parents are too concerned with teenage eating habits and appearance. Doubt, resulting in fear, depression, and lying, seems to be the root cause of these three problems. The problem of addiction is usually also present.

Definition:

Anorexia nervosa—"Anorexia nervosa is generally considered to be a psychosomatic eating disorder of young adults with self-induced severe weight loss, starvation, malnutrition, and emaciation, which can progress to death in 10 percent of the cases without treatment." More than 95 percent of anorexics are females, usually teenagers.[6]

Bulimia—Bulimia is "rapid consumption of a large amount of food in a discrete period of time, usually less than two hours," terminated "by abdominal pain, sleep, social interruption, or repeated attempts to lose weight by severely restrictive diets, self-induced vomiting, or use of cathartics or diuretics; . . . characterized by frequent weight fluctuations greater than 10 pounds due to alternating binges and fasts; awareness that the eating pattern is abnormal and fear of not being able to stop voluntarily; depressed mood and self-deprecating thoughts following eating binges."[7]

Obesity—Obesity is "an excessive amount of adipose tissue 20 percent above the ideal body weight. If the weight should increase to 100 percent over ideal body weight, the point is termed massively, or markedly, obese." Heredity may be a predisposing factor.[8]

Scripture:

I Corinthians 3:16-17; 6:19-20

Information and Principles:

All three of these conditions are a result of a person's being obsessed with food. The anorexic rejects food, and the bulimic and the obese persons crave too much food. Each is a form of addiction. The anorexic is addicted to losing weight and refusing food. The bulimic and the obese persons are addicted to food itself. All three groups want to lose weight, and they do it in four ways.

1. *Self-induced vomiting*—Vomiting can cause physical complications from the stomach acids, causing heartburn or hydrochloric acid burn in the esophagus. It also erodes the enamel protecting the teeth and can cause a burning of the salivary glands. It upsets the acid level of the body, increasing the pH factor and causing numerous physical symptoms from the resulting alkalosis condition. Vomiting also upsets the electrolyte balance and can lead to death because the heart is affected.

2. *Laxatives*—When a person overuses laxatives, the food cannot stay in the intestines long enough to be absorbed, and vital nutrients and electrolytes are lost.

3. *Diuretics (water pills)*—Overuse of diuretics can result in a loss of minerals and electrolytes with an extensive loss of water.

4. *Excessive exercise*—One who over-exercises can become so obsessed with getting in shape that he becomes addicted to the exercise. The loss of water (through sweating) and weight can result in anorexia.

It is estimated that 2 percent of adolescents are anorexic, and another 5 percent are bulimic who may be or may become anorexic. One study of the freshman class of 780 men and 575 women at the University of North Dakota found that the rate of bulimia among men was 1.4 percent and among women, it was 7.8 percent, and 4.5 percent of the women binged once a week or more. Another study at a small college found that out of 287 respondents, 12.6 percent were classified as bulimic and 2.1 percent were classified as having anorexia and bulimia.

The typical symptoms and characteristics of each food-related problem follow.[9]

Typical Symptoms and Characteristics of Anorexia Nervosa, Bulimia, and Obesity		
Anorexia Nervosa	**Bulimia**	**Obesity**
More fanatical about body weight	Preoccupied with body shape	Care about food more than body shape
Turn away from food	Turn toward food	Find solace, comfort, and pleasure in food
Associated with rejection of femininity	Oriented toward traditional families	Feel rejected and in conflict with families
Confident over control of food	Anxious about and afraid of food because more likely to give in to hunger	Love food because of family emphasis on food
Starts at puberty	Usually starts in late teens and early 20s	Usually starts in teen years, although in some cases, late childhood
Dependence and social withdrawal	More mature than anorexics; display sense of independence and professional success; more prone to serious personality problems; are complainers, worriers, and feel guilty more often than anorexics	Feel rejected but put on happy, carefree front
Usually have high intelligence, are achievers, make good grades	Usually have high intelligence, are achievers, make good grades	Usually have average intelligence, are low achievers
Extreme weight loss, emaciation	Overweight but may become anorexic	Steady weight gain above normal weight

Some general principles apply to these three problems.

Depression usually precedes the onset of these three conditions by about six months on the average, and it usually persists throughout the course of the condition. The person needs to be counseled for depression.

There is usually a great deal of deceit connected to all three conditions. The person needs to be confronted with the lying problem.

These three conditions are usually related to the interaction within the family setting; therefore, the whole family needs to be counseled, especially regarding their relationships. Some anorexics are characterized by having an over-controlling parent, especially the father. On the other hand, some anorexics are dependent on authority and do not want to grow up but want to remain children that are still protected and cared for. The diminished breasts and hips, the cessation of her periods, and the increased concern of her parents make the anorexic feel like a little girl again. Eating is the only area of her life she can control and feel safe about.

Usually all three conditions are a rebellion against authority and the control of the parents. Parents need to relax their control in appropriate ways and encourage the person to develop self-control and independence in as many areas of her life as possible.

A person with any of the three conditions needs information about the physical dangers involved. However, because each problem is mainly on the physical and feeling level, information alone will not bring about a cure. The person should be counseled as one would counsel an addict.

All three conditions can cause severe physical problems. Both bulimia and obesity have long-term negative physical effects. In 30 percent of the cases, bulimics become anorexic, and anorexia can result in death.

Solutions:

1. Review the appropriate principles.
2. Get medical help from a qualified doctor who is knowledgeable about the conditions, and work in conjunction with him.
3. Work with the family and encourage them in how to aid the person by (a) not forcing him to eat; (b) not giving in to his peculiarities and attempts to manipulate the environment and behavior of others; (c) not trying to oppose his behavior by imposing additional rules; (d) giving less attention to his food and weight problem (the less attention given, the better chance he has of being cured); (e) expressing honest love through physical and verbal affection; (f) encouraging his decision-making and his taking responsibility for decisions by allowing him to be in charge of his daily routine.
4. Realize that the counselee is ambivalent about getting well and takes comfort in the control and rituals of his disordered life.
5. Help the family realize that hospitalization is the only answer in severe cases.

6. If necessary, counsel the counselee for lying and deceitfulness as discussed in Chapter 15, for addiction as presented in Chapter 18, and for depression in Chapter 21.

Case Study:

A mother came to the counselor about her daughter Corrine, who was thirteen and in the seventh grade. The mother had noticed how thin the daughter was getting and was worried about her because her periods had stopped. (She had matured at twelve.) Corrine was a good cook but refused to eat full meals. She was also a straight-A student who studied constantly. She exercised vigorously, jogging five miles a day. She was a very disciplined girl and set goals that crowded her schedule. She always seemed to be in a rush. She was the oldest girl of four children, with two sisters and a brother. Her father was very controlling and even overprotective of the girls, making most of their decisions for them. He especially gave the girls a lot of attention. The mother worked full-time and was concerned about her daughters because she never had much free time to spend with them.

Case Study Solution:

The counselor suggested that the mother take the daughter to the family doctor for a thorough physical exam. The doctor's report indicated that she was in good health but, at eighty-four pounds, seriously underweight. He diagnosed anorexia. The doctor warned the mother and the daughter that if she got down to eighty pounds, he was going to put her into the hospital because she was in danger of upsetting her electrolyte balance and could die.

The counselor set up a once-a-week counseling session with the girl and emphasized that she could jog only one mile a day, only if she were eating full meals. The counselor also had her keep a list of the type and amount of food she ate.

The counselor went over the "body-temple principle," using the verses related to the body's being the temple of the Holy Spirit. Corrine had been saved at an early age but had never dedicated her life to the Lord. Committing her life to Christ seemed to give her incentive to balance her life and start gaining weight. Corrine also had a habit of lying, which went back to early childhood and which she used effectively to cover her harmful eating habits.

341

The counselor dealt with her about this sin and helped her to overcome it, using Romans 6:11-13.

The mother and the counselor agreed that Corrine had to drop the extra course she was taking in junior high school and two extracurricular activities (that included cheerleading) until her weight improved. The mother agreed to meet with her alone fifteen minutes a day for "mother-daughter talks." Those daily talks helped considerably with a multitude of minor problems. The counselor got the dad to agree to let Corrine make more of her own decisions and to stop doing everything for her.

The counseling went on for over a year until Corrine finally weighed over one hundred pounds. After that time, the counselor started seeing her only once a month until her senior year in high school. That year she relapsed to ninety pounds. The counselor got her parents to agree not to let her go to college until she got up to one hundred pounds. By the end of her senior year, Corrine weighed over 110 pounds and went on to complete a four-year college teacher education program.

Chapter 25

Psychotherapy—
Sophisticated Scam?

Some pastors, counselors, and laymen are hesitant about counseling any serious cases and decide to refer these persons to a psychiatrist who will give them long-term psychotherapy. A Christian psychiatrist or family doctor would be preferred for referral for certain types of persons who need medical treatment or medication. (See Chapter 5.) However, when long-term counseling is necessary, a question immediately arises whether psychotherapy is appropriate for the Christian. It is the belief of many Christian counselors that using biblical principles can better help persons with serious problems when they need long-term counseling. Various studies have shown that psychotherapy, with its antibiblical philosophy, is inadequate to answer people's problems in the secular realm, much less able to help Christians. The following material reveals some of the weaknesses and inadequacies of psychotherapy.

Psychotherapy is a nebulous term which can better be described than defined. It seems to be more of a religion than a science. In Bobgan and Bobgan,[1] Frank is quoted as saying "psychotherapy is not primarily an applied science. In some ways it resembles a religion." Earlier Jung wrote, "Religions are systems of healing for psychic illness. . . . That is why patients force the psychotherapist into the role of a priest, and expect and demand of him that he shall free them from their distress. That is why we psychotherapists must occupy ourselves with problems which, strictly speaking, belong to the theologian."[2] Szasz states, "The basic ingredients of psychotherapy are religion, rhetoric, and repression. . . . It is not merely a religion that pretends to be science, it is actually a fake religion that seeks to destroy true religion."[3]

Psychotherapy has been defined/described in Freedman as follows: "[It is a] form of treatment for mental illness and behavioral disturbances in which a trained person establishes a professional contract with the patient and through definite therapeutic communication, both verbal and nonverbal, attempts to alleviate the emotional disturbance, reverse or change maladaptive patterns of behavior, and encourage personality growth and development. Psychotherapy is distinguished from such other forms of psychiatric treatment as the use of drugs, surgery, electric shock treatment and insulin coma treatment."[4]

In Johnson it is defined/described as the following: "Psychotherapy is the use of a group of techniques to modify feeling, attitudes, and behavior in people. The therapist uses both verbal and nonverbal means of communication to build a relationship with the client. The basic concept of therapy involves understanding—both self-understanding and being understood by another—to achieve relatedness and to relieve emotional pain."[5]

The forms of psychotherapy come in over 250 varieties, from psychoanalysis (Freud) to primal therapy (Janov), with a variety of therapists that practice the therapy.[6] Norman Finkel in his book *Mental Illness and Health* listed twenty-two accepted individual psychotherapy systems and six principle group therapies.[7] They are as follows.

Individual psychotherapies

1. Psychoanalysis—Freud
2. Analytic therapy—Jung
3. Individual psychology—Adler
4. Will psychology—Rank
5. Character analysis, vegetherapy, orgone therapy—Reich
6. Interpersonal psychiatry—Sullivan
7. Direct analysis—Rosen
8. Person-centered therapy—Rogers
9. Existential psychotherapy—May
10. Logotherapy—Frank
11. Gestalt therapy—Perls

12. Fixed-role therapy—Kelly
13. Rational-emotive therapy—Ellis
14. Personal integrity—Mowrer
15. Transactional analysis—Berne
16. Bioenergetics—Lowen
17. Reciprocal inhibitions—Wolpe
18. Implosive therapy—Stampe
19. Social learning theory—Rotter
20. Reality therapy—Glasser
21. Radical therapy—Laing
22. Primal therapy—Janov

Other individual therapies are play therapy (Horney), short-term psychotherapy (Sifneos), EST (Erhard Seminars Training), and other variations, such as the use of dance, animals, gardening, stress-inoculation, and the family.

Principal group therapies

1. Psychodrama—Moreno
2. Analytic group therapy—Slavson
3. Group-centered therapy (no credit given)
4. Gestalt groups—Perls
5. T-group—Lewin
6. Encounter or sensitivity group—Bion, Esalen group.[8]

These individual and group psychotherapy systems, with very few exceptions, have certain ideas in common.

1. They are based on humanistic philosophy; i.e., man can get along without God.
2. They reject man's responsibility for his problems and instead blame environment or class them as an illness.
3. They accept the subjectivism and relativism of psychological thinking.
4. They deny sin and guilt.
5. They neglect and even have hostility toward traditional and religious values.
6. They have an overemphasis on autonomy and self-acceptance.
7. They view virtues as hangups and perversions as preferences.
8. They undermine all forms of authority except psychiatric and bureaucratic.[9]

A description of psychotherapy by Carson is as follows: "Psychotherapy is based on the assumption that, even in cases where physical pathology is present, the individual's perceptions, evaluation, expectation, and coping strategies also play a role in the development of the disorder and will probably need to be changed if full recovery is to take place. The belief that individuals with psychological problems can change—can learn more adaptive ways of perceiving, evaluating, and behaving—is the conviction underlying all psychotherapy. The goal of psychotherapy, then, is to make this belief a reality."[10]

A similar description is found in Davison and Neal in relation to change. "It is primarily a verbal means of helping troubled individuals change their thoughts, feelings, and behavior to reduce distress and to achieve greater life satisfaction."[11]

Both definitions emphasize the idea of the therapist's helping the client to change his thoughts, feelings, and behaviors from one position to another, and generally imply changing to the therapist's philosophical or cultural position.

Rogers advocates no particular position other than some kind of change as being the ultimate purpose of psychotherapy, with growth and actualization as the emphasis.[12] Some, such as Freud, do not advocate change, except in attitude, if the counselee wants to feel comfortable about himself and the lifestyle he has chosen. Of course, if he is not functioning well and wants a behavior change, then that desire will be the goal.[13] Some, like Skinner, would like to change the environment so that it can in turn affect and change the individual.[14]

Many psychotherapists do conduct their treatment on some sort of a scientific basis; however, the extent to which they use science is somewhat questionable. Benner suggests that psychotherapists use a "blend between science, imagination and magic."[15]

Probably the greatest problem of modern psychotherapy is that most systems of treatment do not hold man responsible for his behavior.[16] Past or present environment is blamed, and the problem is labeled an illness for which outside help is required. This idea started with Freud and was called the medical model.

At the end of the Second World War, many servicemen came back "shell-shocked" or with battle fatigue. The Veterans' Administration had to treat these "all-American boys" who had fought for their country and had caved in to stress, supposedly because of the horrible environment of war. Many were actually having problems because of their sinful actions overseas, and the few psychiatrists who gave them treatment that held them responsible for that behavior had a significant cure rate.[17]

The "typical" American boy usually came from a religious and moral background. When he entered the military service and was sent overseas, where he violated moral and religious standards, he was under much stress. The additional stress of war and death caused severe problems in some, who required hospitalization. When the servicemen returned to America with its stricter moral structure, conflict occurred, with resulting guilt.

Most of the psychotherapists who treated these servicemen were trained and hired by the Veterans' Administration. They were trained to use the medical model, and they tried various kinds of therapies, which were carried into the private practice. Very few approached treatment from the moral viewpoint.[18]

Out of this period came many forms of treatment that are used today. With the larger hospitals, the increase in the number of patients remaining in the hospitals, and then the influx of the servicemen, there was a need for more therapists. Most psychotherapists worked in the hospitals and private practice and, other than teaching a course or two, were not connected to a university. So the treatments that were developed were not put under the scrutiny of university research designs.[19]

Most forms of treatment produced results. But the big question was whether the results came about from the psychotherapy administered or as a consequence of other factors, such as the placebo effect or even the deterioration effect, in which the patient is worse after treatment. Various studies seem to indicate that more than two-thirds of the people with mental problems experience recovery without treatment, or "spontaneous remission."

Spontaneous Remission

Landis and Denker's nineteen studies of spontaneous remission compared treatment by general practitioners with the effectiveness of psychotherapy. The figures quoted from these studies agree very well: "The percentage of neurotic patients discharged annually as recovered or improved from New York state hospitals is 70% (for the years 1925–1934); for the United States as a whole it is 68% (for the years 1926–1933). The percentage of neurotics discharged as recovered or improved within one year of admission is 66% for the United States (1933) and 68% for New York (1914). The consolidated amelioration rate for New York state hospitals, 1917–1934, is 72%. By and large, we may thus say that of severe neurotics receiving in the main custodial care and very little, if any, psychotherapy, over two-thirds recovered or improved to a considerable extent. . . . Although this is not, strictly speaking, a basic figure for 'spontaneous' recovery, still any therapeutic method must show an appreciably greater size than this to be seriously considered."[20]

Denker followed up five hundred consecutive disability claims with diagnosis of psychoneurosis, which were treated by general practitioners and not by professional psychotherapists. He found a two-year recovery rate of 72 percent. Eysenck commented as follows:

> Using the two-year recovery figure of 72 per cent, we find that Denker's figures agree exactly with that given by Landis. We may, therefore, conclude with some confidence that our estimate of some two-thirds of severe neurotics showing recovery or considerable improvement without the benefit of systematic psychotherapy is not likely to be very far out.[21]

Compared to this recovery rate of 72 percent through spontaneous recovery and treatment by general practitioners, Eysenck compiled the results of nineteen studies reported in literature covering 7,293 cases that were treated by psychotherapists. These cases covered organ neurosis, psychopathic states, and character disturbances. Schizophrenics, manic-depressives, and paranoid states were excluded. The cure rate was 64 percent. These studies seem to indicate that psychotherapy does not really help most cases and may even hurt some (about 8 percent in this report) and keep them from getting better on their own.

Placebo Effect

In other studies it was found that some persons are cured by the "placebo effect." The placebo effect has greater implications for psychotherapy than for any other type of treatment since both function in whole or in part through the arousal of the expectation of help. Research suggests that the healing effects of expectations are enhanced in psychotherapy when the client has confidence in both the process and the outcome of the therapy.[22]

Shapiro states that at one institution, he conducted a series of experiments on the therapeutic process which illustrates the possible power of the placebo. Over a period of eight years, 1,440 patients were first asked to fill out a long checklist of their symptoms. They were then given a harmless, psychologically inert dose of lactose sugar and told that "they should be helped by this psycho-therapeutic medicine."

After the patients took their medicine, "fifty-five percent of the patients reported that they felt better within the hour of taking the placebo. Thirty percent said there was no change, and fifteen percent said they were worse. As we have seen from studies it [placebo effect] can be a temporary one or not work at all, but it can also be powerful and pervasive."[23] Gross states in the same article, "The evidence is disquieting to therapists. Sugar placebo pills given to unsuspecting neurotic patients often do as well as with psycho-therapy treatments. . . . Between 50 and 76 percent of patients taking only placebos showed improvement, . . . about the same percentage showing positive results for psychotherapy."[24]

Positive expectations regarding the outcome of therapy appear to be as important as expectations regarding therapy process. One study found that the degree of symptomatic relief in psychiatric patients following a single contact with a therapist was related to the patient's expressed expectation that he would be helped. A similar study found a correlation between psychiatric outpatients, estimates of how well they expected to feel after six months of treatment, and the degree of reported symptom relief after an initial evaluation interview.[25] Carson, in his conclusions on the effectiveness of psychotherapy, stated that most psychotherapists view psycho-therapy as better than no treatment.[26] Even so, he adds, the effectiveness is limited by how the therapist, the client, and the client's family and friends view success of psychotherapy and what each considers abnormal behavior.

Deterioration Effect

Some studies reveal the "deterioration effect" in which patients are actually harmed by the treatment rendered. Examining studies that have used control groups with therapy groups, they can now roughly predict the changes likely to occur in the two groups.

Untreated groups		Therapy groups
40%	*improved*	65%
55%	*unchanged*	25%
5%	*deteriorated*	10%

But change was not always beneficial. Ten percent of the therapy cases deteriorated significantly after treatment, twice as many as in the untreated groups. That means one out of every ten therapy patients ended up in worse condition than when he or she began treatment. In half of those cases the deterioration can fairly be blamed on the therapy itself.

Psychotherapy can help—or harm. Assessment of nearly 1,000 cases shows that therapy helps an additional 25 percent but harms another 5 percent of patients. The critical factor may be the therapist's personality and not the type of therapy.

"On the basis of studies that have used such control groups, we can now roughly predict the changes likely to occur in groups of untreated patients. . . . The deterioration among the five percent may be caused by life stress, specific negative experiences, or simply an ongoing process of mental disorder."[27]

The 5 percent refers to the chart above compiled by Bergin giving the percentages related to untreated and therapy groups.

One of the earliest attempts to validate or disprove techniques of psychotherapy also showed the deterioration effect. That study was the Cambridge-Somerville Youth Study, which included 650 underprivileged boys, ages six to ten, believed to be potential delinquents. One-half were in a treatment group, and one-half were in a control group (untreated). "The results were impressive" with the treated group until they checked the untreated control group. "The unpsychologized, uncounseled boys proved to have fewer delinquent episodes than their treated peers."[28] Although the study was cited by Bergin as supporting his conclusion, in his earlier publication Bergin himself had pointed out some serious flaws in the study.[29] Even so, the study seems to have valid conclusions supporting the deterioration effect.

Three Main Approaches Compared with Moral Treatment

The Freudian medical model has prevailed for many years. Gross stated, "There is no doubt that psychoanalytically oriented psychotherapy is the core of most of the psychotherapy done by American psychiatrists today."[30] It has been rivaled in the last thirty years by Carl Rogers's views that man has the resources within to cure himself,[31] and Skinner's behavioristic theories that the right environment can bring about a cure.[32, 33] Jay Adams uniquely describes these different approaches to treatment as the "archaeologist spade, the mirror and the doggie biscuit."[34]

Many forms of treatment can be classed under these three main approaches. Moral treatment, which was the standard treatment in the first half of the 19th century, was very effective, and the cure rate seemed to be as high as 70 percent.[35] When it was at its peak, at least 70 percent of the patients who had been ill for a year or less were released as recovered or improved. Some hospitals reported 80- to 90-percent cure rates. Kindness, patience, attention to needs, and opportunities for expression of creativity were part of this treatment. Then came the larger hospitals, and the discharge rate went down to 5 percent.[36] In the huge centralized mental hospitals that were built as a result of the campaigns of Dorothea Dix, there was a shift from moral treatment to the three main forms of psychotherapy that have continued to develop in the twentieth century.

As already mentioned, the Freudian approach, or the psychoanalytic model, is the predominant form of treatment. The results of this method have not been scientifically proved to be effective as shown by studies supporting spontaneous remission and the placebo and deterioration effects. There may be an occasion when digging up the past may be of some benefit as related in a recent article in the *Reader's Digest.*[37] Some Christian counselors believe that this is not a necessary and beneficial technique for use with Christians. Probably the greatest flaw in the Freudian therapy is that the "digging up" is motivated by the philosophy that man is not responsible for what he does.[38]

The Rogerian, or person-centered, approach to psychotherapy does not give any impressive results either. The approach, which came into vogue in the 1940s, was a new technique. This technique is being increasingly used by therapists and counselors.

This newer approach differs from the older one in that it has a genuinely different goal. It aims directly toward the greater independence and integration of the individual rather than hoping that such results will accrue if the counselor assists in solving the problem. "This newer therapy places greater stress upon the emotional elements, the feeling aspects of the situation, than upon the intellectual aspects. . . . This newer therapy endeavors to work as directly as possible in the realm of feeling and emotion rather than attempting to achieve emotional reorganization through an intellectual approach . . . and places greater stress upon the immediate situation than upon the individual's past."[39]

One of the problems with the Rogerian therapist and client is that there is often a confusion of real love (agape love) with empathy. Agape love looks to meet the needs of others. The Rogerian looks to meet his own need.[40]

The Skinner behavioral approach to psychotherapy is used in treating addictions, phobias, retarded and autistic children, and other problems that cannot be as effectively handled with a verbal approach. One approach cited as least effective for "high treatment effectiveness and cost effectiveness" was the popular method of biofeedback.[41] Skinner believes that all behavior could be changed and controlled by manipulating the environment, and he explained this concept in his two books *Walden II* and *Beyond Freedom and Dignity.* One of the dangers of Skinner's view is that individuals can lose their "awareness of their own freedom and the confidence in their own ability to resist environmental influences" and finally "the ability to direct their own futures."[42] Young children are easily conditioned by punishment and rewards, and most parents use these techniques with good results. The Bible recommends these techniques in Proverbs 3:27; 13:24; 15:23, 30; 22:15; 23:13; and 25:11.

However, Christian parents try to teach the children to take responsibility for their own decisions as early as they are cognitively able. The cognitive behaviorists, modifying Skinner's approach to psychotherapy, have included the decision making by the individual client as part of the therapy. The cognitive-behavior approach was mentioned by Carson as effective for depression.[43]

There are many techniques other than the three most-used ones just mentioned. It seems that psychotherapy in general is not very effective, and there is no significant difference in the forms of psychotherapy and in treatment in general.[44]

Shepherd states that a host of studies have now been conducted which, with all their imperfections, have made it clear that (1) any advantage accruing from psychotherapy is small at best; (2) the difference between the effects of different forms of therapy are negligible; and (3) psychotherapeutic intervention is capable of doing harm.[45]

Garfield also states that "admittedly, we have a long way to go before we can speak more authoritatively about the efficacy, generality, and specificity of psychotherapy. . . . The present results, while modestly positive, are not strong enough for us to state categorically that psychotherapy is effective, or even that it is not effective. . . . Until we are able to secure more definitive research data, the efficacy of psychotherapy will remain a controversial issue."[46]

Research seems to indicate that the form of psychotherapy is not as important as the therapist himself, his training, and the confidence he projects. Tavris states that

> Psychotherapy can be helpful, especially if the therapist is warm and empathic, but sometimes it slows down a person's natural rate of improvement. Most of the time it doesn't accomplish anything.[47]

In another study it was stated that "presumably, through interaction with their therapists they come to feel relaxed, accepted and likeable, and they achieve some confidence and hope."[48] In this same study it was found that when the therapists reported feeling involved, their patients tended to report feeling relieved. Positive patient feelings accompanied therapists' positive feelings and vice versa. According to Bobgan, "patient-therapist compatibility is the best indicator of outcome." "The rapport between patient and therapist is the only variable that has been shown to be reliably significant in psychiatry" and "success in psychotherapy is due to a 'helping alliance' between therapist and patient, not the type of therapy."[49] Even Adams[50] and Brenner[51] give qualifications of a good counselor. It would seem that there is some importance attached to the personality of the psychotherapist or the counselor and the client's response.

Is psychotherapy effective and are pastors and Christian counselors justified in sending people to psychotherapists who are not Christians and are not using the biblical or Spirit-flesh model? In view of the above studies, the answer must be no. The question that immediately follows is, "What can be done about the abnormal, the most serious cases, and those with the bizarre behavior?" The solution is for the Christian counselor, using biblical counseling, to work closely in conjunction with a good Christian physician.[52]

Since the functioning of the physical body and the mind are so closely interwoven, it is very difficult to determine whether physical causes such as anemia, hypoglycemia, allergies, chronic fatigue syndrome, drug reaction, abnormal hormonal functioning, tumors in the brain, or mind causes such as wrong attitudes, guilt, or double mindedness are the source of the problem. A Christian counselor should be well aware of the physical symptoms that indicate a physical cause and should refer the counselee to the appropriate physician, who may refer him to a specialist if there is a need. He should not refer a counselee to a secular psychotherapist.

The pastor or Christian counselor with a knowledge of Bible principles and appropriate techniques in biblical counseling is equipped to handle the mental problems. ("That the man of God may be perfect, throughly furnished unto all good works," II Timothy 3:17.) Mowrer condemned the referral practice of the clergy. He said the "church loses its very excuse for existence . . . as soon as it refuses to go 'all the way' with the person who is in that emotional and moral crisis which we call neurosis and psychosis." Mowrer believes that the clergyman who is not prepared to counsel his people "compounds their feelings of alienation" and fails them.[53] Biblical counseling differs from psychological counseling in spite of the seeming similarities. A number of contrasts are given by

Bobgan and Bobgan. Their final statement is, "The biblical way is God centered and the psychological way is man centered."[54]

It is time for Christians to realize that with the power of the Holy Spirit in them, the principles of the Word of God as their tool, and the love of God flowing in and through them in a counseling relationship, God can bring about healing in a miraculous way. When man's reference point becomes secular philosophies, he then begins to lose the capacity to respond to people in a spiritual manner, which would help them out of their maladjustment. Christian counselors may use secular studies, information, and whatever might be useful that does not conflict with Scripture in counseling, but it is not a necessity.[55] Christian counselors must not be wedded to secular psychology. God's Word is the absolute and final authority and the Holy Spirit is necessary to give the impetus and strength to make a healthy adjustment and needed change. A statement by Kilpatrick puts this warning succinctly: "It's been said he who marries the spirit of the times is soon a widower."[56]

Appendix A

The Secret of Effective Christian Teaching: Bible Action Truths

My father made a profound statement that would later on have a tremendous effect on my professional life and ministry. As a teenage Junior Assistant Scout Master teaching classes in scouting skills, I was interested in how Dad prepared for his classes. At that time he was teaching Time and Motion Study classes at the University of Dayton, Wright Field, and the Standard Register Company. I watched as he made a big flip chart and wrote a simple saying at the top in bold letters—**There is a better way.**

He said, "That is a basic principle, Son, and I will build my lesson on that one general principle." Then he said something that determined the way I was to teach through speaking, counseling, and writing for the next forty-five-plus years: *"The secret of effective teaching is to concentrate on communicating principles instead of facts."* My father went on to explain that the average person soon forgets facts, but principles are more meaningful and more easily retained. Facts are important because they buttress, illustrate, and illuminate the truth; but facts are the medium and not the message. Students tend to forget facts quickly, but principles become the hooks in the mind upon which to hang facts. Principles are the categories under which facts can be filed. Though facts help a learner to understand truth, principles determine behavior.

Principles are foundational ideas, fundamental truths, basic concepts, generic common denominators, and unchanging laws. Principles are not the same as practices. Practices are specific activities or actions that operate in specific situations. Principles should determine practices.

Principles in each subject are easily identified. They are the core ideas, laws, "rules of thumb," or truths and are usually universal in their applications. A principle is the major truth in a lesson under which is grouped the minor points, information, facts, statistics, definitions, questions, and illustrations. Several principles could be taught in one lesson, or one principle might suffice for a series of lessons.

The Christian teacher, while teaching subject principles, puts a strong emphasis on applicable Bible principles. He uses the Bible principles that correlate with the subject matter to give students a Christian world-view. He also teaches principles that best build character and help the students to live lives that please and glorify God. He teaches his students how to search out Bible principles in their devotions and apply them in their daily lives.

As the students study Scripture, the teacher urges them to use the 4M Formula (from Ps. 119:9, 11, 15, and 17): they should *mark, memorize, meditate on,* and *master the principles* that they find in their study. By learning these Bible life principles related to their subjects, students gain not only academic wisdom but also daily guidance and the knowledge of God's will for their lives. The Ten Commandments (Exod. 20:1-17) and the two love commandments (Matt. 22:37-40) are choice examples of foundational Bible principles that should be integrated into every elementary school curriculum.

Bible principles are greater than people, environments, or circumstances. A person who practices Bible principles is not dominated by the attitudes, actions, and reactions of others or by environmental influences or life circumstances that occur.

Bible principles have automatic consequences. If one chooses actions contrary to the principle, he will suffer negative consequences. If he chooses to follow Bible principles, he will finally reap God's blessing. Bible principles give security because they are eternal and unchanging (Matt. 24:35).

Early in the history of the United States, Bible principles were constantly taught to children in the schools, which at that time were connected with churches and run by preachers. The early textbooks reflected this emphasis. The McGuffey Readers, written in 1837 by a Presbyterian preacher and his brother, were full of Bible principles. But around 1850 there was a secularization of education under the influence of Horace Mann, Henry Barnard, and other leading educators. The gospel and the Scripture were no longer the focal point of education; character traits and citizenship were emphasized instead. Revision of the McGuffey Readers in 1857 and in 1879 eradicated almost all the references to Bible principles and salvation. During the first half of the twentieth century, Bible principles were virtually eliminated in many of the churches under the influence of modernists and liberals, who also controlled Christian education in the mainline denominational Sunday schools and churches.

In 1954 Frank Gaebelein, in his book *The Pattern of God's Truth,* called for a revival of teaching Bible principles in every academic subject. In 1963 Bill Gothard, then director of the Hi-C clubs in Chicago, started teaching ten foundational Bible principles which later developed into his Basic Youth Conflicts Seminar. In 1984 he expanded these ten into two hundred Bible principles, which are the core of his Institute in Basic Life Principles. In 1965 Vera Hall and Rosalee Slater promoted the idea of principled teaching as the foundation for their Christian school curriculum. In 1972 the Bob Jones University School of Education developed thirty-seven Bible Action Truths, principles used in the Bob Jones University Press elementary and secondary curriculum. (See the following chart list of Bible Action Truths.) Dr. Ruth Haycock published a pamphlet in 1978 entitled "God's Truth in Every Subject," another listing of Bible principles in the academics. In 1984 she expanded this material into four volumes, and it was published by the Association of Christian Schools International.

This recently renewed emphasis on principled teaching and applying Bible principles is the heart of modern Fundamentalist Christian education. It is the key to training youth "to be conformed to the image" of Christ (Rom. 8:29), equipped to do "the work of the ministry" (Eph. 4:12), and "throughly furnished unto all good works" (II Tim. 3:17).

The teacher is constantly pointing out the application of key Bible principles, for these build character. A person has character when he operates his life consistently on principle rather than on feeling. God has told mankind plainly in His Word how to act and react in every situation. As Christians follow God's principles, they are promised success, happiness, and a full life (Josh.1:8). Therefore, the teacher trains his students to ask in every situation, "God, what would You have me to do?" Even in trials, God promises good to those who love Him, "to them who are the called according to his purpose" (Rom. 8:28).

Students should be encouraged to have a daily morning devotion time (Bible Before Breakfast). It develops consistent discipline, which is essential to character; but more importantly, it directs continual dependence on God instead of self (Ps. 5:1-3, 11-12).

Great Christian teachers know how to teach Bible truths in principle form and how to integrate all other knowledge with this truth. Unfortunately, many Christian schools lack principled instruction based on the Bible's guidelines for action. The thirty-seven Bible Action Truths listed are suggested as foundations for principled teaching and are conveniently classified under eight action-reaction headings.

There are thousands of Bible principles; those listed are the ones most directly affecting character. Of course, these principles are intended for the young person who has been born again and who is being taught the important doctrines of the Faith. Salvation brings the fear of the Lord (Prov. 8:13), which is the beginning of wisdom and knowledge (Prov. 1:7; 9:10).

A balance in using Bible principles is important. When a person overemphasizes one or two Bible truths above all others, his reactions are often warped and maladjusted. There are many different ways of teaching these truths and of integrating them into the curriculum. The proper utilization of Bible principles will enrich the learning of the student and lead to a useful, balanced, and well-adjusted Christian life.

Bible Action Truths

Salvation-Separation

Salvation results from God's direct action. Although man is unable to work for this "gift of God," the Christian's reaction to salvation should be to separate himself from the world unto God.

Understanding Jesus Christ—Matthew 3:17; 16:16; I Corinthians 15:3-4; Philippians 2:9-11

Repentance and faith—Luke 13:3; Isaiah 55:7; Acts 5:30-31; Hebrews 11:6; Acts 16:31

Separation from the world—John 17:6, 11, 14, 18; II Corinthians 6:14-18; I John 2:15-16; James 4:4; Romans 16:17-18; II John 10-11

Sonship-Servant

Only by an act of God the Father could sinful man become a son of God. As a son of God, however, the Christian must realize that he has been "bought with a price"; he is now Christ's servant.

Authority—Romans 13:1-7; I Peter 2:13-19; I Timothy 6:1-5; Hebrews 13:17; Matthew 22:21; I Thessalonians 5:12-13

Servanthood—Philippians 2:7-8; Ephesians 6:5-8

Faithfulness —I Corinthians 4:2; Matthew 25:23; Luke 9:62

Goal setting—Proverbs 13:12, 19; Philippians 3:13; Colossians 3:2; I Corinthians 9:24

Work—Ephesians 4:28; II Thessalonians 3:10-12

Enthusiasm—Colossians 3:23; Romans 12:11

Uniqueness-Unity

No one is a *mere person;* God has created each individual a unique being. But because God has an overall plan for His creation, each unique member must contribute to the unity of the entire body.

Self-concept—Psalms 139; 8:3-8; II Corinthians 5:17; Ephesians 2:10; 4:1-3, 11-13; II Peter 1:10

Mind—Philippians 2:5; 4:8; II Corinthians 10:5; Proverbs 23:7; Luke 6:45; Proverbs 4:23; Romans 7:23, 25; Daniel 1:8; James 1:8

Emotional control—Galatians 5:24; Proverbs 16:32; 25:28; II Timothy 1:7; Acts 20:24

Body as a temple—I Corinthians 6:19-20; 3:16-17

Unity of Christ and the church—John 17:21; Ephesians 2:19-22; 5:23-32; II Thessalonians 3:6, 14-15

Holiness-Habit

Believers are declared holy as a result of Christ's finished action on the cross. Daily holiness of life, however, comes from forming godly habits. A Christian must consciously establish godly patterns of action; he must develop habits of holiness.

Sowing and reaping—Galatians 6:7-8; Hosea 8:7; Matthew 6:1-8

Purity—I Thessalonians 4:1-7; I Peter 1:22

Honesty—II Corinthians 8:21; Romans 12:17; Proverbs 16:8; Ephesians 4:25

Victory—I Corinthians 10:13; Romans 8:37; I John 5:4; John 16:33; I Corinthians 15:57-58

Love-Life

We love God because He first loved us. God's action of manifesting His love to us through His Son demonstrates the truth that love must be exercised. Since God acted in love toward us, believers must act likewise by showing godly love to others.

Love—I John 3:11, 16-18; 4:7-21; Ephesians 5:2; I Corinthians 13; John 15:17

Giving—II Corinthians 9:6-8; Proverbs 3:9-10; Luke 6:38

Evangelism and missions—Psalm 126:5-6; Matthew 28:18-20; Romans 1:16-17; II Corinthians 5:11-21

Communication—Ephesians 4:22-29; Colossians 4:6; James 3:2-13; Isaiah 50:4

Friendliness—Proverbs 18:24; 17:17; Psalm 119:63

Communion-Consecration

Because sin separates man from God, any communion between man and God must be achieved by God's direct action of removing sin. Once communion is established, the believer's reaction should be to maintain a consciousness of this fellowship by living a consecrated life.

Bible study—I Peter 2:2-3; II Timothy 2:15; Psalm 119

Prayer—I Chronicles 16:11; I Thessalonians 5:17; John 15:7, 16; 16:24; Psalm 145:18; Romans 8:26-27

Spirit-filled—Ephesians 5:18-19; Galatians 5:16, 22-23; Romans 8:13-14; I John 1:7-9

Clear conscience—I Timothy 1:19; Acts 24:16

Forgiveness—Ephesians 4:30-32; Luke 17:3-4; Colossians 3:13; Matthew 18:15-17; Mark 11:25-26

Grace-Gratitude

Grace is unmerited favor. Man does not deserve God's grace. However, after God bestows His grace, believers should react with an overflow of gratitude.

Grace—I Corinthians 15:10; Ephesians 2:8-9

Exaltation of Christ—Colossians 1:12-21; Ephesians 1:17-23; Philippians 2:9-11; Galatians 6:14; Hebrews 1:2-3; John 1:1-4, 14; 5:23

Praise—Psalm 107:8; Hebrews 13:15; I Peter 2:9; Ephesians 1:6; I Chronicles 16:23-36; 29:11-13

Contentment—Philippians 4:11; I Timothy 6:6-8; Psalm 77:3; Proverbs 15:16; Hebrews 13:5

Humility—I Peter 5:5-6; Philippians 2:3-4

Power-Prevailing

Believers can prevail only as God gives the power: "I can do all things *through Christ.*" God is the source of our power used in fighting the good fight of faith.

Faith in God's promises—II Peter 1:4; Philippians 4:6; Romans 4:16-21; I Thessalonians 5:18; Romans 8:28; I Peter 5:7; Hebrews 3:18–4:11

Faith in the power of the Word of God—Hebrews 4:12; Jeremiah 23:29; Psalm 119; I Peter 1:23-25

Fight—Ephesians 6:11-17; II Timothy 4:7-8; I Timothy 6:12; I Peter 5:8-9

Courage—I Chronicles 28:20; Joshua 1:9; Hebrews 13:6; Ephesians 3:11-12; Acts 4:13, 31

The 4M Formula (from Psalm 119)

1. *Mark* these Bible Action Truths during your Scripture reading (vs. 9).
2. *Memorize* the verses which best represent the truths (vs. 11).
3. *Meditate* on the verses throughout the day (vs. 15).
4. *Master* these Bible Action Truths in your daily life until they master you (vs. 17).

Appendix B

How to Eliminate Spiritual, Emotional, and Educational Child Neglect and Still Remain Financially Solvent

The most overlooked type of family problem is the preschool child who is neglected spiritually, emotionally, and educationally by a mother who is working full time. If the father is also away from the home a good bit of the time, or if when he is home he is too busy with television to pay any attention to the preschoolers, then there is a spiritual, mental, and educational problem in the making. This type of neglect is increasing at an alarming rate even in Christian circles.

Child study experts estimate that one-fourth of the learning of the child occurs in the first six years. Raymond and Dorothy Moore, after studying 755 pieces of research, indicated that the mother is the best teacher of preschoolers as compared even to a well-qualified day care center or preschool kindergarten.

This early training from mother forms an educational base upon which the other three-fourths of learning occurs. Recent studies indicate that mothers' reading to children in the preschool years helps the children in developing their language and reading abilities in elementary school. Herbert J. Walberg, a leading analyst of education research at the University of Illinois, says that parents have an extraordinary effect on building a child's vocabulary, encouraging a child to read and building a child's character and motivation. Research emphasizes early and intense parental involvement in home teaching as the single most essential element of a child's learning skills. Christian mothers are also laying a spiritual base for the children in these early years by reinforcing the spiritual program of the father.

The trend toward mothers working got started during World War II when mothers went to work in the war plants. By 1950 only 15 percent of the mothers of children under the age of eighteen were working. Sociologists and psychologists were worried then about the educational and psychological effects of these mothers' being absent from the home and not training their children. By 1988, 72 percent of mothers with children under the age of eighteen were working full time, and 69.4 percent of mothers of preschool children were working full time. According to the Bureau of Labor Statistics, these mothers come home from work tired and have an additional twenty-seven hours of housework to do weekly. This does not leave the mother any time or energy to train her preschoolers. The father should be helping out in the home management when the mother is working, but studies indicate that the husband of a working wife helps his wife with home chores an average of only one and half hours a week.

One mother told me that she gets up at 5:45 A.M. every day to get things ready for the day. The children get up at 6:15 and are out of the house by 7:10 A.M. on their way to the elementary school and the day care center. She then reaches work by 8 A.M. She says that she does have an hour for lunch, so she can get a few shopping things done during that time. She gets off at 5 P.M., and by 6 P.M. she is home after having picked up the preschooler and her other children who stayed at a friend's house after school. By the time the homework is finished and the dishes are done, they then get the children to bed by 9 P.M. so that they can get a sufficient amount of sleep. The only time for any family time is on Saturdays and Sundays, but she said they are very busy then with house chores and church activities. They had given up going to prayer meeting because of their hectic schedule, and she is too tired to maintain a proper relationship with her husband.

One mother working at our local self-serve gas station has her very well-behaved three-year-old boy dropped off from kindergarten at 3 P.M. He plays on the top of the counter in the cashier's cage until she gets off at 6 P.M. He at least has some contact with his mother while she collects money at this busy station, but he does not get the playtime he needs three hours a day, six days a week.

Even elementary school children need mother at home when they get home from school for counseling, motivation for homework, and practicing various musical instruments and other skills. Mother ought to be available for love, security, supervision, and day-by-day interchange that answers the thousand and one questions that children have so that their character can be developed. With so many mothers absent from the home, is it any wonder that we have such a high delinquency rate, a lack of moral and spiritual standards, falling educational standards, and a rejection syndrome that causes terrific psychological problems? (See "Hard Truths About Day Care," *Reader's Digest,* Oct. 1988, p. 88.)

Christian mothers want to do right by their children and properly train them in the preschool years, but they are being caught up by the materialistic pressures of the world. They rationalize by saying that they need to pay for Christian schooling for their children, or with the increasing financial needs, they have to work to pay the bills. They reason that if Grandmother is living nearby or the Fundamentalist church has a good day care program, then the Lord has solved the family's financial problems by opening the way for the mother to work full time.

A few years ago a Christian leader did a study on the average working mother not in a professional career. He found that after paying income tax, social security tax, lunch costs, transportation costs, and day care costs, she earned only ten dollars a week for forty hours of work. Another secular study indicated that the family's real income was increased by only 10 percent when the mother worked full time.

A mother's working has an effect not only on the children, but also on the marriage relationship. The wife's being thrown into the immoral business world can put a real strain on the marriage relationship. In 1953 a Kinsey survey indicated that 25 percent of the married women had committed adultery, and 50 percent of the men had committed adultery. A 1980 *Cosmopolitan* survey found that 54 percent of the wives had committed immorality while married. One of the conclusions of the study was that married women working full time were now subject to all the temptations which men regularly experience.

The Scriptures state that men are obligated to provide for their families (I Tim. 5:8). When the wife is earning a good percent of the family income as compared to the husband, this does not help his concept of his role as the provider, the leader, and the one responsible for the welfare of his family; and it begins to erode his position as head of the family. The woman who is married and has children, even though she is a college graduate and has started a career, needs to relegate her career to a part-time effort and take up the higher and more rewarding career of motherhood.

How can mothers of three or four children have quantity and quality time with them and still help out financially without working full time? What principles apply which will help mothers to God's will and not feel guilty about their course of action?

1. Have a right view of money, luxury, and material possessions. Young couples seem to need a new home with all the conveniences and modern furniture to be happy. They also want to have two cars—with at least one of them being new every three years—have cable television, eat out one night a week, have a nice vacation in the Caribbean, and have enough money to make payments on a VCR, camera, boat, and other gadgets. What things does a family really need to serve the Lord and have a happy family life (Matt. 6:19-24; I Tim. 6:6-11)?

2. A penny saved is much more than a penny earned. You do not have to pay additional income tax, social security tax, and tithe on the penny saved. The mother at home can be scanning the newspaper for store sales and bargains, yard sales, and things for sale in the classified ads. Buying things at the proper time of the year, usually in January, can result in a savings of 40 to 60 percent. Using grocery coupons can result in a tremendous savings from 15 to 25 percent on the weekly grocery bill. Buying wholesale at farms, orchards, and farmers' markets in season and canning and freezing the bargains from the bountiful harvest in the family garden can effect a tremendous savings. Many supermarkets sell their bread, fruit, vegetables, and even meat on Saturday night at reduced prices in order to clear the shelves for Monday morning. Dad can learn to make simple repairs on plumbing, electrical, mechanical, car, and carpentry jobs.

3. The mother can think in terms of a part-time enterprise that will earn extra money and yet allow her to have the most time with the children. She can keep several children during the day as long as the number does not get above the state's minimum number for a day care center. She can use her skills with small businesses. She can start a housecleaning service, hiring other mothers to work part time. She can develop money-earning skills, such as cake decorating, sewing and alterations, and make things to sell, such as teddy bears, rag dolls, gingerbread men, and so on.

4. The children can get part-time jobs to help pay for clothes, Christian school tuition, and expenses and to help save for college. Girls can baby-sit, dog sit, house sit, and run a cleaning service for extra money. Buying a spray painting outfit, mowers and lawn care equipment, snowblowers, and other equipment can set teenagers up in a profitable service business. A paper route for boys and girls can give them good business experience as well as relieve the family budget.

5. The father can make good investments in real estate and let the family help in maintaining the rental property and upgrading and refurbishing the property for resale. The wife and children can help in Dad's extra part-time business in everything from rug installation and cleaning business to a remodeling, painting, or sales business. They can answer phones, deliver advertising flyers, and do all kinds of small jobs related to the business.

There are many circumstances in which a woman without a husband has to work. If she or even a married woman must work after her children are in school, teaching might be the best type of work which would not harm family unity and hurt the children. Why? Because the mother is not working when the children are dismissed from school on summer vacations, Christmas, snow days, and so on. She takes them to school when she goes to work, and they stay after school and study until she is ready to go home.

The mother, however, should not work full time while she has preschool children and should work only part-time while she has school children in the home. Her professional career should be put on hold while she fulfills the career of motherhood and helps her husband train the children for God's service. The decision for mother to start or stop working full-time is one of the most upsetting, crucial, child-affecting, and life-changing decisions that can ever be made; and couples should be fully aware of its far-reaching consequences.

Appendix C

Suggestions to Promote Family Unity and Happiness

The mother and father, with the children cooperating, need to make up their minds to list, pray about, and make any changes in their family lifestyle, habits, or relationships that God would have them make. They should also make the following pledge: I intend to put into effect as many of the following suggestions as necessary to insure my family's unity and happiness (Josh. 24:24-25).

1. Have enjoyable, interesting, and challenging daily devotions with my family.

2. Present a godly, positive, and loving testimony in the home, realizing that my children see God in me. I will strive to eliminate negative Devil attitudes.

3. Spend five to ten minutes a day talking individually to each family member.

4. Give one compliment a day to each family member.

5. Have one good family meal together each day at which we dine instead of just eat.

6. Maintain a calm, orderly environment with good music, magazines, books, and stimulating conversation to edify my family.

7. Eliminate or curtail and control television viewing in my home.

8. Have a family night at least one night a week when we play games, sing, picnic, hike, or attend events together.

9. Start and maintain family traditions such as family get-to-gethers, birthday and holiday celebrations, visits or vacations

at special places, holiday meals with traditional foods, and so on.

10. Have a yearly project in which the whole family can participate, such as planting and tending a garden; raising animals; starting a small family business; building a boat, camper, tree house, deck, utility room, or outdoor fireplace; landscaping the yard; putting an addition onto the house; or painting the house.

11. Have a special date with each family member at least once a month.

12. Regularly read or tell character-building and pretend stories to my children to develop their character and their imagination.

13. Have an open-house hospitality attitude and make my home a place where sinners can be evangelized and saints can be comforted and edified.

14. Read one good book each year on some aspect of my marriage or family life and discuss this book with my spouse.

15. Turn off the phone or get an answering machine so that I can control the phone instead of letting the phone control me.

16. Get the family involved in some kind of regular soulwinning ministry, such as a child evangelism class, a bus ministry, children's home services, rescue mission services, jail services, a Sunday school class, tract distribution, or working with a missionary during our family vacation.

It will be difficult to keep all of the above suggestions going consistently. However, it would be good for each parent to evaluate his pledge every six months and to try to implement as many of the suggestions as possible.

Appendix D

Support Groups

With the current emphasis on Christian psychology and psychiatry, support groups have become very popular in churches. Churches began to realize that if they were going to reach the community, they needed to deal with addiction problems. They saw support groups as the means of reaching their own members and new converts—even the unconverted—to get them into the church and under the sound of the gospel.

These support groups exist not only to help cure addictions, but also as a therapeutic aid to anyone who has gone through any devastating or traumatic life experience. The more common support groups in churches today are those for the divorced, widowed, addicted, and terminally ill, such as cancer patients. The big question is whether support groups are of real benefit to a Bible-preaching church by enhancing the ministry of that church in its outreach to the community or whether they are a detriment to the local church by substituting psychological techniques for the power and Word of God?

Effective group therapy was developed in the 1920s and 1930s as a tool of psychotherapy. The first practical support group was Alcoholics Anonymous, developed in 1935 by Bill Wilson and Bob Smith to help alcoholics overcome their addictions to alcohol. There are three foundational ideas that guide this organization.

1. Gaining support from another person who has experienced the same devastation in his life.

2. Affirming their own sense of powerlessness and of the unmanageability of their lives. They believe in a power greater

than themselves to which they need to commit their wills and lives. For the vast majority of AA members, this reference to a higher power or being is a reference to the Judeo-Christian concept of God with His characteristics of creativity and sustaining power. However, this higher power can be an organization such as AA, a life force, or a set of moral principles to which the individual is committed.

3. Getting rid of guilt feelings by admitting to this power, to themselves, and to another human being the nature of their wrongs, and then being willing to make amends to all of the people that they have harmed.

This is supposed to be a continual day-by-day process. AA claims that 50 percent of their members who have gone through their program remain sober and another 25 percent become sober after a few relapses.

Support groups were also designed for the spouses and families of alcoholics. These were called codependents. Several recent books now suggest treatment even for the grandchildren of dependents. Alanon groups and Alateen groups were devised for these codependents. The AA groups were so effective that their support group system was applied to other types of addictions. They base their procedures and methods on two main ideas.

1. *Carl Rogers's idea of ventilating bad feelings.* His maxim is "When bad feelings go, good feelings will flow." So the object in most support groups is to ventilate bad feelings, get them out in the open; only then can you really understand and get rid of these bad feelings. The main difficulty with this idea is that when bad feelings come out, additional bad feelings are going to come from the same place. Verbalizing bad feelings tends to feed them right back into the brain and reinforce the original bad feelings.

   Support groups usually suggest that you bring up painful childhood memories, feelings, and emotions about your parents, brothers, and sisters; or consider rejection feelings that you have had. The Scripture indicates in Isaiah 43:18-19 and 25 that we are not to remember the former things, neither consider the things of old, for God has put them under His blood if they have been confessed. Philippians 3:13 says,

"Forgetting those things which are behind, and reaching forth unto those things which are before." Rehashing the past and bringing up old memories, hurts, and rejection feelings do more harm than good.

2. *There is no real standard of morality or way of judging these feelings other than group approval, and the group is told to accept every expression, no matter how bizarre, as legitimate.* The person ventilating feelings can bring up anything, say anything, or ask anything. However, Ephesians 4:29 says, "Let no corrupt communication proceed out of your mouth, but that which is good to the use of edifying, that it may minister grace unto the hearers." Second Timothy 2:23 says, "Foolish and unlearned questions avoid, knowing that they do gender strife."

One rule of these support groups is usually that there is to be absolutely no fixing; you are there to listen and to be supported by one another and not to give advice. You are there only to share common feelings and concerns. Second Timothy 4:2 says, "Preach the word; be instant in season, out of season; reprove, rebuke, exhort with all longsuffering and doctrine." Paul goes on to say in the third and fourth verses that "the time will come when they will not endure sound doctrine, but after their own lusts shall they heap to themselves teachers, having itching ears. And they shall turn away their ears from the truth, and shall be turned unto fables." We need to turn back to God and His Word and sound doctrine for comfort and help and for victory over sin. Instead of blaming our parents or early childhood and environment for our sin or addiction to sin (or bondage to sin), we need to take responsibility for the sin and make up our minds to follow Bible principles in eliminating the sin.

Most worldly support groups, and even some church support groups, use the Alcoholics Anonymous's twelve steps. This approach is worldly and humanistic and does not deal with the addiction problem or situation the way the Bible tells us to deal with such a problem. Bad feelings are only a symptom of bad mental attitudes and unscriptural thinking. Second Corinthians 10:5 tells us to cast "down imaginations and every high thing that exalteth itself against the knowledge of God and [bring] into captivity every thought to the obedience of Christ." Good feelings follow right actions, right actions follow right decisions, and right decisions follow right mental attitudes. Emotions, desires, and feelings are results of our attitudes, and verbalizing feelings does not change one's thinking or attitudes. The Word of God, when properly applied, is sufficient to solve problems and to give help in time of need (II Pet. 1:3-4; II Tim. 3:16-17).

Spiritual Christians need to help the weaker brother and, certainly, if he has fallen into sin, they need to do their best to restore him to fellowship by getting him to acknowledge his sin, confess it, and forsake it. God's forgiveness is the only real cure for guilt feelings, and God's love is the only cure for rejection feelings that most people have felt at some time in their childhoods. Some feel rejection, of course, worse than others and react very badly with bitterness and even hatred toward the ones who have caused their pain and rejection feelings. Most people feel rejected and are looking for the Christian fellowship of loving, caring, sharing, praying people who will weep with them when they weep and rejoice with them when they rejoice. Unfortunately, we do not always have that kind of Christian fellowship in most of our churches because many activities distract from Christian fellowship, Bible study, and good Bible preaching.

When a person is caught in the bondage of sin, such as addiction, Christian brothers and sisters should rally around that person and pray for him and rebuke, admonish, and exhort him to the point at which he is restored and has gained victory over the sin. When a person is informed of a life-threatening or terminal disease or is involved in a tragedy, people who have been through these situations, tragedies, or difficulties and who know exactly what kind of spiritual and physical help is needed, should help and encourage.

When a number of people in a particular addiction, problem, tragedy, or situation exist in one church, a group can be formed. This group ought to have a leader who is very knowledgeable in the Word of God and who knows how to apply the Bible to the problems at hand. He guides the people with biblical principles on how they ought to act and to react to their particular situations. He puts an emphasis, not on how they feel, but rather on how they should think, what attitudes they should have, and what behaviors and reactions they should practice in their particular situations.

Regarding addicts, the group leader should help them, by the use of Scripture, to learn how to crucify self daily (Luke 9:23), how to reckon themselves dead to sin, how to keep sin from reigning in their mortal bodies, and how to yield their members as instruments of righteousness (Rom. 6:11-14). This solution is the only way to keep sin from having dominion over them and to keep them from coming into bondage to sin, for this is exactly what addiction is.

If your church decides to form or has already formed support groups, be sure that they are based on biblical principles and not on worldly philosophies.

Appendix E

Warning Single Christian Women

Mary was a very talented girl from a good home with solid Christian training and a graduate of an outstanding Christian college. She married a man she had met at college who claimed to have been saved in childhood but was known for his jealousy and bad temper. He would drink on occasion, had smoked marijuana, had a history of immorality with several different women, and was known as a worldly Christian. While Mary was engaged, her friends warned her about him, but she was desperately in love with this handsome, gentle, sensitive, "misunderstood" man and would not listen.

Seven years and three children later, Mary was in a marriage counselor's office bemoaning the fact that her husband drank and physically abused her and the children. He had been involved in a succession of affairs and was having one at that time. He tended generally to be very irresponsible regarding the leadership of the family, although he wanted complete control. He was in debt for many thousands of dollars on his credit cards. He was often away from home hunting, fishing, running off to every ball game in the area, or driving his flashy sports car.

What makes a woman with everything going for her marry a man who is such a loser? All she can see is the romance of marrying this dashing young man who is usually handsome, charming, witty, and smooth-talking. He is exciting to be with, and every date is a thrilling experience with flowers and expensive meals in romantic settings. He is usually a very physical person and gives her a lot of attention, cuddling, touching, and affection on their dates. Parents and friends give warnings about his character and his past performance, but the woman is not interested in hearing anything negative. She will not listen to family or friends.

Usually a man like this is egocentric. This selfishness is evidenced by his need for instant gratification of food, comfort, and sex demands without any regard for the person he is with or the morality of the situation. This man usually has no character and wants to do what he wants to do at any time, whether it is right or not. He is usually jealous and possessive and wants to control the girl's life. The girlfriend or fiancée believes that she is special and very much loved for him to be so jealous and concerned about her. This man is generally not a balanced person but goes to extremes in his thinking or in his habits. There is often some kind of substance abuse in the life of this man—alcohol, nicotine, or drugs. Many times he is a child of an addicted parent. He knows he needs help and is looking for the ideal Christian woman to put the discipline, control, and standards in his life that he has not been able to put there himself.

Why Women Marry These Men

For what reasons would a lovely Christian woman unconditionally accept this type of man?

1. *Father image.* Sometimes the woman who is attracted to a man like this has a father who has had a problem with drink, drugs, sex, physical abuse of women, or dishonesty; when the facts are known, her father is much like the boyfriend that she is dating. Even though her home life looks trouble-free on the surface, there have been longstanding problems in Mom and Dad's relationship, and the mother has shared those problems with the daughter. The daughter goes ahead and marries this man, for women tend to marry men much like their fathers. She is comfortable in coping with this type of man.

2. *Escape from a bad situation.* When marriage is entered as an escape, the girl usually has an attitude problem of rebellion and bitterness. Instead of adapting and adjusting in a Christlike manner, she sees escape as the only alternative because the situation seems hopeless. Marriage to anyone provides

the way of escape. She marries this type of man because he seems to represent security. However, she takes the same rebellious, negative attitudes with her into the marriage.

3. *Wounded dog or therapeutic attraction.* Most women have a compassionate heart, and they want to nurse any stray dog that comes along, especially if it is wounded. Some want to help to heal, even as a mother would a son or a doctor would a patient. This type of woman tends to be crusade-oriented. She sees this young man as a project she can change and correct, especially if the young man has bitterness against his parents during childhood. Her mothering instincts tell her that she can change him by providing the loving environment that he missed in childhood. She feels that she can help and change him, especially if he has drinking and drug problems. She tends to view him as her little boy whom she can love and train to be the ideal husband of her dreams.

4. *Sex guilt.* Many times a woman goes too far physically with this type of man in necking, petting, or premarital sex. She feels guilty about this behavior, for women generally seem to have a much keener conscience than men. Since this is the first man she has had this kind of physical experience with, she feels that if she marries him, she will not feel so guilty. She feels obligated toward him and will go ahead and marry even though she begins to have some serious doubts. Many times before marriage the man will exhibit physical abuse as a result of his extreme jealousy, but she rationalizes it as being her fault since she has probably done something to make him upset.

5. *Lonely woman.* Often a woman feels rejected and unworthy of being loved by any man because of rejection by her father or lack of dates during teen years. She feels so grateful at being considered and loved by this one who finally accepts her that she accepts him no matter what his behavior or lifestyle. Usually this relationship is based on the physical, for she is desperate for any love and affection and wants the security of marriage to ensure that it will continue.

Every unmarried young lady needs to examine her relationships with men to make sure that the above factors are not pushing her down a wrong path. She needs to take decisive action in breaking up an improper relationship—even if the wedding is near—so that she can prevent a bad union and a lot of future unhappiness.

How To Avoid These Men

Choosing a right marriage partner is not entirely an individual's choice. God wants His will accomplished in this important matter. If a woman will prayerfully follow these biblical guidelines, she can be assured of God's leadership.

Never date or marry an unbeliever or a divorced person (II Cor. 6:14-17; Matt. 19:9). There is rarely an innocent party in a divorce. It takes two to make a marriage and two to break a marriage. How badly did the man treat his first wife to make her even think about wanting to run off with another man or just to get out of the marriage? A divorced man brings into his second marriage all the problems of the first marriage. The divorce rate for second marriages is twice that of first marriages, which is high already. Also remember the biblical admonition in Matthew 19 that if a woman marries a divorced person, she commits adultery.

Look at his home background. "Like father, like son" is a trite but very true statement, for boys tend to follow closely the emotional and behavioral pattern of their fathers, even as women are much like their mothers (Ezek. 16:44). A man who does not get along with his mother will certainly not get along with his wife. The woman is also marrying into his heritage. His parents become the grandparents of this couple's children. If he has a drunk for a father or his parents are divorced or they have an unhappy marriage, their life situation is going to have a bearing on this family in the future. As the grandparents of this couple's children, they will be models for bad or for good.

A girl anticipating marriage should visit the boy's home several times in chaperoned situations. She should especially notice the way the boy treats his mother in everyday situations, for he will treat his wife in much the same way after they are married. Any man can put on a good front on dates, but it is his day-by-day actions that make or break a marriage.

Set firm moral standards before ever dating (I Thess. 4:1-7). The couple needs to determine exactly what will take place or will not take place in the physical relationship on dates. The woman should not under any circumstances venture out on the undercut cliff of sensual pleasure with the man and go along with his demands for physical liberties, for this is the way of moral corruption, heartache, and guilt.

Men give love, romance, affection, and touching to get physical attention. Women have a tendency to give physical attention to get the love, romance, touching, and affection that they desire. Women tend to be touch-oriented, whereas men are sight-oriented. Therefore, women ought to make it a point to be modest and discreet in their dress and their actions (I Tim. 2:9-10).

Avoid Devil set-ups (Rom. 13:14). A woman should never be in a man's house alone with him, and he should never be alone in the girl's home with her. They should avoid being in unchaperoned situations on dates. They do not have to take Mom and Dad along, but they should let friends or a crowd be the chaperons. They should not be alone in a room while the parents are asleep in the other end of the house. The Bible talks about avoiding all appearance of evil (I Thess. 5:22), and Romans 14:16 says, "Let not then your good be evil spoken of." Romans 13:14 says, "But put ye on the Lord Jesus Christ, and make not provision for the flesh to fulfill the lusts thereof."

Couples should be discreet and modest regarding talk or actions about bathroom functions and should never talk about sex on dates. When verbal inhibitions are relaxed, one will find that physical inhibitions become relaxed. Then a person can get into some awkward and difficult situations. A woman should never under any circumstances drink alcohol in any form or take drugs, not even for celebrations; for a man knows that if he can get a woman drinking anything alcoholic, even beer or wine, her moral inhibitions are going to be relaxed, and there is a good chance he can get her to do anything he desires.

Check the man's spiritual response before ever starting to get serious. The Christian young man should have a good record of church attendance and activity, have a consistent devotional and prayer life, be an active soulwinner, and be well-grounded in the faith. He should be the one to suggest and lead devotions on the date. He should be the one eagerly praying and seeking after souls and interested in spiritual things. He should have discipline in his life and be actively getting spiritual victories along the way and sharing these with his girlfriend. If he has tremendous spiritual problems, she should not date him because a friend cannot take the place of the Holy Spirit.

Make sure there is agreement in intelligence, spirituality, background, interests, and general attitudes toward life. Amos 3:3, which says, "Can two walk together except they be agreed?" indicates that agreement is necessary in a relationship. Since the husband is to be the leader and decision-maker, he should be of equal or higher intelligence and more spiritually mature. Extremely diverse religious backgrounds or cultures can add a multitude of adjustments that must be made in the early days of marriage. A young man from a struggling economic background who marries a woman from a well-to-do environment can have many financial problems in marriage. Similar interests and attitudes help build the unity that is so necessary in a good marriage.

With these general principles in mind, the Christian woman wants to set the following course for future dates and possible marriage:

1. Think of three or four men who have the right character and meet the criteria which have been set for a husband.

2. Be aware of opportunities for friendly conversation with these men. A woman is generally the better conversationalist and, therefore, should always have several questions that she can ask to spark the conversation. Ideally, the man will respond with the same type of questions. Even on dates, the woman should do her part to keep the conversation going by asking appropriate questions, for men do not like to feel that they bear the entire burden of carrying on the conversation.

3. Be available for dates. If the man asks for a date and the woman cannot go at that particular time, she should suggest another time that she is able to go. Men have fragile egos and hate to be rejected or turned down for a date. If they think that the woman wants to go with them and is not just making excuses, then they will determine another time for a date.

4. When a woman goes on a date, she should make it a good one by being positive and enthusiastic. Men do not like negative women with no energy. A positive, exuberant,

"praise the Lord" attitude is essential. If the man asks for suggestions about where to go on dates, the woman might have several things in mind, taking into consideration the financial cost. Staying at home playing games together over popcorn on a date can set the stage for home activities after marriage.

5. After the date is over, the woman should let the man know how much she appreciated the date and how much she would like to be with him again. She should think of every person dated as a potential mate and work to develop a bond of friendship. Good dating that leads to marriage is nothing more than a friendship developing to the point where the couple finally decides that they are such good friends and get along so well that they may as well live together for the rest of their lives. A good marriage and real love consist of two persons who have a close, intimate, and wonderful friendship and fellowship, sacrificing and unselfishly understanding and meeting the needs of the partner.

6. The woman should have her parents meet the man she is dating and talk over the relationship with them. Parents have a genuine concern for their daughter, and they know her better than anyone else. They can look at the relationship without the glamour of love clouding their vision. The father can pretty well size up this man and give some ideas as to his real character.

7. Let the Lord lead and guide in the relationship. He will show the woman if this is the person she is to marry (Prov. 3:3-5). If God wants the woman to be married (I Cor. 7:32-35), He will bring the right man into her life, and she will know that he is right. If there are serious doubts, then the relationship should be broken. God does not want all women to be married. There is nothing wrong if a woman is not married. God may want the woman to be one of His choice single servants.

By following these guidelines, instead of marrying a disaster, a woman will be able to marry the man whom God has chosen for her and who will be a pleasure to love, honor, and obey.

Appendix F

The Advantages of Home Schooling

Children are born without a philosophy, value system, or religious creed. All of these must be taught in the first ten years of life if the child is going to have any character, standards, or morality. This is an awesome responsibility to parents, for they are literally determining the happiness and future of their children, both present and eternal. The first four preschool years are of vital importance because the child's personality and learning style are set during this time. If mothers, because of working full-time, relegate this essential training to a child-care center where low-paid personnel are in charge of his training, the child will be deficient in the tools he needs to develop to his fullest potential. If they put the child in the public school system, he will be further handicapped because of the many problems of the present system.

The number one problem is the lack of religious and moral standards, which are basic to all education. Some of the present problems of the public schools can be directly traced to taking the Bible (which is the foundation of all moral teaching) and prayer out of the public schools in 1963 and substituting a humanistic philosophy, which is antithetical to the Christian philosophy that served as education's foundation in America. The results have been devastating. For example, college board scores have steadily declined since 1963. Violence against students and teachers has reached an alarming level. "The National Education Association estimates that every day 100,000 [students] carry guns to class; another study reports that 13% of all incidents involving guns in the schools occur in elementary and preschools. . . . Every school day, 6,250 teachers are threatened with injury and 260 are actually assaulted."[1] There is an increasing influence of amoral teachers and peer pressure to use drugs (including alcohol) and participate in premarital sex and sex perversions.

One alternative to the public schools would be private schools, but most nonreligious private schools are very expensive and have the same humanistic philosophy as the public schools. Another alternative might be a superior Christian school. Good Christian schools do not exist to counteract the evils that exist in the public schools. They exist for the unique purpose of giving a Christian education based on the Bible, which guides the students in studying the world from a biblical point of view and teaches them to apply Bible principles in every area of their lives. Life is related to God and all learning is related to principles found in the Word of God. If there is no Christian school in your community that has your religious philosophy and family values, then the only alternative is home schooling.

There are a number of advantages to home schooling.

1. It gives the parents complete control over the teaching of spiritual values that are in line with the family values and religious philosophy.
2. It breaks the institutional monopoly of the public schools. Parents are not at the mercy of whatever school exists in their community, be it public or private, good or bad.
3. The cost is about one-fifth of the tuition of the private Christian school.
4. There is a big savings in time and money spent on transportation. Mothers complain that with two or three children in school, especially junior high and senior high, they are on the run continually, transporting their children to and from school and to the various activities that the children must attend. If they are in sports or band in the school, they have additional transportation problems. If the children use the school bus or public transportation, many precious hours are lost just riding.
5. The instruction can be individualized to fit the learning needs of the child. After a good testing program explained by a competent test administrator, the mother can know exactly what level the child is on in every subject. She can then take

her child where he is, no matter what level, and instruct him from that point.

6. The curriculum can be tailored to fit the interests of the child and the schedule of the family. This flexibility allows the mother to better take advantage of the "teachable moments" that regularly occur in the everyday environment. Since the family is not tied to a calendar or a location, they could travel as a family and learn many geography, history, literature, science, and other lessons firsthand. One father took a sabbatical from his teaching job so that he, his wife, and their three daughters could travel. During a nine-month period, they traveled in an R.V. to every state in the Union (except Hawaii) as well as to eastern and western Canada. The other three months they went to Europe, using the French and German that the girls had learned. The mother and father home-schooled the girls during this year.

7. Home schooling is time-efficient. The same amount of instruction carried on in a regular school can be accomplished at home in one-third to half the time. The mother can be flexible with her schedule.

8. The father can have a greater share of time to train his children. His areas of expertise can augment the mother's as well as direct her teaching. This would help develop family unity.

In their efforts to secure a superior Christian education for their children, more and more parents are opting for home schooling. To do this properly, there are a few factors that need to be considered.

1. *The basic qualifications of the teacher.* Since the mother will be the teacher, she should have a high level of energy, initiative, and determination, above average intelligence, at least a minimum of a high school diploma or the equivalent, and a real love for imparting information and teaching. She should also have time to do this, for it is a full-time job, counting her preparation and grading time; therefore, she should not be working even part-time or be overly involved in community or church work, and she should have a husband who will get involved and help carry the load.

2. *The curriculum and textbooks she uses.* Using public school curriculum and textbooks would be defeating the main purpose

of home schooling. A distinctly Christian curriculum based on the Bible and application of Bible principles to every area of knowledge is essential. Choosing the right curriculum along with the textbooks and teacher's manuals is the most crucial step that parents will ever take in regard to home schooling. The Bob Jones University Press Christian curriculum,[2] with the teacher's manual and textbook in every subject from preschool right up through the twelfth grade, is highly recommended. BJU Press has a great number of supplementary books that go along with the regular textbooks. It has an outstanding reading program, which is phonics-based balanced with comprehension. Its writing program eliminates the difficult transition between printing and cursive writing. BJU Press also has a great support system: calling an 800 number can bring answers to questions in any area or on any grade level, and many of these answers are given by the authors of the textbooks. A unique Christian curriculum for home-schoolers is Bill Gothard's curriculum,[3] which is based on two hundred Bible principles. Some of his innovative and nontraditional ideas are only for "the bold and the brave," but this curriculum is known for its substance and quality. There are several other high-quality curriculums available.

3. *The network and support of other home schoolers.* The beginning home schoolers as well as the veterans need support from a network of other home schoolers. This support can be in the form of sharing techniques, teaching methods, sources of information about field trips, fine arts activities, and historical and literary events and places. Even equipment can be shared and made by other home schoolers who have unique contacts or skills. Libraries, public schools, and other public agencies are always getting rid of useful material and equipment, which usually is given away or sold at a very low cost. For contact with other home schoolers, write to Home School Heartbeat.[4] They can also give you information about laws and procedures governing home schooling in your state.

If you have sufficient reasons and qualifications and the family situation is right, there is no reason that you cannot start home schooling your children.

Notes

Chapter 3: The Brain and the Functioning of the Mind

1. Richard M. Restak, *The Brain* (Toronto: Bantam Books, 1984), 27.
2. Ibid.
3. Edward T. Welch, *Counselor's Guide to the Brain and Its Disorders* (Grand Rapids: Zondervan Publishing House, 1991),100.
4. Norman Cousins, *Head First: The Biology of Hope* (New York: E. P. Dutton, 1989), 71.
5. See note 1 above: 348.
6. See note 4 above: 73.
7. See note 4 above: 74.
8. See note 1 above: 131.
9. Martin Bobgan and Deidre Bobgan, *Psychoheresy* (Santa Barbara, Calif.: EastGate Publishers, 1987).
10. David Hunt and Thomas A. McMahon, *The Seduction of Christianity* (Eugene, Ore.: Harvest Publishing House, 1986).
11. See note 3 above: 33–37.
12. Ruth Beechick, *A Biblical Psychology of Learning* (Denver: Accent Books, 1982), 36.
13. Ibid., 37.

Chapter 5: Physical Causes of Mental Problems

1. Robert D. Smith, M.D., "A Physician Looks at Counseling: Symptoms," *Nouthetic Confrontation* 1 (1975), 84.
2. Edward T. Welch, *Counselor's Guide to the Brain and Its Disorders* (Grand Rapids: Zondervan Publishing House, 1991),110.

3. See note 2 above: 78-79.

4. Helen Klusek Hamilton, ed., *Diseases,* 2d ed. (Springhouse, Pa.: Springhouse Corporation, 1987), 787.

5. Ibid., 793.

6. Ibid., 777.

7. Ibid., 901.

8. Ibid., 900.

9. Stuart M. Berger, M.D. and Michael O'Shea, Ph.D., "Focus on Fitness," *Parade Magazine,* September 7, 1986, 6.

10. See note 4 above: 802.

11. See note 4 above: 804.

12. See note 4 above: 864.

13. John Langone, "Is It a Disease or Isn't It?" *Discover,* November 1985, 102.

14. Stanley L. Englebrandt, "The Little Boy Who Became a Jekyll-and-Hyde," *Reader's Digest,* March 1981, 75.

15. June M. Thompson et. al., *Mosby's Manual of Clinical Nursing,* 2d ed. (St. Louis: C. V. Mosby Company, 1989), 1362.

16. See note 14 above: 77.

17. Leon Jaroff, "Allergies—Nothing To Sneeze At," *Time,* June 22, 1992, 62.

18. Mayo Clinic Health Letter, June, 1988, 6.

19. PRODIGY (R) Interactive Personal Service, April 10, 1992, 10:24 P.M.

20. See note 1 above: 107-61.

21. See note 1 above: 107.

22. Phillip Gold, Frederick Goodwin, and P. George Ghrousos, "Clinical and Biochemical Manifestations of Depression: Relation to the Neurobiology of Stress: Part I," *New England Journal of Medicine* 319 (1988): 348.

23. Philip Elmer-Dewitt, "Depression—The Growing Role of Drug Therapies," *Time,* July 6, 1992, 57.

24. Ibid., 58.

25. Winefred Gallagher, "The Dark Affection of Mind and Body," *Discover,* May 1986, 70.

26. Anastasia Toufexis, "Dark Days, Darker Spirits," *Time,* January 11, 1988, 66.

27. Gertrude McFarland and Mary Durand Thomas, *Psychiatric Mental Health Nursing* (Philadelphia: J. B. Lippincott Company, 1991), 574.

28. See note 26 above: 66.

29. Robert J. Trotter, "Chemistry of Compulsion," *Discover,* June 1990, 26.

30. See note 15 above: 1507.

31. See note 15 above: 1507.

Chapter 6: Detecting: Discovering the Problem

1. Gary Collins, *How To Be a People Helper* (Santa Ana, Calif.: Vision House Publishers, 1976), 50.

Chapter 7: Teaching: Bringing About Change

1. Jay E. Adams, *How to Help People Change* (Grand Rapids: Zondervan Publishing House, 1986).

2. Donald Orthner, *Well Springs of Life: Understanding Proverbs* (Greenville, S.C.: Bob Jones University Press, 1989).

3. See note 1 above: 110.

4. Joe S. McIlhaney Jr. and Susan Nethery, *1250 Health-Care Questions Women Ask* (Grand Rapids: Baker Book House, 1990).

5. J. Norman Wright, *Questions Women Ask in Private* (Ventura, Calif.: Regal Books, 1993).

Chapter 9: Principles Related to the Counseling Process

1. Paul Brownback, *The Danger of Self-love* (Chicago: Moody Press, 1992), 43-48.

2. Wendell E. Miller, *Forgiveness: The Power and the Puzzles* (Warsaw, Ind.: Clearbrook Publishers, 1994).

3. Herbert Fingarette, *Heavy Drinking—The Myth of Alcoholism as a Disease* (Los Angeles: University of California Press, 1988).

4. Ibid., 3.

5. Ibid., 4.

6. Ibid., 5.

7. Ibid., 136.

Chapter 10: Bitterness

1. Carol Travis, *Anger: The Misunderstood Emotion* (New York: Simon and Schuster, 1982), 38.
2. Leonard Berkowitz, "The Case for Bottling Up Rage," *Psychology Today,* 1971, 31.

Chapter 11: Immorality

1. Joseph Fletcher, *Situation Ethics:The New Morality* (Old Tappen, N.J.: Fleming H. Revell Company, 1977).
2. Alfred D. Kinsey et. al., *Sexual Behavior in the Human Male* (Philadelphia: W. B. Saunders Company, 1948).
3. Alfred D. Kinsey et. al., *Sexual Behavior in the Human Female* (Philadelphia: W. B. Saunders, 1953).
4. Judith A. Reisman and Edward W. Eichel, *Kinsey, Sex, and Fraud* (Lafayette, Ind.: Lochinvar Inc. Huntington House Publishers, 1990).
5. Ibid., 25, 62.
6. Ibid., 9.
7. Ibid., 62.
8. Ibid., 182.
9. Ibid., 6-8, 214.
10. Tim LaHaye and Beverly LaHaye, *The Act of Marriage* (Grand Rapids: Zondervan Publishing House, 1970).
11. Ed Wheat, *Intended for Pleasure* (Philadelphia: Westminister Press, 1966).

Chapter 12: Moral and Sexual Problems

1. Judith A. Reisman and Edward W. Eichel, *Kinsey, Sex, and Fraud* (LaFayette, Ind.: Lochinvar Inc. Huntington House Publishers, 1990), 195.
2. *Time Magazine,* April 1, 1974, 38.
3. See note 1 above: 144.
4. Roger J. Magnuson, *Are Gay Rights Right?* (Portland, Ore.: Multnomah Press, 1990), 46.
5. David Gelman et al., *Newsweek,* November 8, 1993, 71.
6. Jean Seligmann, Patrick Rogers, and Peter Annin, *Newsweek,* May 2, 1994, 61.

7. Carol Sue Carter, ed., *Hormones and Sexual Behavior* (Stroudsburg, Pa.: Dowden, Hutchinson and Ross, 1978), 317.

8. Alfred C. Kinsey et. al., *Sexual Behavior in the Human Female* (Philadelphia: W. B. Saunders Company, 1953), 447.

9. Fred Belliveau and Lin Ritcher, *Understanding Human Sexual Inadequacy* (New York: Bantam Books, 1970), 137.

10. John W. Drakeford, *A Christian View of Homosexuality* (Nashville: Broadman Press, 1977), 43.

11. Ibid., 50.

12. Daniel Capon, *Toward An Understanding of Homosexuality* (Englewood Cliffs, N.J.: Prentice Hall, 1965), 115.

13. See note 4 above: 46.

14. See note 4 above: 43.

15. Lorraine Day, M.D., *AIDS—What the Government Isn't Telling You* (Palm Springs, Calif.: Rockford Press, 1991), 254.

16. Ibid., 122.

17. Josh McDowell, *How to Help Your Child Say No to Sex Pressure* (Waco, Tex.: Word, 1987).

18. *Atlanta Constitution,* October 19, 1993.

Chapter 13: Materialism

1. Lewis H. Lapham, *Money and Class in America: Notes and Observations on Our Civil Religion* (New York: Ballentine Books, 1988), 226.

2. Ibid., 108.

Chapter 14: Rejection

1. Charles R. Solomon, *The Handbook to Happiness* (Denver: Grace Fellowship International, 1971).

2. Charles R. Solomon, *The Ins and Outs of Rejection* (Denver: Grace Fellowship International, 1983).

Chapter 16: Imagination and Fantasy

1. Eugene Kennedy and Sara C. Charles, *On Becoming a Counselor* (New York: The Continuum Publishing Company, 1991), 242-50.

2. Lisa Davis, "Murdered Memory," *Health,* May/June 1991, 81.

3. Ibid., 82.

Chapter 17: Doubt: Spirit of Fear

1. Bob Shelton, *God's Prophetic Blueprint* (1985).
2. Philip G. Zimbardo, *Shyness: What It Is, What To Do About It* (Reading, Mass.: Addison-Wesley Publishing Co., 1977), 18.

Chapter 19: Cruel and Irresponsible Men Who Become Wife Abusers

1. Nancy Gibbs, *Time,* January 18, 1993, 41.
2. Susan Forward, M.D., *Men Who Hate Women and the Women Who Love Them* (New York: Bantam Books, 1987), 285.
3. Ibid., 43.
4. Richard J. Gelles, *The Violent Home: A Study of Aggression Between Husbands and Wives* (Beverly Hills: Sage Publications, 1974).
5. See note 1 above: 41.
6. Claire Safran, "Why Men Hurt the Women They Love," *Reader's Digest,* January 1986, 80.
7. Kay Marshall Strom, *In the Name of Submission* (Portland, Ore.: Multonmah Press, 1986), 139.

Chapter 21: Depression

1. Helen Wessel, *Natural Childbirth and the Christian Family* (San Francisco: Harper and Row: 1983), 262.
2. Anastasia Toufexis, "Dark Days, Darker Spirits," *Time,* January 11, 1988, 66.
3. Ibid., 66.
4. John Q. Barcom, *Fatal Choice* (Chicago: Moody Press, 1986), 161.
5. *Atlanta Journal,* March 10, 1989, 12A.

Chapter 22: Husband and Wife Relationships

1. Blaine J. Flowers and David H. Olson, "Predicting Marital Success with *Prepare*: A Predictive Validity Study of Marital and Family Therapy," *Journal of Marital and Family Therapy* 12 (October 1986): 403-13.
2. David H. Olsen, *Prepare/Enrich* (Minneapolis: Life Innovations, n.d.).
3. Ann Landers, "What 100,000 Women Told Ann Landers," *Family Circle,* June 11, 1985, 29.

4. Jeff Giles, Mark Miller, and Charles Fleming, *Newsweek*, March 21, 1994, 71.

Chapter 23: Family Problems Involving Children and Teenagers

1. Walter Fremont and Trudy Fremont, *Formula for Family Unity* (Greenville, S.C.: Bob Jones University Press, 1980).
2. John Stormer, *Growing Up God's Way* (Florissant, Mo.: Liberty Bell Press, 1984).
3. David Sorenson, *Training Your Children to Turn Out Right* (Independence, Mo.: American Association of Christian Schools, 1995).
4. Grace H. Ketterman, M.D., *The Complete Book of Baby and Child Care* (Grand Rapids: Baker Book House, 1986).
5. Walter Fremont, Trudy Fremont, and Gilbert Fremont III. *Forming a New Generation* (Greenville, S.C.: Bob Jones University Press, 1990).
6. Josh McDowell, *Why Wait? Helping Teens Say No to Sexual Involvement* (San Bernardino, Calif.: Here's Life Publishers, 1987).
7. Charles Stanley, *How to Keep Your Kids on Your Team* (Nashville: Oliver-Nelson, 1986).

Chapter 24: Special Family Problems

1. Guy Duty, *Divorce and Remarriage* (Minneapolis: Bethany Press, 1967).
2. Ibid., 130-53.
3. John Murray, *Divorce* (Philadelphia: Presbyterian and Reformed Publishing Co., 1961).
4. Jay Adams, *The Christian Counselor's Manual* (Nutley, N.J.: Presbyterian and Reformed Publishing Company, 1973), 52-62.
5. C. S. Lewis, *Mere Christianity* (New York: McMillan Publishing Company, 1943), 109, 112.
6. Compiled from 1993 and 1994 *Medical Newsletters* and information from the Amercian Anorexia/Bulemia Association, Teaneck, New Jersey.
7. Ibid.
8. Ibid.
9. Ibid.

Chapter 25: Psychotherapy: Sophisticated Scam?

1. Martin Bobgan and Deidre Bobgan, *Psychoheresy* (Santa Barbara, Calif.: EastGate Publishers, 1987), 12.
2. Ibid., 12.
3. Thomas S. Szasz, *Ideology and Insanity* (New York: Doubleday and Company, 1970), 28.
4. Alfred M. Freedman, Harold I. Kaplan, and Benjamin J. Sadock, *Modern Synopsis of Psychiatry/II,* 2d ed. (Baltimore: Williams and Wilkins, 1976), 1324.
5. Barbara S. Johnson, *Psychiatric-Mental Health Nursing* (Philadelphia: J. B. Lippincott Company, 1986), 174.
6. John Leo, "A Therapist in Every Corner," *Time,* December 23, 1985, 59.
7. Norman J. Finkel, *Mental Illness and Health* (New York: Macmillan Company, 1976), 61-62.
8. Ibid., 61.
9. William K. Kilpatrick, *The Emperor's New Clothes* (Westchester: Crossway Books, 1985), 15.
10. Robert C. Carson, *Abnormal Psychology and Modern Life,* 8th ed. (Glenville, Ill.: Scott, Foresman and Company, 1988), 579.
11. Gerald C. Davinson and John M. Neale, *Abnormal Psychology,* 3rd ed. (New York: John Wiley and Sons, 1982), 785.
12. David G. Benner, ed., *Baker Encyclopedia of Psychology* (Grand Rapids: Baker Book House, 1985), 535.
13. Ibid., 891.
14. "Skinner's Utopia," *Time,* September 20, 1971, 47.
15. David G. Benner, *The Effective Psychotherapist* (New York: Pergamon Press, 1982), xi.
16. Rousas J. Rushdoony, *Freud* (Grand Rapids: Baker Book House, 1975), 41.
17. Jay Adams, *Competent to Counsel* (Grand Rapids: Baker Book House, 1970), 15.
18. See note 12 above: 703.
19. See note 12 above: 167.
20. Hans J. Eysenck, "The Effects of Psychotherapy: An Evaluation," *Journal of Consulting Psychology* 16 (1952): 319.
21. Ibid., 319-20.
22. See note 12 above: 848.

23. Joseph Rubinstein and Brent Slife, eds., *Taking Sides* (Sluice Dock, Guildford: The Dushkin Publishing Group, 1988), 283.

24. Ibid., 283.

25. See note 12 above: 849.

26. See note 10 above: 613.

27. Allen E. Bergin, "Psychotherapy Can Be Dangerous," *Psychology Today,* 1975, 98.

28. See note 23 above: 281.

29. G. Nichols Braucht, "The Deterioration Effect: A Reply to Bergin," *Journal of Abnormal Psychology* 75 (1970): 293.

30. See note 23 above: 279.

31. Carl R. Rogers, *Counseling and Psychotherapy* (Boston: Houghton Mifflin Company, 1942), 19-45.

32. See note 14 above: 47-53.

33. Mark P. Cosgrove, *B. F. Skinner's Behaviors* (Grand Rapids: Zondervan Book Company, 1982), 9-14.

34. Jay Adams, *Shepherding God's Flock* (Grand Rapids: Baker Book House, 1979), 159.

35. See note 12 above: 5-6.

36. Ronald L. Koteskey, "Abandoning the Psyche to Secular Treatment," *Christianity Today,* 1977, 20.

37. Peter Michelmore, "Long Nightmare of Ruth Finley," *Reader's Digest,* March, 1989, 97-104.

38. See note 34 above: 107.

39. See note 31 above: 29.

40. Robert Roberts, "Therapy for the Saints," *Christianity Today,* 1985, 25-28.

41. Ronald Melzak, "The Promise of Biofeedback: Don't Hold the Party Yet," *Psychology Today,* 1975, 19.

42. See note 33 above: 112.

43. See note 10 above: 602.

44. John Leo, "Talk Is As Good As a Pill," *Time,* May 26, 1986, 60.

45. See note 1 above: 169.

46. See note 1 above: 165.

47. See note 1 above: 173.

48. Kenneth L. Howard, David Orlinsky, and James Hill, "Affective Experience in Psychotherapy," *Journal of Abnormal Psychology* 75 (1970): 272.
49. See note 1 above: 170.
50. Jay Adams, *The Christian Counselor's Manual* (Nutley, N.J.: Presbyterian and Reformed Publishing Company, 1973), 13, 18-20.
51. See note 15 above: 1-10.
52. See note 50 above: 438.
53. Stephen Quackenbos, Gayle Privett, and B. Klentz, "Psychotherapy and Religion: Rapprochement or Antithesis?" *Journal of Counseling and Development* 65 (1986): 65.
54. See note 1 above: 210-11.
55. Jay Adams, *How to Help People Change* (Grand Rapids: Zondervan Publishing House, 1986), 39.
56. Ivan Thorn, "The Failure of Modern Psychology," *Christian Educator Journal* 24 (1985): 19.

Appendix F

1. Jon D. Hull, "The Knife in the Book Bag," *Time,* February 8, 1993.
2. Bob Jones University Press Home School Division, Greenville, SC 29614; phone: 1-800-845-5731.
3. Advanced Training Institute of America, P.O. Box 1, Oak Brook, IL 60522-3001; phone: 1-708-323-9800.
4. Home School Heartbeat, Box 1835, Leesburg, VA 22075.

Bibliography

Adams, Jay. *Competent to Counsel.* Grand Rapids: Baker Book House, 1970.

———. *How to Help People Change.* Grand Rapids: Zondervan Publishing House, 1986.

———. *Shepherding God's Flock.* Grand Rapids: Baker Book House, 1979.

———. *The Christian Counselor's Manual.* Nutley, N.J.: Presbyterian and Reformed Publishing Company, 1973.

———. *The Christian Counselor's New Testament.* Grand Rapids: Baker Book House, 1977.

Atlanta Constitution, October 19, 1993.

Atlanta Journal, March 10, 1989, 12A.

Barcom, John Q. *Fatal Choice.* Chicago: Moody Press, 1986.

Beechick, Ruth. *A Biblical Psychology of Learning.* Denver: Accent Books, 1982.

Belliveau, Fred, and Lin Ritcher. *Understanding Human Sexual Inadequacy.* New York: Bantam Books, 1970.

Benner, David G., ed. *Baker Encyclopedia of Psychology.* Grand Rapids: Baker Book House, 1985.

Benner, David G. *The Effective Psychotherapist.* New York: Pergamon Press, 1982.

Berger, Stuart M., M.D., and Michael O'Shea, Ph.D. "Focus on Fitness." *Parade Magazine,* September 7, 1986, 4-5.

Bergin, Allen E. "Psychotherapy Can Be Dangerous." *Psychology Today* 9 (6): 97-100, 104 (1975).

Berkowitz, Leonard, "The Case for Bottling Up Rage." *Psychology Today,* 1971.

Bobgan, Martin, and Deidre Bobgan. *Psychoheresy.* Santa Barbara: EastGate Publishers, 1987.

Braucht, G. Nichols. "The Deterioration Effect: A Reply to Bergin." *Journal of Abnormal Psychology* 75 (3): 293–99 (1970).

Bridges, Jerry. *The Discipline of Grace.* Colorado Springs: NavPress, 1995.

———. *Transforming Grace.* Colorado Springs: NavPress, 1988.

Brownback, Paul. *The Danger of Self-Love.* Chicago: Moody Press, 1992.

Burkett, Larry. *Your Finances in Changing Times.* Chicago: Moody Press, 1992

Capon, Daniel. *Toward an Understanding of Homosexuality.* Englewood Cliffs, N.J.: Prentice Hall, 1965.

Carson, Robert C. *Abnormal Psychology and Modern Life,* 8th ed. Glenville, Ill: Scott, Foresman and Company, 1988.

Carter, Carol Sue, ed. *Hormones and Sexual Behavior.* Stroudsburg, Pa.: Dowden, Hutchinson and Ross, 1978.

Collins, Gary. *How To Be a People Helper.* Santa Ana, Calif.: Vision House Publishers, 1976.

Cosgrove, Mark P. *B.F. Skinner's Behaviors.* Grand Rapids: Zondervan Book Company, 1982.

Cousins, Norman. *Head First: The Biology of Hope.* New York: E. P. Dutton, 1989.

Davis, Lisa. "Murdered Memory." *Health,* May/June 1991, 79-83.

Davidson, Gerald C., and John M. Neale. *Abnormal Psychology.* 3rd ed. New York: John Wiley and Sons, 1982.

Day, Lorraine, M.D. *AIDS—What the Government Isn't Telling You.* Palm Springs, Calif.: Rockford Press, 1991.

Drakeford, John W. *A Christian View of Homosexuality.* Nashville: Broadman Press, 1977.

Duty, Guy. *Divorce and Remarriage.* Minneapolis: Bethany Press, 1967.

Edwards, Gene. *The Prisoner in the Third Cell.* Wheaton, Ill.: Tyndale House Publishing, 1992.

Elmer-Dewitt, Philip. "Depression—The Growing Role of Drug Therapies." *Time,* July 6, 1992, 57-60.

Englebrandt, Stanley L. "The Little Boy Who Became a Jekyll-and-Hyde." *Reader's Digest,* March 1981, 75-78.

Eysenck, Hans J. "The Effects of Psychotherapy: An Evaluation." *Journal of Consulting Psychology* 16 (1): 319-25 (1952).

Fingarette, Herbert. *Heavy Drinking—The Myth of Alcoholism as a Disease.* Los Angeles: University of California Press, 1988.

Finkel, Norman J. *Mental Illness and Health.* New York: Macmillan, 1976.

Fletcher, Joseph. *Situation Ethics: The New Morality.* Old Tappen, N.J.: Fleming H. Revell, 1977.

Flowers, Blaine J., and David H. Olsen. "Predicting Marital Success with *Prepare:* A Predictive Validity Study of Marital and Family Therapy." *Journal of Marital and Family Therapy* 12 (4): 403–13 (October 1986).

Forward, Susan, M.D. *Men Who Hate Women and the Women Who Love Them.* New York: Bantam Books, 1987.

Freedman, Alfred M.; Harold I. Kaplan; and Benjamin J. Sadock. *Modern Synopsis of Psychiatry/II.* 2d ed. Baltimore: Williams and Wilkins, 1976.

Fremont, Walter. *Making Your Marriage a Masterpiece.* Bob Jones University Press. 1989. (Six videos: 57 min., 48 min., 57 min., 59 min., 57 min., and 48 min.)

Fremont, Walter. *Teaching Principles Along with Facts: Biblical Character Training.* Bob Jones University Press. 1988. (52 min.)

Fremont, Walter; Trudy Fremont; and Gilbert Fremont III. *Forming a New Generation.* Greenville, S.C.: Bob Jones University Press, 1990.

Fremont, Walter, and Trudy Fremont. *Formula for Family Unity.* Greenville, S.C.: Bob Jones University Press, 1980.

Gallagher, Winefred. "The Dark Affection of Mind and Body." *Discover,* May 1986, 68-74.

Gelles, Richard J. *The Violent Home: A Study of Aggression Between Husbands and Wives.* Beverly Hills: Sage Publications, 1974.

Gelman, David, et al. *Newsweek,* November 8, 1993, 71.

Gibbs, Nancy. *Time,* January 18, 1993, 38-45.

Giles, Jeff, Mark Miller, and Charles Fleming. *Newsweek,* March 21, 1994, 71.

Gold, Phillip; Frederick Goodwin; and P. George Ghrousos. "Clinical and Biochemical Manifestations of Depression: Relation to the Neurobiology of Stress" Part I. *New England Journal of Medicine* 319:348-53 (1988).

Hamilton, Helen Klusek, ed. *Diseases.* 2d ed. Springhouse, Pa.: Springhouse Corporation, 1987.

Howard, Kenneth L.; David E. Orlinsky; and James Hill. "Affective Experience in Psychotherapy." *Journal of Abnormal Psychology* 75 (3): 267-75 (1970).

Hunt, David. *Beyond Seduction.* Eugene, Ore.: Harvest Publishing House, 1987.

Hunt, David, and T[homas] A. McMahon. *The Seduction of Christianity.* Eugene, Ore.: Harvest Publishing House, 1986.

Ingrig, Gary. *Quality Friendships.* Chicago: Moody Press, 1981.

Jaroff, Leon. "Allergies—Nothing To Sneeze At." *Time,* June 22, 1992, 54-62.

Johnson, Barbara S. *Psychiatric-Mental Health Nursing.* Philadelphia: J. B. Lippincott Company, 1986.

Kennedy, Eugene, and Sara C. Charles. *On Becoming a Counselor.* New York: The Continuum Publishing Company, 1991.

Ketterman, Grace H., M.D. *The Complete Book of Baby and Child Care.* Grand Rapids: Baker Book House, 1986.

Kilpatrick, William K. *The Emperor's New Clothes.* Westchester: Crossway Books, 1985.

Kinsey, Alfred D., et. al. *Sexual Behavior in the Human Female.* Philadelphia: W. B. Saunders, 1953.

———. *Sexual Behavior in the Human Male.* Philadelphia: W. B. Saunders, 1948.

Koteskey, Ronald L. "Abandoning the Psyche to Secular Treatment." *Christianity Today* 23 (18): 19-21 (1977).

LaHaye, Tim, and Beverly LaHaye. *The Act of Marriage.* Grand Rapids: Zondervan Publishing House, 1970.

Landers, Ann. "What 100,000 Women Told Ann Landers." *Family Circle,* June 11, 1985, 29.

Langone, John. "Is It a Disease or Isn't It?" *Discover,* November 1985, 102-6.

Lapham, Lewis H. *Money and Class in America: Notes and Observations on Our Civil Religion.* New York: Ballentine Books, 1988.

Leo, John. "A Therapist in Every Corner." *Time,* December 23, 1985, 59.

———. "Talk Is As Good As a Pill." *Time,* May 26, 1986, 60.

Lewis, C. S. *Mere Christianity.* New York: McMillian, 1943.

Magnuson, Roger J. *Are Gay Rights Right?* Portland, Ore.: Multnomah Press, 1990.

Mayo Clinic Health Letter. June, 1988, 6-7.

McDowell, Josh. *How to Help Your Child Say No to Sex Pressure.* Waco, Tex.: Word, 1987.

———. *Why Wait? Helping Teens Say No to Sexual Involvement.* San Bernardino, Calif.: Here's Life Publishers, 1987.

McFarland, Gertrude, and Mary Durand Thomas. *Psychiatric Mental Health Nursing.* Philadelphia: J. B. Lippincott Company, 1991.

McIlhaney, Joe S. Jr., and Susan Nethery. *1250 Health-Care Questions Women Ask.* Grand Rapids: Baker Book House, 1990.

Medical Newsletters and information from the American Anorexia/ Bulimia Association.Teaneck, N.J. Compiled from 1993 and 1994.

Melzak, Ronald. "The Promise of Biofeedback: Don't Hold the Party Yet." *Psychology Today,* 9 (2): 18-22 (1975).

Michelmore, Peter. "Long Nightmare of Ruth Finley." *Reader's Digest,* March 1989, 97-104.

Miller, Wendell E. *Forgiveness: The Power and the Puzzles.* Warsaw, Ind.: Clearbrook Publishers, 1994.

Murray, John. *Divorce.* Philadelphia: Presbyterian and Reformed Publishing, 1961.

Olsen, David. *Prepare/Enrich.* Minneopolis: Life Innovations, n.d.

Orthner, Donald. *Well Springs of Life: Understanding Proverbs.* Greenville, S.C.: Bob Jones University Press, 1989.

PRODIGY (R) Interactive Personal Service, April 10, 1992, 10:24 P.M.

Quackenbos, Stephen; Gayle Privett; and B. Klentz. "Psychotherapy and Religion: Rapprochement or Antithesis?" *Journal of Counseling and Development* 65: 82-85 (1986).

Reisman, Judith A., and Edward W. Eichel. *Kinsey, Sex, and Fraud.* Lafayette, Ind.: Lochinvar Inc. Huntington House Publishers, 1990.

Restak, Richard M. *The Brain.* Toronto: Bantam Books, 1984.

Roberts, Robert. "Therapy for the Saints." *Christianity Today* 29 (7): 25-28 (1985).

Rogers, Carl R. *Counseling and Psychotherapy.* Boston: Houghton Mifflin, 1942.

Rubinstein, Joseph, and Brent Slife, eds. *Taking Sides.* Sluice Dock, Guildford: The Dushkin Publishing Group, 1988.

Rushdoony, Rousas J. *Freud.* Grand Rapids: Baker Book House, 1975.

Safran, Claire. "Why Men Hurt the Women They Love." *Reader's Digest,* January 1986, 77-81.

Seligman, Jean; Patrick Rogers; and Peter Annin. *Newsweek,* May 2, 1994, 61.

Shelton, Bob. *God's Prophetic Blueprints.*

"Skinner's Utopia." *Time,* September 20, 1971, 47-53.

Smith, Robert D., M.D. "A Physician Looks at Counseling: Symptoms." *Nouthetic Confrontation* 1 (8-9): 4-5 (1975).

Smith, Hannah Whitehall. *The Christian's Secret of a Happy Life.* Old Tappan, N.J.: Fleming H. Revell, 1942.

Solomon, Charles R. *The Handbook to Happiness.* Denver: Grace Fellowship International, 1971.

Solomon, Charles R. *The Ins and Outs of Rejection.* Denver: Grace Fellowship International, 1983.

Sorenson, David. *Training Your Children to Turn Out Right.* Independence, Mo.: American Association of Christian Schools, 1995.

Stanley, Charles. *How to Keep Your Kids on Your Team.* Nashville: Oliver-Nelson, 1986.

Stormer, John. *Growing Up God's Way.* Florissant, Mo.: Liberty Bell Press, 1984.

Strom, Kay Marshall. *In the Name of Submission.* Portland, Ore.: Multnomah Press, 1986.

Szasz, Thomas S. *Ideology and Insanity.* New York: Doubleday and Company, 1970.

Thompson, June M., et. al. *Mosby's Manual of Clinical Nursing.* 2d ed. St. Louis: C. V. Mosby Company, 1989.

Thorn, Ivan. "The Failure of Modern Psychology." *Christian Educator Journal* 24 (3): 17-21 (1985).

Time, April 1, 1974, 38.

Toufexis, Anastasia. "Dark Days, Darker Spirits." *Time,* January 11, 1988, 66.

Travis, Carol. *Anger: The Misunderstood Emotion.* New York: Simon and Schuster, 1982.

Trotter, Robert J. "Chemistry of Compulsion." *Discover,* June 1990, 26-27.

Vaughn, John, and Brenda Vaughn. *More Precious than Gold.* Grand Rapids: Revell Book Company, 1994.

Welch, Edward T. *Counselor's Guide to the Brain and Its Disorders.* Grand Rapids: Zondervan Publishing House, 1991.

Wessel, Helen. *Natural Childbirth and the Christian Family.* San Francisco: Harper and Row, 1983.

Wheat, Ed. *Intended for Pleasure.* Philadelphia: Westminister Press, 1966.

Wright, J. Norman. *Questions Women Ask in Private.* Ventura, Calif.: Regal Books, 1993.

Zimbardo, Philip G. *Shyness: What It Is, What To Do About It.* Reading, Mass.: Addison-Wesley Publishing Co., 1977.

Index

A

Abusive men, 239-48
Adams, Jay, 91-92, 96, 329
Addiction, 8, 231-38, 318, 373
Adjustment, 18, 21-25, 27
Adultery, 157-60
Alcoholism, 114
Allergies, 77
Anger, 117-25, 241, 261
Anorexia nervosa, 81, 144, 318, 337-42
Anxiety, 56, 208-14
Assignments, 64, 90, 96
Attention Deficit Disorder and Hyperactivity, 311
Attitudes, 20-21, 23-24, 26
Authority, 333

B

Beechick, Ruth, 45
Belliveau, Fred, 145
Bentham, Jeremy, 32
Bible Action Truths, 361-64
Biofeedback, 352
Bitterness, 38, 56-57, 117-28, 197, 266, 318, 323, 380
Bobgan, Martin and Deidre, 343, 354-55
Brain injury, 74

Brownback, Paul, 111
Bulimia nervosa, 81, 318, 337-42
Burkett, Larry, 65, 291

C

Calcium imbalance, 76
Cambridge-Somerville Youth Study, 350
Cappon, Daniel, 147-50
Children, 305-21
Christian education, 309
Chronic Fatigue Syndome, 77-78
Codependents, 231, 374
Cognitive behaviorists, 353
Collins, Gary, 86
Communication, 45, 278, 284-89
Compulsions, 80, 125-28
Confidentiality, 107
Confrontation, 86
Conscience, 10, 44-45, 55
Cousins, Norman, 31

D

Death, 52, 58
Decision-making, 95
Demon possessions, 54-55